THE XARIPU COMMUNITY

ACROSS BORDERS

LATINO PERSPECTIVES

Gilberto Cárdenas, series editor

INSTITUTE *for*

Latino Studies

UNIVERSITY OF NOTRE DAME

*The Institute for Latino Studies, in keeping with the distinctive mission,
values, and traditions of the University of Notre Dame, promotes
understanding and appreciation of the social, cultural, and religious life of
U.S. Latinos through advancing research, expanding knowledge,
and strengthening community.*

THE XARIPU COMMUNITY

Labor, Migration,

ACROSS BORDERS

Community, and Family

MANUEL BARAJAS

University of Notre Dame Press

Notre Dame, Indiana

Library of Congress Cataloging-in-Publication Data

Barajas, Manuel.
The Xaripu community across borders : labor migration, community, and
family / Manuel Barajas.
    p.   cm. — (Latino perspectives)
Includes bibliographical references and index.
ISBN-13: 978-0-268-02212-9 (pbk. : alk. paper)
ISBN-10: 0-268-02212-7 (pbk. : alk. paper)
1. Indians of Mexico—California—Social conditions. 2. Mexican Americans—
California—Social conditions. 3. Michoacán de Ocampo (Mexico)—Emigration
and immigration. 4. Alien labor—California. 5. Transnationalism.   I. Title.
F870.M5B37   2009
304.8'79407237—dc22

                                                              2009004336

A mi pueblo y a otros que buscan igualdad y humanidad atravesando fronteras injustas.

(To my pueblo and others who seek equality and humanity crossing unjust borders.)

CONTENTS

ACKNOWLEDGMENTS

I want to recognize the people who made the completion of this book possible. Alfredo Mirandé spent enormous amounts of time providing me feedback and mentorship throughout my dissertation work. Edna Bonacich, Scott Coltrane, Devra Weber, and Michael Kearney were also very helpful with their expertise, feedback, and encouragement. I benefited tremendously by the continuous academic and personal support of Refugio I. Rochin, Adaljisa Sosa-Riddell, and Beatriz Pesquera since my undergraduate years at UC Davis. They affirmed the social and academic value of my cultural background and labor migrant experiences. To friends and scholars who helped with feedback, I thank Esther Barajas, Mario Barrera, Katherine Blackmer Reyes, Duane Campbell, Julia Curry-Rodriguez, Verica Dering, Glenn Destatte, Gilberto Garcia, Marlyn Jones, Enrique Lopez, Richard Lowy, Luis Magaña, Cecilia Menjívar, Gabriel Torres, Gregorio Mora-Torres, Luisa Moreno Briseño, Alvaro Ochoa Serrano, Patricia Portillo, Mariano Salcedo Zaragoza, Otis Scott, and Edith Vasquez. I am very grateful to the resource help of UC MEXUS, Ernesto Galarza Public Policy Center, El Colegio de Michoacán, and Instituto de la Revolución Mexicana en Jiquilpan. At the University of Notre Dame Press, I am thankful for the editorial support of Kari Jo Verhulst and for the generous support of Caroline Domingo and Gilberto Cárdenas. For offering me a home during my research in California, I thank my parents (Esther and Luis), sisters (Sylvia, Esther, Evelyn), and brothers (Luis, Jorge, and David), who live in Stockton, California. In Michoacán, my godparents (Carlos Manzo and Juana Pulido) and cousins (Ofelia and Carlos Manzo) hosted me in Xaripu and my great aunt (Esperanza Carrillo Diaz) in Zamora. *Gracias por su hospitalidad.*

This book was made possible by la *cuperacha de todas/os las/los de Xaripu* in both California, United States, and Michoacán, Mexico. *Gracias, mi pueblo. Alitzel eres mi llaves a la felicidad.* Elvia Ramirez, *mi compañera y esposa,* whom I love very much, thanks for your ardent support of me and my work.

Chapter One

INTRODUCTION

Labor Migration, Community, and Family across Borders

An unjust law is a human law that is not rooted in eternal law and natural law. Any law that uplifts human personality is just. Any law that degrades human personality is unjust. All segregation statutes are unjust because segregation distorts the soul and damages the personality.

—Martin Luther King Jr. ([1963] 2003)

On December 16, 2005, the House of Representatives passed House Resolution 4437, which threatened to further militarize the southern border and criminalize as felons undocumented immigrants and those assisting them in any way (Nevins 2002, 61–62, 68–69, 74, 78). Like Martin Luther King a generation ago, the Roman Catholic cardinal Roger Mahony instructed his priests to disobey HR 4437 if it became law, arguing that "denying aid to a fellow human being violates a higher authority than Congress—the law of God" (Fetzer 2006, 698). In 2007, competing interests in the US Congress continued to debate the content of a national immigration act and revealed the historical contradictions of immigration policy, between capital and labor, economic structural demands and nativism, and the ideals of an open society and rigid border control (Calavita 1998; Carens 1998). In line with the historical trajectory of US immigration policymaking,[1] any likely compromise-based immigration act—with its emphasis on border security, exploitable and disposable guest workers, and a burdensome path to legalization—would keep immigrants of color marginalized from the economic and social center of US society for generations to come (Calavita 1998, 98).[2]

This book illustrates the long-term consequences of national borders on both the sending and the receiving societies. It presents an extended case study of the Xaripu community originating from Michoacán, Mexico, and elaborates how various forms of colonialism, institutional biases, and emergent forms of domination have shaped the community's labor migration, community formation, and family experiences across the Mexican and US border for over a century. The Xaripu people generally constitute a transnational community with home bases in both Xaripu, Michoacán, and Stockton, California, and reflect a high level of transnationalism—that is, they feel at home in the two nations and maintain active and fluid social ties across borders. A total of fifty-six persons participated in the formal study on which this book is partly based: thirty-one in California and twenty-five in Michoacán (the concept of transnationalism and the methodology for this extended case study are elaborated in chapter 2).

Among the central questions guiding this book are the following: What historical events have shaped Xaripus' migration experiences? How have Xaripus been incorporated into the US labor market? How have national inequalities affected their ability to form community across borders? And how have migration, settlement, and employment experiences affected the family, particularly gender relationships, on both sides of the border?

People from the pueblo of Xaripu began coming to the United States at the turn of the twentieth century, but it took three generations of migrating before Xaripus began settling permanently in *el norte* (the United States). While US national policy had privileged Western European migration and settlement since the foundation of the United States (Ngai 2004; Bernard 1998), nonwhite colonial subjects were subordinated in both the US society and labor markets through racist policies, norms, and practices (Barrera 1979; Mirandé 1985; Glenn 2002).[3] It was only after the Immigration and Naturalization Act of 1965 ended racist quotas and allowed for family reunification that Xaripu migration changed from chiefly involving male laborers to entailing family migration and eventually settlement. This settlement produced a transnational experience for most Xaripus, though some are more active and comprehensively involved in the actual experience of crossing borders (e.g., communication, remittances, travel, social activities) than others.

In the past three decades there has been much interest in the transnational migration experiences of various groups,[4] including Dominicans (Grasmuck and Pessar 1991), Filipinas/os (Parreñas 2001a), Indians (George 2000; Kurien 2003), Puerto Ricans (Toro-Morn and Alicea 2003), Salvadorans (Menjívar 2000; Mahler 1995), and persons of Mexican origin, who remain the most proximate and numerous immigrant population in the United States (Rouse 1992; Kearney and Nagengast 1989; Smith 2003; López 2007). While identifying the forces that dislocate migrants from their homelands and keep them from being fully incorporated into the receiving society (Espiritu 2003b; Parreñas 2001b), scholars often capture only part of the community experience and overlook the most politically and economically marginalized ones—i.e., the non-migrants who remain in the homeland.[5] This absence of a comparative analysis of migrants and those they leave behind lessens our understanding of the full migration experience (Guarnizo and Smith 1999; Sarmiento 2002). Because the voices of immigrants or transnational subjects are privileged over those of non-migrants in the sending communities, the reality—that their dissimilar cultural and material contexts produce different experiences and at times distort their shared realities—is neglected.

Moreover, by focusing on one side of the border (Hondagneu-Sotelo 1994; Torres 1998; Espiritu 2003b), one area of labor incorporation (agriculture) (Kearney 1996; Zavella 1987; López 2007), one generation of migrants (particularly older ones) (Massey et al. 1987; Rouse 1992, 1996), one gender (Hondagneu-Sotelo 1994), or an essentialist or monolithic view of Mexican migrants (Massey et al. 2002; Portes and Rumbaut 2006), such scholarship offers a limited view of the labor migration and community formation experiences across borders. Thus this cross-national, comparative study of the Xaripu community builds upon these early efforts but attempts to offer a more critical and comprehensive understanding of labor migration, community formation, and family experiences across borders. Unlike in most labor migration studies, I emphasize how colonial domination continues as a social-historical phenomenon that has had a significant impact on the quality of life for Xaripus in both Mexico and the United States.[6]

To do so, I trace the Xaripu community's century-long international migration and detail how it was initiated, how it has transformed, and how it continues to this day. By examining the particular history of the Xaripus I hope to shed light on the experiences of other communities that were similarly dislocated and transformed by social-historical colonial processes. Furthermore, by focusing on this specific community, I attempt to move away from essentialist hegemonic scholarship that homogenizes and erases differences by producing a falsely universal discourse of "Latinos" or "Hispanics" or "Mexicans," which, in truth, obscures social inequities and diversity based on race, class, gender, and national histories.

AN OVERVIEW OF THE BOOK

After this introduction, chapter 2 reviews the scholarly frameworks through which labor migration is typically examined, focusing particularly on the structural (Bonacich and Cheng 1984; Frank 1978; Wallerstein 1974), transnational (Glick-Schiller et al. 1992b; Rouse 1992, 1996; Smith and Guarnizo 2003), and colonial (Blauner 1972, 2001; Barrera 1979)[7] perspectives and offering a conceptual framework I call "interactive colonization" that synthesizes and advances their key concepts.[8] The interactive colonization framework is derived from the social history of Xaripus and employed to understand their labor migration, community, and family experiences across borders. It aims to advance an understanding of their emergent social location between nations and other social structures, and the implications of this location for ending social inequalities rooted in colonialism. This theoretical model accounts for the overlapping forms of colonialism (internal, external, and new forms) and combines three central concepts of labor migration scholarship— colonization (the *longue durée* historical view; Braudel 1980, 25–34),[9] dialectics, and social interaction—to provide a comprehensive, historically grounded, and dynamic understanding of labor migration experiences in the modern world.

The concept of colonization provides the necessary historical context for understanding modern global migration and social relationships, since descendants of the colonized continue to experience economic, racial/ethnic, and gender subjugation and geographic dislocations.[10] The resulting dialectical relations—unequal and exploitative power relationships—create conflict and change in the social interactions that subsequently produce new individual and collective identities. To help illuminate the dynamics of these new identities I employ the Indigenous Nahuatl concept of *nepantla*—a state of being in-between or hybridity—because it captures the collective identity that emerges from being within conflicting material and cultural contexts (León-Portilla 1990, 10; Guarnizo and Smith 2003, 23). Thus the role that those who occupy the *nepantla* position play in advancing or impeding social justice becomes a central issue of analysis in this chapter.[11] The distinction between structural (collective and enduring experience) and situational (individual and temporary level) inbetweenness is important. In the former type, social categories of in-between collectivities—e.g., middle class, mestizas/os,[12] and transnational community—create distinct experiences shaped by collective and shared institutional experiences. Historically, trends show that emergent collective *nepantlas* develop interests distinct from those at the top and those at the bottom. In contrast, at the more individual level, a person's agency and pragmatism work within the existing social hierarchies, and an individual may pursue or be given unique possibilities (token positions) in relationship to those with structured advantages along race, class, gender, and nationality. This individual intermediary position—e.g., contractor, administrator, spokesperson—is predicated on reproducing the status quo and can be terminated if this role is not followed.

Chapter 3 provides a social-historical context for the Xaripu labor migration experiences. Xaripu as a pueblo traces its origins to the Purépechan Empire, and its people's labor migration has occurred within the context of various colonialisms (Fonseca and Moreno 1984; Moreno García 1994). Fifteenth-century European colonialism appropriated Indigenous land and labor (Cockcroft 1998; Keen 1994) and created the first labor migratory movements among Indigenous people in the Michoacán region (Bravo Ugarte 1960). This domination was facilitated by in-between criollos/mestizas(os),[13] who emerged as brokers and/or rivals for the conquering groups.

After Mexican Independence (1821), criollo *hacendados* gained power over the land and continued the suppression of Indigenous communities with the help of *guardias blancas* (hired security). Many of the *guardias* were mestizos—the emerging mixed-race class that would later be favored over more Indigenous communities in the agrarian reforms before and after the 1910 Mexican Revolution (Cockroft 1998; De Bernal 1969; Purnell 1999). Indigenous people were continuously dislocated and forced to migrate even into the twentieth century, particularly after the US-Mexican War and the rise of the US-backed dictator Porfirio Díaz (1876–1910). During this period, the dictator secured Mexico's neocolonial position in the emergent global hierarchy by opening its most valuable resources (mines, petroleum, and railroads) to foreign domination. The overlapping colonialisms of internal-colonial and neocolonial relations created the conditions for the revolution. It was also a major catalyst for international migration.

Around this time Mexican hacienda elites, in association with foreign capitalists, expanded their landholdings by dislocating Indigenous and mestiza/o communities from their lands and converting their populations to migrant wage workers in extractive enterprises producing for export (Moreno García 1994; Fonseca and Moreno 1984; Gonzalez and Fernandez 2003). The construction of the Moreno Railroad Station near Xaripu in 1900 further encouraged Xaripus to begin migrating to the United States. This migration was formalized with the first US-Mexican guest-worker program of 1917–21, which recruited Mexican men to the expanding US agriculture, mining, and steel industries (Barrera 1979; Gómez-Quiñones 1994). Xaripu migration continued to be a largely male reality through the Bracero Program of 1942–64[14] but was ultimately transformed by the 1965 Immigration and Naturalization Act, after which entire families began to migrate north. Although seeking economic improvement in the United States, Xaripus remained occupationally stratified, devalued, and without access to labor protections.

Chapter 4 examines the relationship between racialized work and labor conditions, revealing the logic of colonialism in modern labor relations. I identify three racialized work settings—Mexicanized, diversified, and Whitened—that represent the differing workforce compositions and labor conditions Xaripu migrants experience. The concept of "Mexicanization"[15] describes how wages and working conditions decline as the workplace's labor force becomes increasingly Mexican. Mexican immigrants do not themselves deteriorate the labor conditions; rather, employers devalue Mexican workers and thus decrease both the pay and the quality of the working conditions. Thus, Xaripus did not enter such workplaces as low-cost labor but rather were reduced in value once they were on site. In other words, Mexican labor is not cheap but cheapened (devalued), illustrating the continued logic of colonialism—which, I argue, entrenches and universalizes the racial, gender, and class hierarchies that continue to this date (see also chapter 2).

This labor subordination is facilitated by in-between individuals (e.g., contractors, supervisors, political administrators, etc.), who become brokers and manage the appropriation of surplus value (profit) from those at the bottom. This emergent segment has historically been crucial in the ultimate domination of the colonized. Hence, in the extreme stages of Mexicanization, Mexican supervisors are appointed to manage and supervise the super-exploitation of those at the bottom, thus giving the impression that the employers are fair ("color-blind") and that Mexicans themselves are the ones who keep themselves down—a belief that is often internalized and expressed via the comment *uno mismo se baja* (We keep ourselves down).

This chapter also analyzes the relationship between the racialization of the workplace and labor conditions in two sections: "Colonial Labor in the Fields" and "Out of the Fields." In the United States, thanks to immigration policy, housing segregation, labor market opportunities, and class segmentation, older Xaripus generally remained working in farm labor throughout their lives. Many of their children and grandchildren, however, searched for economic opportunities outside of the fields, particularly at the time of the 1986 Immigration Reform and Control Act (IRCA) and 1994 North American Free Trade Agreement (NAFTA). While their economic opportunities improved out of the fields in comparison to their elders' experiences, their labor experiences also reveal colonial hierarchies—occupational segregation in the service and de-skilled sectors and class segmentation within occupations (Barrera 1979; Segura 1990; Glenn 2002).

Chapter 5 explores how *haciendo comunidad* (building community) across borders works as a strategy by which Xaripus reclaim a fuller humanity. Xaripus' unequal integration as full and equal members of US society keeps many of them oriented toward the homeland even in the twenty-first century (see also Espiritu 2003b). This chapter explores three interrelated concepts in building community across borders: *convivencia, nepantla,* and empowerment. *Convivencia* (affective and egalitarian social interaction) allows Xaripus to construct community on both sides of the border via informal and formal gatherings during *las buenas y las malas* (good and bad times). However, the different experiences between two unequal nations shapes their *nepantla* position for Xaripu *norteñas/os*.[16] Social inequalities and nativist sentiments toward non-whites in the United States (e.g., anti-immigrant, anti-diversity, and anti-bilingual policies in California) create a hostile climate that contributes to their particular *nepantla*. For instance, while young Xaripus reject a one-way assimilation (i.e., conformity with Anglo culture) and seek to reproduce their cultural community in the United States, they have nonetheless undergone material and cultural changes that differentiate them from non-migrants in Mexico.

This social differentiation created by national inequalities becomes a unique source of tension and conflict between transnational Xaripus and non-migrants who remain in Michoacán. While there is evident interest in forming community across borders among transnational and non-migrant Xaripus, social inequalities rooted in national inequities and hierarchies (political, economic, and cultural) strain their relationships.

Today, Xaripus who are able to maintain a fluid and constant movement across the border are generally better off than those who cannot. They are relatively wealthier than non-migrant relatives in both California and Michoacán, and form an emergent in-between group that constructs, to the best of its abilities, a better future for its members. How should this group that exists between unequal power structures relate to those who are advantaged and those who are disadvantaged by an existing social order of privileges (Whiteness, economic hierarchies, and patriarchy) rooted and/or universalized in colonialism? Before pursuing this question in the conclusion (chapter 7), I explore family politics of gender empowerment across borders.

Chapter 6 examines gender equity across borders in relation to the Xaripu family. In the context of globalization and economic restructuring, tremendous stress has fallen on the family, the chief burdens for which have been unequally distributed along gender lines. Two dimensions of gender equity are observed: familial authority and household division of labor. The findings depart from views that assume that through wage labor participation, immigration/settlement experiences, and/or Americanization, women experience more gender equality in the United States (Hirsch 1999; Rouse 1992; Hondagneu-Sotelo 1994, 2003; Min 1997; George 2000; De Genova and Ramos-Zayas 2003). Although reporting more authority than women in Mexico, Xaripa *norteñas* experience a more intense work burden inside and outside the home. So why do they perceive themselves as being more empowered than women in Michoacán? To answer this I first discuss Xaripas' familism and then explore how transnationalism affects the perception of gender equity.

Xaripas' personal experience with transnationalism, I argue, shapes their perceptions of gender empowerment on both sides of the border. For instance, many US-based Xaripus visit Michoacán to relax, go out, and have fun, while the smaller number[17] who live there year-round find themselves with more work during the peak of tourism. Consequently, non-migrants perceive *norteñas* as more liberal—that is, partying all the time, staying up long into the night, and going out for recreation.[18] On the other hand, Xaripus in California, who rarely visit and do not feel as much at home in Michoacán, develop the impression that those residing in Michoacán are more traditional and submissive, particularly women. In contrast, transnational migrants, who maintain more active and continuous social ties across borders, do not see a difference in gender relations.

Overall, Xaripu men remain privileged over women across borders (see also Alicea 1997, 617–19; Orozco 1993, 12–15; García 1993, 23–25) and thus occupy an in-between status in terms of power and valorization as men in the larger society. That is, they possess greater social power than the women in their communities but considerably less authority in the broader work and civic sectors than men of higher socioeconomic classes. Just as national inequalities empower transnational Xaripus over non-migrants in Michoacán,[19] the gendered division of labor inside and outside the home privileges men over women. Gender borders inside and outside the family achieve what national borders do: reproduce hierarchical relationships and unjustified inequalities.

The central objective of this book is to examine what has become of the Xaripu community across borders in the twenty-first century, focusing on their economic, social/cultural, and political integration within the larger emergent nation-states, Mexico and the United States. The interactive colonization model points to overlapping colonialisms and intersecting systems of oppression (racism, patriarchy, and capitalism), and how conflict involves not only polar groups but also emergent in-between individuals and groups that become central in advancing justice or maintaining injustice within labor, community, and family. Chapter 7 theorizes—based on the Xaripu experience—how those in-between unequal nation-states relate to those advantaged and disadvantaged by the global hierarchies rooted in colonialism. It concludes that the project of justice and equality can only be informed and advanced by *las/los de abajo* (those at the bottom), whose vision rests on *un mundo sin fronteras* (a world without borders).

BIOGRAPHICAL SKETCHES OF XARIPU LABOR MIGRANTS

The following biographical sketches exemplify the Xaripus upon which this case study is based and provide insights into the nature and form of their labor migration and settlement experiences over time, elaborating the typical experiences of migrants and non-migrants on both sides of the border. They illustrate how Xaripus' migration experiences have been shaped by their relations to land, work, community, and family. This brief review of the participants' backgrounds helps contextualize the labor, community, and family experiences presented in the subsequent chapters. Participants are divided into four age cohorts based upon their differing border-crossing experiences (base year 2000):[20] *Retiradas/os* (ages sixty-five and older), *Mayores* (ages fifty to sixty-four), *Hijas/os* (ages thirty to forty-nine), and *Chicas/os* (ages twenty to twenty-nine). A total of fifty-six Xaripus were formally interviewed for this study, and here I select cases that typify the experiences of each of the four age cohorts (see elaboration of methods and sampling in chapter 2). The decision to examine Xaripas/os by age cohorts was based on the effort to highlight both historical particularities and generational changes among them.

Transnational Migrants: *Retiradas/os* (Age Sixty-five and Older)

Most of the *retiradas/os* were born to landless peasant families around the time of the Mexican Revolution (1910s) and the Cristero Revolt (1926–29). Their parents had been initially motivated to migrate in search of work intra-nationally during the Porfiriato Period (1876–1910), when *haciendas* and foreign investors expanded their monopoly of land and resources and disrupted and impoverished numerous Native communities. Although many Xaripus migrated to work in neighboring *haciendas*, most remained anchored to their pueblo and returned home at the end of each working season. During this period, a few Xaripus also began migrating to *el norte* to work[21] as a consequence of an increasing global integration with the United States, though immigration policy and occupational segregation kept them in colonial conditions with fewer rights and less freedom to live, work, and move where they wanted (see Ngai 2004; Gonzalez and Fernandez 2003; Barrera 1979).

Thus *retiradas/os* comprised the second wave of Xaripus to migrate to the United States as laborers[22] and are classified as a cohort for several reasons: (1) they were all born landless; (2) they experienced the Bracero Program for longer periods and worked in more diverse occupations than would later generations of migrants; (3) they were sixty-five years of age or older at the time of their interviews; and (4) all of them were considered officially retired even though many continued to work.

The men in this group spent more than half of their working lives laboring in the United States between thirty-eight and fifty-nine years in all (an average forty-nine years). These men were gradually joined in their annual migrations by their spouses and children, particularly after the 1965 Immigration and Naturalization Act allowed for the reunification of families. The women in this cohort tended to work as both farm workers and homemakers. Working within the structures of labor market demands and immigration policies, *retiradas/os'* migration was also mediated by household survival concerns, generation, and social ties (see also Massey et al. 1987; Palacios Franco 1987; López Castro 1986; Curry-Rodriguez 1988; Grasmuck and Pessar 1991). Benefiting from the family reunification provision, braceros and their spouses typically migrated alone the first few years. They would leave their young children with family in Michoacán; if some children were old enough to work, they would come to *el norte,* and the mother would stay back to care for the younger children. As they developed familiarity with resources (health care, unemployment insurance, schools) and built community, all the family members eventually migrated and settled in the United States.

Over time, *retiradas/os'* movement across borders changed from being labor migrants to being transnational migrants.[23] Previous generations of labor migrants had come to the United States primarily to work and continued to view Mexico as their only home. But as the Bracero Program ended and Xaripu migration shifted to include entire families, Xaripus began to settle in the United States, subsequently altering both their migration patterns and their views of home. Significantly, *retiradas/os* shifted from considering California just a place to work to viewing it as their families' year-round home. But even though Mexico is no longer their primary place of residence, *retiradas/os* maintain a deeply transnational sense of identity and consider both Mexico and the United States their home.[24]

Most *retiradas/os* continue to visit Xaripu on a yearly basis and spend as long as three months or more there. They particularly like to be in Xaripu for the pueblo's celebration of the Virgen de la Inmaculada Concepción in January. These trips allow them to avoid the cold in *el norte* during the late fall and early winter and, more importantly, to see relatives and friends who are visiting the pueblo from other places in Mexico or from Chicago, Los Angeles, Texas, or New York—those they would otherwise not get to see. They also get to do things they do not do in the United States, such as farming, acting in theater, and organizing cultural and sporting events.

Profiles of Select Participating *Retiradas/os*

Armando and Carolina were born in Xaripu, in 1923 and 1925 respectively, and married in 1943. At the time of their interview they had nine children, forty-three grandchildren, and twenty great-grandchildren.

Both became naturalized US citizens in 1993, and until their deaths in 2002 and 2003, respectively, they had visited Michoacán annually, usually from November to March. Both were laid to rest in their second home, *el vallé de San Joaquin.*

Armando's schooling went up to second grade, and Carolina completed the third grade. When the Bracero Program was implemented in 1942, Armando joined other Xaripu migrants who had been coming to the United States since the early twentieth century, among them his older brother, who had moved to Chicago in 1926. The brother had encouraged Armando and other Xaripus to settle there, but many of them returned to Mexico during the Great Depression because of economic conditions in the United States and, for some, the ability to capitalize on the agrarian reforms in Mexico that granted them claim to *ejidos* (collective lands) in Michoacán. Armando and a few other Xaripu friends were actually deported in the late 1930s and did not return to the United States until the 1942–64 guest-worker program (see chapter 3).

Carolina's father had also migrated to the United States in the early twentieth century, and she began migrating shortly after the Bracero Program ended. Carolina worked for a few years picking cherries, apricots, and tomatoes in California before returning to Xaripu in the fall of 1966, when she was pregnant with their last child—a baby girl born in 1967. When the baby was nine months old, Carolina returned to work in California; she was able to work until her daughter turned two, when, like many migrant families, she had trouble finding baby sitters and so stopped working in the fields to look after her children. Some of the other women in this situation opted to bring their young children with them to the fields. When her daughter started preschool, Carolina returned to the fields, where she remained until the mid-1970s, when the field strikes began against La Francia grape company in Stockton, California.

Luis was born in 1923 and Nena in 1925. He did not go to school, and she attended for only a few years. Luis first migrated to the United States in 1940; he worked on the railroad tracks for about six months. He later was contracted as a bracero in 1942 with the help of Manuel Carrillo— a Xaripu who worked for the Mexican government and facilitated the guest-worker program. Xaripus remember Manuel fondly because during his visits to the pueblo he would give toys to the children and help men get guest-worker permits. With Carrillo's help, Luis traveled from Mexico City to Juarez, where he was directed to US employers and worked in the asparagus fields in *las islas de Stockton* (Delta River Islands). He continued migrating back and forth, saved a little money, and married Nena in 1950.

Nena's father had been an early migrant to the United States in the 1920s, and she began to migrate north in 1968. Before she started migrating, she struggled to care for her growing family on sporadic remittances and with no house of her own. As has been documented by others (see Curry-Rodríguez 1988; Palacios Franco 1987; Hondagneu-Sotelo 1994), women in her situation often did the impossible—working for subsistence, caring for children, and supporting their migrant husbands when they returned with nothing from *el norte*. Arguably the most difficult struggle these women endured was losing loved ones to preventable illnesses. In Nena and Luis's case it was a daughter who died of pneumonia (Sahagun Sahagun 1967, 23–24).[25]

When Nena first came to the United States, her family lived in a farm labor camp during the six-month working season (April to late October) in French Camp, California, south of Stockton. At the time Nena was forty-four and had six children. Her two youngest children were under five years of age, and she stayed home to care for them while her husband and older children worked in the fields. In 1971, she became pregnant again and, like other Xaripu women, returned to Xaripu to have the baby there. In 1999, her eight children ranged in age from twenty-four to forty-eight. The two oldest sons (forty-five and forty-eight) and the youngest two sons (twenty-three and twenty-seven) still lived with them. Nena and Luis continued their transnational life of living between two worlds and visited Xaripu once a year.

Braceros and Post-Bracero Migrants/Immigrants: *Mayores* (Age Fifty to Sixty-four)

Whereas *retirados* began migrating prior to and during the 1940s and traveled across the United States to work in diverse occupations—e.g., railroads, construction, and farm labor—the *mayores* cohort generally began migrating in the 1950s and were concentrated in the Southwest, where they worked primarily in agriculture. Although some of their parents had access to *ejido* lands in Michoacán in the 1930s and 1940s, very few *mayores* were able to work on them, and so at a young age they followed the structured migration streams north.[26]

The *mayores'* labor-migration experiences are also distinct from those of the *retiradas/os*. Typically the men have worked for all of their adult years in California's agricultural fields, first in the capacity as braceros and then as documented or undocumented residents. The women have also worked for more than half of their lives in the United States. As children in Michoacán, the men would have worked in agriculture and with livestock, while the women would have knitted, sewed, done laundry for pay, and worked as domestics. After marrying, some of the women became homemakers, while some of those whose husbands did not migrate continued to work in the jobs they had held as single women. When families began migrating together after 1965, the women typically worked in the fields while they continued their homemaking labor. Age and injury have forced many of the women and men in this cohort out of the fields and into canneries and packing houses, which they alternate with working in the fields. Now older and worn out, most *mayores* search for lighter jobs like weeding, picking cherries, and packing house or cannery work.

Mayores' visits to Michoacán are more diverse in comparison to the *retiradas/os'*. While many go to Xaripu every year, some go less often, and a minority have not returned. Their movement across the border has taken on the form of visits rather than the more fluid movements and longer stays of the *retiradas/os*. Moreover, unlike *retirados/as'* lengthy annual visits to the pueblo, *mayores* tend to visit only as work schedules, money, and children's and grandchildren's school and work schedules permit. Despite this, most *mayores* share *retirados/as'* sense of being at home in both places.

Profiles of Selected Participating *Mayores*

Gregorio was born in 1938, and his wife, María, in 1941. He completed the third grade, and his wife the fifth, in Xaripu. They married in 1958 and have seven children, ages twenty-two to forty-five, and four grandchildren. Gregorio first came to the United States to work as a bracero in 1956. His father had been among the first Xaripu guest workers in the United States during the 1910s and was also one of the first to benefit from the *ejidos* in the 1930s. Gregorio grew up surrounded by the idea of migrating because many of his great uncles had been migrating to the United States since early in the twentieth century. María was also raised amid migratory experiences—her father and maternal uncles had begun migrating in the early twentieth century. She and their children joined Gregorio on his trips north in 1971 and 1972.

Shortly after this, Gregorio decided to settle the family in California to avoid interrupting the children's education. María recounted how sad and lonely she was, since at that time only a few Xaripu families had settled permanently in California while most other migrant families continued to return to Michoacán at the end of each growing season. Gregorio has not returned to Xaripu since 1972, though his children visit every six to eight years and María had gone with their youngest daughter in 2002, 2003, and 2006. The couple's differing views toward their native land are also evident in the fact that Gregorio became a U.S. citizen in 1969, while María waited until 1993 to do so.

Both Lionel and Christina were born in 1943. He attended school to fifth grade, and she finished seventh grade. They married in 1966 and have eight children and over ten grandchildren. Christina's father had migrated to the United States for work in the 1920s but stopped doing so after the Great Depression because of the extreme racism he had encountered. Christina's father had attained land in Michoacán during the agrarian reform in the 1930s, and when he died in the 1950s, the *ejido* members (the collective land committee) wanted to transfer the land to someone else to work it. But Christina's mother successfully fought to keep the land, after which she tended livestock and cultivated the fields on her own to support her family. Christina observed that this experience greatly empowered her and her sisters, all of whom are very assertive and influential women in their respective communities.

Christina and Lionel migrated to the United States with their children for the first time in February 1972. At that time, they had only four children, who ranged in age from a few months to five years old. They continued to migrate as a family until 1975, when Christina decided to settle the family in Stockton to advance their by then six children's education. Christina and Lionel both became naturalized U.S. citizens in 1993. Unlike her mother and sisters in Michoacán, who worked outside the home and in commerce, Christina worked primarily as a homemaker.

Since settling in Stockton they have visited Xaripu about every seven years, and many of their eight adult children regularly visit Xaripu with their own families. The oldest goes every year.

Martha was born in Xaripu in 1940 and has a fifth-grade education. She divorced her husband because of his infidelity, and they have four children and nine grandchildren. Martha has worked for most of her life in farm labor and grew up surrounded by migrants. When she was young, her father—a blacksmith by trade—would leave finished iron products for her mother to sell so that they could support themselves during his labor migrations to the United States. Most of her brothers migrated north in the 1950s through the Bracero Program. After marrying a man from southern Michoacán, Martha worked as a seamstress until 1972, when she and her husband migrated to *el norte* with their four children. When asked who decided to move to Stockton, Martha explained that her children enjoyed visiting her relatives in Stockton and wanted to live there rather than in Santa María, California. In 1991 she became a naturalized U.S. citizen. At the time of our 1999 interview, eleven people lived in her three-bedroom house, including her estranged husband, who lingered in a makeshift room in the backyard. Martha continues to visit Michoacán almost every year, and with much passion described Xaripu as being *como mi madre* (like my mother). For many years Martha made annual month-long visits to Michoacán, but in the past few years financial limitations, her work schedule, and obligations to look after her grandchildren have prevented her from staying as long.

Danilo was born in 1947 in Xaripu. His migration pattern was different from that of the other men in this cohort. In 1975, Danilo first migrated to California and spent nine months working in Stockton and the remaining three back in Mexico—a pattern he continues to this day. He has never married, and his connections with friends and family in Xaripu, Guadalajara, and Mexico City motivate him to continue migrating back and forth rather than settling exclusively on one side of the border.

Danilo has a higher level of formal education than all of the Xaripus introduced thus far, reflecting the reality that persons who came to the United States at a later age were able to advance their education further than those who had migrated as teenagers or younger. Danilo was raised by a single mother, Margarita, and all of his five siblings are older and married. When he was between six and eleven years old he sold Jell-o and popcorn in the streets of Xaripu, and in 1956 he went to school in Jiquilpan (a city about eight miles west). In 1968, after finishing his secondary education at age sixteen, he moved to Mexico City, where he worked with relatives in a butcher market, continued his education, and began to work as an actor, appearing briefly in the Mexican soap opera *El Mundo de Juguetes* (A World of Toys) in the 1970s. In the summer of 1975, Danilo visited his family in Stockton and took a job in the fields in part to gain firsthand experience as a farm laborer in case a movie role typifying this experience arose.

Danilo continued to travel and work in the two nations until the late 1980s, when a heart problem prompted him to quit working in the fields for good. The fast-paced life in Mexico City and the strain of farm labor in California contributed to his illness. He had worked as a butcher and actor in Mexico from 1963 to 1988 and as a farm worker in California from 1975 to 1994. He stopped migrating sometime between 1986 and 1988, at which point he terminated his acting career and closed his butcher shop in Mexico. The devaluation of the peso, national wage differentials, and family connections also influenced his decision to abandon his work in Mexico City. In California, Danilo worked primarily as a farm worker, doing the most common work among Xaripus: harvesting asparagus, tomatoes, and cherries.

From Migrants to Immigrants: *Hijas/os* (Ages Thirty to Forty-nine)

Participants in the *hijas/os* cohort have had diverse migration and labor experiences. Most came to the United States as children in the 1960s to 1970s, while a few came only after the devaluation of the Mexican peso in 1982 and Mexico City's earthquake in 1985. All of the *hijas/os* are permanent immigrants to California who worked in farm labor as children and teenagers, some of whom continued to work in the fields even after finishing high school. Because many in this cohort were already legal residents at the time the 1986 law was passed, legalization through IRCA was not the major push for Xaripus of this generation to leave farm labor (see also Sarmiento 2002). Rather, their transition from the fields to nonagricultural jobs was largely prompted by their experience with increasingly poor labor conditions during the late 1980s and early 1990s,[27] and also by their higher integration in school and social networks with workers outside the fields in comparison to the older cohorts.

Most of the *hijas/os* spent their first years in the United States in farm labor camps until their families moved into low-income housing projects in the early to late 1970s. As they moved into year-round housing (with some of the *hijas/os* leaving the fields), their families began to stay longer in the United States. Some families immediately became permanent immigrants in the early 1970s, others continued to migrate back and forth for most of the 1970s and early 1980s, and only a few families prolonged their familial migration into the late 1980s. By the 1990s, almost all families considered themselves to be living permanently in Stockton, even though all visit Xaripu frequently—though for shorter durations than before. While most *hijas/os* continue to visit Michoacán, only about half have the sense of having a dual home base in both countries, the way their parents and/or grandparents do. For them, home is generally in the United States, while Xaripu is their homeland and place of origin.[28]

Profiles of Selected Participating *Hijas/os*

Nico was born in 1951 in Xaripu. His father had been a bracero in the early 1940s. Like Danilo, Nico first left the pueblo for Mexico City in 1968; he went to school there and worked part-time as a butcher while maintaining continuous contact with the pueblo. In his interviews he reflected that life was easier in Mexico City during the late 1960s and early 1970s than it was in the 1980s because even laborers could eat meat every day. Business had been good there until the national standard of living declined in the 1980s because of the falling prices of oil and the devaluation of the peso (Krauze 1997; Cockcroft 1998).

In the early 1980s, Nico and his wife, Chelo, who is also from Xaripu, visited the United States with passports and started working in the fields in California. They continued to migrate back and forth until they gained legal U.S. residency status through the Special Agricultural Worker provision that facilitated the legalization of workers who had worked in the fields for ninety days before 1986. They now have four American-born children, ages eleven to seventeen.

Nico, Chelo, and their family's transnational experience is different from that of most of their cohort in that they spend more time on the southern side of the border than in California. Since 1987, Nico, who has a master's degree in education, has worked as a teacher in Michoacán for nine months of the year and as a farm worker in California for the remaining three months. He is one of the few transnational Xaripus who works in Mexico for most of the year. Nico considers Xaripu his permanent home, and he and Chelo want their US-born children to be raised there.

Olivia was born in Xaripu in 1960 and migrated to Stockton in 1973 at the age of twelve. At that time she was the oldest of four children; the youngest was four years old. In 1983 she married Daniel, also a Xaripu, and moved to San Jose, California. They have two children, ages twenty-one and seventeen, both of whom were born in the United States. After eleven years in San Jose, the family moved to Stockton in 1995 primarily so they would be closer to family and community. In doing so, both Olivia and Daniel gave up work benefits and a comfortable lifestyle. Olivia earned an associate's degree from San Joaquin County Delta College, and Daniel studied engineering at the University of Morelia in Michoacán for three years, after which he left his studies because of financial difficulties.

Olivia began to work in the fields of San Joaquin County during summer breaks and on weekends during school starting when she was twelve. She and her siblings initially accompanied their parents to the fields because her parents could not find or afford babysitters. Her father told her to keep all of her earnings, which motivated her to go on working so that she could buy clothing and other items. Olivia recounted excitedly how she bought dresses to go to dances, movies, and "everything" with her friends in Stockton. She contends that her relatively brief experience (six years) in the fields was helpful and did not traumatize her. Beginning in high school, Olivia worked at the YMCA for a few hours each day after school because her parents did not make enough money to provide for her teenage desires. She bought her own car—a 1978 Monarch—in 1979 when she was eighteen, which she recollected with pride: to her mind it illustrates how she had been a survivor who was "independent" and industrious.

Shortly after marrying in 1983, Olivia applied for a job at the post office in San Jose,[29] where she worked from 1984 to 1995, until she moved to San Joaquin, and then transferred to a post office there. She recounted that her would-be employers were impressed by her diverse skills and thus quickly hired her. Olivia became a US citizen in 1978 and Daniel in the 1980s. Their family visits Xaripu about every six to eight years.

Anita was born in 1968 in Xaripu. She finished junior high school in Mexico and went up to the eighth grade in the United States. Anita was only a few months old when she was brought to the United States in 1969. She was the youngest of four siblings, the oldest of whom was then eleven years old. Her mother, Ana, had started migrating in 1966 and would leave her then three children in Xaripu under her mother-in-law's care. When Ana got pregnant with Anita, she decided to return to Xaripu to give birth. This was during the Vietnam War, and she and her husband, Raul, were concerned that if the baby was born a boy in the United States he would be eligible to be drafted into the war when he turned eighteen. The exclusion of farm workers from unemployment insurance, workers compensation, and minimum wage also discouraged her from giving birth in the United States. Anita lived most of her life as a migrant worker, traveling from Xaripu to Stockton every six months until she married in 1991. Anita now has two daughters, aged thirteen and ten, both of whom were born in Stockton.

Anita started accompanying her family to the fields when she was about four years old but did not begin to work full-time there until she turned fifteen. Her experience was typical for this cohort. When she was very young, though her mother would sometimes stay home to care for her or leave her with other relatives, Anita was more often taken to the fields, where she would sleep in the car, wake up, and then get up to look for her family, who were picking cherries or tomatoes. She worked in the fields for the summers and on weekends during the school term. She was an excellent worker, with tremendous discipline and speed picking tomatoes, cherries, or apricots. Once the tomato harvest ended each November, her family headed back to Xaripu.[30]

Anita's family's labor migration ended in the early 1990s, when they settled permanently in *el norte*. Hers was among the last Xaripu families who migrated in the pattern of the Bracero Period: six months here, six months there. Their more permanent settlement resulted from her family's educational goals, decision to get into year-round housing as opposed to seasonal farm labor camps, and shift from the fields to nonagricultural jobs. Since 1997 Anita has worked in the production line in a factory making car lights and other parts for Toyota cars. She now goes to Xaripu every other year for about a week or two when she is able to get time off from work.

Born in the USA: *Chicas/os* (Ages Twenty to Twenty-nine)

Two characteristics differentiate *chicas/os* from members of the older cohorts. First, most of them were born in the United States while their families lived in farm labor camps or housing projects near the San Joaquin County General Hospital in French Camp, south of Stockton. Second, though they all grew up in farm-working families, only a few have had extensive farm labor experiences, and all have permanently settled in California. Roughly half of them visit Xaripu on a regular basis (once every one to three years), while the other half does so infrequently (once every four to six years).

Four of the women in this cohort have university degrees, which is atypical for women and men from Xaripu. Their higher educational attainment appears related to their shared experience as students in a migrant education program that connected them with the Summer Youth Employment and Training Program, a federally sponsored program for economically disadvantaged youth that introduced them to different types of occupational opportunities. These experiences exposed them to work other than farm labor and encouraged them to seek easier and better paying jobs via higher education.

The youth program generally placed girls in public service, teaching, and health-related jobs and boys in janitorial positions, recreational centers, and law enforcement. Possibly as a result of exposure to jobs that require higher education, more young women than young men in this community obtain bachelor's degrees. These young women tend to work in the private sector as clerical workers and sales staff or in public service as educators or health care providers. In contrast the young men generally work in warehouses, factories, construction, landscaping and gardening, and transportation. Their employment opportunities have been shaped by a racialized and gendered labor market that will be discussed in chapter 4 (see Segura 1990; Soldatenko 1991; Parreñas 2001a; Hesse-Biber and Carter 2000).

Profiles of Selected Participating *Chicas/os*

Tita was born in French Camp, California, in 1974. She obtained a bachelor's degree from the University of California, Davis, and completed a master's degree at California State University, Sacramento (CSUS). Her thesis focused on Chicanas/os' educational attainment and the role of multicultural education. While in college, Tita worked as a substitute teacher in Sacramento and Stockton. At the time of our interview, she was single and lived in Sacramento with Valencia, her cousin, who is also a college graduate (Tita got married in 1999).

As a young girl Tita worked a few days picking cherries with her brothers while on vacation from elementary school, shortly after her mother had had a baby (mid-1980s). At the age of fourteen Tita participated in the Summer Youth Employment and Training Program, which gave her clerical training; she worked as a clerk for the school district from 1987 to 1992. In the early 1990s she also worked for migrant education as a tutor. In the fall of 1992 she started school at the University of California, Davis, graduating in 1997. She was a caseworker for Head Start from January to September 1998 before beginning work as a substitute teacher while completing her master's degree.

Tita's migratory experience is that of a second-generation Chicana who maintains symbolic links with Michoacán (i.e., the homeland), rather than that of a transnational migrant (see Espiritu 2003b). She has briefly visited Xaripu three times in her life, at age two, six, and sixteen. Her parents are also infrequent visitors to Michoacán. Tita's home is California, and her short and infrequent visits to Michoacán demonstrate her rootedness to the United States.

Martina was born in Xaripu, Michoacán, in 1972. She was brought to the United States in 1973, and in 1975 her family decided to settle permanently in Stockton. In 1981 they moved to Lathrop, California, where they have lived ever since. Martina married a man from Jalisco, and they have four children. Martina has a bachelor's degree in sociology from University of Pacific, and in 1999 she worked for the Department of Corrections before becoming a full-time elementary school teacher.

Martina has also worked with the criminal justice system as a counselor and as a parole officer. Her early family experiences in Manteca, California, were characterized by conflict with the larger White community and a White police department. I grew up with her brothers in the housing projects in Stockton, and we also worked together in the fields as children in the 1970s and for most of the 1980s. When they moved out of the housing projects into a White working-class neighborhood, they experienced intense racial hostilities. Racial minorities "got jumped" (assaulted) by racially/culturally intolerant youth, and her brothers would often arrive home from school bruised and bleeding. In reaction to the social rejection, they fought back and coalesced with other neighborhood kids into a defensive block, which was inaccurately labeled a "gang" by the local media and police. These experiences influenced Martina's interest in working with youth in a hostile and racist community and her later decision to become a teacher.

Martina worked from 1996 to 1999 as a counselor in youth group homes, and in 1999 she worked for the San Joaquin County Juvenile Department. Martina described her job this way: "[We] change positions every eighteen months. Right now my duty is to place kids with an electronic device to make sure they stay home, rather than confining them in the juvenile facility. There is no room for them there." She quit her job early in 2000 because of what she felt were discriminatory practices in the department and now works as an elementary school teacher. Martina, who is married and has a growing family, visits Michoacán once every four to six years.

Lucina was also born in French Camp, California, in 1976. She is the youngest of eight siblings, is single, and lives with her parents. Lucina and her parents visit Xaripu almost every year, except when they cannot afford to or when she cannot get the time off from work. Lucina has worked mostly in service-sector jobs in restaurants and as a cashier. In 1999, at the time of our interview, she had started to work part-time for the probation department, writing re-institution letters, reading court orders, and working for the DAs office. She enjoyed the work and the work environment, which she described as friendly. But as a part-time worker she did not receive health insurance and noted, "It is very unfair [not to have health coverage]. If I'm not mistaken, all government jobs offer full-time coverage. That's what the part-time workers are fighting for."

Her parents' experiences with work injuries may have heightened her concern about the need for affordable health insurance. Her father, Juan, worked in California's agriculture industry from 1955 to 1995, and Lupe, her mother, has worked in farm labor since 1972. In 1995 Juan was forced to retire as a result of a back injury sustained in 1964 while picking lettuce. Juan was disabled for some time and then went to Guadalajara, Jalisco, to be fitted for a special back-support belt. The canvas belt was about twelve inches wide with metal plates that ran parallel to his spine and was tightened from the front like a shoe lace. Juan wore the belt for back support while working in the fields for three more decades. Despite frustrations with her job, Lucina thinks it would be difficult to find a comparable one with equal pay since she only has a high school diploma.

Connecting the Biographical Sketches to Colonial Dislocations

These biographical sketches provide background context on labor, community, and family relations for the following chapters. Moreover, they illustrate how, though Xaripus have crossed borders for over a century, their movement has changed in form and meaning,[31] especially for younger cohorts. The following chapters on theory and the social history of Xaripus further illustrate how the concepts of "migrant" and "immigrant" are inadequate for capturing Xaripus' experiences crossing borders. The term "immigrant" obscures Xaripus' historical and even ancestral connections with Indigenous people colonized by the Spanish and later by Anglos in the Southwest (Warren 1985, 4).[32] "Migrant" implies transient foreigners coming primarily to work and then returning to their place of origin, while "immigrant" suggests foreigners coming to stay permanently. Older Xaripu cohorts had parents and relatives who worked in the United States for most of their adult lives. These Xaripus were not new to the United States, and calling them either migrants or immigrants obscures their long historical movement caused by American political-economic interventions in Mexico (Cockcroft 1998; Gómez-Quiñones 1994; Gonzalez and Fernandez 2003; Portes and Rumbaut 2006; Sassen 1996b). Their migration parallels Southern Black migration at the turn of the twentieth century—dislocated by monopoly capitalism, agribusiness mechanization, and recruitment by northern industrialists (Bonacich 1976; Du Bois 1903). Occupational segregation in low-wage labor and immigration restrictions maintained Xaripus' continuous migrations through most of the twentieth century, and their more permanent settlement in the United States led to various forms of transnationalism.

The majority of *hijas/os* came to the United States as children who routinely traveled back and forth between Michoacán and California. Through the family reunification provision of the 1965 Immigration and Naturalization Act, women and children began migrating in the mid-1960s. By the late '70s most had settled permanently in *el norte*, though most continue to visit Michoacán as frequently. Younger Xaripus, however, stay for much shorter periods of time. *Chicas/os* generally were born in California, did not work in agriculture, and visit Michoacán less frequently than the older cohorts. Regardless of their citizenship status, most had parents, grandparents, and even great-grandparents who worked most of their lives in the United States.

Chapter Two

THEORETICAL PERSPECTIVES ON LABOR MIGRATION

I was about 17 years of age in 1910. I went alone, hoping that I would make some money. People had already talked to me about *el norte*. A man, who worked a small plot of land on the edge of the pueblo, had gone and returned and went again. He had talked to me about his experience, and, well, I grew anxious to go, and so I soon went after that. What motivated me? Well, I made 25 cents here [in Michoacán], and that was what they paid us. What do you think of that? We were here literally barefooted and naked. We wore *manta* [peasant cloths] and *guaraches* with one strap securing them to our feet. Well, life was tough—that was when people started going and going. I also started going, and then little by little many people began to go. In little time the path was paved. You see now. People don't want to stay here.

    —A Xaripu migrant (Fonseca and Moreno 1984, 139–40)[1]

Why did Xaripus begin to leave Mexico and come to *el norte* when they did? Why did they take almost two-thirds of a century after the first pioneering migrants to settle on a more permanent basis in the

United States? Why do later generations maintain active and meaning-ful social ties with the homeland?[2] And what changes have these Xaripus experienced by living in between different social worlds? This chapter addresses these basic questions by reviewing three major theoretical perspectives and introducing a fourth conceptual framework for under-standing the Xaripu experience.

The push-pull model is one of the most commonly cited explanations for why people immigrate to the United States. Popular with the public, civic officials, and the media, it offers a seemingly common-sense expla-nation of migration—as articulated well by the Xaripu migrant above. The experiences seemingly fits the logic of classical economics in insist-ing that individuals realize that there are more jobs, higher wages, social services, political freedoms, and so forth in America (the "pull") than in their impoverished, politically repressive, and overpopulated third-world countries (the "push") and so leave their homelands to immigrate to the United States.

New economic theories elaborate on the push-pull model by placing rational individuals who seek capital within a web of social relationships—family and community—that limit, enhance, and shape the decision to immigrate (Massey et al. 2002). But though these and other variants of push-pull theories explain individual migration, their limits are too seri-ous to ignore (Portes and Rumbaut 1996; Parreñas 2001b; Gonzalez and Fernandez 2003). They fail to provide a sufficient explanation of mass migration and to elaborate the historical-structural relationships (po-litical, economic, and cultural) between the sending and the receiving societies. This grave omission obscures the history of modern labor mi-gration as a product of global-national inequalities and reflects an in-ability or refusal to recognize that the political-economic conditions of the sending and receiving countries are fundamentally related (Chang 2000; Sassen 2003; Bonacich and Cheng 1984).

The Xaripu community's labor migration experiences exist within a global-historical context of racial, gender, and class inequalities. Three perspectives—structural, transnational, and internal colonial—help ex-plain the migratory processes that have shaped the Xaripu experience. But though each theoretical model highlights an important factor in the migration experience, I propose a framework—interactive colonization—that synthesizes the most cogent contributions of these perspectives and highlights the complex relationships and developments that shape the Xaripu experience.

STRUCTURAL PERSPECTIVES

Contrary to the ahistorical flaws in the push-pull model's explanation of migration, structural theories identify the history of imperialism[3] as the chief cause of mass migration from specific regions of the world. This perspective highlights the causal relationship between capital mobility and labor migration (Sassen 1996b; Portes and Rumbaut 1996; Kearney 1996; Gonzalez and Fernandez 2001, 2003; De Genova and Ramos-Zayas 2003), including how military interventions, labor recruitment, and foreign investment displace people from their homelands and directly contribute to large-scale migrations of both capital and workers (see Fernandez-Kelly 1983; Kay 1989; Gómez-Quiñones 1994; Sassen 1988, 1996b, 1998; Gonzalez and Fernandez 2003).

As Bonacich and Cheng elaborate, capitalism has an inherent tendency toward economic imperialism. Capitalism suffers from long-term, cyclical crises originating "from a decline in the rate of profit, leading capitalists to reduce their investments, which in turn leads to rising unemployment, and so on, in a downward spiral" (1984, 4). These crises are rooted in the intense quest for profits and the corresponding overproduction of a good, which ultimately hurts the price and thus profit. Consequently, employers lay off workers and, with fewer workers, maintain high production levels by lengthening the work day and intensifying productivity through speedups, lowering wages, and/or introducing new technology to displace the high cost of labor. This approach creates both high unemployment and low consumption rates (Bonacich and Cheng 1984, 7–8; Bonacich and Appelbaum 2000, 102–3; Cockcroft 1998, 172– 73). Unable to resolve the crisis from within the nation, capitalists shift production across national borders in search of lower production costs (i.e., labor, resources, and regulations).

Capitalists' interest in foreign resources and their influence on their government have contributed to the politics of empire, which consist of intervening militarily, politically, and/or economically in less capitalistic societies and imposing political-economic structures that benefit the stronger nation (Sassen 1996a, 76–85; Portes and Rumbaut 1996, 272–74; Gómez-Quiñones 1994, 88–89; Cockcroft 1998, 186–90; Hart 2002, 502–3; Gonzalez and Fernandez 2003, 38–45). These interventions disrupt traditional societies and cause emigration. As Bonacich and Cheng argue, "two conditions, the displacement of colonized peoples and the requirement of more labor in the capitalist economy, arise out of the logic of capitalist development. . . . In other words, migration is a product not of discrete and unconnected factors in the sending and receiving societies but of historical connections between the countries. It is not fortuitous; it is systemic" (1984, 2).

While neocolonizing countries develop from unequal global relations, neocolonized nations undergo stagnation and decay resulting from their debts (on imported high-cost capital) to a few investor/creditor nations (Frank 1967, 1969; Wallerstein 1974; Kearney 1996; Cockcroft 1998; Hart 2002; Sassen 2003). At the global level the feudal relationships that were seemingly displaced by capitalistic ones are reproduced metaphorically as a modern transnational sharecropping system. Neocolonized nations produce for the neocolonizers, respond to their consumption needs, borrow credit/capital from them to produce for them, and continuously fall deeper into debt while creating wealth for the neocolonizer elites and the neocolonized intermediaries.

As Portes and Rumbaut note, Mexican immigration "had its historical origins in US geopolitical and economic expansion that first remolded the neighboring nation and then proceeded to organize dependable labor flows out of it" (1996, 274). The authors explain how US imperialism "structurally imbalanced"[4] Mexico by producing mass migration over time. The United States' war against Mexico in 1846–48 reduced Mexico's territory by half and rendered most of its people on either side of the border a source of colonial labor for the United States (see Acuña 1988; Barrera 1979; Hart 2002).

On the Mexican side of the border, the Porfiriato dictatorship (1876–1910) created optimum conditions for the exploitation of national resources by foreign investors, who constructed roads, ports, and railroads that funneled much wealth and labor into the United States. The Porfiriato government accepted its neocolonized status and followed "a process of dependent development" alongside an emergent global empire (Hart 2002, 266). The related expansion of capitalist industry directly contributed to Mexican intra-national and international migrations to the United States (Gamio 1930; Galarza 1964; McWilliams 1990; Gómez-Quiñones 1994; Caulfield 1998; Krauze 1997; Gonzalez and Fernandez 2003; Mora-Torres 2001). US agribusiness, mining, and railroad companies sent representatives deep into Mexico to recruit workers (Gómez-Quiñones 1994; McWilliams 1990; Ngai 2004). Mexican peasants were offered free railroad transportation and cash advances to migrate north. This mass migration was made up mostly of Indigenous people ("Indians") and indo-mestizas/os (Gamio 1930; Ochoa Serrano 1997; Moreno García 1994; Cockcroft 1998). Throughout this process, the construction of Mexican identity in the Southwest United States shifted from that of Natives to a homogenized group of "Mexican aliens" and much later to the collective "illegal immigrants" (Portes and Rumbaut 1996, 274; Nevins 2002, 111–12), particularly after the restrictive Johnson-Reed Immigration Act of 1924 (Ngai 2004, 60–87).[5]

In the twenty-first century, the United States maintains its transnational financial domination of Mexico, which directly contributes to the scope of Mexican emigration to *el norte* (Gonzalez and Fernandez 2003, 54–59; Hart 2002, 432–46). The 1994 North American Free Trade Agreement (NAFTA) formalized "free trade" between the United States, Canada, and Mexico yet particularly disadvantaged Mexico's domestic industries in manufacturing and agriculture (Barndt 2002, 173–75; Thompson 2002; Edelman 2002; Kraul 2002; López 2007, 36–42). In an echo of the Porfiriato period a century earlier, powerful multinational corporations advantageously pushed for privatization, deregulation, and de-tariffing, which hurt the Mexican domestic economy and advanced US capitalists' international control of capital, credit/investment, and profits (Hart 2002, 437–53, 466–74). In a modern form of transnational sharecropping, neocolonized nations (e.g., Mexico) produce wealth and remain in debt while developed ones (e.g., the United States) collect the profits and continue to invest in a global sharecropping system and to push for Structural Adjustment Programs (SAP),[6] which secure such relationships (Sassen 2003, 27–28, 56; Chang 2000, 123–29; Gonzalez and Fernandez 2003, 49–52; Barndt 2002, 173–75). As Cockcroft elaborates,

Capital accumulation for foreign monopoly capital, while originating in the sphere of Mexican production, takes place in the sphere of international money circulation as well (especially through the debt structure). This circulation taps into Mexico's economic surplus and siphons it increasingly into the hands of financial institutions outside of Mexico—further decapitalizing Mexico. Equally important, imperialism uses a nation's debt structure to intervene in the shaping of critical national decisions, such as the use to which oil revenues will be put. (1998, 191)

Assessment of Structural Perspectives

Structural theories' attention to the history of unequal relations between nations and/or global regions and their recognition of how this history has benefited some nations with wealth and development while disadvantaging others with debt and poverty contribute much to a thorough understanding of contemporary migration. While structural views vary in their foci (Brewer 1990, 181; Kearney 1996, 83; Gonzalez and Fernandez 2003, 6–7, 48),[7] their basic insights provide a fuller picture of how global economic integration dislocates people from their homelands (Massey et al. 2002, 144–46; Portes and Rumbaut 1996, 282–84). They also point out how the diverse and conflictive experience of migration transforms migrants' identities by exposing them to different work experiences and social realities (Kearney 1996, 83; Rouse 1992, 1996; Glick-Schiller et al. 1992a and 1992c; Mummert 1999b).

Even though structural theories appropriately point to the powerful macro-level factors that contribute to migration, they fail to sufficiently explain the exploitation of foreign laborers and the racism and sexism that underpin this exploitation. For instance, they do not fully account for why capitalists exploit foreign laborers more and pay them less than domestic workers. Migrant workers from neocolonies do not set the low wages for themselves; indeed they travel hundreds and thousands of miles from home in search of higher wages. Their material experience in their homelands compared to that in their new country partly explains why immigrants accept low wages and poor working conditions. But migrants do not set out to displace domestic workers, nor are they necessarily absorbed as cheaper labor through supply and demand economic principles (Ngai 2004, 106–9).[8] (For more on this topic, see chapter 4.)

Structural views' near-exclusive focus on how the political economy shapes labor migration neglects the roles of racism and patriarchy and considers their impact secondary to the basic and all-determining economic relationship. Underestimating the significance of racial dynamics in shaping modernity—i.e., the creation of nation-states, capitalism, and culture/identities (Winant 2001; Quijano 2000)—impedes a full understanding of modern labor migration (Espiritu 2003b). The modern nation-states that emerged from colonialism developed concepts of citizenship, boundaries, and rights that excluded, segregated, and marginalized racialized Natives and women (see Glenn 2002; Nevins 2002; Delgado 2003). These countries have differentially incorporated immigrants into the nation on the basis of race, class, gender, and national origin (Espiritu 2003b; Ngai 2004; Zolberg 2006). For instance, Xaripu men migrated for over two-thirds of a century before they and their families began a general settlement process in the United States. This migration pattern was shaped by racist/sexist labor markets and immigration policy acts,[9] though Xaripus' social networks with their community, family, and friends across borders produced unique settlement and migration experiences within the more general trend.

TRANSNATIONAL PERSPECTIVES

Transnational perspectives bring the analysis of migration closer to the subjects of migrants and their communities by focusing on their social ties (networks) across borders.[10] Complementing the macro-structural perspective outlined above, transnational theories examine more personal-level and interactional-level processes in migration[11] and consider the social context—local community, family, and personal factors—that influences individual migration decisions. Scholars who adhere to this framework ascribe more personal and collective agency to migrants, which helps nuance the more deterministic models of migration posited by structural theorists (Rouse 1992, 31; Palacios Franco 1987, 13; Arizpe 1978, 247; Hondagneu-Sotelo 1994, 6, 15).

Transnational migration scholars regard migrants as people embedded in extensive and fluid social networks (economic, political, and cultural) that exist across national borders. Though scholars have not reached consensus over the content range and nature of transnationalism (Guarnizo and Smith 2003, 3–4; Menjívar 2004, 1–2; Fouron and Glick-Schiller 2002, 171), some have tried to map out variations in its practice and magnitude: from occasional to habitual, from selective to comprehensive activities, and from a personal to an institutional level (see Levitt 2001, 199).

Some scholars view transnationalism as a new phenomenon resulting from the increased internationalization of the economy and advances in technology (see Glick-Schiller et al. 1992c; Portes and Rumbaut 1996; Hondagneu-Sotelo and Avila 1997). But others point out that transnational migration existed long before the new advances in transportation and communication took place (Torres 1998, 171–72, 182; Gledhill 1999, 32; Guarnizo and Smith 1999, 87–88; Gómez-Quiñones 1994, 71, 73, 88–92; Castillo 1994, 36–37). Weber, for example, notes, "Transnationalism is not completely new. . . .While distance and lack of communication cut off some immigrants from their native countries, many others maintained meaningful familial, social, and economic contacts with their hometown" (1998, 211). More qualified claims acknowledge this history but stress that transnationalism has been intensified in direct relation to neocolonialism; advances in technology; reincorporation by sending nations that promote tourism, remittances, and investment; racist nativism in receiving societies that contributes to a sense of non-belonging; and the development and persistence of social networks across borders (Parreñas 2001, 80–81; Espiritu 2003b, 70–71; Guarnizo and Smith 2003, 24; Goldring 2003, 166–170, 189; Smith 2003, 205, 207; Tyner 2003, 68, 73). This latter focus on the nature of social ties has occupied much of recent scholarly attention. Particularly helpful for our purposes, Massey and his co-authors' assessment of Mexican migration (1987) identified six facets of the development of migrant social networks across national borders.

First, dislocated by structural transformations (see Arizpe 1981; Fonseca and Moreno 1984; Massey et al. 1987; Grasmuck and Pessar 1991; Sassen 1996a, 1996b, 2003; Cockcroft 1998), migrant pioneers create social ties between the sending and receiving societies. Though individual agency and household politics have some impact upon the form of migration, an elite network of actors—i.e., transnational corporate elites—has the power to determine who migrates on a larger scale, such as professionals or laborers, men and/or women, particular national origin(s) and not others (Parreñas 2001; Portes and Rumbaut 1996; Tyner 2003; Sassen 2003). Thus the migrant's individual agency in determining whether and where to go is limited by existing structures of opportunity—i.e., labor market, national policies, and community support—that determine whether migration takes place on an individual level or becomes a large-scale phenomenon. Moreover, the development of migratory social networks is shaped by racialized and gendered global labor market demands, whereby core country administrators recruit—often aided by the sending country—third-world men into agricultural work and women into service and domestic employment.

Second, over time migrants develop a social infrastructure that facilitates mass migration (Glick-Schiller et al. 1992a, b; Rouse 1992, 1996; Portes and Rumbaut 1996, 2006). The pioneer migrants set the stage for a large-scale migration as cross-sectional networks develop (Massey et al. 1987). Social networks, constituting social capital, reduce the costs of migrating as migrants engage in reciprocal/mutual aid activities (Grasmuck and Pessar 1991, 13; Massey et al. 2002, 18–21). As Massey and his co-authors observe, "Each act of migration creates social capital among the people to whom the migrant is related, thereby raising the odds of their migration" (2002, 19).

However, migrants' political status, labor market opportunities, and the quality of their networks in the receiving society greatly affect the advantageousness of their social capital (Menjívar 2000, 148–58; Portes and Rumbaut 1996, 82–92). For instance, Menjívar (2000) documents the varying value of migrants' social ties among Salvadorans who are undocumented and who experience low-paying and unstable service jobs along with intense nativism (see also Espiritu 2003b; Chavez 1997). Under such circumstances, Menjívar observes, Salvadorans' "social capital may be drained under extreme conditions of poverty, because exchanges with friends and relatives become highly irregular" (2000, 156). Moreover, social networks are not equally accessible to all social relations: they are fluid and are rearranged as some connections are lost and others are gained.[12]

Third, household life cycles influence the survival strategies that shape families' labor-migration patterns. Age, marital status, number of children, and other life changes affect a household's labor-migration decisions and experiences (see Palacios Franco 1987, 43, 58–59; García et al. 1982, 52–53; Sarmiento 2002, 158–60, 179). Grasmuck and Pessar, for example, document how the shift from subsistence living to commercial farming production in the Dominican Republic reduced the need for large families in farming, which encouraged the sponsorship of sons' emigration and relegated non-migrant women to domesticity and economic dependency (1991, 139–47). Sarmiento also observed that the developmental cycles of Tzintzuntzeño families' (that is, Purépechans from Michoacán) significantly shape their migration and settlement processes (2002, 179).[13] Being married and having children encourages migrants to pursue family reunification, either by continuing the migration to see family or by bringing the entire family over. Moreover, stable employment and the number and ages of children also mediate family's migration and settlement patterns (Sarmiento 2002, 184).[14] With steady employment, large families are more likely to settle in one place to secure a better education and home stability for their children.

Fourth, international migration eventually becomes a self-sustaining social process whereby migration experiences affect persons' attitudes, family survival strategies, and community structures (Portes and Rumbaut 1996; Massey et al. 2002). As Massey and his colleagues contend, "Once the number of network connections in a community reaches a critical threshold, migration becomes self-perpetuating because each act of migration creates the social structure needed to sustain it" (2002, 20). Portes and Rumbaut likewise note, "At some moment, networks across international borders acquire sufficient strength to induce migration for motives other than those that initiated the flow" (1996, 276). Modern migration thus becomes "self-initiated" or "self-perpetuated," and the "gap between modern consumption standards and the economic realities of backward countries plus increasing information about work opportunities abroad provide enough incentives to generate an almost limitless supply of would-be migrants" (Portes and Rumbaut 1996, 275).

Fifth, temporary migration becomes permanent settlement in the receiving society. Initially migrant workers return to their homeland communities, but over time they establish social, institutional, and economic ties in the receiving society that transforms their migration into settlement (Espiritu 2003b; Hondagneu-Sotelo 1994; Hagan 1994). However, this settlement does not completely cut social ties with the homeland, particularly for the first generations and for some members of subsequent generations (Levitt and Waters 2002, 13–18; Rumbaut 2002, 79–89; Kasinitz et al. 2002, 119).

Sixth and lastly, return migration keeps transnational ties alive and problematizes dualistic models of migration that depict migrants as having a home base in only one geographical site (see Kearney 1996). Roger Rouse (1992), for instance, documented how Mexican migrants from La Pitaya, Michoacán, and Redwood City, California, maintained transnational ties between both places. Some who had settled in the United States returned permanently to La Pitaya when they retired; others did so when they felt they had saved enough money to run a small-scale farming operation in Mexico, some when they were deported by the INS, and others according to changes in family life cycles (see also Glick-Schiller et al. 1992a, c; Kearney 1996; Weber 1998; Mummert 1999). Remittances reaffirmed connections between migrants and their sending communities and encouraged further migrations to support house constructions and other community projects in La Pitaya. Thus sojourners and settlers were not simply from here or from there, because extensive social ties across the borders created a single, bi-locational community (see also Rouse 1996, 254):

> Through constant movement back and forth, the energetic efforts to reproduce involvements across space, and the accompanying circulation of money, goods and services, the municipio, Redwood City and the other settlements in the United States had been woven together so tightly that, in an important sense, they had come to form a single community spanning the various locales, an arrangement I have referred to elsewhere as a "transnational migrant circuit." It was the circuit as a whole that constituted the main arena in which Aguilillans developed and maintained social ties and the primary setting in which they orchestrated their lives. Moreover, while its continued existence depended on the efforts of those who actively reproduced their transnational connections, its workings exerted an effect on everyone who lived within its compass. (Rouse 1992, 45)

To summarize, transnational social ties typically originate from migrants' structural dislocation from their native country and their subsequent incorporation as low-wage workers throughout the globe. Migrants' marginal status and sense of non-belonging in receiving societies further enhance their social and emotional ties to the homeland, to which they routinely remit cash and gifts to family (Espiritu 2003b; Goldring 2003; Parreñas 2001b; Levitt and Waters 2002). Although over time migrants generally move toward settlement (Rumbaut 2002, 91; Mahler 2003, 78–80), some actively preserve their transnational ties and thereby create what Rouse calls "transnational migrant circuits" and others have called "transnational social fields," which shape the thoughts, feelings, and behavior of both migrant and non-migrants in the sending and receiving societies (see Mahler 2003, 75–76; Levitt 2001, 197; Fouron and Glick-Schiller 2002, 172–73).

Assessment of Transnational Perspectives

Social networks link sending and receiving societies, give agency to migrants and households, maintain transnational migration, and circulate social resources. But recent scholarship has problematized simplified descriptions of households/networks as cohesive and unified, since these obscure the social differentiations that exist within immigrant communities (e.g. along gender, generation, and class lines) and neglect migrants' unequal access to these social ties, power, and resources (Grasmuck and Pessar 1991; Hagan 1994; Hondagneu-Sotelo 1994, 2003; Alicea 1997; Menjívar 2000; Parreñas 2001b; Mahler 2003). For all of their merits, social networks are not always supportive, and poverty can weaken or dissolve social ties. What is more, national policies, labor market demands, and the receiving community all affect the form and nature of social networks and thus the resources that migrants will have available upon their arrival.

Transnational theories also direct attention away from the continued social-economic disparities that exist across the borders and that are the primary stimuli of migration by emphasizing the role of social networks in advancing or even causing migration (Menjívar 2000; Parreñas 2001b; Gonzalez and Fernandez 2003). Although social networks facilitate migration, claims that modern migration is primarily self-initiated and not induced by political-economic interventions and relations as in the past neglect historical and structural factors (Chang 2000). The problem arises from these scholars' tendency to separate today's migrants from both history and contemporary nation-state policies—e.g., structural adjustment programs and free trade agreements—and instead focus on individual-level short-term events—e.g., family migration mediated by social networks—removed from broader historical and structural trends. In doing so, social network analysis fails to demonstrate how social ties alone sustain migration without controlling for the impacts of unequal national conditions and relationships between sending and receiving societies.[15] A comprehensive explanation of migration needs to account for nation-state policies and practices within a historical context of global domination (Kearney 1996; Sassen 1988, 1996a, 1996b, 1998; Quijano 2000; Gonzalez and Fernandez 2003). Thus as Menjívar points out, "The task in analyzing immigrant social networks is, then, to consider both the structural parameters that delimit social action and the individual responses to broader forces as informed by social positions and ideologies" (2000, 36).

Lastly, Rouse's idea that migrants "come to form a single community spanning the various locales, an arrangement I have referred to elsewhere as a 'transnational migrant circuit'" (1992, 45)[16] misses the social differentiations that fragment transnational communities. Cultural and material inequities arise between migrants and non-migrants, and labeling them "a single community" obscures the emergent social distances that exist between them. The idea of a seamless circuit is further complicated by the reality that transnational migrants experience different material and cultural contexts from those of non-migrants—experiences that in turn shape differing senses of self and community as well as distinct beliefs and behaviors.

INTERNAL COLONIALISM

Colonialism—as a comprehensive project of domination with long-lasting effects—is one of the most powerful events shaping modern labor migration experiences and by extension complex social differentiations among members of the same extended communities. Indeed, as will be elaborated below, internal and neocolonial experiences have shaped Xaripu migration to *el norte,* and have influenced intra-community relationships (i.e., within the pueblo) in a manner that is analogous to the relationships between "house" and "field" colonial subjects.

The internal colonial model (hereafter referred to as IC) views labor migration from the social-historical perspective of colonialism. Colonialism shaped contemporary inter- and intra-national inequalities in and between Mexico and the United States and has consequently influenced who migrates and how they are incorporated into the receiving society.[17] IC examines multiple sources of oppression and thus reflects empirical reality more accurately than the other models surveyed thus far (Carr 1997; Omi and Winant 1994; Barrera 1979). Moreover, it proceeds from the realization that nation-building has not been a project bringing diverse people together with equal rights and protections as citizens, but rather has structured hierarchies of racial, gender, and class privilege in modern nations and emergent global social structures (Espiritu 2003b; Glenn 2002; Ngai 2004; Nevins 2002; Winant 2001). By highlighting the dialectical relationship between the colonizers and the colonized within the nation-state, IC underscores multidimensional forms of oppression (Almaguer 1971; Mirandé 1985; San Juan 1992). In what follows, I conceptualize IC, assess its utility for interpreting labor migration, and propose an alternative conceptual framework: interactive colonization.

Conceptualizing Internal Colonialism

The concept of internal colonialism is both distinct from and related to colonialism and neocolonialism (see Feagin and Feagin 1999; Quijano 2000). Colonialism is generally understood as a comprehensive project of domination in which colonizers used force to appropriate the land, labor, and resources from another people; imposed a social order (political-economic system and culture) that privileged them over the colonized subjects; and ruled the colony or colonies from outside of the actual territory (see Memmi 1965; Blauner 1972; Almaguer 1971; Sosa Riddell [1974] 2001; Barrera 1979; Mirandé 1985, 1987; Glenn 1994a; Castillo 1994; San Juan 1992, 1998). In the Americas, colonizers took the lands and surplus-value labor of Natives and organized a racist and sexist division of labor[18] that exploited the colonized in plantations and haciendas (Almaguer 1994; Cockcroft 1998; Gómez-Quiñones 1994; Glenn 1994a; Winant 2001). From the start, the Natives resisted and fought for liberation from oppression.[19] But colonialism proved difficult to dismantle, and other varieties often supplant it, particularly neocolonialism and internal colonialism.

Neocolonialism describes what occurs when a colony gains independence from its colonizer but nonetheless remains politically and economically subordinated to other powerful nations.[20] In the case of Mexico, after gaining independence from Spain in 1821, the weak and emerging nation-state remained vulnerable to other empires, particularly its neighbor to the north. The United States immediately warned Europe through the 1823 Monroe Doctrine to stay away from Indo America,[21] and by 1848 it had taken over half of the Mexican territory. The United States subsequently aided President Juarez during the French invasion of the 1860s and then neocolonized the remaining half of the Mexican territory by monopolizing its infrastructure and valuable resources (Hart 2002; Gonzalez and Fernandez 2003). This new form of colonialism was less costly (Grosfoguel 2003a) and more manageable[22] than a complete military takeover like what the United States had done earlier in the Southwest.

Internal colonialism is the condition that developed for Natives and slaves after the American colonies gained their independence from their colonizing kingdoms. While American-born colonists found freedom from the unequal treatment of their previous owners, slaves and Indigenous people remained powerless in the emerging nation's internal systems of social domination and went from being externally colonized to being internally colonized within their geographical space.[23] Although some scholars prefer the term "postcolonial" to classify Indigenous people who went from being externally colonized to being integrated as nation-state members (e.g., Mexicans after the 1848 Treaty of Guadalupe Hidalgo), that term obscures the continued unequal treatment experienced by those who effectively remained colonized subjects long after formal or legal racial domination ended.[24]

In *Racial Oppression in America*, Blauner, who popularized the term "internal colonialism," underscores the centrality of institutional racism in the United States.[25] Although formal domination, such as de jure racism and national-origin quotas for immigrants ended with the civil rights acts of the '60s, the content of colonial domination persisted in institutional practices, as evidenced in the social devaluation and segregation of minorities in employment and education as well as in the media and government (San Juan 1998, 162–63). Racial and ethnic inequities continue in individual and organizational norms, values, and practices sometimes referred to as the "privileges of whiteness" (McIntosh 1997)[26] and are preserved through a "possessive investment in whiteness" (Lipsitz 1998).[27] This racism has created unearned advantages and rewards for Whites and disadvantages and liabilities for racial minorities (Feagin and Vera 1995; Feagin 2000; Kivel 1995; Lipsitz 1998; McIntosh 1997; Wellman 1977). The historical roots of these inequities are obscured through ideologies of individualism and meritocracy (Crenshaw 1995; Carr 1997; Winant 1994, 2001), which shift attention away from the legacy of slavery and institutionalized racism and on to individual and cultural deficiencies among minorities.

Adding complexity to these overlapping colonialisms is the reality that neocolonized nations can also have internal colonies. Many Indo American countries that gained independence from Spain and Portugal, for example, subsequently entered into a neocolonized relationship with stronger empires like the United States, England, and France. These neocolonized nations also reproduced social hierarchies within their borders that originated from their earlier colonizers (see Bonfil Batalla 1996; Ochoa Serrano 1997; Alvarez del Toro 1988; Moreno García 1994).[28] However, these new administrators were not fully in control of their nations' resources, which became monopolized by foreign neocolonizers. As elaborated in chapter 1, Porfirio Díaz brokered the appropriation of national resources to the United States in the pursuit of dependent development (Cockcroft 1998; Hart 1998; Gonzalez and Fernandez 2003). Díaz believed foreign investors would help Mexico's economic development by building its infrastructure (roads, railroads, communication); instead they came to control most of the national resources and used the infrastructure to funnel out the wealth, using the peasants at all levels of production (extractive labor, transportation, service) to fuel the development of the United States. In the process, colonial laborers were generally dislocated from their land and became highly exploited migrant workers in the most difficult and least rewarding jobs in both Mexico and the United States (Cockcroft 1998; Ngai 2004).

In *Race and Class in the Southwest,* Barrera documents the internal colonial experience of these dislocated people (Chicanas/os) in the United States and assesses that "Chicanos are members of all classes in the United States, but form a subordinate segment within each class" (1979, 214). As evidence, Barrera points to Chicanas/os' ongoing labor exploitation, categorically lower wages, and occupational stratification in agriculture, service, construction, and other job sectors (see also Barrera 1979, 216–19; Glenn 1994a, 145, 148; Vélez-Ibáñez 1996, 65–72). This experience continues in the twenty-first century (Chacón and Davis 2006; Levine 2006).

Assessment of Internal Colonialism

The internal colonial model illustrates how emergent nation-states continued to subordinate Indigenous people and slaves, who later gained formal freedoms and inclusion as members of the nation but remained in de facto relationships of domination, excluded from valuable resources, and devalued as a people. Nevertheless, three critical questions about IC provide a basis for my proposed alternative model: (1) Do the internally colonized exist as a single and homogenous community? (2) Are the internally colonized spatially bounded? And (3) do dualistic concepts—e.g., "them" and "us"—limit IC?

First, though the "internal colony" is often described as a group that shares common experiences, including racism, which create a common sense of "us" across classes, not all members of the group share the same interests or experiences. Rather, members' experiences are shaped by racial, gender, and class differences. Consequently, IC has been dismissed for not accurately representing the history of racial minorities in contemporary times (Acuña 1981, vii) and for reducing Chicanas/os to monolithic victims (Gonzalez 1999, 4–5; Gonzalez and Gonzalez 2000, xii–xiii; Montoya 2000, 187). Although this critique neglects the long-lasting impacts of colonialism (Mirandé 1985; Glenn 1994a; San Juan 1998), it encourages a close examination of the historically diverse experiences within the internal colony[29] that challenge the notion of a unified "us."

A second critique of IC contends that the internally colonized must be confined or bound to a specific geography (Moore 1976; Omi and Winant 1986; Cervantez 2003), which therefore excludes seemingly "voluntary" Mexican migrants. Furthermore, according to this critique, spatial and social segregation is no longer rigid or legally enforced, and high rates of interracial marriages are common. While these are important developments, occupational, educational, and residential segregation continue in contemporary society.[30] Moreover, rigid physical and social apartness was not absolute even during classical colonialism. Mixing among slaves and masters was common, and the offspring typically became an intermediary group (Jacobs 1987; Winant 2001; Ochoa Serrano 1997). *Ranchero* elites often intermarried with the new White colonizers in Texas (Montejano 1987; Limón 1994), California (Pitt 1966; Camarillo 1979) and other Southwestern states (Vélez-Ibáñez 1996). Thus some could move in and out of internal colonies, though the freedom to do so was shaped by race, class, and gender (Limón 1994, 61–62, 100–101). Indigenous persons, poorer people, and women were more constrained and regulated in their movement.

Lastly, a serious critique highlights that IC maintains a dualistic and static framework in examining group conflict, e.g., colonized versus colonizers, dependent versus developed nations, and core versus periphery regions. This critique also relates to IC scholars' neglect of the internal diversity within the "colonized" and "colonizers," which results in simplified discussions of "them versus us" and breaks down potential alliances among those at the bottom of the colonial-rooted social hierarchies.

MOVING BEYOND TRADITIONAL PERSPECTIVES

Though structural, transnational, and internal colonial frameworks offer much to explain labor migration experiences, all can benefit from a more comprehensive analysis. Structural views tend to treat global regions as being made up of undifferentiated people (ignoring internal diversity by race/ethnicity, class, and gender) who are subjected to the same dislocations and homogenizing forces of global capitalism. This model also ignores the internal colonial experiences within both neocolonized nations and neocolonizing empires. Its simplistic understanding of migration from above (capital) and below (labor) is confined to the evolving relations of capitalist production, which neglects or subsumes the roles of patriarchy and racism—forces that have shaped the patterns of global capitalism and development within and across nations.

Contrary to the structural approach, transnational perspectives emphasize individual- and community-level networks as key factors shaping modern international migration. Yet their stress on social networks obscures the continued significance of global inequality and its central role in international migration experiences. Furthermore, the claim that migrants and their social networks create a unified community across (or transcending) nations is problematic. This view simplifies the emergent changes that occur between those who remain in the sending society, those who have settled permanently in the receiving society, and those who continuously move across borders. It is thus crucial to analyze the range of social experiences that exist on both sides of the border in order to more fully understand transnational experiences, particularly those of the most marginalized, such as the internally colonized in neocolonized nations.

IC offers a helpful corrective to both structural and transnational views in that it contextualizes institutional and social processes by highlighting colonialism and its social consequences, particularly the universalizing of economic exploitation, patriarchy, and racial domination (Sosa Riddell [1974] 2001, 362–64; Almaguer 1994, 109–11; Pollard 1993, 178–79). IC scholars, however, tend to blur the conflicts and differentiations that exist within groups and have neglected patriarchal oppression as part of the colonial project. Therefore, notions of a unified internal colony and its dualistic nature need to be rearticulated within other conceptual frameworks.

INTERACTIVE COLONIZATION

This book examines colonial subjects who cross borders from their neocolonized (sending) nation to the neocolonizers' (receiving) country. As Chicana scholar Sosa Riddell insightfully observed, "The migration of Mexicans in large numbers to the areas north of the Río Bravo did not mark an end to [their] colonization experience. It simply meant that Mexicano-Chicanos . . . added a second one to their existence" ([1974] 2001, 364). Even though much of the Xaripu experience can be assessed using the neocolonial and internal-colonial frameworks,[31] I enlist a new model, "interactive colonization" (XC), that combines critical aspects of the theoretical perspectives outlined above and places the Xaripu experience within interacting forms of colonialism. For instance, Xaripus migrated to *el norte* as internally colonized subjects within a neocolonized nation. Though they were recruited as "imported colonial labor" (Ngai 2004, 94–95) to the United States, their migration allowed them to escape the neocolonial subjugation of Mexico. This experience placed them in between a neocolonized and neocolonizing nation. Although incorporated into the United States as unequal members, they experienced greater levels of social and economic power than their relatives in Michoacán, creating social inequities, distances, and conflicts within the Xaripu community (see chapter 5). Hence, XC examines relationships of domination within and between groups and then analyzes how migrants experience unequal social spaces and subsequently are transformed by their transnational experiences. In what follows, XC is outlined, and the emergent "in-between" status (*nepantla*) is elaborated.

Interactive colonization combines the colonial, structural, and transnational frameworks, highlighting their three central concepts (colonialism, dialectics, and interactionism) and underscoring the independent and interrelated systems of oppression. These relationships of domination have been effectively theorized by various scholars: Omi and Winant's racial formation (1994), Evelyn Nakano Glenn's integrated framework (2002), Eduardo Bonilla-Silva's racialized social system (2001), Patricia Hill Collins's categories of analysis and connection (2003), and Kimberlé Crenshaw's intersectional theory (1993). These theorists offer slightly variant articulations of how the meaning and significance of race and gender get shaped at the levels of structure/institution, interaction/individual, and representation/signification, and how unequal power relations contribute to racial and gender formation.[32]

XC adds to this scholarship in four key ways: (1) by stressing that race, gender, and class are all social-historical constructs universalized by colonialism; (2) by identifying the central unit of analysis as social interaction; (3) by breaking away from analytical binaries such as "base

~~and superstructure" or "them versus us"; and (4) by adding complexity to the study of migrant colonial labor through an exploration of the internal diversity and emergent social formations found among migrant communities.~~ In what follows, I outline XC's major principles.

Colonialism

XC proceeds from "the fact of colonization" to understand contemporary social inequalities that exist between and within nations (Mirandé 1987, 222). I use the term "colonialism" rather than "imperialism" for the following reasons: (1) it recognizes the socio-historical construction of nation, race, class, and gender; (2) it comprehensively examines social domination, not just within the economic sphere; (3) it applies to feudalism, capitalism, socialism, etc.; (4) it notes that national subjugation includes groups within a nation (i.e., internal colonies) as well as between nations (i.e., colonialism or neocolonialism); and (5) it underscores "oppression"[33] as opposed to "influence" and "competition," since these latter terms suggest neutrality or even the naturalness of social domination.

The colonialism under which Indigenous people suffer can be understood "as a historical and social project aimed at destroying the humanity of such peoples" (San Juan 1992, 45). A materialist worldview fueled such colonial projects. The *Chronicles from Michoacán*, for example, documents the first colonial encounters with a Purépecha chief:

> When Olid saw them, he chided the Cazonci [Purépechan Chief]: "Why do you bring so little? Bring more. You have a lot of gold. Why do you want it?"
>
> At this the Cazonci questioned his principals [advisors]: "Why do they want this gold? Their gods must eat it, that could be the only reason they want so much." (De la Coruña 1539/1541, 82)

The Cazonci was puzzled by the valuation of gold and the accumulation of wealth and thus concludes: "their gods must eat it." This passage depicts not only the appropriation of wealth from the Natives, but also the clashing worldviews that illustrate how materialism, which today fuels global capitalism, is not a universal or a natural condition. Rather it reflects a social-historical specific relation/value that was spread through colonial projects (Almaguer 1994; Zinn 1999; De la Coruña 1538/ 1539).[34]

XC situates labor migration experiences within a global context of forced inequalities. Migration flows to the core regions are stimulated by neocolonialism (Fernandez-Kelly 1983; Sassen 1996; Gonzalez and Fernandez 2003). In other words, as Portes and Rumbaut stress, the "pull" of the US lifestyle is not the primary factor in modern migration: "Despite the universal appeal of Western consumption standards, the specific historical ties between receiving and sending countries—primarily the impact on the latter of colonial and neo-colonial episodes—continue to be clearly reflected in the major immigrant flows today" (1996, 275). To be sure, the top sending countries of immigrants to the United States during the 1990s all have experienced colonial and/or neocolonial interventions by the United States. Specifically, the top five sending countries of legal immigrants were Mexico, Philippines, China/Taiwan, South Korea, and Vietnam; the top two sending countries of undocumented immigrants were Mexico and El Salvador; and the four main countries sending refugees were Vietnam, Laos, Cambodia, and Cuba (Portes and Rumbaut 1996, 274–76; Sassen 1996a, 76–85).

Dialectics

The method of dialectics offers an analysis of how multiple and conflicting social relations create tension and change, and it is thus central to understanding migration experiences in a global context of unequal national, gender, racial, and class relationships.[35] Much scholarship, however, conceptualizes dialectics in the deterministic and dualistic terms of "base" and "superstructure" rather than relationally. This take is grounded on Marx's primary premise that "before everything else come eating and drinking, a habitation, clothing and many other things. The first historical act is thus the production of the means to satisfy these needs, the production of material life itself" (Marx 1970, 48). From this premise, scholars deduce that the base of society, conflated with economic relations, primarily determines the superstructure: culture and ideas (Burawoy 1979, 14; Gómez-Quiñones 1977, 5; Kearney 1996,

12–13; Robinson 2003, 4, 13). In other words, the material base has primacy over the superstructure of culture and ideas in shaping history.

Exemplifying this Marxist interpretation, Carr (1997) argues that the base (presumably the economy) creates and shapes the superstructure (essentially all ideologies), including racism and patriarchy. Accordingly, any efforts to eradicate racism by targeting the superstructure are merely reformist in nature (Carr 1997, 10; Burawoy 1979, 18–19). Along a similar Marxist premise, yet with a different take on the significance of the "superstructure," Roediger elaborates, "If, to use tempting older Marxist images, racism is a large, low-hanging branch of a tree that is rooted in class relations, we must constantly remind ourselves that the branch is not the same as the roots, that people may more often bump into the branch than the roots, and that the best way to shake the roots may at times be by grabbing the branch" (1991, 8). But though Roediger offers more weight to the significance of the branch in helping uproot the problem, he still reproduces the dualistic ideas of base and superstructure.

Gonzalez and Fernandez also illustrate this dominant view: "Laws, policies, degrees of enforcement, and other 'macro' structures are merely expressions of the 'subjectivities' of US legislators, officials of the Departments of Justice, Labor, Agriculture, and Treasury, the Border Patrol, and Mexican political leaders. These actors themselves respond to the active desires of other life economic actors, such as business leaders and associations of large agribusiness interests" (2003, 97).

But Bertel Ollman offers another interpretation of dialectics in his work *Alienation* (1976). Ollman argues that the "base" does not necessarily mean the most important structural factor influencing society, but rather points to the factor being examined at the moment (1976, 3–11). Thus the economy interacts with other "modes of production," as he notes: "All the evidence is that Marx manipulates the size of his factors, alters his classificational boundaries, to suit his changing purposes. An extreme instance of this, which starkly sets out the dimensions of our problem, is his claim that 'religion, family, state, law, morality, science, art, etc.' are 'particular modes of production' (Marx 1844)" (Ollman 1976, 10).

In this light, patriarchy and racism are not merely ideological constructs and/or products of economic relations, but rather have a material base in concrete actions along the same lines as the economy does. Societal institutions produce and reproduce patterns of social behavior that form the material basis of society.

In this way, base and superstructure are false dichotomies, because one without the other ceases to exist and because both imply a material basis.[36] Any type of organization that produces enduring patterns of behavior can be considered to be making and maintaining a material base or structure. It follows that relations of economic production actively interact with other modes of production such as patriarchy and racism. Furthermore, capitalism, as a mode of production, reproduces not only class relations but also multiple structures of stratification (e.g., racial and gender inequalities).

This dialectical analysis advances our understanding of the labor, community, and family experiences and transformations of migrants. In the Xaripu case study, a dialectical analysis considers how capitalism, racism, and patriarchy shape Xaripus' work, community, and family experiences across borders; how Xaripus experience race, class, and gender in the labor context (chapter 4); how their transnational community and identities are shaped by intersecting systems of domination (chapter 5); and how the family experiences a context of social inequalities across borders, particularly in the area of gender relations (chapter 6). In short, the Xaripu experience with work, community formation, and family transformation cannot be reduced to one basic social relationship (class), because it has also been shaped by national, cultural, racial, and gender relational and power inequalities.

Interactionism

An interactionist perspective helps explain how labor migration in a global context shapes the sense and form of persons and communities. Where the dialectical analysis examines individual, group, community, institutional, and national relationships that exist in tension because of social inequalities, the interactionist view offers insights into the formation of the community, family, and self. It complements colonial and dialectical analyses by explaining the emergent transformations of a transnational "Mexican" community. As outlined by George Herbert Mead ([1934] 1962) and Herbert Blumer (1969), this framework highlights the significance of human interaction in the development of symbols, meaning, and emotions.[37] Mead and Blumer both insist that interaction with self, others, nature, and/or things creates a social experience that becomes the subject of reflection and meaning. Thus, the self, mind, and community are constantly in-the-making (emergent). For migrants, the creation of personal symbols, meaning, and emotions is shaped by dialectical relationships rooted in colonialism.[38]

An interactionist perspective also reinforces and complements the dialectical approach. Both frameworks highlight the importance of social relationships in the making and/or changing of the self, family, and community. But the interactionist approach elaborates how beliefs and behaviors are socially constructed and emergent (in-the-making), while the dialectical perspective stresses how unequal power relationships (in terms of economic, racial, gender, and cultural factors) privilege one social influence over another (e.g., Western over Indigenous) and may create conflicting ideals within a person or society, although they often produce new emergent social forms. All of these dialectical and interactive processes occur within a historical context of colonialism and form the foundation of the XC framework.

Xaripu migrant experiences have been shaped by a history of colonialism, dialectical relations, and emergent social relations and formations (e.g., *nepantla*). Social oppression across national borders produced new social relations and cultural formations that place some in an "in-between" social location related to nation, culture, and class. While neocolonial relations caused Xaripus to migrate to *el norte*, when migrants returned to their pueblo, they were no longer the same but rather occupied an in-between position and were materially more advantaged over non-migrants. A discussion of the centrality of those "in-between" and the emergent condition of *nepantla* follows.

In-Between "Them" and "Us": *Nepantla*

Scholarship on colonialism tends to stress the dichotomous outcomes of national oppression, yet discussions that reduce colonialism to "them versus us" are problematic. One such example is Memmi's suggestion that there are no "in-betweens" among the colonized and the colonizers. He defines colonization as a relationship that creates profit and privilege for the colonizers or usurpers (1965, 7–10, 91) while it allows some of the colonized to move up within the new colonial order and "sell out" to the colonizers: "The recently assimilated place themselves in a considerably superior position to the average colonizer. They push a colonial mentality to excess, display proud disdain for the colonized and continually show off their borrowed rank, which often belies a vulgar brutality and avidity. . . . [By] choosing to place themselves in the colonizer's service to protect his interests exclusively, they end up adopting his ideology, even with regard to their own values and their own lives" (16).

Similarly, Fanon (1967) emphasizes that internal colonization produces a "them" and "us." He documents how colonized people from Martinique experience internalized racism as a result of economic exploitation and cultural repression, which produce "colonized minds" that experience self-hatred. Fanon's chief concern was thus to help "the Black man free himself of the arsenal of complexes that has been developed by the colonial environment" (1967, 31). He observed that when a Black person returned to Antilles from France, his family awaited with curiosity to see who would arrive: the family member they knew or a newly transformed "European." Fanon concludes: "The Negro is appraised in terms of the extent of his assimilation, it is . . . understandable why the newcomer [returning native] expresses himself only in French" (1967, 35).

Similar to the colonial binaries reproduced in the Black colonial experience, Barrera, Muñoz, and Ornelas contend, "the apparent semipermeability of the colonial barrier for Chicanos is illusory, since there is no escape from the colonial status for an individual as a Chicano" (1972, 485). Thus, one is either a colonized or colonizer. Mirandé further argues, "Typically the cost of acceptance into mainstream society and upward mobility for colonized people has been rejection of both their cultural heritage and ethnic identity: a choice, in other words, between subordination and cultural genocide" (1985, 5). Thus individuals caught between the colonized and colonizers who are capable of "passing" as mainstream—contingent on their class, culture, and race—become instrumental in reinforcing the hegemonic social order by adopting the manner of speech, customs, and so forth of the dominant culture. I argue, however, that in-betweens are not simply victims nor forever fixed to be instruments of the colonizers.

I use "in-between" as an analytical term to emphasize persons or groups that occupy intermediary positions between those "at the top" (with power, resources, and status) and those "at the bottom" (poor and stigmatized). In-between positions can be situational (individual and brief) or structured (collective and lasting), and their form and nature are contingent on race, culture, gender, and class.

The situational status applies more to individuals and implies a sense of temporariness and flexibility to act in diverse ways, though the selected options are constrained by the social structures of race, class, gender, and nation. From the margins, a farm worker becomes a contractor or manager to agribusiness, or a person of color advocates for policies of sameness (e.g., anti–affirmative action) that secures Whiteness as the privileged norm. Situational in-betweens benefit from financial rewards, but they cannot escape their structured marginality (along race, culture, gender lines). Those with some privilege can side with those with less power and status and can play key roles in advancing justice. Because they have more social and spatial mobility, these situational in-betweens can have much influence in bringing about social change. For instance, some in-betweens have used their structural advantages (race, class, and/or gender) to advance the interests of those from the bottom. For example, Bartolomé de las Casas advocated for the human rights of Indigenous people; Marx and Engels, the working class; White abolitionists, Black slaves. Hence, persons with structured privileges can play a significant role in advancing justice, though they remain privileged by the structured hierarchies, and they can leave the just cause without completely losing their racial, gender, and/or class privileges.

While everyone can occupy an intermediary position with variable levels of power, the most significant in-between positions are those that are structured and that shape collective behaviors. Structured in-between positions are more fixed along the lines of race, gender, and class and create a more distinguishable set of experiences that separates those in-between from either polar side. For example, the mestiza/o experience is distinct from the Indigenous or European experience, and the middle-class experience is different from the working-class or capitalist experience.

In this case study, I argue that the Xaripu experience in-between two unequal nations produces a collective *nepantla* position for *norteñas/os*

(US-based Xaripus) who are transnational. For instance, transnational Xaripus monopolize land and power in Michoacán, while most of the pueblo's permanent residents depend on their *norteña/o* relatives for employment, business, and remittances. Transnational Xaripus thus form an emergent in-between group whose social networks of influence in their community across borders empower them over their non-migrant fellows (Mummert 1999a; Zabin et al. 1993; Portes and Rumbaut 1996; Rouse 1992; and Massey et al. 1987). Their position in between unequal nations may reflect the competing and contradictory interests of both areas. At first, the outcome of this middle position is never certain for the individual, since conflict and confusion can create new lines of action for the intermediaries (see Cockcroft 1998, 228–29) and since the condition of *nepantla* emerges from competing structural locations (Anzaldúa 1999, 100–1; León-Portilla 1990, 10–11; Loewen 1995, 107; Mirandé 1997, 60). Nevertheless, as this in-between position becomes normalized, it creates unique social forms that separate the transnational group from non-migrants on either side of the border (see chapter 5).

In the transnational family, Xaripu men also hold in-between social locations in part because they benefit from the patriarchal structures that persist across borders, including access to higher wages than women and benefiting from the latter's unpaid domestic labor. Yet their patriarchal privilege does not translate into substantive social power outside of their families or communities. Indeed, some scholars have reported a relational decline in status for men and increase in empowerment for women in immigrant families (Pessar 2003; Hondagneu-Sotelo 1994), and certain aspects of Xaripus' self-reports seem to validate this finding. However, when one examines actual actions, division of household chores, and the transnational context of these perceptions, the picture of women's empowerment becomes less optimistic. Hence, in chapter 6, I explore how Xaripu men's in-between social location in the United States maintains male privilege and how women's in-between position vis-à-vis those from Michoacán contributes to their perception that they are more empowered within their families than women in Michoacán, even though *norteñas* have comparatively more intense work and home burdens.

To understand Xaripu labor migration experiences one must examine the emergent in-betweens within a global context of unequal national relationships and the in-betweens' role in the making of history and advancing social justice. Their social-political direction is never certain: Will they advance the interests of those at the bottom, the interests of those at the top, or their own?

METHODS

A Multi-Locational Extended Case Study

This book is based on an extended case study of the Xaripu transnational community that has home bases in Xaripu, Michoacán, and Stockton, California. A total of fifty-six persons participated in the formal study: thirty-one in California and twenty-five in Michoacán. Of those formally interviewed, the overwhelming majority (fifty of fifty-six) had stronger Indigenous appearance (broad nose, dark and thick hair, and dark brown skin), and only a few (three) had a visible European appearance (narrow nose, light complexion, and lighter brown hair) and about the same number (three) had strong Black features (broad nose, fine curly hair, and dark brown skin).[39]

The study was multi-locational with the field research taking place in both countries (see Mummert 1999a, 17–18; Guarnizo and Smith 1999, 104–5). Members of the Xaripu community have been migrating to the United States for at least a century, and, as members of a transnational community, Xaripus have multiple social ties—familial, cultural, political, economic, and/or emotional—that span the US-Mexico border (Glick-Schiller et al. 1992c, 1). Most Xaripus consider themselves to belong to the communities on either side of the border and maintain strong connections to family, friends, community, and institutions in both Michoacán and California, though some maintain these links more actively than others. Further, many of the families are binational, and their members have various residential statuses—US-born and naturalized citizens, documented and undocumented residents, and dual national citizens.[40] In the present day, most families who reside permanently in the United States are comprised of legal residents and US citizens, since many of those who were not able to attain legal status through the Immigration Act of 1965 (family reunification provision) later did so via the amnesty and special agricultural worker provisions of the Immigration Reform and Control Act of 1986.

My analyses of Xaripus' life experiences are based on primary and secondary sources: interviews, scholarly research, newspaper reports, reports of demographic and economic trends, county and state agricultural reports, personal letters, and home videos. Linking personal biographies to historical structural events places Xaripus' labor migration experiences within broader social, economic, and political processes. As Burawoy observes, this approach allows us to "unmask appearances, link the part to the whole, the past to the future, and thereby shatter the appearance of naturalness and inevitability in the present order of things (here, intra-national/international inequalities)" (1979, 7). This study uses the social interaction between persons, between individuals and institutions, and between institutions (e.g., work, community, government agency, family, etc.) as its units of analysis in order to understand the influences such exchanges have on both individual and group-level thought and action.

Various qualitative methods were used as part of this multi-locational case study, including in-depth interviews, participant observation, and informal interviews, in order to gain a deeper understanding of labor, migration, community, and family experiences across borders (see Burawoy 1991 and Burawoy et al. 2000). All of the participants' names and biographical information have been changed so as to maintain confidentiality, except for two participants whose biographies are well-known both within and outside of the Xaripu community. All interviews in Mexico were conducted in Spanish, and those in the United States were conducted in English and Spanish, depending upon the interviewee's preference. Interviews took place in respondent's homes, restaurants, parks, the plaza, or wherever the participants felt most comfortable.

Study Design

Interviewees were selected through a purposeful sampling technique in order to include respondents from diverse occupations, ages, and immigration backgrounds and experiences (see Tables 2.1 and 2.2 in the appendix). Respondents were initially contacted by phone or by personal visits to their homes, and they were then asked to participate or to refer potential participants who might fit the diverse characteristics of the community (age, generation, gender, occupation, etc.). Although snowball sampling was not necessary in California because of my familiarity with most families, it was beneficial in Michoacán because of my infrequent visiting patterns (I have visited every seven years, from 1973 to 1999). My field research in Michoacán took place during May and June 1999 and January 2000 and for two weeks in July 2001. This longitudinal approach was useful in documenting changes among the participants and observing them in different social contexts (e.g., when *norteñas/os* were absent in Michoacán). In California, field research and interviews were conducted from January to April 1999 and from September to December 1999, though most interviews were done throughout 2000 and completed in January 2001. I maintain contact with many of the participants through home visits and participation in familial and community celebrations.

In California, most Xaripus in Stockton—in fact every person I approached—were interested and excited about helping me research their life experiences as workers, migrants, and families. At times I even sensed a degree of resentment from those who did not get interviewed when somebody else in his or her family did. I explained that I was trying to capture diverse experiences from different age cohorts, and that if I interviewed one member over another it was not a deliberate rejection but rather a matter of who was there when I went to interview or phoned to schedule an interview. Trying to find nonrelatives to interview was a challenge. Most Xaripus are kin-related—our grandparents were cousins, or our relatives were related in some way. Thus I am related to most of the participants of this study, as a nephew, (first, second, third) cousin, godson, grandson, *compadre*, or friend. Rapport was not difficult to establish, since past and present relationships and shared experiences served as bridges for conversation.

In Michoacán, I also felt connected to the pueblo. I have great aunts and great uncles, cousins, and friends whom I feel strongly connected to through our *convivencia* and shared familial biographies, and we have stayed in touch through letters and telephone calls. Xaripus made me feel part of the community and often invited me to eat with them, stay over, and even take a shower in their house. Kinships relations were always affirmed by older and younger Xaripus, and most were friendly and generous.

During my research in California, I stayed in the homes of my parents, brothers, and sisters, who live in Stockton. In Michoacán, my godparents (Carlos Manzo and Juana Pulido) hosted me in Xaripu and my great aunt (Esperanza Carrillo Diaz) in Zamora. I also spent a few nights in my parents' unoccupied adobe house in Xaripu.

Sample

In 1981 Fonseca and Moreno (1984) took a census of Xaripus (whom they referred to as Jaripeños) living in Stockton's Sierra Vista housing projects and counted 624 persons (about 117 households). Many other Xaripu families lived in other low-income housing including *los campitos* (farm labor camps) and Conway housing projects, and some had begun to move to neighboring south Stockton communities: Crow Valley, McKinley and Mariposa areas, and Lathrop. The Xaripu population has increased significantly since the 1980s. Most of the families I interviewed had doubled in size since the 1981 census was taken, and conversely the population in Xaripu, Michoacán, has declined drastically. Estimated at 1,349 in 1822 and 2,800 in 1873 (Fonseca and Moreno 1984, 70, 77, 79), the population in Xaripu dropped precipitously during the international migrations of the twentieth century (1900–30, 1942–64, and 1965 to the 1980s), most particularly after the Immigration and Naturalization Act of 1965. The 2000 *XII Censo de Población y Vivienda* (a regional census) registered 641 people living in Xaripu.

For analytical purposes, I have classified Xaripus in one of four possible age cohorts that capture their historical labor migration experiences, using 2000 as the base year: *retiradas/os* (ages sixty-five and above), *mayores* (ages fifty to sixty-four), *hijas/os* (ages thirty to forty-nine), and *chicas/os* (ages twenty to twenty-nine) (see chapter 1). The California Xaripus included in my study are made up of five women and four men in the *retiradas/os* age cohort, four women and four men in the *mayores* cohort, four women and three men in the *hija/o* cohort, and six women in the *chica* cohort. The Michoacán group contains four women and two men in the *retirada/o* age cohort, two women and five men in the *mayores* cohort, four women and one man in the hija/o cohort, and four women and three men in the *chica/o* cohort.

The use of Xaripu cohorts highlights both historical particularities and generational changes. The popular term "bracero" (guest worker) clouds important distinctions between *retiradas/os* and *mayores*. For instance, the older Xaripus migrated before the 1940s and generally worked in the railroads, steel factories, and agriculture. They also tended to travel across the United States. The younger braceros, in comparison, were sons and nephews of the older migrants, and their migration was concentrated in the Southwest (particularly California), and they primarily worked as farm laborers. *Retirada* women typically experienced about twenty years of seasonal separation from their migrant husbands, whereas the *mayores* were separated from their husbands for a shorter time span of about ten years. Once Xaripu women began migrating to the United States, *mayores* worked over twice as many years in farm labor than *retirada* women, who became primarily homemakers. The longer separation from the migrant men and wage labor experience possibly structured a more rigidly gendered division of labor within families in which the men effectively told their wives, "You take care of the younger children and house, and the older children and I will work." In addition, a distinction between the *chicas/os* and *hijas/os*, who may be siblings, is that the younger ones were born in the United States and did not have a direct farm labor experience. These qualitative differences are better captured by a cohort analysis than by a generational one, since the cohort typology reflects diverse life experiences and historical contexts.

Other distinctions between Xaripus in California and Michoacán were their marital and employment statuses (see Figure 2 in the appendix). While twenty-three of thirty participants in California were married, nine of twenty-five in Michoacán were married. Eleven of twenty-five in Michoacán and five of thirty in California were single.

Furthermore, though Xaripus on both sides of the border are generally working-class, a few from Stockton occupy middle-class (mostly service and clerical) occupations. More Xaripus work in commerce in Michoacán than in California, specializing in a variety of formal services such as *tienditas* (stores), restaurants, meat markets, dairy production, and pharmacies. Some engage in informal activities; they are produce sellers, *sobadoras/es* (healers), *albañiles* (masons), hair stylists, and domestic workers. In California, a few Xaripus were formally self-employed, operating restaurants and meat markets. Many more worked informally as bakers, cooks for parties (e.g., *carnitas* and *birria*, that is, deep fried pork and goat meat in a special sauce), mechanics, hair stylists, yard workers, and construction workers.

Interestingly, in 2000 there were more Xaripu professionals in Mexico than in the United States, including doctors, dentists, engineers, lawyers, and pharmacists. I counted five medical doctors in Michoacán and only one in California, one dentist in Michoacán and none in California, one pharmacist in Michoacán and none in California, and so on. Many of the Mexican-based professionals had parents who had been labor migrants to the United States and whose remittances contributed to their education. In the 1980s, as a result of Mexico's weakened position in the global economy, a few of these professionals (primarily teachers and lawyers) left their occupations to work as laborers in the United States.

Most of the Xaripus in California are employed year-round, compared to about half of those living in Michoacán. Seven were unemployed in Michoacán, whereas everyone was employed in California, though some held part-time or temporary positions in the service sector, agriculture, or factories. Women and men living in Michoacán find more work during December and January, when Xaripus from California visit and create employment opportunities in domestic work, restaurants, construction, etc. Non-migrants are actively employed when business activity is stimulated by the tourism of *norteñas/os*.

Research Instruments

Open-ended questions focused on experiences with migration, work, community, family, and gender relations across borders (see Barajas 2002). An open-ended question, for example, was *¿Quién manda en la casa?* (Who has the authority at home?), while semi-structured questions focused on the amount of household chores family members performed weekly. The in-depth interviews, on average, were two hours long (the shortest was one hour, and the longest took five and a half hours). With the exception of three interviews, all interviews were recorded on audio tape and fully transcribed.

In addition to the in-depth interviews, I conversed informally with over a hundred Xaripus about my research questions. These informal interviews helped verify information from the formal interviews, clarify themes and processes, and identify diverse experiences within the Xaripu community.

Participant observation also supplemented the formal interviews. This consisted of involvement in social activities as a member of the community being studied. This approach was facilitated by my insider status and by my full participation in both communities in Michoacán and California during informal social gatherings, community meetings regarding hometown projects (e.g., restoration of the 1692 church in Michoacán), soccer and basketball games, and community celebrations. Field notes were typically sketched out daily and developed further each night. Among the topics examined were typical daily activities and social interactions between migrants and non-migrants, men and women, and various generations.

As an insider of the Xaripu community, I benefited from my shared experiences in farm labor (every summer from age four to twenty), living in the same neighborhoods (1973–87), and participating in celebrations and social gatherings (from infancy to present). Participant observation helps grasp the fuller meaning of human experiences within a context of social inequalities. This experience was an asset in determining the reliability and validity of some interviews. I could observe individuals' interactions in a more natural state without having their behavior modified (censored or magnified) to impress an outsider scholar. Direct observation offered important insights about what people say and what people actually do, contextualizing the research findings and revealing power inequalities. For example, when asking about how people felt when working in farm labor when the border patrol came, a couple of respondents said they felt nothing or that they found it humorous seeing people run: *"me la curo cuando viene la migra"* (I am amused when the border patrol comes), and *"me da risa de verlos correr"* (I laugh when I see people running). Having witnessed them in the fields on such an occasion, I knew they had reacted differently from what they reported. Rather than laughing or feeling indifferent, I saw them being quiet, looking down, and staying busy as if to become invisible in spite of their legal residency. When I questioned them about it, one admitted that he avoided looking up or at the border patrol officers so as not to draw attention to himself. The other interviewee mentioned feeling scared and angry at the same time. In order to make sense of the inconsistencies between self-reported and actual actions, observations offered more valid information than the initial self-report and led to further conversation.

Being an insider as a Xaripu also has a possible drawback. My insider status could potentially conceal phenomena that would be more accessible to outsiders, such as information that respondents might consider too embarrassing or delicate to risk revealing to a member of the family. Though I tried to overcome this problem by reassuring participants of the study's strict confidentiality, I cannot know whether being an insider provided me with greater access to private information than I would have attained had I been unknown to the community. Overall, however, my insider standpoint provided me with clear advantages, as Patricia Hill Collins (2004) and Sandra Harding (2004) have suggested about such situations. I knew who the Xaripus were and where they lived, understood the dense web of community ties and the personal conflicts, and had intimate knowledge of their day-to-day struggles at work and within the community. In general, Xaripu participants had *confianza* (trust) in me, and my cultural proficiency in the community's unique linguistic and cultural expressions helped reduce errors of interpretation in their oral and behavioral communication.

Validity, therefore, was sought in this investigation through deep and genuine understanding of a people's experience within a context of social inequalities and through a triangulation of methods—in-depth interviews, informal interviews, and participant observation. It was through these various research tools that I examined Xaripus' life experiences at work, in the community, and with family across borders.

Chapter Three

A SOCIAL-HISTORICAL CONTEXT OF XARIPU'S LAND DISPLACEMENT AND LABOR MIGRATION EXPERIENCE

Xaripu, my ancestral pueblo, has changed tremendously over the centuries: from a Purépecha center to a "Mexican" pueblo. My grandfather Elias, during one of our last visits before he passed away in October 1991, told me, *Mi abuela era tarasca*[1] *y no hablaba español* (my grandmother was Purépecha and did not speak Spanish). His father, Pomposo Barajas, wore *calzon de indio* (Indigenous trousers), and his mother, Bartola Muratalla, was from San Antonio Guaracha, which was known to have relied on African slaves during the colonial period. Indigenous and mestiza/o (a mix of Black and White) ancestry are part of Xaripus' heritage, though the Indigenous prevalence is documented in church and public records[2] and also evident in their appearance, language, and customs. While influenced and altered by major historical events, their collective identity as Xaripus remains strong: their Indigenous heritage, which has blended with other ethnic influences, distinguishes them from their surrounding communities in Michoacán.

This chapter examines the social history of Xaripu and traces the transformations experienced by Xaripu across time. I provide the social-historical context that contributed to their migration patterns in both Mexico and the United States and also examine their incorporation as a racialized people into a global labor market and society.

ORIGINS OF XARIPUS

Xaripu[3] is a pueblo in the northwest region of Michoacán, Mexico, whose history predates the modern nations of both Mexico and the United States. Three distinct peoples occupied the lands surrounding present-day Xaripu—the Purépechans inhabited the geographical area along today's central-western state of Michoacán by the Pacific Ocean, the Mexicas occupied the eastern and southern areas bordering Michoacán, and the Chichimec tribes dominated the northern areas (López 1981). Xaripu lies southeast of Xiquilpa and southwest of Xacona, {and it appears in both Abraham Ortelio's 1579 map of New Spain, "Theatrum Orbis Terrarum" (see Figure 1 in the appendix), and Theodore de Bry's 1595 "Americae Pars Quinta."[4] (The presence of Xaripu on these historical maps is important since the pueblo is not typically shown on modern maps.)

The Purépechans had linguistic and cultural practices that were distinct from the Nahuas (Chichimeca/Mexica), who dominated Mesoamerica (Wolf 1959, 41–44; De la Coruña 1539/1541, xiii), though there are evident links between their culture and both southern and northern Indigenous people (Wolf 1959, 44; Pollard 1993, 8–9; Warren 1985, 8). For example, their metal art and use of tools were similar to those of the Quechuas from Peru and Columbia. A sixteenth-century account notes that they were especially advanced with "welding, alloying, casting, soldering, and plating," and their work with copper was particularly sophisticated at a time when metal work was unusual in Mesoamerica (De la Coruña 1539/1541, xiii–xiv). This technology possibly helped them successfully defend themselves against the Mexicas several times in the centuries before European colonialism. Purépechans also shared linguistic forms with the Quechuas from Peru and the Zunis from New Mexico (De la Coruña 1539/1541, xiv; Warren 1985, 4), and resembled their Chichimecan neighbors' ethnographic characteristics (Warren 1985, 8).[5]

The ties between the Purépechans and the Nahuas are described in the sixteenth-century *Relación de Michoacán* (the Chronicles of Michoacán). The *Relación* tells of Taríacuri—who was born to a Purépechan mother and a Chichimecan (Nahua) father—unifying Michoacán's Purépechan core and expanding its territory into periphery zones (De la Coruña 1539/1541, 113–20, 133). Between 1250 and 1350 CE Taríacuri and later descendents secured the Pátzcuaro basin (the core), which served as Michoacán's political and military center (Pollard 1993, 88–91). Its periphery areas became tributary lands overseen by *caciques* (local administrators), which included Teco, Otomi, and Chichimecan settlements (Pollard 1993, 92–105).

Purépechans gradually resettled from the core to the periphery to integrate and secure the newly acquired territory in Mexica areas. As Pollard (1993, 103) documents, "Such resettlements are known to have occurred from Jacona to Jiquilpan, to Tarecuato, and to Periban. . . . Smaller resettlements are known to have been made within the heartland and along the military borders, apparently to enlarge local populations in the face of active military threat." In 1450, the Purépechan state incorporated Xiquilpan, a Chichimecan village about 5 miles northwest of Xaripu, and named it Guanimba or "place of toasted corn" (Ochoa Serrano 1999, 18–19; López 1981, 109), while Guarachan, another Chichimecan village about 3.5 miles north of Xaripu, was acquired during the same period, and named Guaracha (today, Villamar), meaning "place of dancers" (Alvarez del Toro 1988, 20–21; Moreno García 1994, 90).

By 1500 the Purépechans controlled the area that roughly makes up modern Michoacán (Pollard 1993, 88, 90–93).[6] The limited historical data on Xaripu during this era (1250–1521) suggest that the pueblo was situated within the northwest border of the Purépechan Empire (Ortelio 1579; Pollard 1993; Fonseca and Moreno 1984). Xaripu was separated from the Chichimecan zones by two large hills, and its strategic location in a very volcanic rocky terrain, where axes and arrows are still found, suggests that it possibly served as a military post for the Purépechans.

Today Xaripu, like several of its neighboring communities (Tarimoro, Tumbiscato, Cuameo, etc.), maintains many Purépechan cultural influences, including its village name. Its residents' identity remains oriented toward the pueblo and its religious celebrations, which they collectively organize and finance.[7] While the Indigenous language has been lost, their Purépechan heritage is reflected in their continued use of words such as *chancharra, charanda, chocho, chunde, cokocha, corunda, huchepo, pachichi, curuko, curupo, ecuaro, guarache, jóchica, tambache,* and *timbiriche* (Ochoa Serrano 1999, 20).[8] Xaripu's Indigenous culture is also expressed in special foods such as *huchepos* and *corundas* (special types of tamales) and their devotion to saints, including the Virgen de Guadalupe, which closely resembles the reverence to diverse Indigenous deities and spirits that some attest helped facilitate the transition into Catholicism (Garcia Canclini and Villalobos 1985).

Liborio Castañeda Medina's romantic poem "Un Rincón Michoacano," published December 24, 1983, captures Xaripu's Purépechan heritage (Salcedo Zaragoza 1988, 8):

Al canoro tañer de las campanas   At the sound of melodious bells
se despiertan muy frescas sus mañanas   a cool morning awakens
rizadas por el sol del nuevo día,   breezed by the sunlight of a new day,
radiante de esplendor, luz y poesía.   radiantly splendid, light and poetry.
Un kiosco, un jardin, un campanario . . .   A kiosk, a garden, a bell tower,
Las cuatro apariciones del sanctuario,   the sanctuaries of four apparitions,
palo-bobos, flores que se mecen   curious-trees, flowers that sway,
a ese rincón purépecha enaltecen.   elevate that Purépechan corner.
De lejos contemplé el río Tarecuato,   From afar I see the Tarecuato river,
y de cerca a Xaripu, pueblo grato   and from here, Xaripu, pleasant pueblo
de rojizos tejados coloridos   of reddish-colored clay roofs
sombreados por naranjos florecidos.   shaded by flowered citrus.
Y fui a la Tecomaca y a la presa   I went to the Tecomaca and to the reservoir
mis ojos admiraron su belleza;   my eyes admired its beauty;
a la barranca fui, quedó encantada . . .   to the cliff I went; enchanted . . .
De Xaripu, mi lira emborrachada.   of Xaripu, my lyric intoxicated [with pleasure].

This poem situates Xaripu within a *rincón* (corner) of the Purépechan geographical territory. Its verse describes the pleasant climate, plaza area, gardens, sanctuaries, and reddish clay roofs of a small adobe pueblo connected to Tarecuato (another Purépechan pueblo) by a river and preserved for ages by a water spring called La Tecomaca. These romantic images, however, neglect the violent forces that transformed the people of Xaripu into landless and racialized subjects of alien colonizers and future nation-state empires.

THE COLONIZATION OF MICHOACÁN (1521)

In 1521, the Spanish and their Indigenous allies defeated the Mexicas, and quickly expanded into Indo America in pursuit of wealth, justifying their violence in the name of God (see De las Casas 1552, 31–32, 41, 50–52, 107, 116; Warren 1985, 46, 53, 57; Keen 1994, 7–8; Cockcroft 1998, 19). By the time Cristóbal de Olid was preparing to extend the Spanish conquest into Michoacán early in the summer of 1522, the Purépechans were preparing to defend themselves (De la Coruña 1539/1541, 70). But Cuinvolverángri, or Don Pedro Panza, who served as a close advisor to the young Purépecha chief, Tangaxhuán II, and as an ambassador to Tenochtitlan, the Mexicas' capital city, soon discouraged such resistance. Don Pedro had witnessed firsthand the devastation the Mexicas had suffered at the hands of the Spaniards, and Xanaqua, a Mexica interpreter for the Spanish, advised the Purépechans that war would be futile (De la Coruña 1539/1541, 72–73; Warren 1985, 34, 38, 46). Thus Don Pedro discouraged Chief Tangaxhuán II from fighting the Spanish, in spite of the elders' and warriors' ardent opposition and distrust of the Spanish (Warren 1985, 46–48). As the European colonizers approached Michoacán, Don Pedro went from pueblo to pueblo disbanding the estimated eighty thousand to two hundred thousand Purépechan warriors who had been ready to fight (De la Coruña 1539/1541, 73; Warren 1985, 46–51; Cook and Simpson 1948, 29). Michoacán's leadership was not willing to suffer the same fate as the Mexicas (Warren 1985, 50; De la Coruña 1539/1541, 74), and the colonial forces immediately established a new social order.

After their conquest, Nuño Beltrán de Guzmán, a Spanish colonizer, killed the Purépechan chief and coerced Don Pedro to assume a broker position to establish control of Michoacán and neighboring areas (Alcalá 2000, 690; De la Coruña 1539/1541, 80–81, 99–100; Krauze 1997, 48). Don Pedro governed Michoacán and directed the Purépechans to join Pedro de Alvarado's colonizing forces and to fight the Chichimecas north of Michoacán (See Alcalá 2000, 686–91; León-Portilla 1995, 73–77, 86–87; De la Coruña 1539/1541, 71, 90, 99–100; 1538/1539, 29). The strategy of incorporating Natives into the colonial forces further facilitated Spanish domination (León-Portilla 1995, 73, 86; Warren 1985, 227; Shorris 2004, 76). Nonetheless, as Indigenous resistance and widespread discontent grew in the 1540s (Cockcroft 1998, 35–41; León-Portilla 1995, 10–11), ethnically diverse and often conflicting Indigenous nations began to realize their common fate under colonialism. As others have pointed out, they were becoming the first racialized "Others" (Winant 2001; Zinn 1999).[9] León-Portilla documents how some Indigenous nations—not in the sense of modern nation-states but in terms of pueblos and collective identity as a people—began to form alliances against colonial domination:

> Their acts and screams of war revealed the tiredness and anger against the vexations they had been subjected to. It was a clamor that began to be heard in other places, such as Michoacán, Tlaxcala and the heart of the conquered country [Mexico]. . . . We saw—through Gerónimo López's [encomendado] letter—that Zacatecos, Caxcanes and other related nations with them, had initiated contacts with the Purépechas from Michoacán and the Nahuals from the high central plains, among them some Tlaxaltecas and Mexicas, to form an alliance of war. (1995, 10–11)

While some Indigenous nations formed alliances with each other and resisted the Spaniards, others strategically adopted the culture of the colonizers in the hopes of lessening the violence. This acculturation, however, did not necessarily lead to increased safety or equality within the colonies. Bartolomé de las Casas (1552) documented how, in the face of brutal conquest, some Natives strategically converted to Christianity in the hope that doing so would prevent the colonizers from violently entering their territories. One pueblo burned their idols and allowed the Franciscan friars into their pueblo, believing that the colonizers would not attack fellow Christians. But as de las Casas recorded, the Spaniards invaded anyway, after which the Natives "rose up in angry revolt and the entire population joined them in opposition to the Franciscan friars. Some Indians came to them saying, 'Why did you lie to us, falsely telling us that no other Christians would enter our lands?'" (1552, 86).

In the case of Xaripu, the colonial forces established control over the pueblo by the late sixteenth century. The account by Franciscan friar Antonio de Ciudad Real of the 1585 visit by the general commissioner, Friar Alonso Ponce, to the territory provides one of the earliest known written accounts of Xaripus:[10] "[Ponce] got there before sunrise to another pretty pueblo named after the Indians Xaripu, attended by the San Augustines, three leagues away from Tarécuato; he passed by without stopping" (Ciudad Real 1976, 27–28). In 1586, Friar Alonso Ponce again passed through Xaripu from Tarécuato:

> Having walked three leagues in which he passed two or three creeks and a fountain, he arrived after sunrise to the pueblo Xaripu that was attended by the San Augustines. Xaripus came out to receive him with the music of trumpets, and at the entrance of the pueblo, the people gathered waiting for him to pass so as to get his blessing, and those who could not be there went out to a crossroad at the pueblo's exit for the same purpose. They had swept all the streets where the priest commissioner would walk, and before he reached the pueblo they had removed many rocks so as to pave the road, all with so much devotion that even those with no devotion helped. The priest commissioner passed through, and went by two or three creeks and traveled another three leagues to the pueblo and convent of Huanimba, called Xiquilpa in Mexican tongue, where he was well received by all the religious people. (Ciudad Real 1976, 85)

This Spanish account omits the enormous devastation brought upon by the first century of European colonialism (Borah 1951; Cook and Borah 1960, 3, 50–56). Indigenous people were violently displaced from their lands and subjected to an *encomienda* system,[11] where they experienced extreme labor exploitation and social injustices as slaves and later as landless peons (See Borah 1951; León-Portilla 1995; De las Casas 1552; Fonseca and Moreno 1984; Warren 1985; Keen 1994; Cockcroft 1998; Purnell 1999). Their communities existed within an exploitative colonial-labor system (Borah 1951; Barrera 1979; Warren 1985), and those who fought or escaped the *encomienda* system were killed or pushed into unproductive lands, where they starved (León-Portilla 1995; De las Casas 1965; Cockcroft 1998).

In 1542, the new laws of the Indies changed the *encomienda* system into a *repartimiento* system that officially ended Indigenous slavery and regulated tribute (Keen 1994, 34). This new system, however, had many loopholes, and the enslavement, abuse, and exploitation of Indigenous people continued throughout and beyond the colonial period. During this era, Natives suffered extremely high mortality rates (Keen 1994, 14; Krauze 1997, 37; Cockcroft 1998, 20). From 1519 to 1650, over 90 percent of the Indigenous population in central Mexico was killed off by European violence, disease, slavery, and starvation—reduced from 20 million to 1.5 million (Cook and Borah 1960, 3, 50–56).[12] By 1586, the population of Xaripu had been reduced by about 60 percent, dropping to around 150 people (Fonseca and Moreno 1984, 60).

The depopulation of Natives threatened Spanish profits that depended on Native labor tribute (Cockcroft 1998, 20–21). The colonial elites sought to remedy their labor shortage by importing slaves from the Congo, Angola, and Cape Verde (Keen 1994, 23, 28; Ochoa Serrano 1997, 70; Cockcroft 1998, 37). Expressing concern over a labor shortage, Viceroy Velasco wrote to King Philip II of Spain on April 6, 1595:

> Until now much of the need of the Spanish was met by the abundance of foodstuffs and others supplies. However, since the Spanish who consume are many and the Indians who produce are few, supplies have become so short that this year no one has come forward to contract to supply meat, for neither sheep nor cattle are to be found. All supplies are becoming scarce and are rising in cost so fast that before many years this land will experience as great a dearth and want as now exists in Spain. (Quoted in Borah 1951, 23)

In a second letter addressed to the Count of Monterrey a few months later, Velasco further expressed his economic concerns relating to Indian labor: "Especially notable is the harm which comes from the Indians' failure to raise crops, for in addition to the rising cost of foodstuff, the lack of them [even at high prices] will be the ruin and destruction of this land. . . . For the Indians to sow and cultivate their lands (which are abundant and fertile) is a matter of the greatest importance for this realm and one which should be given special attention in the future" (quoted in Borah 1951, 23).

So even as the Indigenous population was decimated, the Spanish continued to demand high productivity and to profit from their labor, and eventually that of African slaves (Borah 1951, 1–2, 22–23, 26–28; Keen 1994, 9–11; Cockcroft 1998, 22–23, 26). Alonso de Zurita's account from 1556 to 1566 reveals that *encomenderos* pushed the Spanish Crown to raise the tribute quota and relax labor regulations so that they could get more out of the surviving Natives (Keen 1994, 12–13). Thus, from the mid-sixteenth century to the end of the eighteenth century, the Crown's annual tribute from Indo America increased from approximately a hundred thousand pesos to over one million pesos (Keen 1994, 12–13).

Even when the Indigenous people were at their lowest numbers in Mexico, they continued to greatly outnumber the Spanish (León-Portilla 1995; McWilliams 1990). In 1646, they made up 74 percent of the population (1.27 million); Indigenous-White mestizas/os accounted for 6.3 percent (109,042 persons); Black-White mestizas/os,[13] 6.8 percent (116,529); Blacks, 2 percent (35,089); and White *peninsulares*/criollos,[14] 10.6 percent (182,348) (Aguirre Beltrán 1972, 234). But around 1821, after three centuries of colonialism, only 60 percent of the Mexican population was classified as Indigenous; over 23 percent and a growing number as *castes* (diverse mixtures); and a smaller percentage as criollos (Whites) (Ochoa Serrano 1997, 38).

In Xaripu the 1778 Jiquilpan church's archives of confessions and communions registered 182 Natives, 16 Spanish, and 730 Black-White mestizas/os (Ochoa Serrano 1997, 78). Jiquilpan's church did not differentiate between those living in the pueblo and those from surrounding communities. Using 1792 tribute records from Zamora (an administrative city) and 1798–1800 Xaripu church baptism records, Fonseca and Moreno report similar figures as above and note, "Xaripu was predominately an Indian pueblo, without overlooking the large [Black-White mixed] segment, who was the second largest group followed by the Spanish as the third group. In addition, during these documented years three Indian-White *mestizas/os* were also registered in Xaripu" (Fonseca and Moreno 1984, 70). The predominantly Indigenous pueblo's church served surrounding communities with religious services and a hospital (Fonseca and Moreno 1984). Considering their large numbers and high likelihood of interaction, the mixing of Natives and Africans was likely underreported.

European colonialism forced Indigenous people (and Africans) to migrate by displacing them from their land. During this colonial period in Michoacán, the Guaracha latifundium engulfed part of Xaripu's communal land from the northeast, and after Mexican Independence smaller-scale criollo and mestizo landholders' *ranchitos* (small family farms) occupied much of the southwest portion of the pueblo's lands (Fonseca and Moreno 1984; Moreno García 1994; De Bernal 1969; González 1995). To subsist, Xaripus were forced into servitude with a land-owning clergy and an *encomienda*, and later into semi-feudal (wage) relations with the Hacienda Guaracha and other more distant haciendas (Moreno García 1994; Ochoa Serrano 1999; De Bernal 1969). Thus, Natives and later mestizas/os became labor migrants as a result of land displacement through colonial conquest (Bravo Ugarte 1960, 10, 22–24, 27).

MEXICAN INDEPENDENCE (1810)

In the late eighteenth and early nineteenth centuries, Spanish Crown officials launched an *Inspección Ocular en Michoacán: Regiones Central y Sudoeste* (Close Inspection of Michoacán; Bravo Ugarte 1960). The purpose of this report was to inform the governing and policing forces of twelve county-like regions in the Purépechan zones of Michoacán about the social conditions of Natives living under their authority (Bravo Ugarte 1960, 8). The conditions described were typical of other areas of Mexico during the late eighteenth and early nineteenth centuries.

[Santiago Tupátaro's] population includes 22 tributary Indian families, who appoint their mayor and council and who work principally as peasants in mills and *haciendas*, cutting firewood, growing corn and wheat, because they lack sufficient lands of their own; since their indigenous lands have been reduced significantly. Natives are forced to expatriate themselves in search of sustenance; they are sad victims of unhealthy conditions . . . are reduced to 49 tributary Indians, who name their mayor and council for the collection of royal tributes. They work as peasants in mills, cutting firewood and growing small amounts of corn, because to their bad luck the *Hacienda* de San Nicolás has expanded into their land, reducing it in size and to the poorest quality. They do not have a choice but to migrate from their localities and to search for sustenance in unhealthy climates that destroys their population little by little. (Bravo Ugarte 1960, 23–25)

In this social context Bishop Manuel Abad y Queipo of Michoacán, Mexico, warned the king of Spain in 1799 about the escalating racial tensions between the Whites and the brown masses:

The Spanish make up about 10 percent of the total population, and they alone control all the property and wealth of the Kingdom. The other two classes that make up ninety percent can be divided in three, two castes and one of pure Indians. Indians and castes are employed in domestic services, in agricultural jobs, and in the ordinary ministries of commerce and the arts and other occupations. That is, they are servants and laborers of the first class. Consequently, there exists between them and the first class conflicting interests and values which is normal among those who do not have anything and those who have it all, between the dependents and the lords. . . . The color, ignorance, and misery of the Indians place them at an infinite distance from the Spanish. (Quoted in Alvarez del Toro 1988, 61–62; see also Bravo Ugarte 1960, 9; Krauze 1997, 82–85; Cockcroft 1998, 48–49)

The growing tension that Bishop Abad y Queipo alerted his king to eventually erupted in a revolt in 1810. Landholding criollo elites and clergy (such as Miguel Hidalgo)[15] reacted to the increasing financial pressures imposed by the Spanish Crown's Consolidación de Vales Reales (Consolidation of Royal Vouchers) in 1805 (Krauze 1997, 83–84; Cockcroft 1998, 46–48)—an effort to actively collect debts owed to the church, so as to finance its wars in Europe. The Spanish and criollo landholders in Mexico who were affected by these royal collections fumed (Cockcroft 1998, 47). As Cockcroft notes, "Landowners had long objected to the 'protection' the Crown had offered Indians and Indian village lands, wanting instead to extend their *haciendas* in a free and open market. Many *hacendados* and middle-size landlords began thinking seriously of political autonomy for Mexico" (1998, 49).[16]

The frustrations of both the brown property-less and the White propertied thus converged in *el Grito* (declaration of independence) against the Crown of Spain. In between the structured hierarchies of a European kingdom and the colonized, criollos strategically sided with the Indigenous against Spain, but protected the haciendas and White privilege in the process (Krauze 1997, 91–100; Cockcroft 1998, 48–50). Thus the independence gained in 1821 was primarily a victory for criollos and mestizo elites, who maintained their land and social privileges in the transfer (Ochoa Serrano 1999, 95–114; Krauze 1997, 84, 97–98, 109, 112; Bonfil Batalla 1996, xvi). As Benjamin Keen documents, "The *hacienda* easily survived the Wars of Independence; indeed, it improved its position after independence as creole *hacendados* took advantage of the lapse of Spanish protective legislation to acquire by various means the lands of neighboring Indian communities" (1994, 16–17).

Ongoing racial and economic inequalities spurred further Indigenous rebellions. González (1995, 47) documents racial conflicts in Michoacán in 1835, in which seven criollo ranchero families appropriated land from the Mazamitla Natives, who numbered about 177. After being ignored by the authorities, the Mazamitla took matters into their own hands and, with rocks, sticks, and machetes, reclaimed their land. Moreno García (1994, 112–13, 143) also recounts Guarachita Indigenous protests against the Guaracha *hacendados* about five miles north of Xaripu.

These conflicts were not particular to Michoacán. For example, Yucatán's War of the Castes, which started in the mid-1800s and continued into the twentieth century, "was a racial, territorial, and ultimately, historical conflict between the Maya Indians and the sparse White population of the Yucatán" (Krauze 1997, 145; see also Shorris 2004, 67–69). In 1848, while Mexico was militarily occupied by the United States of America, these racial conflicts spread to central areas of Mexico, as Krause notes, in the form of "sporadic warfare between the villages (inhabited by *mestizos*, but with deep indigenous roots) and the *haciendas* for possession of the land" (1997, 145). Cockcroft further notes, "Hoping to stem such peasant rebellions, many prominent families collaborated with the US invaders, thereby hastening the defeat of a Mexican officer corps reluctant to fight and thousands of aroused peasants and workers who genuinely defended the nation's honor" (1998, 67). Through the Treaty of Guadalupe Hidalgo in 1848, the Mexican elites in the Southwest expected full citizenship and all related rights that went with it.

Under these circumstances, elites in Mexico possibly saw less to lose under US neocolonialism than with a peasant Indigenous revolution. Consequently, in Mexico, elites from all political bents feared the revolutionary potential of the brown masses and thus advanced seemingly inclusive notions of "we Mexicans" and *patria* (fatherland). In a similar way that the language of "melting pot" and "American" is used to deny social differentiation in the United States, the guise of a unified national Mexican identity effectively maintained the social inequalities (Lugo 1995, 40–41; Gutiérrez 1999, 19–20). The use of in-between brokers facilitated the process of establishing this social order. The emergence of a Zapotec (Benito Juarez) and later a mestizo (Porfirio Díaz) as executive rulers of Mexico facilitated the nation-building project (Cockcroft 1998, 69; Gutiérrez 1999, 3–5). They followed the model of US liberalism (as had some of their earlier predecessors) and began the process of nation building through legal frameworks and militarism (Shorris 2004, 177–78). In effect, Juarez and Díaz consented to a neocolonial order.

Liberal reform laws following Mexican independence and throughout the nineteenth century continued to attempt to lessen Church and Indigenous communal control over the land (Cockcroft 1998, 72–73; Shorris 2004, 176–78). For instance, the Colonization Law of 1833 attempted to reduce the Church's land control and to divide it among the peasants who worked it (Menchaca 1995; Gonzalez and Fernandez 2003). Whites and mestizas/os, however, were favored over Indigenous communities with land for *ranchitos* (Cockcroft 1998; Menchaca 1995; González 1995). As Purnell notes, land privatization was furthered by the Lerdo Law of 1856, which allowed "independent small holders to acquire further communal holdings either through legal purchases or through the various sorts of frauds and coercive measures so commonly associated with liberal reform" (1999, 41; see also Cockcroft 1998, 71). In 1883 and 1884, the *baldío* (empty land) laws encouraged *hacienda* expansion into supposedly unused land, dislocating Indigenous communities who inhabited it (Purnell 1999, 40–41; Quiñonez 2001, 251–52; Cockcroft 1998, 72–73). Both sets of laws increased criollo and mestizo family *ranchitos* at the expense of communal Indigenous lands (Purnell 1999, 42; González 1995, 54), and Whites and mestizos were favored with land and state support over Indigenous communities (Forbes 1982, 52–53; Menchaca 1995, 7–8; Purnell 1999, 40–44; Cockcroft 1998, 71–73). As Cockcroft notes, "*Criollo* (and some *mestizo*) landowners were thus able to achieve what not even the colonial elites had been able to do: take over the vast majority of Indian land!" (1998, 72). All of these forces were at play in Xaripu as well. The vast majority of the pueblo's inhabitants share-cropped and served the few who owned everything: the Hacienda Guara-cha, three families, and the Church (Fonseca and Moreno 1984, 86–91).

THE MEXICAN REVOLUTION (1910)

After Mexican independence, Indigenous communities remained sub-ordinated to Mexican powerful elites, and their nation, by and to foreign interests. These overlapping colonialisms of internal-colonial and neo-colonial relations—i.e., interactive colonization—created the extreme conditions leading to the Mexican Revolution in 1910. In that year, Emiliano Zapata, descendant of the Anenecuilco Indigenous pueblo, was called upon by his pueblo elders to reclaim their lost lands (from 1607), because, since 1895 a Spaniard *hacendado*, Vicente Alonso Pinzón, had become more oppressive, taking over more Indigenous land and refusing to rent them land to subsist (Krauze 1997, 275–78). After several centu-ries, Anenecuilco was no longer ethnically and linguistically a purely In-digenous community, but its collective memory as a pueblo and sense of indignation caused by displacement, exploitation, and insult reached a threshold during the Porfiriato Period and spread throughout Mexico.

The privatization of land ownership intensified during the Porfiriato Period (1876–1910), when Mexico increasingly came under the control of domestic and especially foreign monopolistic forces (Hart 2002, 168, 266–67; Gonzalez and Fernandez 2003, 29–32; Shorris 2004, 187, 198, 209–210). The social inequalities that had been prolonged and deepened in postindependence Mexico heightened during this era. From 1876 to 1910 the dictator Porfirio Díaz brokered a foreign-controlled "moderni-zation" project that, by the late 1800s, had dislocated thousands of In-digenous peoples from their native lands (Hart 2002, 257–67; Gonzalez and Fernandez 2003, 42–43). The Porfiriato (Díaz's administration) con-solidated the power of large landholders and foreign investors, and expropriated masses of peasants from their village lands as railroads ripped up the countryside, and haciendas expanded their export production (Silva Herzog 1960, 40; Weber 1998, 214–15; Cockcroft 1998, 83–90; González and Fernandez 2001, 11; 2003, 38; Mora-Torres 2001, 1–2). In 1905, Díaz devalued the peso from one US dollar to fifty cents, which hurt both domestic workers and businesses while benefiting foreign investors (Hart 2002, 264; Ochoa Serrano 1995, 15). Foreign capitalists eventually monopolized Mexican mines, oil holdings, banks, and railroads and left the cane, corn, and cows to the Mexican *hacendados* (Hart 2002; Gonzalez and Fernandez 2003; Shorris 2004). By 1910, only about 3 percent of the Mexican population owned agricultural lands (Galarza 1964, 18; Weber 1998, 215; Cockcroft 1998, 82; Hart 2002, 262–63), and Indigenous people and mestizas/os were forced to extend their intranational and international migration in search of subsistence wages (Gamio 1930; Purnell 1999; Fonseca and Moreno 1984; Mora-Torres 2001).

During the Porfiriato Period and the revolution that followed (1910–17), one-tenth of the Mexican population moved permanently to the United States (Acuña 1988, 188; Mirandé 1985, 49). As railroads transported rich minerals and other resources to the United States, labor migrants followed (Florescano et al. 1983, 135; McWilliams 1990, 156–57; Gómez-Quiñones and Maciel 1998, 32–33), many of whom were recruited by US employers and Mexican intermediaries (Cockcroft 1998, 86; Zamora 1993, 11–19). Thus the dramatic increase in migration was directly related to the US interventions that reconstructed Mexico as a neocolonized nation—first through military conquest and then through the appropriation of its national resources (Gonzalez and Fernandez 2003, 45–49; Hart 2002, 235, 257–67; Portes and Rumbaut 1996, 274–75; Shorris 2004, 198).

This neocolonialism had a profound impact on Xaripus and their labor migration. As poverty intensified in the new colonial context, Xaripus began extending their internal migration to haciendas in Guaracha, Los Reyes, and Tierra Caliente, Michoacán, where they worked seasonally for subsistence wages (Fonseca and Moreno 1984). The Hacienda Guaracha, the closest and largest employer of Xaripus and other neighboring Indigenous communities, had already displaced them from their land during the colonial period—possibly no different from Zapata's pueblo

(Moreno García 1994; Alvarez del Toro 1988; Fonseca y Moreno 1984; Ochoa Serrano 1999). But around the time of the Mexican Revolution, Xaripus had begun seeking higher wages in more distant haciendas in Los Reyes and Tierra Caliente (Fonseca and Moreno 1984, 94–95), which took, respectively, a day to almost three days to get to.

The material poverty experienced by Xaripus was a frequent topic in my interviews. Personal stories about looking for, craving, and preparing food were very common. In one such conversation with a Xaripa elder about her childhood, she recounted how she and her younger sister had captured a chicken that had flown into their dirt patio. Knowing its owner would come looking for the bird, one of the girls hid it under a bucket and then sat on it to keep it from running away. When the owner arrived at the house in search of his chicken, the girls denied having seen it. Believing them, the owner left, and the girls lifted the bucket only to discover that the chicken had died from asphyxiation. The girls then surgically removed an egg from the dead bird and shared it for a meal.

Modesta Salcedo, a one hundred-and-five-year-old woman from Michoacán provided another glimpse of the social conditions that stimulated intra-national and international migration among the Xaripu. Modesta, who was born on February 24, 1895, and died ten months after our interview in November 2000, recalled: "*Antes había mucha pobreza. No se diga . . . la gente andaba con calzones parchados*" (There was a lot of poverty before. People walked around with patched up peasant pants). They filled pillows with old rags, and when their pants tore, they would open the pillows to look for patching material. She especially remembered a gift her mother had given to her as a little girl: "My mother bought me a *reboso* [shawl]. It was a great gift. But I didn't have something to tie a donkey with, I didn't find a rope, and I used the *reboso*. The donkey tore the *reboso*, and I was left with nothing." She then laughed with gusto that she was able to survive that misery.

Modesta's parents were seasonal migrants to *el norte chiquito* (the little United States) in Tierra Caliente, Michoacán. Tierra Caliente was given that nickname because it was a key migration site before the "big" *norte* became migrants' main destination. In Tierra Caliente, migrants experienced extreme labor exploitation working in the rice fields and frequent illnesses. Many of the Xaripu elders I interviewed recalled relatives who died while working there and others who came back near death from severe cases of fever. Modesta's father had worked in the rice fields in Tierra Caliente, and her mother had been a cook there for the campesinos. Modesta did not migrate with them but remained in Xaripu until she married in 1917, after which she moved to the western periphery of the pueblo, *el Rincón de Xaripu,* where she lived most of her life in a small adobe house. Modesta's main job consisted of grinding corn and making tortillas for commerce.[17]

Margarita was born in Xaripu in 1910, and her father also migrated seasonally to Tierra Caliente to work in rice fields for a hacienda. In the late 1910s, her father returned to Xaripu with a severe fever and soon died, leaving behind his wife and five small children. Margarita's mother became the sole breadwinner, working as a domestic and making chocolate for the local market. Margarita and her sisters also started working at a very young age. In 1927, she married a Xaripu migrant to the United States, when the dollar equaled two pesos.[18] After she married, she stopped working outside the home until her husband was violently killed in the pueblo in 1931. She tearfully recounted that he had been drinking and fighting when somebody shot him. At the time Margarita was twenty-one and pregnant with their third child.

About three years later, Margarita had a baby with another Xaripu *norteño.* But she refused to marry her boyfriend because his brother accused her of being *interesada* (financially motivated) because she already had three kids. A proud woman, she decided to support all of her children alone. Later, one of the richest men in the pueblo gave her a sewing machine, and she slowly taught herself how to sew: *"Ahí solita comencé a coser, ahí solita, ahí solita, y comencé."* (There, by myself, I started to sew, alone, alone, and I learned to sew.) Margarita worked as a seamstress and dress designer from 1935 to 1975, when she joined most of her children in the United States.

Xaripu international migration intensified during the 1910 Mexican Revolution and the 1917–21 US guest-worker programs (Zamora 1993; Gutiérrez 1996; López Castro 1986; Fonseca and Moreno 1984). The Moreno railroad station, built in 1900 near the Hacienda Guaracha, where many residents of Xaripu worked for wages (Moreno García 1994; Fonseca and Moreno 1984; De Bernal 1969), linked the pueblo to other train stations in central Mexico[19] with routes to the United States (Zamora 1993, 11–12). As communication and transportation improved between the rest of Mexico and the United States, economic and labor conditions encouraged more Xaripus to migrate north for work.[20]

This migration was shaped not only by class factors but also by race and gender. In the early twentieth century it was mostly Xaripu men who migrated and who were recruited by US industries. Manuel Gamio described the typical Mexican migrants to the United States in this era as: "*mestizos* and . . . full-blooded Indians who make up the greater part of both unskilled and skilled labor and the tenant and share farmers" (1930, 197). This ethnic composition is not surprising given Mexico's predominant Indigenous makeup (Forbes 1982; Gonzalez 1999; Shorris 2004). In 1921, Whites made up about 20 percent of the Mexican population; Indigenous people, 40 percent; and mixed-race people, 40 percent (Ochoa Serrano 1997, 38). Indeed, Modesta told me that most Xaripus in that era were "*prietos como indios pero hablaban español*" (dark like Indians, but spoke Spanish). Margarita reflected that only three families owned land property in Xaripu in the 1920s[21] and also commented, "*En este siglo las familias más poderosas fueron blancas. Como todo el tiempo . . . hubo poca gente blanca en Xaripu*" (In this century the most powerful families were White, like always . . . [though] there were few Whites in Xaripu).

As the nation-building project advanced after the Mexican Revolution, cultural diversity was repressed and the melting-pot ideology of Mexican-ness advanced. Though some of the Xaripu interviewed recalled that their parents and/or grandparents spoke the Purépechan language,[22] by the late 1950s only half of the Mexican population still spoke "their mother tongue, one or another of the autochthonous Indian Languages" along with Spanish (Wolf 1959, 44). Transnational experiences also contributed to the growing sense of Mexican identity, though ethnic distinctions within the Mexican label continued, as Weber elaborates: "This sense [of Mexican-ness] . . . did not preclude deep divisions and bitter conflicts among Mexicans who differentiated among themselves on the basis of ethnicity, region, class, gender, and their length of residence in the United States. For the most part, however, Mexicans operated within a community bound together by common identities and notions of cooperation, sharing, and mutuality" (1998, 218).

Xaripus also migrated in groups, and their US experiences over time moved them toward accepting the "Mexican" identity—though they remain Xaripu-identified and oriented (see chapter 5). One migrant shared how his personal decision to migrate influenced other Xaripus, revealing a collective orientation[23] that is typical of Indigenous communities: "In a trip that I took in 1920, in which many Xaripus also went, we were about twenty persons from this pueblito. Although I'd preferred to travel alone, that time I went with more because they would tag along. A train passed by and many of us left, but it wasn't that I had invited them to come along, it was just because I was leaving, and so many people also left" (quoted in Fonseca and Moreno 1984, 146).

From 1900 to 1920, most of the Xaripus who migrated went to Illinois (Chicago) and Indiana (Gary), and from 1920 to 1930 they also went to Texas (Fort Worth, Dallas, San Antonio), Kansas (Topeka, Newton, Kansas City), Indiana (Indiana Harbor), Colorado (Denver, Platteville), Michigan (Saginaw), Pennsylvania (Pittsburgh), and Nebraska (Fonseca and Moreno 1984). These migrations occurred in several stages. First, migrants would reach the US-Mexico border area, where they would work to earn money to migrate to Chicago. From Chicago they eventually traveled to other industrial cities in Indiana and Pennsylvania. During this period, northern industrialists also recruited African Americans from the Southern states to work alongside of the Natives/mestizos(as) from Mexico and the Southwest, subjecting all of them to unfair working conditions vis-à-vis their European immigrant counterparts (Barrera 1979; Bonacich 1976; Ngai 2004; Zamora 1993).

The direction of Mexican migration was reversed during the Great Depression, when many of the first-generation international migrants were repatriated and/or deported to Mexico through the Mexican Repatriation of 1931–34 (Galarza 1964; McWilliams 1971)—though some Xaripus did settle permanently at this time in Chicago, Illinois, and Colton, California. When I visited family in Michoacán in January 1991, a great-uncle, Serafín Barajas (1905–95), told me about his return to Mexico during the Great Depression. He had been working for a steel company in an eastern industrial city, and a tall European immigrant became upset that a "Mexican" was employed there with him.[24] After constant harassment, pushes, and invitations to fight, Serafín agreed to step outside and settle this once and for all. The tall man led the way, and Serafín grabbed a pipe and hit him in the back of the head. Soon after, Serafín returned to Michoacán for good.

AGRARIAN REFORM IN MEXICO (1917–1930s)

The implementation of Emiliano Zapata's 1917 Plan de Ayala (land reform that involved breaking up haciendas and giving land to the peasants) had proven to be a great challenge in the immediate postrevolutionary period (see Alvarez del Toro 1988; López Castro 1986; Moreno García 1994; Purnell 1999). Large landholders stridently objected to it and issued violent threats against those who tried to claim land under its terms. The Catholic Church also condemned it and warned the faithful against taking what it considered to be other people's property (Fonseca and Moreno 1984; Moreno García 1994; López Castro 1986). Jesus De Bernal, who played the organ in the Xaripu Church at the time, recounts in his autobiography, *Tierra Mía* (1969, 88), that at this time Mass usually concluded with the following benediction: "May God our Father enlighten us with an understanding, so that we can comprehend that only by living in conformity to his mandates and obeying everything our bosses and superiors demand, can we in this life have a beautiful death, and in the other life, see and enjoy the eternal prize. This is what I wish for everyone, in the name of the Father, the Son, and the Holy Spirit. Amen."

De Bernal also describes a demonstration of disregard for the Church's support of the wealthy in San Antonio Guaracha, just east of Xaripu, where most of the people displayed indifference toward the hacienda's sponsored religious celebration, Misa del Buen Temporal (Mass for a Good Season). He writes: "As it says, the 'Mass for a Good Season' had as an objective a prayer to God so that He would bring plenty of rain to grow corn, grasses, and especially optimum fruits. But since these would invariably go to the *hacienda,* the campesinos saw the festivities with indifference . . . , since the only benefit they could expect were loans in the form of credit and corn from the *hacienda* that was deducted from their part of the crop as sharecroppers" (1969, 189).

De Bernal's radical musician friend Teodoro Acevedo also displayed this evident criticism of wealth disparity:

[Teodoro Acevedo] appeared to be 25 years old. He was thin and discolored, with a broad mustache with curled tips, black like his hair and eyes. He wore a coarse cotton shirt and peasant pants. He wore *huara-ches* [leather sandals] and a wide straw hat. His dress was completed with a sarape, folded lengthwise and carried over the shoulder. Since he spent most of the day playing a guitar, he became a good player, and so his guitar skills were sought joyfully by Xaripus for entertainment or when gallants serenaded their girlfriends. On such occasions, it was difficult to make him play, but when he did, he usually received some pay for his services. He had radical ideas, so profoundly rooted that he preferred not to eat than to work, according to him so as to not make the rich richer with his work. (De Bernal 1969, 34–35)

De Bernal also tells of enjoying the hospitality of his friend Doña Adelina Abarca and how critically observant she was of the local priest's ability to eat meat every day:

> I was often invited to eat, and regularly received eggs and fried beans completed with *cotijense* cheese and *chile de molcajete*, accompanied by tortillas just heated in a *comál*. Rarely did I eat so deliciously as in Doña Adelina's house! On occasions, she would say afflictively, "I don't give you meat, because this you might eat every day in the priest's house." But I knew that she didn't give me stews, because of her own financial limitations. For this reason, every now and then I took her a piece of meat that I could afford. (1969, 47)

The combination of poverty and *hacendados'* resistance to land reform extended the revolutionary conflicts into the postrevolutionary period. The communities neighboring Xaripu were directly affected by these conflicts, but not the pueblo. Xaripus only remember one close attack by Ines Chávez García, a Pancho Villa rebel with his own armed men, in San Antonio Guaracha.[25] A great-nephew of *guardias blancas* (hacienda hired-hands), who had been posted to protect San Antonio Guaracha, shared with me his family's oral history about the early Agrarian Reform period:

> My grandmother's brothers hid on the hills near San Antonio [an extension of the Hacienda Guaracha], and as the Inez Chávez's men [one of the revolutionary groups challenging the haciendas' monopoly of

wealth and land in the area] got close to it, [my great-uncles] started shooting at them. . . . They were killing those rowdy Indians, and they made them turn back. But this *vieja mitotera* [old shrew] ran towards [the Indians] and told them, "*Hijos de la chingada* [sons of bitches], don't be *pinche* [cowards]—they are only three *cabrones!*" So they went back, and killed [my] two great-uncles.

De Bernal's autobiography mentions this same event and recounts that on December 17, 1917, Chávez García raided San Antonio Guaracha: "'Viva Inez Chávez García!' came to our ears . . . followed by screams. We realized, then, that who attacked us were not Samaniegos or González [other revolutionary leaders], but Inés Chávez García who led about one thousand men. . . . Our escape would be through the north towards *la presa* [reservoir]. Hit well before we reached it, I began to name my partners to know whether all were present. . . . A cold wind of death embraced our bodies" (1969, 174).[26] Six of the sixteen men defending the Hacienda (extension) of San Antonio were killed in the attack (176).[27] After attacking San Antonio Guaracha, the revolutionaries proceeded to the Hacienda Guaracha just three miles north of Xaripu, where they burned a sugar cane/alcohol distillery. Chávez García's rebels did not raid Xaripu, and some rumored this was because the pueblo had been supportive of the revolution (De Bernal 1969, 9). But Moreno and Fonseca (1984) point out that the Chávez García forces were primarily directed against the haciendas. The social unrest continued through the 1930s and eventually pressured government administrators to actively enforce Zapata's Plan de Ayala land reform.[28]

The reverse migration and deportations during the Depression coincided with, and possibly contributed to, the agrarian reform movements of the 1930s in Mexico. A significant number of Xaripus began to make land claims under the newly enforced Agrarian Reform, and some took up arms to obtain *ejidos* (collective land grants) under its provisions (Fonseca and Moreno 1984, 106–11). Indeed, as other scholars have pointed out, Mexican migrants' revolutionary experiences and communal social networks in their native land were extended into the United States, making them key labor activists in US agriculture (Weber 1998; Zamora 1993). According to Weber, in the 1930s Mexicans made up "75 to 90 percent" of the labor activists in the San Joaquin Valley strikes (1998,

224; 1994, 146–47, 159–61). The impact of these transnational experiences flowed in both directions, as Weber notes: "While their Mexican experience influenced events in the cotton fields, the workers' experiences in the United States also affected political life in Mexico" (1998, 224).

The first land claim made by Xaripus was on November 29, 1929, by a group of eleven persons, eight or nine of whom had at one time migrated to the United States in the early twentieth century (Fonseca and Moreno 1984).[29] Their experiences of workplace injustices on both sides of the border had fostered their political and labor activism in both the United States and Mexico (see Weber 1998, 219–29; Zamora 1993, 3–9; Gómez-Quiñones 1994, 72–73). The Hacienda Guaracha was determined to enlist every possible means to oppose and reduce the land claims, which substantially slowed down the process of acquiring land (Moreno García 1994, 144–46, 203–35). The hacienda was able to legally use a census to determine eligibility for land: only family men who worked in agriculture and who neighbored the hacienda (Fonseca and Moreno 1984, 107–8).[30] The census indicated that of the 789 registered Xaripus, 198 could be counted as heads of households, and only 126 of those fit the requirements that gave them the right to claim land (Fonseca and Moreno 1984, 107–8). Other legal mechanisms for avoiding the distribution of land consisted of transferring land to family and friends (See Moreno García 1994, 230–31).[31] Illegally, the hacienda hired *guardias blancas* to maintain order through repression, scaring people off of the disputed lands and intimidating *agraristas* (land reform claimants) (Fonseca and Moreno 1984, 109; Moreno García 1994, 189, 207).

On April 2, 1934, definitive *dotaciones* (land grants) in Xaripu were approved by President Abelardo L. Rodríguez, and in August of the following year an engineer drew the *ejido* boundaries (Fonseca and Moreno 1984). Finally, on February 25, 1937, the definitive *dotaciones* came into effect. Nevertheless, the Agrarian Reform made no radical change in the socioeconomic status of the Xaripu population.[32] *Hacendados* used the law, politics, and repression to obstruct the redistribution of land, and when they were forced to comply with the reforms, they would cede only the poorest and most unproductive tracts of land (Krauze 1997; Moreno García 1994; Alvarez del Toro 1988; Fonseca and Moreno 1984). The great majority of the pueblo remained landless, while the few persons who had acquired *ejidos* lacked both quality land and the means to cultivate it. Small *ejidos* in postrevolution Mexico were guaranteed to fail. While big *hacendados* produced for export and received low-rate fees for railroad transportation, the high cost of transportation closed the doors of the US and Mexican markets to small *ejidos* (Gonzalez and Fernandez 2003).

Besides the minimal impact of the Agrarian Reform on Xaripus, most of the beneficiaries of the land distribution were from mestizo pueblos.[33] For instance, in the mestizo pueblo of San José de Gracia most families obtained land grants by 1926, though initially many were not excited to claim *tierra ajena* (someone else's land) (Gonzalez 1995, 186). So while mestizos sought and/or received *dotaciones,* many Indigenous pueblos had not forgotten their historical land displacement by colonialism and neocolonialism; they sought the restitution of their historical land claims rather than *dotaciones.* After a long struggle some did, like Guarachita, now Villamar (see Fonseca and Moreno 1984; Purnell 1999; Moreno García 1994; Alvarez del Toro 1988).

In the Xaripu case, by the time the Agrarian Reform was implemented in the 1930s, they had little memory of their historical displacement and thus sought *dotaciones.* The repression of Indigenous identity that began with their cultural colonization under the Augustinians in the first century of Spanish conquest (see Fonseca and Moreno 1984, 59; Krauze 1997, 74, 80) was furthered by the structured inequalities of the new nation that valorized the European heritage over the Indigenous (León-Portilla 1990). As Zabin and her coauthors observe, "Colonial and post-colonial history has left Mexican Indigenous peoples with fractured social identities, which in rural Mexico are often limited to village of origin rather than membership in an ethnic group defined by a common language and culture" (Zabin et al. 1993, 9; see also Kearney and Nagengast 1989).

Xaripus overall remained landless and impoverished in Mexico, and thus continued and broadened their international migration during the Bracero Program (1942–64). This guest-worker program significantly transformed the pueblo into a labor migrant community for generations to come, altering notions and expressions of identity and community (see chapter 5).

BRACERO PERIOD (1942–64)

At the outset of World War II, the United States arranged with Mexico an Emergency Farm Labor Program, or Bracero [literally arm or working hands] Program, that remained operative until 1964. Signed into law on August 4, 1942, by President Roosevelt, Agricultural Labor Law No. 45 established the Bracero Program to supply Mexican laborers to compensate for farm labor shortages resulting from the war (Menchaca 1995, 90; Driscoll 1999, 54). Mexico set certain conditions for the guest-worker program: (1) the program would guarantee the rights of both Mexican workers and US citizens; (2) braceros would be employed only if the US Secretary of Labor officially confirmed labor shortages in the United States so as to protect the prevailing wages and working conditions of domestic workers; (3) braceros would be exempt from service in the US military; (4) contracted workers would be protected from racism and unfair labor conditions; and (5) a defined work contract, housing, food, and travel arrangements for return to Mexico would be provided to braceros (Gutiérrez 1995, 133–34; Driscoll 1999, 54–55).

As Gutiérrez explains, on "September [29] 1942 the program began quietly with the transportation of 1,500 Mexican contract workers from the interior of Mexico to the sugar beet fields outside Stockton, California. The number of Mexican workers contracted grew steadily throughout the war years, from 4,189 in 1942 to a peak of 62,091 in 1944. By 1947 nearly 220,000 braceros had worked under contract in the United States, almost 57 percent of them on large-scale corporate farms in California" (1995, 134; see also McWilliams 1990, 237–38). In 1942 Xaripus began migrating through the Bracero Program to Stockton, where relatively good wages and plenty of work left an early and overall good impression.[34] In addition to finding higher wages than in other areas, the Xaripus I interviewed told me that the Farmer Association center in Stockton easily connected the braceros with work and that the climate was pleasant—neither too hot nor too cold. Although braceros were not free to choose their employment destination, they learned how to get contracts in favorable areas, usually with the help of growers. One of the early Xaripu migrants recounted,

A Grower's Association sent us to a farm labor camp near some islands by Stockton and Lodi. There they did give us food and there was
little to complain about. They fed us until we were full; we were
treated more humanely and not like animals as in most other places.
The pay was better. . . . From there I returned to Xaripu to get married
and from that work I built my house—I bought a lot and built my
house. . . . I worked in that island for six years: six months there and
six months here. (Quoted in Fonseca and Moreno 1984, 185)

Xaripu males migrated primarily to California and Texas, though
Texas was boycotted in the early part of the Bracero Program (1943–47)
because of its extreme racism and unfair labor practices against Mexicans (López Castro 1986, 53–66; Gutiérrez 1995, 139–41). After World
War II ended, agricultural lobbyists in the United States persuaded their
government to extend the program indefinitely through Public Law
No. 78, which was enacted in 1951. The contracting centers were moved
from central Mexico (Federal District, Irapuato, and Guadalajara) to the
border area (Hermosillo, Empalme, Mexicali, and Chihuahua), and the
traveling costs were shifted from the US government to the workers,
who had to pay for their own transportation to the border area. One of
the early Xaripu migrants (in the 1910s) recounted the dehumanization
experienced in this phase of the second guest-worker program.

I took two trips in the [second] Bracero Program. I was losing my vision that's why I decided not to continue going. The last year that I
went, the inspectors took a long time observing me. I noticed that
people who were my age were not taken to the corral to be physically
examined. They would just look at me. About 50 people were rounded
up, and they pulled out all the good people, all the young people; and
those of us who were older were left behind. I was one of those who
got left behind, and that was my last year. (Quoted in Fonseca and
Moreno 1984, 165)

Those denied a guest-worker contract faced a tremendous financial
crisis upon returning home, since many had borrowed money to make
the trip to the contracting areas on the border, whereas those selected to
work experienced further degradation—growers treated them like animals. One Xaripu reported:

We were treated horribly. We were taken to a corral from where we were contracted. In El Centro [California], like buying a bunch of cattle, horses, or donkeys, we were enclosed in a corral and then [the contractors would] say [to the growers] "you go to see which one you like. You choose the one that you like." We were treated like that even though we were not animals. That is how they treated us. As if they were choosing a nice animal, the growers entered the corral and selected one out of all those people. (Quoted in Fonseca and Moreno 1984, 179–80)

Braceros also faced many hardships on their way to and from work in the United States. For instance, Armando, whom I interviewed in 1999, migrated as a bracero in the early '40s, and his wife, Carolina, joined him in 1966. He was not the first in his family to migrate to *el norte*, and Carolina's father had been an early Xaripu migrant in the 1910s. Armando recalled his first migration experience:

That first year we went to Kansas City. I came with Pascual, *el Tambor*, who helped Guillermo sell meat, my sister Mariana, *la Llegua*, Teorrema, *el Barañas*, Cruzito's brother. We then left Kansas City, and we went to Chicago. We worked on the railroad tracks there. There were older Xaripus who lived there already, including an older brother of mine who came in 1926 or earlier. . . . They would tell us that we should try to get legal residency papers. In the first few years [of the Bracero Program] they wouldn't ask one whether we wanted to renew the bracero contract. . . . When we had been there for six months they threw us out. . . . Within eight months of our return to Michoacán, several [Xaripus returning to Mexico] were killed in a railroad car accident when some pipes exploded. They were buried in Indio around 1946.

Another migrant interviewed, Luis, was seventeen in 1940, when he first migrated to the United States and worked on the railroad tracks for about six months in Westmoreland, Pennsylvania. He was later contracted as a bracero in 1942 with the help of Manuel Carrillo, a Xaripu state worker who helped many of Luis's generation get contracted as braceros. Luis traveled from Mexico City to Juarez, where he was directed to US employers and worked in the asparagus fields in Stockton's Rough and Ready Islands. He continued migrating, saved a little money, and in 1950 married Nena, whose father had been migrating north since the 1920s. Luis remembered,

> We worked from sun up to sun down. They told us we would earn more money, but then the check came out lower than anything. . . . Sometimes in the camps there were about a thousand workers. They would only feed us junk there. Can you believe it? They cooked the beans in barrels without washing them. They fed us pork feet and stinky chickens. Porfirio Serrano had been a cook, and he would tell us, "Don't eat the pork feet, because I washed them and couldn't remove the stink. Who knows what they used to get rid of the smell!"

On top of this inhumane treatment, farm workers received grossly low wages. According to Menchaca, "Government surveys indicate that between 1942 and 1964, when the Bracero Program was in operation, farm labor wages remained the lowest in the country. . . . It was not until 1984 that the Fair Labor Standards Act of 1938 was applied to farm workers, making most of them eligible to receive the federal minimum wage" (1995, 91).

In their later years in Michoacán, some of the first generation of Xaripu labor migrants, by then retired, would routinely gather to reminisce about their past and discuss politics. These men were among the first *agraristas* and guest workers in the United States during the 1900s and 1920s.[35] During the evenings they met on National Street near an adobe jail in the middle of Xaripu to discuss world politics, particularly US-Soviet relations (this was during the Cuban Missile Crisis in the early 1960s). Usually, they formed two debate groups—*los Rusos* and *los Americanos*—who took sides on the political economy of the world. *Los Rusos* outnumbered *los Americanos* by a ratio of two to one. This mismatch was not surprising, considering that most of these men had spent half a century working in *el norte*, where they witnessed de jure racism and exploitation, and in their view Russia was more oriented toward workers' rights.

The families of braceros in Xaripu—the elders, women, and children—did not see immediate benefits from the Bracero Period. Poverty and death were commonplace for most of the migrants' families. Almost all of the older families I interviewed had lost children and family members to preventable illnesses. According to Dr. Luis Velasco Vargas's medical thesis (1945, 24–25), no medical doctors served the* pueblo during the 1940s, though several midwives assisted with births. The most common illnesses, in order of frequency, included malaria, gastrointestinal disturbances, avitaminosis, dysentery *amibiana*, typhoid, extreme coughs, pneumonia and bronchopneumonia, pulmonary tuberculosis, and typhus. The highest mortality rates were attributed to exhaustion or bile problems for adults and colic or diarrhea for children (Velasco Vargas 1945, 14).

Nena, whose father had been one of the early migrants to the United States in the 1920s and whose husband, Luis, was a bracero, recounted her struggles during the Bracero Period. She raised a growing family on sporadic remittances from Luis, and relatives eventually helped her purchase a small rocky lot of land on the outskirts of Xaripu to build an adobe house.

> I did not rent for very long. The house is about my son's Lupe's age [forty-six years], because in 1950 they made the dirt road by where my house got built. I bought it there. . . . I think with the hope of settling there. It was very rocky. Well, consider what it cost me, [900 pesos]. I remember I did not have the money. Lupe Vesello, a woman who was called *la Tomata*, lived by there and asked me if I wanted to buy it. First, she had asked the neighbor, Lionel, but he had no money, nor had I any, but my mother went to Rumaldo, and Rumaldo lent me the money. Then, I bought the rocky piece of land. . . . Then Luis returned as a bracero and built me the house there. He started to make adobe bricks with his brothers, and he made the house. When my son Lupe was born, I had a house. The house has been there ever since.

Nonetheless, life was not easy for Nena, especially when Luis would get held up trying to get to the United States for work. She recalled the struggles of raising kids alone:

> Navigating alone with so many kids. When Luis was [working in the United States], I did not suffer because he sent us whatever he could,

but when he was delayed in Empalme trying to cross, sometimes he could not send us anything. The little we had ran out, and we suffered a lot. I suffered a lot alone. . . . I remember that I would take all my kids to get firewood. All of us went to the highlands for wood so that I could use it to make tortillas for the children. . . . Well, we suffered because I was alone with my kids, but little by little I always had food to give my children—with a lot of suffering because it is tough to manage with so many young kids alone. I remember that they got sick with the measles, and my little girl of one year and a half died. Lalo, my son, was also about to leave me [die], and Lupe, my other son, was also very sick and . . . I was without a cent. Luis had just left to the US, and I had nothing [money nor medicines] to treat them with. My daughter died because I had no medicines. Sometimes the doctor was not there. . . . It was from bronchitis, she left me. She lost her breath and left me. I had nothing.

In another interview with an older Xaripu woman, María told me about her father and maternal uncles, who began migrating to the United States in the 1920s and 1930s, and her husband, Gregorio, who began migrating as a bracero in 1954. As a young girl, María helped with home chores like making tortillas, washing laundry, carrying water from *la tecomaca* (the spring), and so on. Her mother, Licho, was a sickly woman afflicted with a variety of ailments, particularly muscle aches. Her father, Victor, earned just enough to subsist in Michoacán, but when he migrated as a bracero, his remittances and gifts significantly improved his family's life. María characterized her father as a very good provider. However, around 1954, after traveling to Empalme, Sonora, in the hope of once again being hired as a bracero, Victor was denied a contract because health inspectors found he had a hernia. He had borrowed money to travel to the border area and could not repay it for a long time. This was during "Operation Wetback" in 1954, when border enforcement and deportations increased, reducing the number of unauthorized farm workers and directing them into a regulated Bracero Program (Ngai 2004, 154–56). Crossing over to *el norte* became very difficult for the undocumented—and eligibility for the guest-worker program with a hernia, impossible.

María lamented that there had been no good paying jobs for her in Xaripu, and she recalled how she earned what she could for her family by knitting, making quilts, and doing other similar work. She also ran errands to the store for neighbors, carried drinking water from *la tecó-maca* for her neighbors, and cleaned houses, especially for migrant families. "When there was just not enough [money or food]," María recalled, her mother washed laundry for a *guarachero* (sandal maker) but "would quickly get sick washing other people's clothing, because they smelled bad." So María would wash the laundry in a river in her mother's place, while Licho stayed home with the other children. María could not remember how much she earned washing and ironing, but she did remember that her earnings were used to help out her family. "That's how it was, when one was left without anything."

When María married at age sixteen in the late '50s, she no longer needed to work outside of the home because her nineteen-year-old husband, Gregorio, sent her money from his work in the United States. She continued to knit and make quilts, but was now self-employed. María found doing her own work instead of working for other people empowering, and reflected: "Now my work was to take care of my children." She visited her family and relatives daily, helping her ill mother and younger siblings.

POST-BRACERO PERIOD (1964–1980s)

By the end of the Bracero Program, many Xaripus gained legal residency in the United States with the help of some of the farmers for whom they worked. But the growers' motives were not selfless. Gregorio, for example, attained legal US status with the help of a German grower who had been impressed with his work and endurance irrigating fields in Dixon/Davis, California. Gregorio performed the job of two persons for the price of one, but in spite of the exploitation, he felt indebted to the grower. This changed when Gregorio planned his yearly visit to see his family in Michoacán in the early 1960s, and the grower threatened to call the border patrol and tear up his residence papers if he did not return to work after his trip. Upset, Gregorio went to the

Immigration and Naturalization Service and asked if his employer could terminate his legal residency. When informed that he could not, Gregorio did not return to work for him.

After the Immigration Act of 1965 ended the racist quotas of the Immigration Act of 1924 and allowed for family reunification (see Ngai 2004, 21–55), the pattern of male migration transformed into family migration,[36] as Xaripu women began migrating to the United States as well. This change affected the seasonal migration patterns too, since concern over children's education, stress over family separation, and access to housing became increasingly important. In the early years of this transition, children were frequently left in Mexico in the care of relatives or older siblings while their parents were working up north. For example, when María first migrated to the United States with Gregorio in 1970, they left behind their four children, who joined them three years later. Such family separations put tremendous strain on parents and children alike. A letter from a father working in the United States to his eleven-year-old daughter back in Michoacán conveys the immense concern parents had for their children's education and safety:

August 12, 1972

Olivia Gonzalez,

My dear daughter with much joy I write this letter to say hi to you and your little brothers and to hope you are well. Your mother and I are well. Daughter I got your letter which informed me that you are doing well, for which I am very happy.

Daughter you ask me if you should enroll Rafita [her three-year-old brother] in preschool, enroll him. And also enroll yourselves in school in time so that you can attend. As soon as you find out about registration go and sign in! Olivia, tell me if the house gets wet inside when it rains. Take much care of your little brothers and don't let them stroll too much on the streets and don't let them go swimming in la presa [reservoir]. Receive a million hugs and kisses from me and your mom. Attentively your father who loves you all very much, Gregorio Gonzalez

The pains of separation were particularly felt by migrant mothers who were away from their children for the first time (see Parreñas

2001a; Hondagneu-Sotelo and Avila 1997; Sarmiento 2002). Maria, Gregorio's wife, developed high blood pressure during these separations. Meanwhile, care for non-migrant children—feeding, babysitting, and educating—was performed by family members with very limited resources in Michoacán. For instance, the eleven-year-old addressee in the letter above had been left with her three younger brothers in the care of an eighteen-year-old aunt, whose own family totaled ten members.

Twenty-four year-old Valencia recounted her childhood experiences of moving back and forth between California and Mexico during this era.[37] Born in French Camp, California, in 1975, Valencia was the third youngest of seven children. During her primary school education, Valencia was sent to live with relatives in Michoacán for the school year and would rejoin her family each summer in Stockton. She completed part of her elementary and junior high school education in Michoacán but did all of her high school education in the United States. She recalled:

I was born in the United States, but we lived six months in Mexico and six months here [in California], and when I turned fourteen years old, I decided to stay here. Before this, I spent three years in Mexico going to school. Then when I turned fourteen, I started high school here. I wanted to stay, but I was telling myself, "My God, I'm going to start school, and they are going to place me in a class with the children who don't know much." Because when I was in second grade, they used to place me with the children who didn't speak English—in the group that didn't know a lot, right? I didn't want to be in that little group because I was not a dumb girl. . . . But I got placed there. And I thought, "now that I will be returning to school in California they will place me in the slow class with children who know little." I didn't want to be in that class. I would think, "I have to buy a language program like *Inglés sin Barreras*, so that I can learn to speak and not be placed in such a class." I was extremely stressed, because I did not want to be in a class with children who were behind.

Though Valencia excelled in school in both Michoacán and California, her experiences illustrate how migrant children face educational barriers from both the migratory experience and lack of support in US schools.

Irrespective of the child's learning ability, migrant children were not introduced to core educational courses such as history and science because of their limited English proficiency.

The strain of a fragmented education prompted many migrant families to settle more permanently in the United States. In the late 1960s and 1970s, Xaripu families who migrated for work lived in farm labor camps and would return to Michoacán each fall, when the harvest season ended and the farm labor camps closed. But eventually some families decided to stay in the United States for most of the year because they did not want to interrupt their children's education. Most bracero families I interviewed reported that their children's education was the primary reason they decided to stay permanently in the United States.

Once families moved into year-round housing, Xaripu migration patterns began to change (see also Chavez 1992, 180–81). In some cases, only part of the family migrated, while other members remained in California; whereas with others, the whole family reduced the amount of time they remained in Michoacán each year from months to weeks. But education and housing opportunities were not in themselves sufficient causes for more permanent settlement.[38] Rather, the growth of crops like tomatoes and grapes offering year-long job opportunities and the new farm labor rights gained in the 1970s made settlement possible in the United States. As Palerm (1991, 7) documents, "The vast majority of California-based farm workers settled between 1975 and 1985 after a lengthy experience as migrant farm workers. That settlement indeed was encouraged by the new opportunities created by the proliferation and expansion of fruit and vegetable specialty crops" (see also Allensworth and Rochin 1999, 50, 57).

Before the expansion of value crops in California, Xaripus had migrated to Oregon and Washington to pick cherries and apples.[39] They lived in the fields, slept in tents and cars, and bathed in open-water ditches. In the 1970s some of the Oregon growers began to provide migrant workers, now with families, more comfortable housing arrangements, in part to maintain a reliable and "cheap"[40] supply of workers. Some Oregon growers recruited Xaripu workers from Stockton, California, as this letter attests:

May 17, 1970

Mr. Gonzalez!

I hope that this letter finds you and all your friends in good health. I would appreciate it if you would let me know if you and your friends are planning to come to Oregon to pick cherries this year. People are calling in for jobs already, so I will need to know how many cabins to hold for you as soon as possible. We have a good_crop this year—so far—much better than last year. If you are coming I can use 20 pickers at least and if more come I am sure they can find plenty of work. The crop is going to be very early this year probably about 15th to 20th of June.

I do not want El Coyote [a Xaripu] this year. He is too hard on fruit spurs. Please write or call collect as soon as possible, so I will know whether or not to hold jobs and cabins for you. Sincerely Yours! Bud Zulke [signed]

But as 1970s farm workers' activism and the increased acreage for value crops[41] in California affected the passage of favorable state policies (see Palerm 1991), Xaripus began settling in California and stopped migrating as regularly to Oregon and Washington (see also Hondagneu-Sotelo 1994; Sarmiento 2002). The United Farm Workers successfully lobbied for the California Occupational Safety Act (1973),[42] federal and state unemployment insurance for farm workers (1974/1977), and the Agricultural Labor Relations Act (1975) (Villarejo et al. 2000, 2; Rosenberg et al. 1995, 16–17; Menchaca 1995, 133; Palerm 1991, 14). The last act permitted farm workers union representation for the first time in US history. These farm labor gains, along with the family reunification immigration provision (1965), permanently altered Xaripus' migration patterns (see also Sarmiento 2002, 85–91).

CONTEXTUALIZING XARIPUS' LABOR MIGRATION IN THE HISTORY OF COLONIALISM

Fifteenth-century colonialism began a destructive project of conquest for wealth in the Americas, whereby the colonizers appropriated land, resources, and labor by force. This large-scale and continuous conquest dehumanized Natives and began a history of racial formation—the organizing of society along a social hierarchy and division of labor based on the social constructs of race/ethnicity (Omi and Winant 1994). Colonialism shaped our modern world, including the world economic system, the hierarchy of contemporary nation-states, and the social constructs of racial identity (Wallerstein 2003; Winant 2001). From the time of Spanish colonialism, Xaripus have migrated to other lands to work (Bravo Ugarte 1960; Fonseca and Moreno 1984). In the context of neo-colonialism, particularly during the Porfiriato Period, Xaripus extended their intra-national migration in Mexico and eventually were incorporated as colonial subjects in *el norte*. Their migration experience has been shaped by interactive colonial contexts and emergent unequal nation-state relationships. In the twenty-first century Xaripus are no longer labor migrants and have generally settled in the United States, though most maintain active social and emotional ties to Michoacán.[43]

Chapter Four

THE LOGIC OF COLONIALISM IN MODERN LABOR RELATIONS

For two-thirds of the twentieth century Xaripus were recruited as colonial labor to the United States.[1] After the Bracero Program ended in the mid-1960s, they continued to labor under colonial conditions in the agricultural fields, where they remained highly exploited, underpaid, and without access to labor rights.[2] In spite of their residential status and semipermanent settlement in the United States, *retiradas/os* and *mayores* generally remained working in farm labor throughout their lives.[3] Many *hijas/os*, however, searched for economic opportunities outside of the fields, particularly at the time of the 1986 Immigration Reform and Control Act (IRCA) and 1994 North American Free Trade Agreement (NAFTA). Though *chicas/os* were under age eighteen during this period and generally did not work in the fields, they were also affected by their families' occupational and residential segregation. While younger Xaripus' economic opportunities improved compared to their elders, their labor experiences also reveal colonial hierarchies—confined largely in service and other de-skilled job sectors and experiencing further class segmentation within these occupations (Barrera 1979; Segura 1990; Glenn 2002). These inequities become evident when examining the relationship between the racialization of the workplace and corresponding labor conditions (wages, productivity, and work schedules). This chapter analyzes this relationship from the standpoint of Xaripus[4] and classifies their labor experiences as Mexicanized, diversified, and Whitened. These experiences are discussed in two sections in this chapter: "Colonial Labor in the Fields" and "Out of the Fields."

The Mexicanization experiences are documented both in and outside field occupations, whereas the diversified and Whitened experiences are observed only outside the fields. Furthermore, I do not document the process of diversifying and Whitening an occupation as I do for the Mexicanization of jobs. However, I work from the assumption that in a diverse city with a notable presence of minority groups,[5] a nondiversified occupation—i.e., one that employs predominantly one racial group—is not a natural condition, and neither are racially segregated communities (Massey and Denton 1993, 41–61; Lipsitz 1998, 13–14; Allensworth and Rochin 1999, 16, 49–52, 58). The absence of diversity is a consequence of a past and present history of practices with institutional or individual bias—such as recruitment, interview processes, and tests[6]—and unwelcoming or exclusive work environments that keep occupations generally homogenous.

COLONIAL LABOR IN THE FIELDS

In *Racial Formation in the United States,* Omi and Winant (1994) elaborate how race as a social historical construct has been shaped by institutional and representational processes in which unequal power relations determine the emergent racial formations. These authors conceptualize racialization as the assigning of specific racial meanings and values to an ethnic group, whose members through social-political struggles may shift and change the content of the racial ascription.[7] Along these lines, I use the term "Mexicanization"[8] to illustrate how people of Mexican origin, as well as the work that they do, become similarly racialized in the United States.[9] Although the findings of my case studies are not inferential, they fit the general national patterns of the devaluation of Mexicanized occupations—particularly those that are feminized in both private and public spheres (see Levine 2006, 7–10; see also chapter 6).

The Mexicanization of labor occurs when Mexicans become a majority of the workforce and wages and working conditions subsequently deteriorate. According to Elaine Levine (2006, 7–10), all occupations (except skilled construction work) whose workforces experienced an increase of at least 25.6 percent in Mexican composition resulted in significantly lower median weekly earnings than found in the general population. It is important to stress that Mexican immigrants do not themselves deteriorate labor conditions,[10] but rather racist employer and state practices and norms devalue Mexican labor and negate their humanity.[11] This distinction adds a critical qualification to the body of classic labor scholarship documenting how racial minorities are used to segment (Barrera 1979; Gordon et al. 1982; Menchaca 1995) and/or split the labor market (Bonacich 1972, 1976; Wilson 1980; Miles 1989). The dominant theses advanced in this scholarship argue that racial minorities were historically cheapened (Roediger 1991) and that they were later incorporated into the labor market as cheap labor (Bonacich and Cheng 1984) for the purpose of depressing wages. However, I propose that racial minorities are not merely incorporated as low-cost labor but rather reduced in value at the work site. In other words, Mexican labor is not cheap but devalued—illustrating the continued dehumanizing logic of colonialism (see Ngai 2004, 106–9).

The interactive colonization model (XC) recognizes the complexity of the labor experiences of Xaripus. As outlined in chapter 2, XC highlights how interactive systems of domination (race, class, and gender) have been persistently universalized since the colonialism of the fifteenth century. XC also underscores the continuity of emergent forms of domination rooted in colonialism—though with changing ideological justifications: from Social Darwinism to color-blind racism (Carr 1997; Bonilla-Silva 2003)—and moves beyond polarized conflicts between the "haves" and "have-nots" in the workforce by highlighting the role of emergent intermediaries, who often facilitate the appropriation of wealth and social control of labor. For example, in the advanced stages of Mexicanization, Mexican supervisors are appointed to manage and supervise the exploitation of workers, which helps give the impression that the employers are fair ("color-blind") and that Mexicans themselves are the ones who keep each other down.[12] These dynamics are clearly evident in the agricultural fields.

Mexicanized Labor in the Fields

Although farm labor has historically been an exploitative and poorly paid occupation for all people (regardless of race and nationality), class oppression interacts with racial and gender systems to create variable experiences within different groups in ways that are significantly shaped by their colonial histories. For instance, Filipinas/os and Mexicans were both colonized and neocolonized in their homelands, and subjected to internal colonial experience as imported colonial subjects in the United States in the early twentieth century (see chapter 2). Their shared experiences with racial hierarchies and labor exploitations created a more devalued and unstable position for them than their fellow Dust Bowl and Eastern European migrants during that period (Ngai 2004, 76–87). Both Filipinos and Mexicans earned less for doing the same job, and they were also vulnerable to deportations and repatriations (See Weber 1994; Espiritu 2003b; Ngai 2004).[13] Indeed, colonized people have historically been even more restricted in their occupational opportunities (Barrera 1979; Mirandé 1987; Segura 1990; Menchaca 1995), thus keeping them in agriculture for longer periods and in numerically higher proportions than other ethnicities in the general population.

Since the 1970s, farm labor employment has remained constant, but Mexican workers have become the overwhelming majority of the workforce (Mines 2006, 1–3). Surveys by the California Assembly, University of California Employment Development Department, and National Agriculture Workers Survey document this shift in California's agriculture over three decades (Mines 2006, 2). In 1965, the US farm workforce was 44 percent White, 46 percent Mexican, 7 percent Asian/Native American, and 3 percent Black; in 1983, it was 4.5 percent White, 87 percent Mexican,[14] 7 percent Asian/Native American, and 1 percent Black; and by 1995, it was 1 percent White, 98 percent Mexican, and 1 percent "other." Immigration policies have significantly contributed to this Mexicanization of the fields (Ngai 2004, 128–31). The Immigration Acts of 1917, 1921, 1924, and 1934 excluded Asians, Eastern Europeans, and Africans from entry to the United States, and the guest-worker programs in 1917–21, 1942–64, and 1986 (IRCA) specifically recruited and replenished agricultural workers from Mexico.

In further explaining the ethnic replacement in farm labor, Mines (2006) suggests that poor working conditions and declining wages over time have failed to keep veteran farmworkers in agriculture, while the opening of other low-skill, nonagricultural jobs provided an escape from agricultural work. However, Mines does not explain why it is mostly recent Mexican (and fewer Central American)[15] immigrants who have replaced other ethnicities and veteran farmworkers. Alternatively, Zabin and associates (1993) attributed this shift to the agribusiness structure that continuously replaces various ethnic groups with more exploitable labor, suggesting that Chinese, Japanese, Filipinos, and others were used to depress wages until each group was displaced by another. They thus argue that in the late twentieth century, Mexican-origin mestiza/o labor was being replaced by Indigenous Mixtec labor, though mestizos dominated intermediary roles—contractors and supervisors—and discriminated and exploited the Indigenous people (Zabin et al. 1993, viii; Johnston-Hernandez 1993, 50).

But though mestizas/os are privileged over more Indigenous people on either side of the border, these scholars' claims are problematic. To begin with, the anticipated "ethnic replacement"—i.e., a new more exploitable racial group—has yet to supplant "Mexicans" in the fields (Villarejo et al. 2000, 7). To this day, Indigenous and indio-mestizas/os alike continue to occupy the bottom jobs in the United States, though without question the Indigenous groups who maintain their languages and traditions experience greater discrimination. What is more, categorizing early "Mexican" migrants as mestiza/o erroneously transforms a diverse ethnic/racial group into a monolithic entity (Lugo 1995; Forbes 1982; Bonfil Batalla 1996). For instance, early in the twentieth century Gamio (1930, ix, 197) observed "full-blooded Indians" and indio-mestizas/os migrating from the central states of Mexico to the United States.[16] In *The World of the Mexican Worker in Texas*, Zamora (1993, 120) describes a railroad general superintendent who refused to negotiate with Mexicans union workers: "He would have found the demands just and reasonable if they had been submitted by Anglo workers. But since they [Mexicans] were *indios*, the demands were unacceptable." Hence, the migration of Mexican-origin Indigenous to work in the United States is not a recent phenomenon, and their distinctiveness from mestizas/os was noted among scholars and US public officials.

What is more, racist differentiations of Mexicans intensified as their population increased in the United States. Menchaca in *Mexican Outsiders* (1995, 74) documents how, as Mexican migration to the United States increased in the 1920s and 1930s, government officials began to pay increasing attention to how to racially classify and segregate them, including in the educational system.[17] In 1927 and again in 1930, California Attorney General Ulysses Sigel Webb opined that "it is well known that the greater portion of the population of Mexico are Indian and when such Indians migrate to the United States they are subject to the laws applicable generally to other Indians."[18] But in 1935 the California legislature legally differentiated Mexican students according to their skin tone, as Menchaca reports, and "officially segregated some Mexican students on the basis that they were Indian while it exempted 'White Mexicans.'"[19] Thus Indigenous-looking people from both Mexico and the US Southwest were identified as "Mexican."[20] Though the few who could pass as White were purportedly given the advantages of being White, they were still discriminated against because of their social proximity to Indigenous people, which was assumed to indicate racial and/or cultural impurity and thus inferiority.[21]

As farm labor in the United States has become overwhelmingly Mexicanized, workers have experienced higher levels of economic instability and exploitation. The fact that farm labor has become Mexicanized has contributed to the extreme deterioration of labor conditions as evidenced by Xaripus' farm work experiences, in spite of the labor laws that were extended to them in the latter part of the twentieth century.[22] The colonial logic in modern labor relations suppresses their humanity and the enforcement and protection of their labor rights and health. Thus, Mexicanization of the farm occupation illustrates the continuity of colonial oppression in modern labor relations through the devaluation of their labor, unstable work schedules, and exemption of labor/political protections to workers, particularly undocumented residents.

LABOR CONDITIONS IN CALIFORNIA AGRICULTURE

Farm labor is possibly unmatched in offering low occupational pay and dangerously exploitative work[23] and in creating disenfranchised undocumented workers. These conditions are extensively related to the rigid profit-orientation of agribusiness. Corporate farms, markets, and packing/canning companies, who are the principal profiteers in agriculture, rely on the contractors who occupy intermediary positions (Rothenberg 1998, 12) to serve as labor-cost buffers and to facilitate the appropriation of wealth from farm laborers (see Bonacich and Appelbaum 2000, 136–40). Contractors compete with each other for contracts with growers, and to win they lower the labor costs by reducing the workers' pay. Indeed, at the same time that the number of labor contractors in the industry increased, farm work piece-rate wages[24] declined dramatically from an average of $7.11 an hour in 1989 to $5.01 in 1991 (Villarejo and Runsten 1993, 28; Osterman 2005a, A6). Other strategies contractors use to profit from workers include undercounting their piece-rate production or hours worked and more often keeping some workers— without their knowledge—off of the payroll[25] to avoid paying taxes and social security deductions (Rothenberg 1998, 97). In addition, after a day's work many contractors and supervisors purchase piece-rate units at a lower rate (e.g., five cents less) from workers who need immediate cash and then transfer the labor benefits—unemployment insurance and social security funds—to a contractor's (or supervisor's) family member who may not be working at the time but who will profit from someone else's labor.

Although the word *contrato* (contract) is commonly used by farmworkers to refer to work paid by the piece rate, it wrongly suggests a negotiated and detailed work arrangement between workers and employers. In reality, the contract is an empty construct that carries no mutuality or economic stability but rather invites many labor abuses. Farmworkers generally lack the power to negotiate wages and labor conditions with their employers. The contractor who functions between the worker and the owner buffers risks and costs to agribusiness, and his social-cultural proximity to labor—as someone who was once a farmworker himself and who comes from the same community as the workers—facilitates the creation of a more manageable and often loyal workforce. Hence, the contractors' authority stems not only from the companies who employ them but also from the fact that many workers identify with them. Workers consider this person one of their own and often an example of success.

Armando, a Xaripu man in his mid-seventies who was interviewed for this study, shared a conversation he had on a plane with a farm labor contractor, Sancho, while traveling to Mexico. Sancho is a big contractor in San Joaquin County but, according to Armando, very envious of a

Xaripu, Chente, who had landed a supervisor position with the Triple E tomato company.[26] In Armando's words,

> Chente had been big in the tomato company, and many people did not like him, but the people from Xaripu would defend him. For example, I had talked to Sancho, who is from Jalisco, who did not like Chente at all. We talked a good while because we were traveling to Mexico. Sancho said that he did not lose the hope of taking over Chente's job. He did not know that another Xaripu was near and traveled with us. The other Xaripu told Sancho, "You are very mistaken if you think that you can displace Chente. He does not speak English and he did not go to school, but he is very intelligent. . . ." Sancho asked, "Where are you from?" The Xaripu said, "Xaripu, and I have known you for a long time, you are very envious, but Chente has much knowledge of his job [and] that's why it is impossible for you take over his job." . . . [Xaripus] protect each other so as to help themselves find work.

Although the positive aspects of these worker-contractor relationships can include friendship, employment opportunities, respect, and social support, the negative outcomes include a higher tolerance of exploitation. A friendly contractor may gain the loyalty of his workers (as illustrated above with Chente) and exert tremendous influence on them, encouraging them to endure harsh labor conditions such as working longer than they would normally to help finish picking a large field to meet the contractor's production goals. Workers in turn often obtain more consistent employment in a very unstable occupation. Nonetheless, farmworkers face widespread, systemic abuses, including the illegal appropriation of their time without compensation, lack of enforcement of labor regulations, and legal exemption from labor rights offered to all other workers.

The appropriation of workers' time without compensation is a prevalent illegal abuse under *contrato* work. Although licensed contractors are familiar with their legal obligations to workers, they violate the law anyway by taking advantage of uninformed and often disenfranchised undocumented workers. These illegal practices are widespread, and labor rights are not enforced,[27] because of workers' lack of knowledge of their rights and also because workers do not complain for fear of losing their jobs or being deported. A common violation is not compensating on-call employees for the time they spend waiting to begin work, even though this is mandated by federal law (Rosenberg et al. 1995, 104).[28] On-call-time abuse often occurs during the fall tomato harvest in the San Joaquin Valley. Workers are told to be at the fields at six or seven AM yet are not permitted to start work until the recommended temperature for picking tomatoes is reached—often not until nine AM or later. Furthermore, when they do begin to harvest, they are often further delayed in starting to work because loading trucks may not arrive on time, and so the workers lose from a few minutes to half an hour or more waiting to empty out their tomato-filled buckets.[29]

Other labor violations consist of denying workers various forms of legally entitled compensation. For example, when farmworkers finish picking a particular field, they are sent to another one, which can take ten to thirty minutes to get to, but they are not compensated for the time traveled or for the use of their own car and fuel (Rosenberg et al. 1995, 103).[30] In addition, when rain stops work after just a few hours, workers are not paid for the remaining half day's work, even though this is mandated by California law (Rothenberg 1998, 19). Labor codes are further violated when piece-rate pay does not add up to the minimum wage rate required by law,[31] and so workers earn less for a day's work than they would if they were they being paid the hourly minimum wage.

Farmworkers also face labor abuses that are legitimated by law, since they are exempt from certain aspects of its protection (Fonseca and Moreno 1984; Rothenberg 1998; Villarejo et al. 2000). Historically, farmworkers were excluded from the National Labor Relations Act of 1935 (union representation, strike, and collective bargaining rights) until the mid-1970s because agribusiness successfully lobbied Congress against their inclusion (Rosenberg et al. 1995; Menchaca 1995). Also, the Fair Labor Standards Act of 1938 was not applied to farmworkers until 1984, at which time they finally became eligible for the federal minimum wage and other workplace protections (Menchaca 1995, 92; Rothenberg 1998, 208–9).

But even with these advances, laborers still will work continuously for weeks without getting a day's break[32] because field workers are not covered by the Industrial Welfare Commission's Order 8, which asserts that employees who work seventy-two hours per week are supposed to receive a twenty-four-hour break thereafter (Rosenberg et al. 1995, 108).[33] Moreover, farmworkers do not receive overtime pay because they are excluded from the legal provision that would otherwise mandate that they be paid one and a half times more than the average pay after working more than forty hours a week (Villarejo et al. 2000, 10; Rothenberg 1998, 208–9).

The greatest abuse against workers, however, is the devaluation of their labor. Though wages have generally declined (in terms of real dollars) for almost everyone in the United States over the past thirty years, they have particularly dropped for farmworkers (Collins and Yeskel 2000, 2005; Rothenberg 1998). Free-market economists claim that supply-demand market forces place the values and prices for commodities, including labor. But they do not sufficiently explain the devaluation of farm labor.[34] The supply-demand logic postulates that if there is a demand for a commodity in low supply, its value will go up. However, this principle has not applied historically to farmworkers, even when they are in high demand and agribusiness actively recruits them. For instance, during World War II, when growers claimed labor shortages and the United States recruited braceros from Mexico, farm labor wages were significantly depressed (Menchaca 1995, 90–92; Ngai 2004, 139–43; and Chacón and Davis 2006). More recently, agribusiness have lobbied for a type of guest-worker program that addresses labor shortages in farm labor and requested fewer regulations and lower pay requirements for workers:

> The National Council of Agricultural Employers has written to the [US presidential] administration to urge changes like speeding up the H-2A application process, easing housing requirements for guest workers, reducing the required wage for these workers and increasing the types of work they are allowed to do—poultry processing might be included, for instance. Grower groups have also urged the administration to ease requirements that they run newspaper advertisements to determine whether American workers want the jobs. (Greenhouse 2007, 16)

The devaluation of farmworkers therefore reflects the political power and economic interests of agribusiness instead of market forces setting the price of commodities (Rothenberg 1998, 208–9; Ngai 2004, 106–9, 133–37).[35]

Indeed, analysis of the industry indicates that production and corporate profit have increased substantially over the last four decades, while farmworkers' wages have declined (National Farmers Union 2005, 15–16).[36] But while California crop acreage and profits increased substantially from 1960 to 1989 (Palerm 1991, 42–49; Rothenberg 1998, 20, 59–60; Villarejo and Runsten 1993, 16) and vegetable and fruit production doubled from 1970 to 2000 (Villarejo et al. 2000, 10), real wages for the workers harvesting these crops have declined. In "California's Agricultural Dilemma: Higher Production and Lower Wages," Villarejo and Runsten (1993, 24) reported a more than 40 percent decline in real wages in the raisin grape and fresh tomato harvests. The US Department of Agriculture also reported that California farmworkers' earnings generally declined by one-sixth from 1978 to 1992. At the national level during this period, annual real income among farmworkers employed by contractors declined by 25 percent (Villarejo and Rusten 1993, 24). Throughout the 1990s, over half of all farmworkers lived in extreme poverty, earning from $5,000 to $7,499 a year (Zabin et al. 1993, vii, 1, 17, 24–26, 31–32; Rothenberg 1998, xvii, 95; Villarejo et al. 2000, 23), and by 2005 the median family income for farmworkers had not risen above $10,000 (Mines et al. 2005, 7).

In addition to earning such low wages, farmworkers and their families are exposed to dangerous pesticides and hazardous labor conditions (Johnston-Hernandez 1993; Rothenberg 1998; Watson 2002; Wright 1990; see also United Farm Workers of America 1992). According to the US Bureau of Labor, from 1970 to 2005 disabling injuries almost doubled in the nation from 2.2 to 3.7 million, and agricultural work had the highest fatality rates (31.5 percent) of all occupations (US Census Bureau 2008b).[37] Yet injured farmworkers are frequently uncertain of the compensation they are due, or they fear that filing a claim will result in losing their job or being deported. Villarejo and associates found that of the 19 percent of agricultural workers who experienced an on-the-job injury and were compensated by California Workers Compensation Insurance Systems in 2000, only one-third knew that their employers had such coverage (2000, 8). Mines and Kearney found in their study that "Tulare County farm workers who suffered on-the-job injuries preferred to treat themselves instead of filing a workers compensation claim or, in a disturbing number of pesticide injury cases, chose to continue working without treatment if that was physically possible. Immigration status and fear of losing income undoubtedly influence such individual decisions" (1982, 98–99). Moreover, in the early years of the twenty-first century, about 70 percent of adult farm laborers in the United States had no health insurance, and only 7 percent receive any form of public assistance, e.g., Medicaid, Medicare, Healthy Families, etc. (Villarejo et al. 2000, 8, 31–32, 41; Mines et al. 2005, 13).

Xaripus' agricultural experiences reflect these broader trends; in fact, all of this study's participants reported a decline in personal productivity and real income from 1970 to 2000. Their working conditions worsened within the larger economic context primarily because of an oversupply of workers (see Villarejo and Runsten 1993, vii–viii), the increased mechanization of jobs, and, most importantly, the globalization of the agriculture industry.

The oversupply of laborers stems in large part from the Immigration Reform and Control Act (IRCA) of 1986, whose passage encouraged an oversupply of farmworkers to come to the United States, which thus reduced the amount of work available to each worker.[38] IRCA alone did not prompt people to migrate from Mexico (Villarejo and Runsten 1993, 18); rather, the effects of global capitalism such as the devaluation of the Mexican peso, the reduction of public services, and the elimination of labor protections in Mexico pushed Mexicans from their homelands. IRCA simply directed Mexican migrants to agricultural work through the Special Agricultural Workers and Replenishment of Agricultural Workers provisions,[39] which resulted in the complete Mexicanization of California's fields by 1995 (Mines 2006, 2). With more workers crops were harvested more quickly, but general earnings decreased for the field workers. For example, the workday of all the farmworkers I interviewed declined during this time by 25 percent (from eight to six hours a day), and their work week was reduced from about six days to less than five.[40]

The mechanization of field crops also contributed to the underemployment and unemployment of field-workers (Villarejo and Runsten 1993; Mines 2006).[41] For example, in 1994 cucumber pickers in the Stockton area were displaced by a harvesting machine—a technology that pushed more workers into the tomato harvests (Mines 2006, 7–10),[42] only to have new tomato planting methods in the twenty-first century subsequently eliminate the need for workers to weed those fields (Mines et al. 2005).

Both of these developments occurred within an increasingly global-ized agricultural industry that was motivated to produce more for less and to expand their market sales internationally. In the 1980s, California agribusiness increased their vegetable and fruit production as well as their exports, particularly to Europe and Japan (Villarejo and Runsten 1993, 3, 8, 16; Mundo Hispano 1992, 13; Magaña 1993, C1). In addition, agribusiness shifted the production of some fruits and vegetables—like tomatoes, broccoli, and cauliflower—to Mexico, while simultaneously maintaining high levels of production in the United States. In spite of this higher agricultural production in labor-intensive crops, farmwork-ers experienced declining earnings in California and throughout the na-tion. Agribusinesses' ability to produce crops abroad and to lobby for favorable legislation domestically to remain globally competitive—such as deregulation, guest-worker programs (H-2), tax cuts, and government subsidies—has also had an adverse affect on farm workers. Moreover, NAFTA worsened the plight of farm workers on both sides of the bor-der. In Mexico, it disrupted many farmers—unable to compete glob-ally and without tariff protections—and encouraged their migration to the United States (Cockcroft 1998, 169, 179–84; Brecher et al. 2000, 76–77; Bonacich and Appelbaum 2000, 5–7; Sirota 2006; Barndt 2002, 176–77). Similarly, in the United States "investment farms" monopo-lized agricultural production and hurt smaller family farms (Rothenberg 1998, 66–67).[43]

Farmwork

These global market politics have reinforced the structure of farm labor exploitation within which many Xaripus must labor. The rise of corporate power in the past thirty years has restructured the economy in ways that have increased and concentrated profits among corporate elites, while workers have lost real income, job security, and the enforce-ment of labor rights (Collins and Yeskel 2005). These declining labor conditions had harsh consequences for Xaripu workers. Nine out of the twenty-six workers I interviewed in California had suffered a disabling injury. Two-thirds of these injuries occurred in the fields, and the other injuries equally spread among a packinghouse, a roofing tile factory, and a post office. In 1998, a year before my research began, three Xaripus died at work—two in the fields and one in a factory.

The first of these, El Nono, began migrating to the United States in the final years of the Bracero Program and was in his mid-fifties when he passed away. His father had worked in California for most of the Bracero Period (1942–64) and had a tremendous influence among Xaripus. Some say that he was the first to move into the housing projects in Stockton in the early 1970s, and that many Xaripu families soon followed him. Nono was also very popular among Xaripus. After many years of laboring in the fields, he got sick while working in the tomato fields and was taken to the hospital, where he subsequently died of a brain tumor. Exposure to high levels of pesticides, lack of early medical intervention, and work-related stresses all contributed to his early death.

The second farm labor casualty was Sotero, who was similar in age and migration history to Nono. Sotero collapsed of exhaustion while working in the tomato fields, and he died later in the hospital. Sotero had high blood pressure but worked in the fields despite the risks because of financial need. The third fatality was Keletos—a young man in his early thirties who was married and had two children. His death took place in a factory; I elaborate his story in the next section (Out of the Fields).

Though Xaripus have worked in most types of fruit and vegetable crops in California, most have worked longest in asparagus and tomato fields. According to Alejandro, a bracero from the 1940s, most asparagus workers are between eighteen and fifty years old—a logical age range, since picking asparagus is backbreaking and extremely difficult. Workers pick long rows of asparagus for about eight hours a day, using a long knife.[44] The picker must bend down for long periods of time, cutting asparagus with the blade and placing them in small bunches in the field row.

The asparagus harvest begins in March and ends late in June. Work starts at six AM and stops around six PM, seven days a week. Workers are paid by the piece rate ranging from $4.00 to $5.25 per thirty-five-pound box. In 2007, a pound of asparagus sold for $2.99 at a Safeway grocery store, and thirty-five pounds, for $104.65. When there are many fields to be picked, people work for over ten hours a day. According to Alejandro, people harvest an average of fifteen to twenty boxes on most days, and twenty to twenty-five boxes when the crop is good.[45] Alejandro began picking asparagus in 1952 and amazingly lasted into the late 1990s—only by then he worked as a foreman. To this day three of his children, who are all around fifty years old, continue to work picking asparagus.

In the tomato harvest, the other major crop that Xaripus work, people are paid by the bucket. Wages depend on many factors, including the market price of a tomato bucket, the quality of the crop, the weather, the number of hours worked, the number of people working, the number of truckloads, and the experience of the picker (see Tables 4.1 and 4.2 and Figure 4 in the appendix for more details). Picking tomatoes involves every muscle in the body and requires tremendous mental discipline to endure the hardships. Kneeling or stooping over, pickers move along a fifteen- to twenty-five-yard tomato row, sifting through dense, strong-smelling tomato plants. They must comb the plant vine by vine in search of the right size, color, and quality of tomatoes. Then, using both hands, they quickly grab a tomato or two, thumb the stem off, and, with a fast twist of the wrist, throw it into the bucket that is always close at hand. Once two buckets have been filled, together weighing between fifty-five and sixty pounds, the worker must carry them to a dump truck waiting some thirty yards away. Unloading the tomatoes entails swinging the bucket four to five feet up to another laborer, who then empties the produce into the truck bin.

Getting to the truck is also a challenge. The path to the truck is scattered with smashed tomatoes, and maintaining balance under the weight of the full buckets strains one's arms, legs, and neck. Workers must walk across mud and rough clods of dirt while dodging fast-moving farm workers and the insults of a foreman who thinks one is moving too slowly. After a day's work few laborers have energy to do anything else.

Luis, who had been an early Xaripu migrant from 1942, worked for over fifty years in farm labor, particularly in the tomato harvest. Though Luis retired in 1995, two of his sons continue to pick tomatoes in the Stockton area, and thus he continues to have direct knowledge of the working conditions. In our 1999 interview, Luis commented that the mistreatment and poor pay of farmworkers have not changed over the past five decades but have actually worsened—in his view resulting from the IRCA's guest-worker program and globalization of agricultural production.

Luis was working in the fields when IRCA came into effect and witnessed firsthand its immediate impact—the oversupply of workers—on labor conditions. Prior to IRCA, he recalled, they had worked at least five days a week for over eight hours a day. By the early 1990s, the entry of new workers had reduced their work week to four to five days a week, about five hours a day. To make ends meet, families had to become more flexible and look for work with multiple employers within the same week, often working in several different sites on the same day.[46] For instance, some workers picked cucumbers in the early morning (from about five to nine AM) and then went to harvest tomatoes from nine thirty AM to three PM. In some cases, family members split up and worked for different employers in order to have income. In this context, children became crucial economic contributors, especially during school vacations and weekends. This need for every family member to work prompted many Xaripu families to rely upon networks and flexible family structures to ensure that child care and other familial concerns were attended to (see also Sarmiento 2002).

Some of the Xaripu *mayores* I interviewed described how they piece together field jobs throughout the year. Those who do not visit Michoacán every winter spend the cold season (December through February) pruning a wide variety of fruit trees, including grapevines in San Joaquin and Stanislaus counties in California, for which they earn sixteen to thirty cents per tree. In March they work tying up grapevines and then move on to weeding fields in San Joaquin County for minimum wage ($6.25 per hour in 2000). Late May to early June, they pick cherries, earning $2.25 per small box (thirty pounds) and $4.25 to $5.00 per large box (fifty pounds). Others pick apricots from June to July ($0.90 to $1.00 per two buckets, about thirty pounds each). Late June to early November, most pick tomatoes, while a smaller number pick cucumbers from late June to August, and some work in vegetable or fruit packinghouses. In November, some pick green peppers, apples, or pears or work in other field-related jobs.

Xaripu men and women generally work in similar crops, except during the late fall and winter, when farm work becomes scarce. Then the men assume the wage labor for the family. Despite this, many of the women I interviewed talked about how much pride they derive from outperforming men in physical farm labor, including María, a member of the *mayores* cohort:

> When I first started picking tomatoes (in the 1970s), my husband carried my buckets for me, [but then] I got tired of just picking and picking tomatoes. So I told him to carry his own and that I would carry my own. We were then always in competition, and I always beat him, and I felt very satisfied because I would win. Before carrying my own buckets, we picked together about 300 tomato buckets or more and I felt he produced twice as much as me. But when we worked independently I saw that I could do more than him.

A higher number of Xaripu women than men were also employed in packing and cannery jobs. Although farm labor was generally perceived as *mas pesado* (harder), packinghouses and canneries presented new labor challenges—e.g., highly regulated work spaces without the freedom to talk and move as they did in the fields—and also faced economic restructuring because of global market competition.

Packing and Canning

Over the course of the decade spanning 1990–2000, total employment in the US agricultural industry declined by 32 percent (US Bureau of the Census 2003; Levine 2006, 8). The 1994 passage of NAFTA changed the balance of exports and imports of fruits and vegetables (canned, frozen, and fresh) and increasingly shifted their production to Mexico (US Department of Agriculture 2007a, 8, 16–19). The lower labor costs, year-round production, and neoliberal policies mandated by the trade agreement (e.g., privatizing collective land, eliminating trade tariffs, and cutting state subsidies to small farmers) benefited large foreign and national commercial interests (Barndt 2002, 175–77). From 1994 to 2005, vegetable imports to the United States increased from 2.3 to 5 million metric tons, and fruits and nuts, from 6.3 to 9.5 million metric tons (US Department of Agriculture 2007b). In contrast, vegetable and fruit exports from the United States rose slightly, from, respectively, 2.5 and 3.7 million metric tons to 3 and 4 million metric tons. US tomato production (fresh and canned) was particularly affected by the comparative advantage of Mexico (Barndt 2002, 176, 178; US Department of Agriculture 2007a, 1–4).

While tomato cannery work was a move up from the fields, the industry was affected by this growing global competition and economic restructuring, which had a very direct impact on a predominantly female workforce. Gendered occupational segregation is more salient in the canneries and packinghouses than it is in the fields. This division of labor reflects notions of gender differences in strength—an idea that is not as prevalent in the fields, where men and women alike pick and haul heavy boxes of produce. In the canneries, however, men generally hold the positions of authority and those involving technology (e.g., mechanics, assemblers, forklifters, truckers), while the majority of women work sorting and packing tomatoes or as office secretaries.

Cecilia—in the *hija* cohort—grew up in a family of farmworkers. Both of her grandfathers began migrating to the United States for work even before the Bracero Program; her father came north during the guest-worker program (late 1950s), and her mother joined him in the 1970s. While Cecilia and her younger siblings grew up working in the fields alongside their parents during summer vacations and weekends, she went straight to work for a Tri Valley tomato cannery when she finished high school in 1988 until she was laid off in 1999. Then married and with two children, Cecilia had been working the same number of hours and days each week since graduating from high school: eight hours a day, seven days a week.

The cannery job had offered a sort of economic and health security that the fields had not given Cecilia's parents. She described it this way: "When you have worked ninety days for the company, and join the union, you get health insurance coverage and a raise." But these comparative advantages did not last. In 1999 Tri Valley Growers began laying workers off in response to the growing economic difficulties (overproduction and low prices of commodities). The next year it filed for Chapter 11 bankruptcy protection, and then rehired some of its former employees for lower wages as part of the bankruptcy reorganization conditions until it finally shut down later in 2000 (Sinton 2000).[47] One of the nation's largest farmer cooperative and fruit/vegetable canners dating back to the 1930s, the company had employed about 9,500 seasonal and 1,500 full-year workers in the California Central Valley. However, in a neoliberal global context, powerful retailers (e.g., Safeway, Albertsons, and Kroger) merged and dictated commodity prices, and NAFTA advantaged the largest multinational corporations over smaller domestic producers. Consequently, many canneries in the Sacramento and San Joaquin regions relocated or closed (Sinton 2000).

Though Cecilia speaks English fluently and was brought from Michoacán as a child, she continued in agricultural-related work even after losing her cannery job. In fact on the day of our interview, she had been picking cherries. Her field and cannery labor have been interspersed with low-paying service jobs at Kmart and Toys R Us, mostly in a temporary capacity. When asked about employment opportunities and the possibility of finding other kinds of jobs in Stockton, Cecilia indicated that there were few employment opportunities in the area but also expressed some optimism. She said, "It all depends on whether you switch to something you know how to do or to something that is new to you, which would be more difficult to do. But I think that with time one can reach one's goal." Recognizing that what she knew—i.e., agricultural work and service-sector jobs—had no future, she hoped to go back to school in the fall and specialize in health care.

Lupe, in the *mayores* cohort, also entered cannery work during the IRCA period. She estimated that about 75 percent of the workers at her cannery were Mexican. She also observed that though most workers are assigned similar types of work sorting fruits and vegetables, English speakers have more mobility and are often placed in laboratories and offices, which are perceived as easier and better paid positions. For example, she described how, when a White English speaker and a Mexican bilingual worker compete for the same job, the White candidate is favored, despite the fact that the overwhelming majority of workers are bilingual or Spanish dominant. Lupe finds it senseless that English is privileged at work when so many of her coworkers do not speak English and thus may miss important information about working schedules and other company concerns.

Lupe started working for the cannery in 1991, at which time she was paid $6.50 an hour. By 1999 she was earning $9.00 an hour and worked an average of eight hours a day, seven days a week, but in recent years productivity demands had intensified because the cannery downsized the number of employees (including Cecilia). Before the layoffs, Lupe observed, "twelve people sorted tomatoes per belt, and now seven people do the work of twelve."

Cannery work is physically intensive and monotonous. Workers stand for eight to ten hours a day with their heads bowed down over a conveyer belt, straining their necks and eyes to inspect the tomatoes that rapidly pass by. First timers especially often feel nausea and dizziness while they look at the shifting and endless number of tomatoes on a conveyor belt. The fast pace and the monotony are enforced by the managers, who reprimand workers if they talk to each other or if they sort with only one hand.

Between 1998 and 2001, María, who was in her late fifties, worked for Delta Pre-Pack Company—a packinghouse in French Camp, California. She and the other women primarily sorted tomatoes, while the men put the produce in boxes and moved the tomato boxes to and from the sorting area. Her coworkers were mostly Mexicanas and a few Filipinas. No White or Black women worked at the packinghouse. Unlike in canneries, packinghouse workers had no union and were all paid minimum wage.

In 1998, María worked six to ten hours a day. Her schedule changed on a daily basis according to the production goals of the company. Though the production level remained constant during her tenure, like Lupe, María and her fellow workers were pressured to sort with both hands and prohibited from talking on the production line. On one occasion, a Mexican supervisor in his late thirties gestured to María to stop talking. He told her she was talking too much, and then he went to a restroom nearby. When he came out, he was fanning himself and gestured to her that it was hot. María felt that her supervisor was gesturing to her this way in an effort to connect with her after reprimanding her because he was embarrassed that he had told a woman his mother's age to shut up. (He had never said anything to her before.) So she waved to him to come over to her and then told him, "You say I talk too much, but look, you speak with your mouth, and you work with your hands." He said, "Okay, okay, there is no problem." Although the rules were enforced, María reclaimed her dignity by pointing out that it was unfair to demand that she and her coworkers not socialize while working in a monotonous job for long periods of time.

In another incident, María's blood pressure was high, and so she decided to work on a slower moving belt so she would not have to move her hands as quickly. But because the workers generally rotated from the normal fast belts to the slower one, one of her coworkers informed a supervisor that María was "playing dumb" to avoid work. The supervisor—a Mexican woman who did not earn much more than the other workers—aggressively scolded María for evading work and demanded that she rotate to a faster-running belt. María refused and was reported to a higher supervisor (a White man), who accused her of wanting to make "easy money" without working and threatened to fire her without compensation. This incident illustrates how the worker—the source of wealth for the company—can be defined even by her coworkers as a liability, despite the fact that she worked from nine AM to ten PM, six days a week, earning only minimum wage and with no additional benefits.

The super-exploitation of workers creates competition and divisions among them, and they seek to get the easier jobs (e.g., the slow belt) or to receive the favor of their supervisors via reporting a "bad" worker. As labor conditions worsen, the company selects supervisors from within the pool of exploited workers as intermediaries to enhance labor control and to give the impression that the company is not biased. Thus, unable to change the working conditions within an unstable, low-wage occupation, workers pursue what seems to them more feasible: immediate and personal gains within their exploitative setting, which creates envy, resentment, and disunity among the workers.

Over the past thirty years, hours, wages, and working conditions have declined in both the fields and the packinghouses and canneries where Xaripus labor. While canneries—the most racially diverse workplaces of the three—offer better wages and stability than "Mexicanized" packinghouses, the late '90s saw a series of closings and reductions in the workforces. Though cannery production remained stable, the reduced workforce was required to work longer and harder hours to meet output demands. These practices of downsizing and increasing individual productivity weeded out the senior, higher-paid workers, many of whom had no choice but to seek minimum-wage jobs elsewhere. In the face of overwhelming structural forces of global agribusiness, economic restructuring, and anti-labor and anti-immigration policies, workers remain in colonial conditions—occupationally stratified, exploited, and poorly compensated.[48] Like in the past, they also resist these injustices.

Resistance

Though Xaripus have lacked formal political power in both Mexico and the United States, they have maintained a spirit of resistance against economic injustices. This resistance to political and economic disempowerment is evident in their history of labor activism, particularly in California. In the late 1960s and early 1970s, most Xaripus joined the United Farm Workers Union (UFW), cofounded by César Chavez and Dolores Huerta, in strikes against tomato growers in San Joaquin County. The United Farm Workers successfully pushed for the California Occupational Safety Act (1973),[49] federal/state unemployment insurance for farmworkers (1974/1977), and the Agricultural Labor Relations Act (1975) (Rosenberg et al. 1995).[50] These significant gains improved labor conditions for farmworkers (Villarejo et al. 2000, 2; Rosenberg et al. 1995, 16–17; Menchaca 1995, 133; Palerm 1991, 14). They also affected Xaripus' migration patterns. Thanks to the improvements they brought, as well as the family reunification immigration provision of 1965, a significant number of migrant workers in the 1970s decided to stay for longer periods and/or on a more permanent basis in California.

With the help of the UFW, Xaripus and other farmworkers succeeded in getting the price paid per tomato bucket raised from twenty to thirty cents in 1974 (Fonseca and Moreno 1984, 252). But the UFW's organizing efforts declined during the early 1980s, when they began to concentrate their limited resources on a grape boycott and a campaign against pesticide use (Hastings 1990; Zachary 1995). Nonetheless, though farm labor rights were formally achieved in the mid-1970s, worker rights were rarely enforced in the fields, and the need for organized labor continued. Thus rank-and-file farmworkers began forming self-help organizations. These self-help movements appealed to farmworkers, according to Ventura Gutierrez—the president of the Border Farm Workers Union in Coachella, California—because "workers want to organize, [but] see [that ...] the UFW isn't around. The workers aren't going to wait around, like priests don't wait around for God to save souls" (Johnston-Hernandez

1991). These movements were widespread, as Johnston-Hernandez reports: "Thousands of farm workers from North San Diego County to Salinas to Stockton are organizing themselves in tiny self-help clusters. Reminiscent of the so-called Mexican 'mutualista' associations at the turn of the century, the new model 'is based on self-help, rather than an institutional approach,' according to Alfredo de Avila, training director at Oakland's Center for Third World Organizing and a former UFW executive" (1991).

In Stockton, California, La Asociación Campesina Lázaro Cárdenas (Farm Worker Association Lázaro Cárdenas) was founded in 1983.[51] Drawing upon early organizing examples (like the UFW) and their own experiences with labor organizing, Xaripus and other farmworkers sought to improve their labor conditions in the San Joaquin Valley through this association. A third-generation Xaripu labor migrant named Luis Magaña, a cofounder of the effort, became the first director of the association. Luis's father had been a bracero in the early 1940s, and his maternal grandfather worked in Indiana and Illinois during the 1920s. Luis himself began to migrate in 1969, when he was about thirteen years old. In a report on agricultural workers, Luis reflected that, "From my first years as a farm worker I became critical of the bad labor conditions and inhumanities we face as migrant laborers" (Magaña 1996, 1). Labor conditions worsened during the Reagan Administration of the 1980s, further encouraging activism among some farmworkers. In an interview with me, Luis described his first act of labor resistance in the tomato fields in 1982:

We went to work for a contractor [named] Alfaro. . . . I rarely worked with him. I usually worked for the Triple E tomato company. Anyhow, we had been working in the fields, and we were not making even minimum wage. We were picking red tomatoes that day, though Alfaro's crew also picked green tomatoes. . . . I was with Fidel [a Xaripu who came as a bracero in 1952], and he said, "Well we aren't making anything, *que la chingada*! [What the f...!]. They should increase our piece-rate price, *compa* [partner]. . . ." And I asked him, "Will you back me up?" And he said, "All the time, *compadrito*!" Then I went and got up a truck, and began to yell, "*Compañeros* [partners], we are working for free, let's stop!"

I was concerned [our fellow workers] wouldn't support the stoppage, and so I continued screaming, "Look at this situation!" The checkers[52] didn't say anything, and the first workers began to stop. *La Rata* stopped, then your [the author's] father stopped, and so others followed. When I was shouting, a foreman went towards Fidel and asked him, "Why do you bring people who give us problems?" And Fidel got angry, and said, *"Que la chingada, ustedes están acostumbrados ha chingar* [What the f..., you guys are used to f... exploiting us]." A big argument ensued. Fidel argued fiercely with the big foreman. The following day I didn't go back, but they paid more.

La Asociación Campesina Lázaro Cárdenas became noticeably active in the fields of San Joaquin County and won three major strikes in 1983, 1987, and 1989 (Nichols 1991). The UFW joined the 1983 strike effort, which successfully gained a five-cent price increment per tomato bucket (from $0.35 to $0.40 cents a bucket). In 1991, Luis Magaña successfully pushed for the organization of ten such farm labor associations, including the one he cofounded, into the Alianza Campesina (Farmworker Alliance) to address workplace concerns and community needs (Johnston-Hernandez 1991, 1993; Torres Delgado 1995, 3). The alliance was formed, Magaña explained, because "we can't count on government agencies any more because they can't represent undocumented farm workers" (Johnston-Hernandez 1991). On top of the fact that these farmworkers were constantly abused in the fields, the government agencies denied them public services. Thus, the Alianza's activism adapted to respond to the broad social and labor concerns of migrant workers (Torres Delgado 1995, 3; Johnston-Hernandez 1993, 51).

The globalization of agribusiness, however, created significant barriers to all labor activism. By the early 1990s, the UFW had lost all contracts with grape growers in California, and its union membership was on the decline (Arax 1994, 42), from an estimated eighty thousand in 1973 to about twenty thousand in 1993, the year of Cesar Chavez's death (Claiborne 1997; Sneider 1997; Johnston-Hernandez 1991, 1993). In San Joaquin County specifically, efforts by the Alianza and farmworkers to improve the tomato piece-rate pay failed in 1991. The price remained static at $0.45 cents per bucket throughout the 1990s up until 2005, when it increased by a mere 5 cents, far behind the rising cost of living.

In 2007, the piece-rate pay had not changed—$1.00 for picking fifty pounds of tomatoes. Safeway sold one pound of house tomatoes for $3.50 and fifty pounds for $175.00.[53]

While union membership in general has declined with the dominance of global capitalism and its influence on national policies (Chuck and Yeskel 2005, 66, 78–81, 87, 100), the waning influence of farm labor activism over the last twenty years is also due to border politics and cultural/social distances between workers. IRCA (1986) channeled migrants—who had been displaced by structural adjustment programs in Mexico—to the fields, which complicated ongoing organizing efforts because work was scarce and many of the new arrivals needed the assistance of contractors/employers to gain legal status via the special agricultural worker provision (Magaña 1988; Johnston-Hernandez 1993; Runsten et al. 1993, 1–6). The vulnerability of undocumented farmworkers, who risk deportation, has also hindered organizing efforts (Magaña 2001a; Soldatenko 1991). Furthermore, traditional unions have frequently failed to understand the cultural diversity of farmworkers, in particular Indigenous ones, and this failure has impeded their efforts to attract them as new members. Recognizing this problem, Magaña and the Alianza tried to privilege in their organizing efforts the cultural standpoint of the most marginalized within the fields, as he recounted in our April 2001 interview:

When we begin to work with the more Indigenous and accept them as they are, you win them over. That was the deficiency in the UFW's movement, which made an effort to adapt the Mexican migrant experience to their Chicano movement. Now they understand Mexican workers somewhat, but now there is the Indian, and they have to do that cultural sensitization once again, because there are no Indian leaders being incorporated into the Union . . . [just] as there were very few Mexican migrants in Chavez's union . . . with the exception of Elizeo Medina and a few others. There were few Mexican migrants in the administrative board. In the fields the UFW incorporated organizers with initiative. The body was made up of us—those from rural Mexico—and so it was something of a shock [that] the leadership was not composed of Mexican migrants. Sometimes the rank and file wanted to do things along their cultural expressions, while the leadership wanted to be in line with the structure of US unions. But in spite of this . . . the rank and file began to [have] influence, and that is why [you had] the image of the Virgin de Guadalupe, the flags, the symbolism of the Mexican [incorporated into the efforts], but now that symbolism is no longer as useful. Now it is necessary to seek other forms to organize the Indigenous. Like the Zapatista movement uses words that the Indigenous people can identify with. For instance, Sub-Comandante Marcos[54] poetically says, "Those of the color of the earth, we are those of the color of the earth," and the Indian feels good. . . . What is important is the base [the common folk]. Or you divorce yourself from the base to talk in the language of those at the top [the privileged], and that is the question that many representing the leadership of movements forget. They want to think at the "high level" of the system. But the Indian is now working here in Stockton, and you also see this diversity elsewhere.

In spite of the challenges of organizing a newer labor force, there was awareness that social realities were different—both within the agricultural structure and for workers—and that to combat an unfair social structure the Alianza had to accommodate the needs of those most vulnerable within it: the Indigenous workers, their families, and children. In 1992, La Asociación Campesina Lázaro Cárdenas became Organización de Trabajadores Agrícolas de California (OTAC) (California Farmworkers Organization) and broadened its mission to respond to the anti-immigrant political climate of the 1990s. According to its mission statement, OTAC's Proyecto Binacional Lázaro Cárdenas "is an organization born from the initiative of the migrant workers themselves to provide mutual support to each other from their places of origin in Mexico to their places of residence in the United States."[55] At the turn of the twenty-first century, OTAC has advocated for reparations for braceros who, between 1942 and 1949, had 10 percent of their paychecks deducted for savings (for a total of about $500 million): over half of them were never reimbursed by US and collaborating Mexican banks (Connell and Lopez 2001a, A1; 2001b; Smith 2001; Puerner et al. 2001; Obsatz 2001).

In 1994, the UFW, under the new leadership of Arturo Rodriguez, also returned to organizing farmworkers in the fields (Arax 1994, 42).

Responding to declining wages, worsening labor conditions, and shrinking union membership, the UFW organized five thousand new members within the first year of Rodriguez's tenure (Zachary 1995). In 2002, the UFW successfully pushed for an Agriculture Labor Relations Act amendment that allowed for state mediation when growers and workers cannot reach a settlement, though to this day it is being aggressively fought by a coalition of growers (Osterman 2005a, A6). In 2005 the union reported having twenty-seven thousand members—about seven thousand more than in 1994 (Osterman 2005b, D1; 2005a, A6). Although numbers remain significantly lower than they were in the 1970s, this increase is admirable given the enormous political power and flexible global mobility of corporate agribusiness.[56]

Xaripu agricultural workers overall report a difficult time getting by in the twenty-first century. Their labor power in the fields, packinghouses, and canneries has been weakened by the dominance of global agribusiness and the economic restructuring that has left agricultural workers vulnerable to low wages, unsafe labor conditions, and economic insecurity. These oppressive conditions have roots in historical colonial relationships that have changed in expression but not in substance: Indigenous tribute to the Crown during colonial times has become tribute to big corporations in modern times. Only through collective efforts, exemplified by the United Farm Workers and grassroots organizations such as La Organización de Trabajadores Agrícolas de California that mobilize around broad social justice issues and across borders, will the marginalized have a chance to challenge their subordination. But though most young Xaripus participated in these field struggles while growing up in the 1970s and 1980s, many have since left the fields in a unique historical period—the entrenchment of neocolonialism.

OUT OF THE FIELDS

Young Xaripus generally moved out of the California fields during the late twentieth century. In 1982, in compliance with the International Monetary Fund's debt conditions, Mexican neoliberals functioned as intermediaries and partners to global capitalists in imposing austerity on the national budget by cutting public expenditures, and in devaluing the

peso to encourage foreign investment. The loss of social services and decline in the peso's value made it hard for the average Mexican to simply
make ends meet. The 1985 earthquake in Mexico City only made matters worse, and by the mid 1980s, many in the Mexican middle class had
become poor (Levine 2006, 2–6; Shorris 2004, 574; Sirota 2006). Without
viable alternatives at home, Mexican immigration to the United States
began accelerating in 1985, with sixty-one thousand going north in that
year alone. By 1988, the number had risen to ninety-five thousand (Chavez and Martinez 1996, 27–29). Among these thousands were some
Xaripus who had lived comfortably in Mexico as teachers, butchers, lawyers, small business owners, and university students prior to the economic shifts of the early 1980s.

Efforts to regulate and control these dislocated migrants of globalization produced the contradictory Immigration Reform and Control Act
of 1986 (IRCA) (Calavita 1998). While including employer sanctions to
deter migration,[57] the Special Agricultural Workers (SAW) and Replenishment of Agricultural Workers (RAW) provisions secured a workforce
for US agribusiness. These provisions, combined with declining labor
conditions, encouraged younger Xaripus to search for employment opportunities out of the fields. Their exiting agriculture, however, was not
accompanied by a racial/ethnic replacement of the farm labor workforce
(as discussed above). Rather, they were replenished by Mexican migrants, some of whom were highly educated and had been professionals
in Mexico and who now labored side by side with old-time farmworkers
from the Bracero Period. While newer migrants, particularly the more
educated and urbanized, worked briefly in the fields and then transitioned to other economic sectors, old-time, career farmworkers—such as
Xaripu *mayores* and *retirada/o* cohorts—remained in farm labor. The
occupational shift among younger Xaripus, nonetheless, was important
because their new experiences out of the fields reveal how occupations
become racialized and affect labor conditions.

A crucial process documented in the Xaripu case was how the changing racial composition of work over time relates to labor conditions. In
what follows, I examine the relationship between the racialization of occupations and labor conditions, and classify work settings as Mexicanized, diversified, or Whitened. I highlight experiences that exemplify
each racialized occupation classification. I thus argue that the unique

historical racialization—from natives to aliens (Mirandé 1987; Nevins 2002; Ngai 2004)—continues to shape Mexicans' gender and class experiences across occupations.

Mexicanized Labor Out of the Fields

Xaripus who left the fields entered occupations that offered more employment stability and higher pay, but those conditions were not fixed. While many companies had been undergoing economic restructuring (as in agriculture), their racial composition clearly preceded the nature and level of labor exploitation.[58] The process of Mexicanization and the ensuing changes in labor conditions are evident in Xaripus' work experiences at the Death Tile factory. On December 3, 1998, Keletos—a thirty-three-year-old from Xaripu who left the fields in the late 1980s—was killed while working in a roofing tile factory in south Stockton. Keletos worked at the Death Tile factory and had been working the night shift from six PM to six AM seven days a week, with only one day off every other week. After his death, friends and neighbors said that he had been exhausted the week of the accident. Other Xaripus who worked with him reported that Keletos had asked the company for help loading the three-thousand-pound pallets onto trucks, but no one else had been assigned to that duty. Exhausted, overworked, and lacking sufficient administrative support, Keletos was hurrying to load pallets in the dimly lit warehouse when he backed his overloaded forklift into a parked truck, crushing him to death under the weight of the pallets.

Elías, in the *hijo* cohort, was a friend and neighbor of Keletos who also worked at the Death Tile factory. His experience sheds light on the changes in the factory that contributed to that fatal accident. Over the course of several interviews, Elías recounted his experiences in the factory and talked about the changes that took place as the workforce became predominantly Mexican. Elías graduated from high school in 1981, and though he is bilingual, he prefers to speak mostly in Spanish. He started to work for a roofing tile company in 1989, at which time most of his coworkers were White or Black. He was paid $6.50 an hour, and three months later he got a raise to $7.00. At the end of his first year of work, Elías was earning $8.35 an hour. In 1991 the company closed and reopened under a new name—Death Tile Company—which kept the previous company's administrators and management and then rehired workers at $6.50 an hour. Many of the new workers hired were Mexican immigrants. Although the workplace was becoming Mexicanized, the easier and better paid positions, including management and supervisory ones, were still held by non-Mexicans.

More established workers were resentful of the newer workers,[59] believing, partly because of a racialized nativism, that the newer workers had less right to work in the same space (Feagin 1997, 30–31). For instance, Elías shared an incident in which he suffered from a cold and a headache, and asked a supervisor if he could go to the restroom. The supervisor told him to wait for the next break, and Elías replied angrily, "I know you don't care about my health, but I do! *Pinche Gringo.*" But while recounting this experience of perceived racial mistreatment, Elías himself referred to the newer workers as *puro mojarras* (mostly "wetbacks"), despite the fact that all had proof of residency after IRCA (1986).[60] Elías seemed to want to distance himself from the more marginalized Mexicans by emphasizing their difference—*mojarras*—even though he himself was not able to escape the racial formation that made him a perpetual alien within a historically racialized nation (Glenn 2002; Nevins 2002; Winant 2001).

As the workforce at Death Tile became Mexicanized, workers were obligated to work up to twelve hours a day, seven days a week, averaging about seventy hours a week. While the factory became more than twice as productive as before, its mostly Mexican labor force was paid about 25 percent less than when they worked for the previous company. The deteriorating working conditions—more hours, fewer breaks, and a faster pace—compelled most of the White and Black employees to leave the factory, and so supervisory and other positions (mechanics, painters, and forklifters) gradually opened to the increasingly Mexican workforce.[61] By this stage, the company had increased production to the highest levels ever. Elías recalled, "When I first started, and Whites and Blacks worked there, we would produce like eighty pallets a day. Now with only Mexicans working we produced like two hundred plus pallets a day. At first, the machine would run 80 tiles per minute, later 110 tiles per minute. Also [before] I earned $8.35 an hour . . . , [and] when only Mexicans worked, we earned about $7.00 an hour."

In the mid-1990s, Elías's coworkers would frequently go over to his house after work for a few beers to talk about their workplace, especially the unfairness of their new supervisor, whom they nicknamed *la Tortuga*. Though the company had significantly increased the levels of production and work hours, Elías and his coworkers focused their frustration on *la Tortuga's* assertion of authority and his *barbero* (brownnosing) orientation toward the employers. For example, on trips to Michoacán, he would purchase some of the finest tequila for the higher-level management back at the plant. Moreover, he obeyed company orders to pressure workers to be more productive, which Elías and his coworkers resented.

By this time, Elías was earning just $8.35 an hour after seven years of working for Death Tile. Frustrated by his low pay and a stressful working environment, in 1996 Elías transferred to a different factory, Money Tile Company, which promised to pay him $9.00 an hour (this company merged a year later with Death Tile to become Money-Death Tile Inc.).[62]

Soon after Elías began working at the Money Tile Company, he witnessed a similar process of Mexicanization to the one he had seen at Death Tile. He recalled that when he had started at the company in 1996, the workforce was diverse and comprised of equal numbers of Whites, Blacks, and Mexicans. He worked about forty to fifty hours a week and earned $9.00 an hour, and the factory produced a hundred pallets of roofing tile a day.

In contrast, by 1999 most of the factory workers were young Mexicans. At this time, Elías was earning $10.64 an hour, but worked sixty to seventy hours a week at an accelerated production level. The company had increased production to two hundred pallets a day without hiring more workers, and thus the now predominantly Mexican workforce was expected to work sixty to seventy hours a week.

Elías also noted that the division of labor had changed since the company had become more Mexicanized. When the workforce was diverse, he recalled, "everyone did similar types of work," but at the time of our 1999 interview, the few non-Mexicans in the factory primarily worked as forklifters, while "most stackers are Mexicans." Stacking, the most difficult and strenuous job in the factory, involves repetitively lifting tiles from a moving belt on to pallets. Injuries are common, but employers usually succeed in arguing that such muscular injuries could be caused by something other than the work setting. Making matters worse, in March 2001 Congress, with President Bush's support, ended "the first federal job safety rules targeting repetitive-motion injuries" (Anderson 2001a; see also Anderson 2001b; Greenhouse 2001). The Money Tile Company also discouraged workers from filing injury claims by offering quarterly bonuses (e.g., a turkey for Thanksgiving) for no-accident records, which successfully motivated workers to discourage others from reporting injuries in order to get a bonus. Elías reflected, "In this new company [Money], hours have also changed since I started working. There is more production, from a hundred to two hundred pallets. Production has increased per minute. Machines have been accelerated. Yet," he insisted, "everything is better here. The company is newer."

This positive assessment shifted in a later conversation, during which Elías expressed resentment over workers being forced to work overtime; he told me that if they refused to do so, they were threatened with not getting paid holidays. The fear of confronting the company's unfair practices was great, since most workers were afraid to lose their jobs, given the limited employment opportunities in the area. In the late 1990s cannery workers—including Xaripa spouses—had been losing their cannery jobs (as a result of Triple E's bankruptcy and similar causes). This fear was evident when the Xaripu Death Tile employee, Keletos, was killed. Several Xaripu coworkers had complained about the bad working conditions and felt that the death could have been prevented with adjustments to the work setting and organization (i.e., more rest days, shorter working hours, more lighting, more forklifters, etc.). However, when the time came to demand changes in the company, most workers feared losing their jobs.

Some of Keletos's coworkers refused to testify against the company, and some, including Elías, redefined the situation and blamed the workers for accepting the exploitation. For example, when I asked about accidents at work, Elías reflected, "In the Death Tile, when I first started working, someone cut off his hand. Keletos died because he was a workaholic. He didn't want to miss a day of work." I asked, "Was the one who cut his hand also a workaholic?" Elías responded, "No, because the machines were not as safe as they are today. They didn't have an emergency shut-off switch. Now they do. People were too ambitious. They didn't want to take days off." Thus, Elías blames the workers for not wanting to miss a day of work. Yet workers with young children to support, such as Keletos, could not afford to skip work.

When I asked whether workers would be interested in union representation, Elías observed, "It would be better to have [a] union, but it is difficult to bring one in . . . because the company is too strong. . . . They have already tried to bring one into the company. The company is too powerful. Here they wanted to start one, but it didn't take off." The threat of closure and intimidation are common strategies a company uses to discourage unions at work (Collins and Yeskel 2005, 80–82), and in this particular case the supply of willing workers in economically hard times may have complicated unionization. Elías reflected on this last point: "*Esta cabrón para que te encuentres un trabajo de $10.00 ahorita!* [It is difficult to find a $10 an hour job today!] Everywhere you go they pay at the most $8.00. In most of the warehouses, such is the case. There were two *Chicanitos* [US-born Mexicans] who came to work at Money Tile. One said he had worked for a warehouse and the other for the railroads and construction, and they commented that the work is tough and the pay is low. In this company, you suffer but you get better pay." Even so, Elías assessed that working conditions had deteriorated drastically over time, and commented, "The Money Tile Company makes a lot of profits. The company used to pay better. Some stackers earned up to $15.00 an hour in the 1980s." In 2000, they earned $6.50.

Elías's work experience reveals how large companies organize their labor to maximize their profits. The two companies he had worked for in the past sixteen years merged in 1997. Both companies became more exploitative of their workers—paying them less and demanding longer and harder hours—after their workforces became primarily Mexican. However, Death Tile—which was fully Mexicanized by the end of Elías's tenure with them—had a higher rate of workplace abuse than Money Inc.[63]

In 2005, Elías injured his back while stacking tiles and was immediately sent to a company doctor. No major injury was found, and he was told by the company to stay home for a while. However, because his accident cost his fellow workers their periodic bonus (about $100) for a no-accident period, Elías was anxious about facing his coworkers. Though

the bonus policy supposedly promotes safety at work, it has clearly negative outcomes for those who do get injured at work. Elías decided not to
return to the factory, and a general foreman was delighted to be rid of a
health-risk worker with sixteen years of employment and referred him
to another factory.

Elías's work experiences reflect a common tendency among workers to attack the least powerful instead of the real source of their problems. Even though Elías was aware of who benefited from his exploitation,
he often directed his feelings of frustration and impotence toward the
powerless newcomers in his midst—for example, when he referred to
his new coworkers as *puro mojarras*. Throughout our conversation,
Elías revealed a situational in-between status: on the one hand, he is a
foreign-born immigrant without US citizenship, but on the other he is a
documented immigrant and thus felt that he had a proprietary claim to
his job that the "Others" in his factory should not enjoy.[64] This was also
evident when I asked how the hours had changed over time at Death
Tile. He grew defensive and insisted that workers had a choice in signing
the contract or not. "When you begin to work, they give you a contract
asking you to work the hours they need you, and you decide to sign it. I
started to work four days: two night-shifts and two day-shifts. I worked
forty hours." Elías emphatically did not want to frame his experiences
within a victim's framework but instead insisted, "I chose to sign the
contract." At the same time, he could clearly see that his company benefited from paying its workers less than it previously had, and he identified with workers who had unsuccessfully tried to unionize the factory.

At an electronics factory in Stockton, Anita—a Xaripa in the *hija*
cohort—surveys her coworkers and notes that Whites and Japanese hold
the management and office staff positions, while Mexicans along with
Filipinos and other Southeast Asians work in production. In all, about
twenty-six women and just three or four men work in the factory. The
staff speaks only English, whereas most of the workers are bilingual. To
get a job there, Anita and her fellow production workers had to complete
a training program. The workers are between thirty-five and fifty years
old, and most have a high school diploma.

Anita began working for the factory in 1997, at which time she earned
$8 an hour, and received a $0.50 increase after three months. In her first

year at the factory, production demands began to increase, and the company started requiring more hours from the workers. To encourage loyalty among the employees, the management told workers that the company was growing fast and passing many tests, and Anita believed the company had a good future. This strategy is highly effective during periods when manufacturing jobs are rapidly declining in the United States. As Michael Burawoy (1979, 29) observed, some workers "come to regard their future livelihood as contingent on the survival and expansion of their capitalist employer, [and] they will also come to accept theories of profit that reflect the experiences of the capitalist seeking profit through the sale of commodities." By the end of the twentieth century, when employment insecurity had become the norm, the company's request for loyalty/productivity and promise of shared prosperity continued to have an integrative effect on some workers.

In November 1998, Anita's hours were increased from eight hours to ten hours a day, and her work week from five to six days. These changes took place at the same time as the number of Mexican employees increased in the factory. On my visit to her house, Anita had just gotten home from work around three thirty PM, when she received a call asking her to return for a second shift. Although Anita was quite upset over not getting to spend much time with her two daughters, she did not consider the possibility of refusing to work a second shift. Workers are exploited not simply through force or consent but also by the lack of opportunities that trap them in unfair labor relationships. During the late 1990s in San Joaquin County, companies in agriculture (Triple E) and manufacturing (Money-Death Tile) were undergoing economic restructuring, and thus job security was a significant concern.

By the twenty-first century Anita's company's workforce had become predominantly Mexican, and she was promoted to supervisor. Soon, conflicts and jealousies with the production workers developed, as they directed their frustrations over their labor exploitation at her. However, Anita's generous and friendly personality has facilitated managing a highly efficient and generally cooperative labor force. Her value to the company has been recognized: she was sent with a group of managers to share their organizational strategies and successes at other factories abroad.

Diversified Jobs

Many of the Xaripus who have higher education have been able to find better employment opportunities in jobs not typically held by racial minorities. Martina—a member of the *hija* cohort—exemplifies this experience. From 1996 to 2000 she worked at the San Joaquin County Juvenile Corrections Department. The department was ethnically diverse, and employees of different races did similar types of work. At the time she started her job, the department was hiring young counselors who had recently graduated from university, and most supervisors were over fifty years old. A few employees were bilingual, and most of the workers were men.

When Martina began her job, she worked eight hours a day, five days a week, and earned $10.25 an hour. By 1999 she was earning $14.15 an hour. The department saw a jump in its workload starting in 1998, when a strict judge began sentencing youth to longer times in juvenile corrections. This judge's actions fit the larger social context of the state at that time, including Governor Pete Wilson's 1997 bill package of "get tougher" juvenile crime laws (Rodríguez 2001, 44).

When asked if race and gender influenced job opportunities in her workplace, Martina said no, though she noted that the supervisors did differentiate along gender lines in some circumstances: "[The treatment] should be the same, but many times it is different because we have to respond to emergency calls for different units, and sometimes the supervisor asks one to stay and not participate because one is a woman." While Martina observed different role expectations for men and women at work—where women are perceived as less able to deal with potentially physical threatening calls—she had no problems with the differential treatment. Martina commented, "You never know how many are involved in the fight or whether they are carrying something in their hands or whether they are going to settle down when one gets there." Nonetheless, it is interesting to note that gendered roles were reproduced at Martina's workplace in ways they were not in the fields.

In 2000, Martina quit her job at the Corrections Department after growing frustrated over an unfair shift assignment. Specifically, she had been consistently assigned to work the evening shift (from two to ten PM) ever since she had started working there, even though her contract stated that she and her four female coworkers (all of whom were White) were to rotate the shift among themselves.

According to her husband, Martina chose not to pursue legal action but instead to put the negative experience behind her and move on. Her decision reflects the lack of institutional support for dealing with racist work environments, which discourages legal action against public and private employers. While Martina initially did not perceive any bias at work and expressed satisfaction, she later reassessed her perceived color-blind work environment and realized that she was being singled out and unfairly assigned the late shift.

Other Xaripa women, however, recounted experiences with more overtly hostile work places. Rosalía, a Xaripa social worker, has worked for a high school health center under Delta Health Care since August 1998. The clinic offers services and information to young women and according to Rosalía, is staffed by "a diverse group. Except the executive director is a White person." She attributed the racial diversity of her office to the nature of their clientele: "A lot of people who are of different races come to the clinic, and there has to be diverse employees." Rosalía further elaborated that most workers were female and bilingual because they deal with ethnically diverse women and a range of issues in women's health care. Despite the apparent valuing of diversity in this work setting, Rosalía experienced a hostile work environment and recounted the ethnic bias she perceived her boss to have:

> I sometimes feel my boss wants to push me out. The supervisor wants me to get so frustrated [that I will] quit. . . . I feel he does it on purpose. He tries to push me so that I could just say, "Forget about this," and it does bother me, but I am not just quitting because of him or anything like that. I mean, I'm not thinking of quitting, but it can happen. I can quit. My contract ends in July, and I have a feeling that he wants to get me very pissed off before then, so that I can just say, "Forget it." He has something against me, and I am not quite sure what it is. I really think he does not like Mexicans. I really do, because he treats me pretty bad, but the other Mexican, she acts more White than anything, and I am always talking about Mexican this, we are going to do this . . . for the Mexicans and for the Hispanic girls and

stuff like that. And it seems that he has a lot of hatred for them or something. That's what it seems like.

At the time of our 1999 interview, Rosalía had been earning $12 an hour, or about $96 a day, since she had been hired. Her pay had not increased, she reflected, because "they don't change. . . . They are really tight on their budget. They don't like to give raises." But Rosalía was not optimistic about finding a better job in Stockton. "Job opportunities are not very good because the pay is bad. The better paying jobs are in the Bay Area, but the cost of living there is high." She went on to describe how her education was no guarantee of finding a better job. "Even with a BA I had trouble finding a job last year, so it doesn't really matter what you have. It just depends who you know." It should be noted that all of the Xaripu women I interviewed who had college degrees earned better pay and had an easier time getting jobs than those without college degrees, whose pay and employment options were even more limited.

Expanding upon her observation that connections matter more than education in the Stockton job market, Rosalía described the ethnic divide in the community and talked about how this often translates into a lack of understanding between White staffers and Mexican and Black clients at agencies like hers:

A lot of people [in Stockton] are scared to talk to each other, it seems. The races are diverse, but the people don't communicate with each other, because when they have a Mexican American day—for example Cinco de Mayo—you never see any Black people there or any White people there. People just don't communicate with each other. And so . . . [in places like social service agencies] the White people don't know what the Blacks have gone through, they don't know what the Mexicans have gone through, and yet they work in those places. [And] sometimes these agencies don't hire the people that are needed to take care of [minorities], or if they do, they are not qualified. . . . And so sometimes they just don't know who to hire; they don't hire the right people; and the people who should be hired they get some lesser job; there are just not a lot of opportunities. . . . Also, if you know people, you are going to hire your friends also, so sometimes the situation is just not fair. They hire the people who are not qualified because they are friends.

Thus, Rosalía, like other Xaripus, observed that discrimination limits employment opportunities and underscores racial intolerance and exclusionary practices against Mexicans. She believed that those in positions of power tend to hire people they can relate to, such as Whites or assimilated racial minorities, rather than those who are most qualified for the job.[65] Even when Mexicans and Blacks are hired in her agency, Rosalía suggested, they are relegated to the "lesser jobs."

Whitened Jobs

The process of racialization, as elaborated earlier, assigns meanings/values and thus treatment to specific ethnicities which translates into differing occupational values and labor conditions based on the racial composition of the workplace. I use the classifications of Whitened and Mexicanized to highlight the social or unnatural construction of worth (i.e., pay and labor conditions) of the job, and to suggest that the same occupation—requiring the same skills and experiences—will be treated differentially according to the racial composition of a given workforce.[66] This chapter illustrates how an occupation remains Whitened through an institutional culture that privileges sameness (i.e., Whiteness)[67] as normal and hurts those different and most distant from the norm, especially if they threaten the social order.

The Xaripus I interviewed who work in Whitened job settings had higher wages and better job security than those who work in Mexicanized or even diversified workplaces, but also experienced intense forms of racial bias and emotional abuse. These racialized labor experiences—unwelcoming environment and differential treatment—keep some occupations ethnically and racially homogenous. From the several accounts of Whitened jobs I came across in my field research, I have selected the following example because it highlights the typical experiences of these workers and offers a longitudinal case of such a workplace.

When Olivia transferred to the San Joaquin Post Office in 1994,[68] she was the first Mexican-identified person to work full-time at her new site, where twenty-two of her coworkers were White; two, Black; and one, Filipino. At the time, the Post Office employed about 50 percent women and 50 percent men, most of whom were between twenty-five and sixty years old. Everyone but Olivia was a monolingual English-speaker, and so when Spanish-speaking clients came into the office, Olivia was the only one who could help them. Because of this, she often worked more than the rest of her coworkers yet received no extra pay for her bilingual skills and more difficult schedule. Moreover, there were many other work environment dynamics—besides the unfair work assignments—that, from Olivia's standpoint, constituted clear hostile and racist treatment.

Olivia was titled a "flexible" employee, even though she was a full-time worker, and was thus expected to help everyone, including mail carriers and counter clerks. She was assigned a split-shift schedule, which had her work from five to nine AM and then return from two to six PM. The only employee assigned to a split shift, she worked this schedule for four years, despite repeatedly requesting a change. She described how they kept her on this schedule because other workers either refused or were unqualified to cover the window during those shifts:

There was another person who had a home difficulty. Wendy had a son who was disabled. She got stressed in the post office window, or I don't know what, but she didn't want to do the window anymore . . . from nine AM to six PM, and since I was the only one qualified for the window without being a regular, they assigned me to it. But there were times that they needed me both in the morning and evening. That's when they gave me all those split schedules because they didn't have others who could do what I could. Later, they sent a White guy who was also part-time flex (PTA) for training, and then it was he and me with this schedule. But he didn't like the window, so they would assign me more to the window than him.

Olivia's schedule only changed when she filed a racial discrimination claim with the Equal Employment Opportunity Commission (EEOC) on the basis of being both the only Chicana on staff and the only person assigned a split-shift schedule. Though she would eventually withdraw her formal grievance, at the time she informed those included in her complaint that she was filing it, which prompted her supervisor to finally take her off of the split-shift schedule. However, this did not end Olivia's perceived unequal treatment based on race. She then worked from five thirty AM to two PM, five days a week, but was the only one assigned two separate days for break—Sunday and Tuesday. She thus continued working on the busiest day of the week (Monday) and was given the slowest day off (Tuesday). Moreover, after her EEOC complaint, she was assigned—more than her coworkers—tasks involving repetitive and awkward movements using office machinery, and had to lift boxes throughout the day.

In recounting her experiences, Olivia was quick to characterize herself as a fighter who has never been passive but was always ready to stand up for her rights. Nonetheless, after the threat of the EEOC claim passed, the postmaster continued to favor White workers who were temporary and part-time over Olivia, who was a career post office worker. He would justify sending a part-timer to paid workshops during work hours by claiming that it was because she (a White woman) had been hired before Olivia, even though the other worker was not a full-time worker or career employee. According to Olivia, the postmaster knew that what he was doing was wrong, or he would not have bothered trying to justify his discriminatory actions. Olivia described the hostile environment she faced each day before she filed the EEOC complaint:

> There was another person who . . . got a job. . . . She had a White mother and a Black father, and she would be White or Black according to what was more convenient. She was with the union, and when she came to this job, things got more difficult for me because she was more familiar with the union. She would get everyone against me. There was a time when everyone seemed to be against me. She got together with Wendy, Mary, and another one, and those three with a young male supervisor turned against me. Everything became difficult. The union did not do anything, or [accused me of] not going to [them].

Olivia's distrust of the union here was striking, since she had otherwise spoken favorably of its role in her workplace. The previous postmaster at that site had demanded more from the women, asking them to clean the Jeeps and do other work that was not expected of the men. Infuriated, the women went to the union—a move Olivia supported—after which the union pressured the postmaster to stop his unfair labor practices. But when she faced a racist and hostile work environment, Olivia did not feel she could seek support from the union, since many of its members were good friends with her main antagonist.

This is when she opted to file a complaint with the EEOC. But this process was also discouraging. Olivia summed it up as "a lot of paperwork," and went on to say that the "EEOC instead of helping adds to one's headaches." The EEOC—the government entity assigned to enforce the nation's anti-discrimination laws—cannot handle its caseload. According to Savage (2002), the EEOC "intervenes in less than one percent of the job bias cases filed each year." Out of the 79,896 complaints of employment bias filed in the year 2000, only 402 developed into lawsuits by the commission. Though private lawyers can and do file discrimination claims, the concentration of people of color and women in lower-paid occupations makes it unlikely that they can afford to hire such firms to go up against well-established public or private corporations.

As Olivia talked about her experience with the EEOC, her facial expression and vocal tone shifted from strong and confident to frustrated and hopeless. Her mouth tightened and trembled as she spoke, and her eyes welled with tears. Her voice became shaky as she continued,

> With so much paperwork, you send [it in], and they send twenty other things to fill out. Instead of helping you come out of a problem, they add to the problem by giving you other problems. I got tired, and called them by phone. I talked to a woman from Richmond; I told her that I needed to talk to someone. She said that they no longer made cases through site visits, and that everything was now done by paper, letters, and phone. And I told her that I really needed someone to come and talk to me. She said that she herself would come to see me, but that I might not like what she had to say.

Olivia attributes the EEOC worker with changing her life, but not in the way one might expect:

> [The EEOC worker] was also White. When she came, we talked. . . . She was the person who has helped me the most in my life, the way she talked to me. Over the phone she sounded very hard, and then she talked to me in June 1998. She told me, "If you want to pursue the

case, you will pursue it, or if you want from today on to erase it and forget it, and continue ahead and try. . . . Well, things are going to change for you." Well, I decided, I told her, "I am going to leave the case because if I proceed with it, it is going to continue being a lot of paperwork, and my burden is not going to end." In fact that day I spoke with her was like a new beginning in my life. I said I am going to forget everything, and I went to work, and I told the persons involved, "You know I had an EEOC complaint, and you were on it. I'm going to leave it because I want to, and for no other reason. I'm going to leave it and try to make things different." And everything changed for me. *(Olivia begins to cry.)* Things happened—last December all the temporary personnel left, and everything changed. Wendy transferred. . . . Everything changed. These people did not disturb me, but the people who left were the ones who were hurting me. And can you believe that they left and my life changed?

When asked what the EEOC representative did to "help," Olivia said, "nothing," but that her words had given her comfort and another view of the situation. She helped Olivia remove herself from the "victim status," where she felt sorry for herself; Olivia was grateful for this because she prefers to think of herself as a winner and not a loser. Olivia commented that it is not because they are White that she criticizes them, because she knows that even within her ethnicity people can be racist against their own people. For example, "Wendy was Mexican through her mother and White by her father; maybe because of this she didn't like me, because she did not identify with Mexicans anything at all. She was very volatile and immature and would try to please others, like a little girl." Olivia's coworker displays a situational in-betweenness. Although passing as White, she could momentarily claim being Mexican, but did not identify with Mexicans and expressed stereotypical biases against Mexicans, seeing them as "aliens" who drain public resources. Thus Olivia considered her immature because, in a social context where cultural difference was repressed, her coworker felt the need to play up her sameness with her predominantly White workforce. Olivia's brownness and Mexicanized-English accent apparently limited her fit at work.

Though Olivia was able to recognize the complexity of racial and identity politics at play in her workplace, it is clear that the split-shift schedule she was assigned to for four years was discriminatory because before and after it ended for her, no other person qualified to do the work she had been assigned to do. Sometimes employees were needed in the morning, but the administrators did not split their schedules to respond to the service needs of the post office. All the workers maintained continuous work hours, while Olivia had been ordered to a split-shift schedule by her administrators. Unfortunately, the discrimination at work did not end after her split shift did, and the unfair distribution of work assignments continued.

Olivia's labor experiences reveal a clear pattern of racial discrimination that affected her emotionally and that contributed to her physical deterioration. Though she did not realize it at the time, the social abuse and labor exploitation had taken a toll on her physically as well as mentally. The heavy lifting, and the fact that she worked on the busiest days and was given the slower days off, contributed to her being diagnosed in October 2000 with severe physical health impairments. Although her doctor recommended that she be assigned to lighter duties, the postmaster insisted that no light duties existed at the office, and so after sixteen years of working for the post office, Olivia was forced out of the job in 2000. At forty, her movements and strength resemble those of someone twice her age. She can only stand up for brief periods of time, cannot hold a telephone without getting fatigued and switching hands, and has no strength in her hands for grasping and opening jars.

RACE, GENDER, AND COLONIALISM IN MODERN LABOR RELATIONS

The racialization of work significantly relates to labor conditions and wages. Older Xaripus, along with a few younger ones, remain colonial labor working with *puro Mexicanos,* whereas younger ones who moved outside the fields do not escape the colonial relationships subordinating them within stratified occupations and labor segmentation. Although entering more diverse and (fewer) White-dominated jobs, all Xaripus experienced social marginalization and unfair work burdens based on race and gender. The most extreme labor exploitation, however, was experienced by those in occupations undergoing Mexicanization.[69] In such work sites, the company employs mostly Mexican workers,[70] increases production without increasing the number of workers,[71] adds more hours and days of work per week, reduces benefits, and assigns coworkers to positions of authority. This last characteristic seems to be a critical and historical element that facilitates the ultimate control of a subordinated group—the construction of an intermediary position that serves as a buffer and model for others.[72]

Globalization and economic restructuring are not color-blind processes: they reflect the continuation of traditional, interactive, and emergent forms of colonialism. The racial and gender composition of the workforce mediates the labor experiences at the work site. Minorities are devalued in ways beyond economic relations. Jobs that have been Whitened, as opposed to Mexicanized, pay better and have lower levels of physical exploitation, yet they are more exclusive and intolerant of racial diversity. Whitened jobs, particularly in male-dominated workplaces, are less welcoming and open to racial/ethnic minorities. Few Xaripus entered Whitened occupations, and more were employed in diversified jobs in public services: Public Housing Authority, Department of Education, San Joaquin County Juvenile Department, and Department of Probation. The occupational concentration of Xaripus in service jobs also reflects labor stratification and class segmentation (see Hesse-Biber and Carter 2000, 54–57; Rosenblum and Travis 1996, 304–5; Soldatenko 1991, 76; Segura 1990, 58–61; Levine 2006, 7–10).

Legal status, educational attainment, and generation partly explain labor experiences. Although most Xaripus were documented, the undocumented experienced the most exploitative and unstable economic sectors of the economy. They were more vulnerable to the costs of deportation, lost wages, lack of health care, no social security, *nervios* (nerves), etc. Educational differences further shape Xaripus' labor conditions.[73] In my 2000 interviews, those who had graduated from college earned from $96 to $116 dollars per day, whereas those who had only completed high school earned about $60 a day, and those without a high school diploma made less than minimum wage—about $34 a day. Among those with similar educational levels, the ones in the more Whitened and male-dominated jobs earned the most.[74] The highest income earners were not college graduates or US-born Xaripus, but the few who occupied Whitened occupations.

Generation does not fully explain racial occupational patterns among Xaripus, because they directly and indirectly[75] have worked in the United States for almost a century, and their occupational segregation has been largely entrenched through labor market and immigration policies that blocked their full integration as equal members of US society. Beyond human and cultural capital, racial and gender structural biases (e.g., labor market, immigration policy, and media) continue to affect wages and working conditions (Avalos 1995, 29–37; Hesse-Biber and Carter 2000, 67–72). Jobs themselves do not carry an inherent value,[76] but rather who performs them (contingent on race, gender, and class) too often determines the status and rewards associated with them. The devaluation of workers and occupations reflects the logic of colonialism in modern labor relations.

Chapter Five

HACIENDO COMUNIDAD ACROSS BORDERS

Xaripu *norteñas/os* have crossed national borders for over a century, and their concept of home has correspondingly changed over time. For the first two-thirds of the twentieth century, most Xaripus considered Michoacán their home and the United States a place to go temporarily for work. In the latter part of the twentieth century, the concept of having a home base in both nation-states emerged for many Xaripus, and thus their sense of "home" shifted to include both: *soy de aquí y de alla* (I am from here and from there). In the twenty-first century, social ties remain strong across borders and continue to move fluidly back and forth to and from Mexico. These transnational Xaripus generally return to Mexico in order to relax, go out, and have fun. There they experience a cultural freedom that they lack in the United States,[1] where their humanity is reduced to devalued workers (as discussed in chapter 4; see also Bellah et al. 1996). Their unequal integration into *el norte* has partly motivated this ongoing movement across national borders (Barrera 1979; Parreñas 2001b; Espiritu 2003b; Goldring 2003).

This chapter contextualizes and conceptualizes Xaripus' transnational experience[2] and explores key themes in their formation of community across borders, including: (1) *convivencia* (quality and intimate social interaction); (2) *nepantla* (emergent identities);[3] and (3) empowerment. It also shows that Xaripus' ability to construct community within and across nations is significantly shaped by race, class, and gender differentiations as well as by national inequalities.

CONTEXTUALIZING AND CONCEPTUALIZING XARIPU
TRANSNATIONALISM

The history of the pueblo Xaripu predates the founding of the nation-states of Mexico and the United States (Fonseca and Moreno 1984). Although the pueblo was transformed by European colonialism, slavery, peonage, and later neocolonial inequalities, the emergent ethnic/racial identities of the Xaripus reflect a shared and collective history that to a great degree continues to this date. Nonetheless, contemporary international migration has created more divergent experiences among folks of this pueblo, which have resulted in profound changes in identity and self-understanding. The Xaripu community's international migration experience predates the Mexican Revolution, when Mexican hacienda elites expanded their land holdings in partnership with foreign investors and thereby dislocated Indigenous and mestizo communities from their lands (see chapter 3). As a result peasants were converted from subsistence farmers to low-wage laborers in haciendas that produced for export (Moreno García 1994; Fonseca and Moreno 1984; Gonzalez and Fernandez 2003). To find work Xaripus began migrating within the nation, and after the construction of the Moreno Railroad Station near Xaripu around 1900, they began to migrate across the border to work in the United States. This migration was formalized with the first US-Mexican guest-worker program (1917–21), which recruited Mexican temporary workers for the expanding agriculture, mining, and steel industries. Xaripu migration continued through the Bracero Program (1942–64) and was then further transformed by the 1965 Immigration and Naturalization Act, after which entire families began to join the men in migrating north (McWilliams 1990; Galarza 1964; Chavez and Martínez 1996). In the post-Bracero Period (after 1964–65) legalization of residential status and family reunification made it easier for Xaripu families to begin settling more permanently in California, which effectively transformed their labor migration to transnational migration in the late twentieth century and into the twenty-first.

As discussed in previous chapters, Xaripus' transnational migration has intensified as a result of neocolonialism, advances in technology, reincorporation by sending nations,[4] racist nativism in receiving societies

(Feagin and Feagin 1999; Chavez 1997),[5] and mature social networks across borders (Espiritu 2003b, 70–71; Guarnizo and Smith 2003, 24; Goldring 2003, 166–70, 189; Smith 2003, 205, 207). To frame the discussion of the Xaripu case it is important to first establish a working definition of what comprises a transnational community, even though no consensus exists on the content range and nature of transnationalism (Guarnizo and Smith 2003, 3–4; Menjívar 2004, 1–2; Fouron and Glick-Schiller 2002, 171). Some scholars, noting the lack of clarity in what forms a transnational community, highlight the centrality of social relations based on migrants' shared history, interests and meanings, and place of origin and destination (Guarnizo and Smith 2003, 13, 26–27; Mahler 2003, 73–76; Goldring 2003, 173, 175; Smith 2003, 198, 200–202, 226). Others have mapped out variations in its practice and magnitude: from occasional to habitual (infrequent to frequent), from selective to comprehensive activities (one purpose to many), and from personal to institutional level (private to public and organizational) (see an excellent review by Levitt 2001, 199). Despite this ongoing debate, there is general agreement that the term "transnational" describes migrants who have extensive and fluid connections (economic, familial, social, and cultural) across national borders (Kearney and Nagengast 1989, 1; Glick-Schiller et al. 1992a, ix, 1992c, 1–2; Rouse 1992, 45; Chavez 1997, 62; Hondagneu-Sotelo and Avila 1997, 550; Parreñas 2001b, 28–29; Trueba 2004, 39–42).

Robert C. Smith's suggestion that "a community can be said to exist because its members agree it exists, and because they use it as the 'unit of discourse' and emotion within which they feel they belong" (2003, 226) also provides a helpful lens through which to understand the Xaripu community. Its transnational members fit this description but go beyond the concept of "imagined community"[6] in that they (1) have a dual home base or sense of home in two nation-states,[7] (2) maintain physical, mental, and/or emotional connections with both regions, and (3) make material, cultural, and emotional relations constant and active across the border. As we will see, Xaripus in the older cohorts reflect these characteristics more fully than the younger ones.[8]

As noted in chapter 1, thirty of the fifty-six Xaripus who participated in this study had settled permanently in California, twenty-three of whom travel to Michoacán frequently (once every one to three years) or somewhat frequently (once every four to six years) and seven of whom do so infrequently (every seven or more years). In interviews they offered a similar range of reasons across cohorts as to why they settled in the United States—employment, family, and education for children—and almost all highlighted economic factors as their primary reason for having done so. For example, Rosalía, a member of the *chica/o* cohort, explained, "We settled because my mother bought a house in California [and] because we see that there is a better future here than in Mexico." Her contemporary Tita reported, "My dad wanted to stay here because there were more opportunities for us." And Cecilia likewise responded, "There are more job opportunities and more money" (see also Chavez 1992, 26–29).

Family considerations also played a vital role in a family's decision to settle in the United States. A young Xaripa, Cecilia, indicated that "I think that [people started to settle] because of their children; parents thought that there was a better future for their children [in the United States]." Older Xaripus agreed. Nena, a *retirada*, shared, "We spent six months here and six months there . . . until we got a house in the Sierra Vista housing projects, and then we did not go to Mexico as much because the children were in school and I did not want to have them here for six months and then take them there for six months. They were not learning here or there." Lionel, a member of the *mayores* cohort, also echoed this view: "I was able to support myself in the United States, and in the pueblo I wasn't able to. To me it was a better change from Mexico to here. In 1975, that's when we settled here. I used to come and go. . . . We stayed for the children, so they could go to school. I called them in 1970, and in April of 1971, I brought them here."

Christina, Lionel's spouse, further elaborated that when they first came, they had three children, ranging in age from a few months to three years old. Her family continued migrating until 1975, when Christina decided to stay permanently in Stockton to help their now six children's education. Though Christina's family was among the first to make a conscious effort to settle more permanently in California, their decision occurred as the structures of opportunities changed for them. Although education had always been desired, the structures of opportunities—i.e., working conditions, state benefits, and unemployment insurance—permitted a more permanent settlement and a continuous education for children. These seemingly individual decisions marked a change in migration trends among Xaripus, from labor migrants to transnational migrants.

Despite having common reasons for settling in the United States, the transnationalism experienced by US-based Xaripus varies in intensity and according to people's particular life circumstances. For instance, birthplace is no longer as influential in shaping visiting patterns as financial circumstances, work schedules, and school constraints.[9] Moreover, cultural factors like language and religiosity partly explain the level of transnationalism.[10] Specifically, Xaripus who still speak Spanish fluently or even predominantly maintain a stronger sense of belonging and more active relationships with relatives abroad than those who have become English-dominant. Similarly, those who are religiously active are more motivated to return to the pueblo to participate in its patron saint's day celebrations than those for whom such observations are less meaningful.

Generally, Xaripus of the older cohorts held to similar traditions and beliefs as the elders in Mexico, while the younger ones had undergone greater changes in language, style, and ideology.[11] Older Xaripus, not surprisingly, move back and forth between Michoacán and California more fluidly than do younger Xaripus and tend to regard Xaripu as not simply a place to visit but also a place in which to live. This orientation was apparent in their longer stays in the pueblo and their self-reports of being *de aquí y de allá* (from here and from there). Most *retiradas/os* visit Michoacán every year and stay for as long as six months. Only health problems and/or child-care obligations reduce these visits. But though the frequency and duration of their visits have not changed significantly since the Bracero Period, their sense of home has shifted to now include both places.

Alejandro, who is seventy-seven and first came to the United States as a bracero in 1942, shared, "We settled here because of the life conditions; it is easier to support yourself here than in Mexico. I do go to Mexico every year just to be over there, because it isn't so cold over there. This year I stayed for five months." Margarita, age ninety, had married a *norteño* migrant in 1927 and first visited *el norte* in 1970. She commented, "I'm a naturalized US citizen, but I want to be from here and there, from the two sides."

Some of the Xaripus who were raised in the United States talked about how growing up in *el norte* had shaped their acculturation and their transnational orientation. According to Valencia, "I think that by living here one acquires other customs, and that people who have just arrived from Mexico see us as a little bit strange." These changes include language usage, dress style, and music tastes, among other things. In contrast Olivia, who only visits Michoacán once every seven or more years, reflected wistfully on her childhood in Xaripu: "We have lived most of our life here [in the United States]. If you ask me about my life, I have more memories of the United States than Mexico. I only have memories of my early childhood in Mexico. I was happier over there than here." Olivia's fond memories of happier times in Mexico, or "symbolic transnationalism,"[12] might partially stem from the experiences of nativism and bias at work in California that she was recovering from at the time of our interview (see chapter 4).

In the Xaripu case, a few respondents did express ambiguity about where their permanent home was. In one such case, Rosalía, a second-generation Xaripa, expressed uncertainty regarding her family's permanence in the United States. She shared, "My mom wanted to move back to Zamora and open up her own business. She said that life in the United States is boring. You can't just go around in the streets and stuff like that. So that is the reason she wants to go back. But since everybody didn't want to go back—my dad is so used to life in the United States, his family is here, only one of his brothers lives in Mexico . . . —I don't think he would want to go back."

Rosalía's mother's experience of feeling constricted in her movements and thus bored contradicts the idea that immigrants find greater freedom and spatial mobility in the United States (Hirsch 1999; Hondagneu-Sotelo 1994; Rouse 1992). Indeed, most of the Xaripa women I interviewed indicated that holding a job with long hours, little pay, high-stress levels, and inconvenient work schedules limits them from going out and socializing (see chapters 4 and 6). US-based Xaripus of all ages also noted that high crime rates further discourage people from walking in their neighborhoods. The overall sense was that there was more violence, robberies, and drugs on the streets.

María, in her fifties, talked about her two teenage children and how she was happy that they did not want to go out of the house: "They don't want to go out, and I do not encourage them. I think it is good that they don't go out, because the world is so lost that they could offer my children some *cochinada* [junk, suggesting drugs]. The boy, I wish he did not even go out. I am very happy that he does not have too many friends in this neighborhood, and that he does not go out. I worry that someone can give him drugs." Martha also reflected on an incident in her neighborhood where a driver was speeding and burning tires on the streets: "When he parked just there [near the apartment], many police officers arrived to arrest him, physically assaulted him, and even beat up children [who were] bystanders. Many more were arrested. They [police] treat the youth badly." Although recognizing the danger posed by the driver, Martha was significantly moved by what she perceived to be police brutality of innocent bystanders, whom she identified as children. The general sense was that their working-class Stockton communities were unsafe for their families.

In contrast, in Michoacán women take evening walks with their friends in the pueblo or sit outside their house or in the plaza, and older men sit on the plaza benches discussing work and politics. Parents generally felt more at ease about their children, who are allowed to play in the plaza and on the streets from morning until late at night, with no worries about gangs, drugs, and traffic. People know each other, and they take a village approach to raising children—though it feels intrusive to *norteño/a* children who visit.

Xaripus in Michoacán have more diverse views about migration and, not surprisingly, are a bit less romantic about Mexico than those who live in the United States. Most of the elders expressed no interest in living in the United States, including those (mostly men) who had worked in the United States for all of their lives and others (mostly women) who had never been. In contrast, almost all of the younger people interviewed in Michoacán said they wanted to move out of the pueblo. In general, these younger people wanted to head north in search of higher wages (see Palacios Franco 1987, 47; López Castro 1986, 19; Cornelius 1976; Bustamante 1978), to be with family, and/or to escape boredom. When asked why they wanted to leave for the United States, Conchita (age twenty-four) replied, "I am not in school or employed [here]. In the United States, I will have more opportunities to work. I do not want to stay here forever, or wait for someone to come and marry me, and that's it. I want to do something with my life first, rather than just be here forever." Paula (age twenty) said she wanted to leave in order to "go out and work, and not remain here just waiting for remittances. If you have money, you do not wait to see if they will send money or not." Blanca (age twenty-three) elaborated, "Having one's own money, well I say I would be prouder to know that it is mine, and not that it was sent to me. It is different to earn money than just receiving it." Antonio (age twenty) simply said, "I want to go to *el norte* because of the earnings."

A few younger people in Michoacán said they were not interested in settling permanently in the United States, and some did not want to go at all. For example, Lorena expressed concerns about the cultural changes she had witnessed among *norteña/o* youth, and she associated many bad habits with the United States. Miranda, who is married and who occupied a governing position in the pueblo at the time, reported that she had not considered leaving Xaripu because her father would have disapproved of it, even though he had died in the 1980s. Miranda was accustomed to life in Michoacán, and even if she wanted to emigrate, she noted, it might not be possible, because of her lack of legal documentation. These few examples notwithstanding, the clear trend among the young residents of Xaripu is that they want to leave the pueblo for work to *el norte*.

Thus it was not surprising to find that people who live in Michoacán year-round express concern that the pueblo is becoming a ghost town. In one street alone, only four of the approximately twenty houses were inhabited year-round. Strolling through Xaripu,[13] I found that this situation was widespread. Only about a quarter of the houses were inhabited, and even these were occupied by only a part of the family.

But though many of the pueblo's remaining residents want to migrate to *el norte* in search of economic empowerment, numerous US-based Xaripus continue to look to the pueblo as a place of welcome and reprieve. For instance, Olivia and Rosalía's mother wanted to return to Michoacán to escape the hostile and unfriendly work and community environments they inhabit in California.[14] Whereas Olivia found refuge in symbolic (mental) transnationalism, Rosalía's mother, like many other people of her generation, takes annual trips to Michoacán. A site of seeming contradictions, Michoacán serves as a break from a stressful and materialist *norte*, while its unemployment/underemployment and inflation created by migrants' dollars and local low wages have squeezed the young out of the pueblo.

Most of the young people I interviewed in Mexico sought to break from this economic dependence. To be sure, those in Michoacán significantly depend on remittances from relatives in *el norte* and on the work opportunities occasioned by their visits back to the pueblo, and many clearly dislike the dependent and unequal status[15] that becomes manifest in migrant and non-migrant social interactions.

BEYOND SOCIAL INTERACTION: *CONVIVIR*

After a century of transnational experiences, transformations of identities and relationships among non-migrants in Michoacán, transnational migrants, and settled Xaripus in California can be expected. Though scholars have documented that transnational community members negotiate or establish common grounds and form meaningful communities in the different localities through activities such as hometown projects, fund raisers, and family connections (remitting to and visiting relatives) (Guarnizo and Smith 2003, 13; Smith 2003, 198, 204; Goldring 2003, 174–75), a single community across borders is, indeed, difficult to maintain in the face of global inequalities (see also López Castro 1986; Kearney 1996).[16]

Among the theoretical models that explicate how transnational community members establish a common identity and sense of community despite being geographically separated, the symbolic interactionist perspective is particularly helpful to the Xaripu case. This interpretive lens elucidates how labor experiences, migration, and social networks interact to shape notions (meanings and symbols) of community, family, and self within a context of national inequalities (Charon 1998; León-Portilla 1990; Shibutani 1955; Blumer 1969; Mead [1934] 1962). The sense of self that emerges therein arises from a person's or group's unique social location and relations within structures of national, racial, cultural, gender, and class inequalities (Omi and Winant 1994; Lowe 1996; Guarnizo and Smith 2003). However, for all of its merits, symbolic interactionism does not sufficiently account for the affective realities at play in these social processes. Thus it is helpful to employ the concept of *convivir* in order to more fully explain the ability or inability of constructing community across borders.[17]

Convivir means literally to experience life together, and thus to laugh and cry together *en las buenas y en las malas* (in good times and bad). It is through *convivencia* (the act of *convivir*) that transnational communities are constructed. Social inequality and domination, however, complicate *convivencia*. While some Xaripus maintain a sense of community through their continued *convivencia* across borders, others lose this because of the growing social inequalities between the two locations. The social distances are rooted in relationships of domination at various personal, communal, and national levels.

Though Xaripus continuously build communities through *convivencia* in both California and Michoacán, living in and experiencing different and unequal worlds has produced new social transformations among transnational migrants. These transnational migrants experience an emergent *nepantla*—a hybridity that will be discussed below (see Lowe 1996, 67; Mahler 2003, 92, 94; Guarnizo and Smith 2003, 23, 27; Smith 2003, 209). Furthermore, they achieve relative empowerment compared to their non-migrant counterparts on both sides of the border. In what follows, *convivencia*, *nepantla*, and empowerment are examined in Stockton, California and Xaripu, Michoacán.

CONVIVENCIA

The idea of *mis raíces* (my roots) suggests an awareness of shared history and memories tied to a community and geographical space. But while this sense of *raíces* facilitates identification with the pueblo, it does not foster the ongoing development of the community. Rather, *convivencia*—the ongoing social interaction, shared culture, and affection in the making of community—provides a more substantive foundation for building community. Thus, though Xaripus generally celebrate their *raíces*, they construct community through *convivencia* in California and Michoacán.

The meaning of "community" reflects the definers' emotions, attitudes, symbols, and desires. While shared meanings, symbols, myths, interests, and emotions are central to building community (Gutiérrez

1999, 19; Guarnizo and Smith 2003, 13; Goldring 2003, 174), they are inherently dynamic and change according to the varied experiences and locations of a given community's members. For example, Marixsa Alicea (1997, 607–10) documents the contradictory meanings ascribed to the "homeland" by Puerto Rican women living on the mainland United States. While these women had experienced unfair burdens of patriarchal oppression in Puerto Rico, their marginality in the United States distilled their desire to return to their homeland for security and comfort (see also Espiritu 2003b). Alicea thus concludes that, "faced with race oppression and conditions of poverty in the United States, [these women] make a place for themselves, in part, by salvaging some things from their past and from the home territory that 'can be made new'" (1997, 610).

This seeming contradiction was also evident among the elder Xaripus. After more than thirty years of settlement in the United States, most of them retain an idealized vision and affection toward Xaripu in spite of the memories of what caused them to migrate in the first place. In California, María, who was a *mayor* and an infrequent visitor to Mexico, elaborated on what belonging to the Xaripu community meant to her: "Xaripu is my home, my land, my roots. I feel part of the Xaripu community. I am a Xaripa, even though I do not go or anything. . . . When I see people from Xaripu that I know, I do not see them as people from Xaripu but as my family. Back in Xaripu all the people talked to each other; everyone knew each other. I see them as my family, as if we were one family." Martha, who is also in her fifties but who is a more frequent visitor to Xaripu, captured the emotional intensity and connection with her homeland: "Xaripu is my mother. It means what my mother means to me, and in a similar way I will defend her, and let no one say anything [bad] about Xaripu, because I'll be there with a gun. I was raised there, I grew up there, and I got my education there, the little I got. I lived my life there very happy, happy, happy . . . with no main attraction other than the plaza and home, the water spring, and that was all. There I felt happiness living among the people from the pueblo. I felt content, I felt happy, and I got along fine."

As other scholars have noted, living in a context of racial, class, and gender oppression is frequently the driving force behind migrants' desire for another homeland and thus their movement across borders

(Parreñas 2001a, 2001b; Espiritu 2003b; Goldring 2003). Xaripus not only re-create this ideal homeland in their minds but also continue to visit Michoacán almost every year. How have these connections and meanings affected the children who were born or have lived most of their lives in the United States? And how have these connections to Michoacán affected the young non-migrants who reside there? Participants' varying understandings of the meaning of "Xaripu,"[18] "belonging," and "unity" help provide answers.[19]

In California, the word "Xaripu" generally meant "roots" to the younger cohorts; as one said, "[Xaripu is] my roots and the place where my parents are from." Another commented, "It means my heritage, my history, my origin, because both my mother and father are from Xaripu." But "Xaripu" was also defined as a people who live in many places. Julia, who is in her early thirties, was brought to the United States as a baby, and frequently visits Michoacán, reflected both meanings in her answer: "[Xaripu is] a pueblo that I like very much. It is a pueblo that has been growing, because Xaripu is everywhere. I like Xaripu, and I like to visit." Valencia, who is in her mid-twenties, was born in California, and is an active transnational (she visits Michoacán at least once very three years and perceives herself as belonging in both nations), elaborated, "The Xaripu community varies a lot, and it is very big. There are those who are from Xaripu and live in Xaripu; there are those from Xaripu who live outside the pueblo, such as in Mexico City or the United States, and who go to Xaripu for two to three months a year; and there are those from Xaripu who never return to Xaripu. It is a very large community. But Xaripu means my heritage, my history, and my origin."

Xaripus in Michoacán defined "Xaripu" in similar ways as those in California had. One young woman said, "It is my pueblo. No matter how ugly it may be, I see it as very pretty, and I don't like people to talk bad about it. But even then, I want to leave." A second reflected, "I want to leave it, but it will also hurt me to do so. I do love it." And the third agreed, "Me too, I want to leave, but just for a while, because of boredom, and then return." They generally wanted to move out because of lack of employment opportunities and boredom, even though they expressed affection and interest in returning to the pueblo. Three young men similarly indicated that though they like Xaripu, they, too, wanted to leave the pueblo to earn more money. Two years after these interviews, two of the young men and one of the young women had migrated to *el norte*.

Although Lorena, who is in her early thirties, expressed no interest in emigrating, she did not share the general affection for Xaripu. Rather, she talked about the long history of hardships that her family experienced when they first moved to the pueblo from a nearby community. Lorena observed that class and social differentiations in the pueblo were sharp and that the poor did not get much respect. Indeed, despite the fact that most Xaripu grandparents (1900s migrants) and Bracero generation parents (1942–65) were born landless, migration has created social and resource differentiations within the pueblo: those without relatives abroad are among the most impoverished and marginalized. Thus Lorena did not socialize with many others in the pueblo, and she said that the economic insecurities—underemployment and low wages—made her feel disconnected from the pueblo.

A couple who had been living in the pueblo for about ten years also indicated that they did not feel part of the community because they believed people were not interested in change and they felt excluded as "outsiders." But their major complaint was directed toward the *caciques*[20] and *norteñas/os* who acted as if they owned the pueblo.

A few of the Xaripus interviewed did express such kinds of rigid notions of community that distinguished the insiders with *raíces* to the pueblo from the outsiders who were not born there. However, Samuel, the town doctor, made a point to express his disapproval of the "them and us" distinctions. He explained that because Xaripu was like a county for all the other communities or *rancherías* that have historically visited Xaripu for Church, medical, and market services, these other communities were also part of the pueblo:

One hundred percent of those participating in celebrations in the pueblo are from Xaripu. Well, maybe 95 percent; there are always people from the *rancherías* [outlying areas] here, but they are from the same county district. I want to explain something to you. Xaripu for me is the entire county, and we have that tendency to separate ourselves. We [Xaripus] always think that those from el Fresno are one and those from Tarimoro others, and those from Cuameo Chico still others, and those from la Presa and San Miguel others. Here the

county of Xaripu includes forty *rancherías*. [However] we divide ourselves. We say you are from here and you are from there, but no.
Xaripu is the county. We are all from here.

To be sure, Samuel's unique social location as a doctor who receives pa-
tients and makes home visits throughout the surrounding communities
may have influenced his interpretation of the boundaries of Xaripu. In
this, he reflects Anzaldúa's (1987) observation that persons who cross
mental and/or physical borders seem to transcend narrow definitions of
community based on territory in ways that people who remain within
these borders do not (Gutiérrez 1999; Bonfil Batalla 1987, 1996; Lugo
1995; Feagin 1997; Rosaldo 1997).[21] Nevertheless, Samuel's context of
reception—i.e., his political status, occupational opportunities, and social
ties—also affected his sense of belonging and made it easier for him to
expand his notion of home to include those outside communities in
which he worked (Portes and Rumbaut 1996; Menjívar 2000; Espíritu
2003b).

But most Xaripus in Michoacán expressed a sense of belonging to the
Xaripu community for more visceral than geographical reasons. For instance, Antonio, who was born in a neighboring community, said he belonged there "because *convivo* with them." Conchita commented, "I feel
part of Xaripu because more than anything, my grandparents, my roots
are from here." Miranda shared, "This is where I was born, and from the
day I opened my eyes, I have not seen anything else but Xaripu. I am
much attached. I went briefly to Morelia [Michoacán's capital], and I
thought of staying. And at times I dreamed of coming back to my house,
here with my mother . . . in Xaripu." She returned, and has stayed to
this date.

In California, social inequalities have deeply affected Xaripus' sense
of belonging to both their particular and their larger societies. Their ongoing occupational, residential, and educational segregation facilitates
their continued *convivencia* with other Xaripus, even among younger
US-born generations. A great majority of those interviewed reported
that over 80 percent of their friends were of Xaripu origin, and many of
these were relatives.

Nonetheless, for some of the Xaripus who have settled in California,
the sense of belonging to the Xaripu community has changed over time.

For instance, Martina, who was born in Xaripu and raised in Stockton, talked about how she had grown apart from Xaripus in California. When asked whether she felt a sense of community, she replied, "Not really, because we grew up apart from the Xaripus." Martina had been active in Xaripu festivities while growing up, but after her marriage with a non-Xaripu and moving away from the larger Xaripu community, her *convivencia* declined, and she grew apart from them. In contrast Rosalía, who was born in the United States and had grown up relatively apart from the core community in Stockton, later married a US-born Xaripu. Afterwards, she became more involved with Xaripus in California and began to visit Michoacán regularly. Her visits to Mexico integrated her more fully into the Xaripu transnational communities in both California and Michoacán. Rosalía described how she slowly began to feel part of the community: "[I didn't feel part of the community] until now that I got married, because [my husband] loves to go every year, and since the marriage I had to go back and forth very often. And everybody made me feel like I belonged there. But if I was an outsider coming for one day, I wouldn't think I was part of it. Do you know what I mean? I guess who is staying there and the way people treat you make you feel part of it. Before I didn't, and now I do."

Tita, a second-generation immigrant who visits Michoacán infrequently, also reported that her experience of *convivencia* with the Xaripu community shifted while she was growing up. From kindergarten to the eighth grade, Tita went to schools with few Xaripus and developed very strong friendships with girls from her neighborhood. She had strong bonds with Betty, Lorna, and Lilly, and they regularly called each other at home, frequented each other's birthdays, and nagged their parents to transport them to each others' houses. But Tita's relationship with them changed when they started high school. According to Tita, they all got bused to a north Stockton high school along with a large Xaripu student population (over a hundred), who also got bused from the south. All of a sudden, Tita was in school with many of her Xaripu cousins and friends and so knew more of her classmates than did her childhood friends. Xaripu youth often greeted her, "Hi Tita!" and invited her out: "We're going to off campus for lunch. Do you want to come?" According to Tita, though her childhood friends were also invited to socialize with Xaripus, the bonds of her friendship with them weakened.[22]

While visiting "el Camano," who was thirty-five at the time, I observed how active Xaripu relations are. Camano lived with a cousin in his own house just around the corner from my parents' house in a Stockton community, where within half a square mile about twenty-five to thirty Xaripu families reside. El Camano, as most Xaripus and friends call him, got home from work around four PM, after a ten- to twelve-hour workday at a roofing company. He carpooled with a coworker known as *la güera* (the light skinned one), who after work would frequently come in for a beer before heading home. Camano's house was like a bachelor's pad where Xaripu friends who worked in the same factory, fields, warehouses, or grounds-keeping jobs would stop by. On a typical day, soon after he got home, one friend after another—Gabino, el Bule, el Zambo, el Topo, la Morsa, el Alacrán—would stop by, stay a while, talk about the workday and job opportunities, have a beer or two, and then go home. Later in the evening, the same friends or other ones would come over to watch sports and talk about work, women, work, each other, work—and argue and laugh. Sometimes before Camano had arrived home, his friends would be waiting for him outside of his house. A few close cousins had their own keys. In this particular neighborhood, there are at least three other such houses where young Xaripu men fraternize and visit each other.[23]

In interviews in both Michoacán and California, Xaripus expressed a general feeling that there was unity within their community in their respective locations. In California they agreed that there was unity *en las buenas y en las malas* (in the good times and the bad times). Olivia commented, "When something happens, people are always there offering support, like when there is an accident or someone dies. People go to see them, and it feels as if we were one family." Valencia elaborated this common perception about unity within the Xaripu community:

> Definitely yes [there is unity]! You have to go to a funeral to see for yourself. If someone dies from Xaripu, all the pueblo of Xaripu from Stockton is at the funeral. It might have been centuries that you hadn't talked to that family. Also at weddings Xaripus get together. If someone gets married, wow! Even though you might not know who that particular person might be, if you don't get invited you get offended. Also at the weddings all Xaripus are there. I think that there is

affection because the majority of Xaripus who immigrated to the United States came here to Stockton. They continue to come to Stockton. It's a feeling of security and survival, being together in a foreign country—that is why there is so much unity. In addition . . . one is related to everyone, and if they aren't relatives, they become related by marriage. Strange, but Xaripus continue to marry Xaripus.

Per Valencia's observation, five of the eight younger Xaripus interviewed in Stockton were married to persons of Xaripu origin, and the three who were married with non-Xaripus had actively incorporated their spouses into the community. As Valencia noted, the two universal events that bring Xaripu people together are weddings and funerals. Several respondents reported that people gathered "for the good and bad times such as birthdays, weddings, accidents and deaths." Funerals of community members in Stockton are usually attended by hundreds of area Xaripus and by relatives from Michoacán who make the trip north to pay their respects. On some occasions, the deceased are brought from California to Michoacán for burial. For example, Keletos, who was killed in a workplace accident in Stockton (see chapter 4), was buried in Xaripu, Michoacán, where most of his family resided.

The entire community is also involved in organizing weddings. *Padrinos* and *madrinas* (godparents) help plan the large social events by finding reception halls, making food preparations, buying drinks, hiring musicians, organizing special dances or social activities within the event, designing and making decorations, and so on. Celebrations are funded by *cuperachas*—monetary and service support donations that are collected from family and community members. This collectivism has the added effect of ensuring a high level of Xaripu attendance at such events.[24] For example, Valencia recounted a cousin's wedding in which roughly 200 of the 250 invitations distributed by the bride alone (not including the groom's invitees) were given to Xaripu-origin relatives and friends. The reception was held in a community hall with a capacity of 850, and around ten PM the hall was so overcrowded that security would not allow in latecomers.[25] Such high attendance is typical,[26] and it is common for two major Xaripu events to be held in one day; for example, there might be two weddings or a wedding and a *Quinceañera*[27] taking place at two different south Stockton halls. Although families try to avoid time conflicts, factors such as the availability of dance halls, church schedules, and vacation time sometimes make them inevitable. When there are overlapping events, people feel conflicted about whose celebration to attend and so often make time for both.

The principle of cooperation through service or monetary aid is a well-established Xaripu tradition. Even those respondents who said they did not feel like part of the community agreed that *"gente del pueblo cupera"* (the people from the community cooperate). *Encargados* (task volunteers) go around asking people to help. As Julia described, "They ask you, 'How much do you want to cooperate with?' They ask you like that, and then they write your name and how much you gave." *Cuperachas* also cross borders, as Valencia shared. "There was going to be a ceremony to inaugurate the new priest in Xaripu [Michoacán], and here at St. Linus Church [in California] they were asking us for money. And someone from Xaripu went around asking for money from a lot of people from Xaripu, then took that money to the Xaripu parish and made a grand feast for the parishioners in Michoacán."

This kind of cooperation facilitates a sense of unified community both within the local manifestations of the Xaripu community and across the border. Xaripus in Michoacán also reported that people generally cooperate in times of need. Chana elaborated, "I like the people, though we can be very conflictive. We fight, we argue, but when there is something we want to do, such as a celebration, we support each other and get along well. That is why I like Xaripu." Similar to what people reported in California, major social events are open to the whole pueblo. It was common for the priest to use the church tower speakers to announce a wedding celebration to the pueblo, and the people were expected to attend and to bring their own chairs. Other events like Mother's Day, community theater performances, school graduations, Easter, Independence Day, Los Reyes Magos (Three Wise Men), pueblo fiestas, and cultural weeks also bring people together.

Larger celebrations also draw intra-national and international migrants back to Xaripu. For example, the week-long religious celebrations honoring Virgen de la Inmaculada Concepción draws large crowds during the last week of January.[28] Community folks, local commerce, and church volunteers organize the celebrations (see also Sahagun 1967, 13). The elders, youth, children, and merchants each have a special day in which they participate in a *peregrinación* (procession) that begins from the pueblo's main entrance road and ends at the church with a Mass, usually followed by a big evening dance in the plaza. During the week communities and *rancherías* surrounding Xaripu are each scheduled for an afternoon or evening in which they process from their community to Xaripu in honor of the pueblo's patron saint. These *peregrinaciones* include floats with religious and cultural themes affirming community values and beliefs, and are accompanied by school bands and community members playing music and singing religious songs. "La Guadalupana," a song dedicated to the Virgin of Guadalupe, can be heard every day for the duration of the celebrations. Most of the celebrations reflect a Purépechan heritage in both the music and *viejito* (the elder) masked dancers (see García Canclini and Villalobos 1985).[29]

Not all of the Xaripus interviewed felt that the community was unified, however. These persons noted that local politics and other community issues like water rights and street construction had created divisions in the pueblo. Moreover, most Xaripus acknowledged that not everyone in the pueblo or in the Stockton diaspora got along with one another, even though the majority consistently stressed that in times of need people were supportive (see Goldring 2003, 180–82). And though Xaripus on either side of the border cooperated with one another in orchestrating community festivities and observations, conflicts about how to use celebration moneys were not infrequent.

Community formation among Xaripus largely occurs through *convivencia*. Nevertheless, social inequalities, particularly those related to international migration, create divisions within the community that reduce the level of cooperation in addressing the needs of the pueblo. While Xaripus display *convivencia* and create community in both California and Michoacán, constructing a single community that transcends borders has been challenging (Rouse 1992, 45).

NEPANTLA

Many postmodern and assimilation theories alike predict that over time, immigrants move away from their ethnic/racial community and toward hyper individualism or an American culture of individualism.

According to the postmodern view, in an increasingly global and multi-cultural context, transnational identities and communities fragment, split, and multiply as persons move in and out of diverse and competing social relations (Limón 1994, 106–17).[30] In such an interconnected world, migrants experience diverse social contexts and assume fluid multiple identities (Goldring 2003, 167; Smith 2003, 202, 227–29), often according to what side of the border they find themselves on—e.g., employee here and boss there (Parreñas 2001b, 150–52; Kearney 1996, 145–47); agabachados (Americanized) in Michoacán and "Mexicanized" in California. The multiple identities and fluidity of the postmodern self hint at a move away from ethnic and collective identification to a form of hyper individualism. In a way, this postmodern view affirms the dominant theory of assimilation, which postulates that immigrants eventually become culturally and structurally integrated as individual members of the nation with equal access to both rights and opportunities to succeed (Mirandé 1985, 186–88; Feagin and Feagin 1999, 30–35). In other words, immigrants are expected to move away from their ethnic/racial communities and become individual Americans.

These individualistic interpretations of identity formation neglect the normalizing forces of structured inequalities and how their "dominant meanings" maintain social hierarchies.[31] Racial, class, and gender hierarchies remain entrenched across borders and produce relational identities[32] and practices that persist even in a supposedly "postmodern" (i.e., borderless) world (Glenn 2002, 13–14; Guarnizo and Smith 2003, 11, 20–23; Guarnizo and Smith 1999, 100–103). In this context of domination, where minorities are devalued and exploited, community building reflects forms of resistance and empowerment (Castells 1997, 8–12; Espiritu 2003b, 86–87; Goldring 2003, 167–79, 189).[33] Thus, as scholars of ethnic and race relations have elaborated, community formation offers minorities a refuge from racism in American society.[34]

In a similar way, the Xaripu community in both California and Michoacán serves as a refuge for transnational Xaripus from the dominant meanings that devalue and suppress ethnic diversity. Within this context, Xaripus' identities neither are replaced by more individualized ones nor remain static (e.g., Anzaldúa 1987; Rouse 1992, 1996; Limón 1994; Torres 1998; Besserer 1999). Rather, within the various manifestations of their community, transnational Xaripus are modestly able to affirm and reproduce their culture while pragmatically adopting language and other skills that ease their personal and familial life conditions within the dominant society. This qualified cultural adaptation is also a form of resistance against linear assimilation—a unidirectional move from their parent culture to American culture—and thus a conscious opposition to being reduced in social worth (Espiritu 2003b; Goldring 2003; Castells 1997; hooks 2004; Collins 2004), as in the process of being devalued within the labor context (see chapter 4; Sassen 2003, 45). They do not conform to the expectations of assimilation; rather, the interaction between their comparative social marginalization and their desire for ethnic survival produces new social formations—*nepantla*—among transnational Xaripus. This collective *nepantla*[35] is aptly characterized by León-Portilla as a state of being in between two cultures and thus not belonging fully to either but rather creating a new culture that is a mixture of the two (1976 and 1990, 10).

To be sure, the unequal power relationships between minorities and the dominant society complicate the retention of a parent culture (Lowe 1996; Parreñas 2001b). Moreover, even if linear assimilation were to be considered desirable, ethnic minorities' experiences with occupational, residential, educational, and political subordination make achieving this cultural state improbable (Barrera 1979; Espiritu 2003b). Nonetheless, transnational Xaripus who occupy this social location exercise some degree of personal agency and freedom in determining how they will self-identify. By some accounts this Chicana/o experience in the United States exemplifies a *nepantla* condition, whereby those in-between competing influences create a third space that affirms their unique realities and self-image (such as unique dress and linguistic styles blending different cultural influences) (see Mirandé 1997, 60–61; Anzaldúa 1999, 101–5). The Xaripu transnational experience also produces *nepantla* through occupying different material and cultural contexts.[36]

Although *convivencia* helps maintain meaningful relations across borders (see Guarnizo and Smith 2003, 13; Smith 2003, 198, 204), the transnational experience has created inequalities and conflicts between transnational Xaripus and non-migrant Xaripus.[37] These tensions reveal how difficult it is to maintain the unity of a pueblo that has been divided by a border marking a global hierarchy, in part because the divergent experiences of transnational and non-migrant Xaripus create a *nepantla* condition for the former that grants them privileges and powers not enjoyed by the latter. Moreover, emergent inequalities and conflict reflect the changing social locations (nationality, class, and culture) of transnational Xaripus who experience two unequal worlds and who become transformed by both realities.

In what follows, transnational Xaripus' *nepantla* is explored through field observations and two questions: Is there unity between migrant and non-migrant Xaripus? And how do Xaripus from California and Michoacán view assimilation into Anglo society? By exploring perceptions of unity among non-migrant and transnational Xaripus, I examine how they personally understand unity or lack of unity within the community. Although they report that the community is unified because of kinship ties and participation in collaborative projects, both non-migrant and transnational Xaripus recognized that this fragile unity reveals an emergent *nepantla* among transnational Xaripus. Another way to explore this social location is by analyzing the notion of assimilation, more commonly referred to among Xaripus as "Americanization" (which is understood as losing one's parents' culture) or *agabachar* (becoming Whitened). Views of assimilation provide insight into how Xaripus see each other and how they interpret the cultural distances they experience within the dominant US culture.

In California, Xaripus had various impressions about whether there was unity between those who visit Michoacán and those who live there. "Unity" was not necessarily understood as entailing closeness, and their *nepantla* position was identifiable in their perceived distance from those in Michoacán. While all of the people who were asked the question "Is there unity between migrant and non-migrant Xaripus?" agreed that they enjoy seeing family in Michoacán, many also observed evident distances:

[People who live in the pueblo and we who live in California are] united like normal people, but that does not mean that there is closeness. Those in Mexico only see those who are from here at the most three months [a year]. . . . But the youth visit only for up to four weeks at a time. It is not sufficient time to come to know a person well, to be able to say there is closeness. (Martina)

There is unity because we have relatives. . . . All of us have relatives in Xaripu. But let me tell you that there are differences. Yes, you can feel the differences between the Xaripus from there and those from the United States. There is resentment, because the *norteñas* act very crazy—that's what the girls from Xaripu say: "There are a whole bunch of girls out late at night. Oh, *que locas*. They drink and smoke." There is resentment. . . . Generally [migrants and non-migrants] do not mix very much, though they talk to each other, they know each other, they greet each other, because they go every year and they see each other. But when they go sit down in the plaza, they do not mix very much. (Valencia)

Yeah, there's unity [between the two groups] because they are related. But [those in Michoacán] probably don't like the way [the *norteños/as*] go to Xaripu because they try to show off their clothes and . . . they bring new cars and trucks, and they fix up their houses and stuff like that. So they try to show off. And people there sometimes actually get offended or get pissed off. Actually I have heard a lot of this. I mean they get along fine except there is a minority there who talks [badly] about Xaripus who go every year. (Rosalía)

Transnational and non-migrant Xaripus experience social distances from one another because of the lack of continuous interaction and because the former tend to visit Mexico to go out and have fun, which they have a greater capacity to do because of the social inequities that exist between the two locales. While many of the Xaripus in California interviewed identified such tensions, most felt that generally the two groups reconciled their differences, particularly in times of need. Cecilia observed, "I see that they like each other very much. . . . Whatever the case, they help each other."

Interviews with young people in Michoacán confirmed the observations made by those in California that people in the pueblo were very critical of transnational Xaripus. For example, Antonio noted that migrants who know non-migrants in Michoacán may talk to them when they are in town, but generally distances arise even between relatives. According to another young interviewee, during the pueblo's festivities in January the non-migrant youth feel excluded by *norteñas/os* and tell each other, "Let them form their own groups, and we can form our own." Another reported that while youth from Mexico and the United States do talk to each other, they tend to form their own social circles. This is particularly evident when visiting *norteñas/os* go off on trips and non-migrants are excluded, either intentionally by not being invited or indirectly, because they do not have enough money to come along even when the *norteños* invite them. Lorena noted that even migrants and non-migrants who had been good friends when they were younger tend to grow apart.

I asked the young people in Michoacán whether these distances arise only with those from the United States or also with people who have migrated to other parts of Mexico. According to Antonio, there is more *convivencia* among Xaripus who live in the pueblo and those who live elsewhere in Mexico because they are closer to equal, whereas those from the United States tend to "discriminate against non-migrants more." Non-migrants feel excluded and put down by *norteños/as* because they use English, overdress, and/or show off material wealth.

Miranda recounted a particular conflict between young *norteñas* and non-migrant women regarding their participation in the *peregrinaciones*. In her view, the *norteñas/os* were given the favorable roles of walking with the Mexican and US flags at the front of the *peregrinación*, and thus the non-migrants felt excluded. Some of the women in the pueblo thought they were overlooked for the position because their dresses were not as nice. In another incident Miranda recalled the local priest put a halt to *norteñas'* fashion displays at church, largely because he did not like the revealing and stylish dresses they were wearing to church. So he said, "This is not a fashion parade; this is the house of God, and we are all the same," and he asked that they come as they should or that he would walk out of the church. According to Miranda, some young women left the church, and the dress etiquette concern was resolved at least in that case.

Rita further illuminated the tensions between permanent residents of the pueblo and transnational visitors. She felt that the *peregrinaciones* had been more respectable in the past, when people were more in tune with the spiritual significance of the events. Now, she claimed, migrants' committees collect dollars to organize the events and pay others to create their religious floats. Rita contended that these floats are among the worst presented compared to those from the *rancherías,* who still put effort and sacrifice into making their own. In contrast Xaripu *norteños/as,* according to Rita, focus more on raising funds and organizing entertainment, and, if money was left over, "they drank it up to the sounds of Mariachi." Rita frowned, "Why then do they use the Virgin as a pretext, no? The Virgin is not an apron!" From this she concluded that migrants do not care about the general welfare of Xaripu and are more interested in being entertained. She reflected, "There are a lot of needs in the pueblo, even though they do not see them" (see Smith 2003; García Canclini and Villalobos 1985).[38]

The differences in economic power between *norteños/as* and permanent residents of Xaripu are further evident in the comparative size and luxury of the former's houses. During a stroll in the plaza, I met an older Xaripu man who had never migrated to the United States. After talking about our common *raíces* and the struggles with poverty, hunger, cold, and death that Xaripus had generally shared in the past, he said, "I worked here all my life, and with these two hands I built my small house and supported my family. But look across the street at that big two-story house." Pointing to it, he continued with sharp and watery eyes, "The owners didn't really earn it—they cheated, and they used money from over there to build it, while I worked for mine from here." He objected to the fact that his labor, no less skilled, was devalued in the global economy.

In contrast, Nadia, an older woman in Michoacán, had a more positive view of the unity between migrants and non-migrants. She praised the collective spirit of both transnational and non-migrant Xaripus: "One group gets together and says, 'We're going to bring the music.' Another group gets together and says, 'We'll get the fireworks.' Some do one thing and others another, but one thing is for sure—they come out much unified." Nadia also believed that unity existed because many continue to use *apodos* (nicknames) with each other, reflecting *confianza* (trust). There is even a street in the pueblo informally known as the zoo street, where nicknames like *el chango, la rata, el tlacuache, la cococha, la zorra, el burro, el águila,*[39] and so on highlight physical or personality traits of the people who live there.[40] Often Xaripus do not know the formal names of people they have known all their lives even if they know other intimate details about them.

Nonetheless, social inequalities hurt *convivencia* among Xaripus across borders. *Convivencia* is difficult to maintain when *norteñas/os* achieve comparatively higher social and economic power and seemingly abuse their advantage through behaviors that are interpreted as flaunting their wealth—e.g., wearing stylish, expensive clothes, jewels, shoes; taking new, big cars back to Mexico; and constructing large houses. These impressions are rooted in nation-state inequalities that have privileged those from the North at the expense of those from the South. At the local level, such inequities are apparent in transnational migrants' increased political-economic influence in the pueblo and construction of large houses that remain uninhabited for most of the year (see López Castro 1986, 19–22; Mahler 2003, 88–92; Goldring 2003, 174–83, 190; Smith 2003, 205, 217–18).

The economic and social advantages that transnational Xaripus enjoy when visiting Michoacán are not sustained when they cross the border and return to the United States. The contrasting disadvantage Xaripus experience in the context of the broader US society holds them in an in-between social position within two unequal nations. This *nepantla* experience was further captured through Xaripus' views about assimilation in *el norte*. Non-migrants from Michoacán and transnational Xaripus map themselves in contrasting ways to American culture, revealing the latter's *nepantla*.

Norteñas/os' views on assimilation, generally understood as the giving up of parents' culture or "Americanizing," further illustrate this emergent social location in between two unequal worlds. Xaripus' acculturation in the United States has been shaped by their labor migration experience and their residential segregation in Stockton,[41] both of which have reinforced a dense web of social ties that allow them to reproduce culture and shield them from negative stigmas more isolated immigrant families are subjected to. When asked "What do you think about those children who become assimilated?" Xaripus in California uniformly agreed that linear assimilation was undesirable for young children but that learning English and educational attainment were highly valuable. About highly assimilated children, Tita suggested: "Something was mis-

sing in their home. I think that if they become assimilated, that is because they feel embarrassed of their own culture and race. Some type of
communication was missing. The parents did not communicate that well
with them. Something was missing! It is not right to assimilate. I believe
they were weak by erasing their roots and in just trying to be like those
here."

Valencia offered a less negative appraisal of "Americanized" children,
but also held out the importance of remembering where one came from:
"I think that children become Americanized because they want to belong to a group. That is why they wear baggy pants and style their hair
in a particular way. . . . It is a defense mechanism to try to belong. I do
not see anything wrong with it. What I find wrong is when you want to
forget your culture, heritage, roots, and you forget to speak Spanish or
that you do not feel like speaking it. It doesn't matter if a person becomes Americanized, as long as they do not forget where they come
from."

Cecilia insisted that assimilating was "wrong, because one is Mexican
and it is in our blood." She went on to say: "It is okay to speak English
and whatever you want . . . but never assimilate. But when my daughter
speaks to me in English, I respond to her and everything in English, and
she knows where she can speak English and where not. Like when there
are people who don't understand it, I think that it is bad manners to
speak it, because they can think one is talking bad about them. And they
feel bad."

These women, along with most of their younger cohort in California,
shared the opinion that maintaining their parents' culture was important. Indeed, all of the young second-generation respondents echoed the
unfavorable views toward linear assimilation. Many observed that some
Mexican traditions had been lost—for example, los Santos Reyes and
Día del Santo (Three Wise Men and Saint's Day)—while others were
gained—e.g., birthdays, Thanksgiving, and Santa Claus—and that their
way of living is different from those who live in Michoacán. While cultural maintenance was important to all of these young transnationals,
cultural conflicts frequently occur between age cohorts. Older children
sometimes feel that their younger siblings do not show respect to their
elders or are picking up bad habits in dress style and language. While
those in the *hija/o* cohort—now ages thirty to forty-nine—in the 1970s

and 1980s seemed to emulate the *cholo* style,[42] younger Xaripus in California today have more diverse cultural orientations that incorporate aspects of Black and other Chicano influences in dress style and music. At the same time these youth maintain an interest and affection for *"lo Mejicano,"* be it music, food, or family and community celebrations.

On my visit to a Xaripu house in Stockton, for example, three brothers in their mid- and late-twenties, who were all born in Stockton, were sitting in front of their garage talking about their experiences in the housing projects and their subsequent move to a predominantly white neighborhood. As they talked with each other, they mixed Spanish and English and switched back and forth between the two, but conversed mostly in English. Though they no longer lived in the housing projects, they still reflected the *cholo* style in their preference for low-rider cars, oldies and old school music, and dickie pants and white polo shirts. They also enjoyed *corridos (norteño* Mexican music) and took pride in their "Mexicanness."[43] One of the brothers, Chon, mentioned that a friend of theirs pretended not to understand Spanish even though he spoke it at home. Chon expressed disgust, saying, "He plays dumb." His friend's acculturation was not the concern, as Chon and his brothers all spoke English to each other, but rather his friend's assimilation of a value system that devalues part of their "Mexican" heritage.[44]

Some of the Xaripus interviewed in California revealed how they have adjusted to living in between two cultures. Cecilia, who was brought to the United States as a baby, described how her daughter—who speaks English and Spanish at home—switches to speaking only Spanish when non-English speakers are present. Another young woman, Lucina, mixed the two languages and switched back and forth throughout the interview with fluency and ease. Still another, Rosalía, conducted the whole interview in English but discussed how it was important to retain culture and knowledge of Mexican history. Thus the choice to speak English did not necessarily indicate a favorable view toward assimilation; on the contrary, these Xaripas stressed the importance of maintaining cultural celebrations to prevent being linearly assimilated into a value system that devalues who they are. But though most Xaripu *norteños/as* embrace cultural differences as reflected in their multicultural/bilingual skills and cultural hybridity, a majority disapproves of a one-directional assimilation that requires the erasure of their parents' culture. In response, young transnational Xaripus have generally combined and integrated forms and practices from both US and Mexican culture in ways unique to them.

Xaripus in Michoacán also uniformly disapproved of assimilating "American ways" and perceived Xaripu *norteñas/os'* use of English as an indication of such assimilation. A common perception was that *norteños/as* use English when they visit the pueblo to arrogantly assert their superiority and cultural distance from Mexico. A few, however, recognized that those who visit Xaripu in general are bilingual and that if they make mistakes when they speak Spanish and are ignorant of cultural traditions and norms, it is not fully their fault but rather that of their parents. Here are some typical concerns:

There was an incident last year during the cultural week whereby they passed with the flag and people from over there, who are originally from here, did not pay respect to it. People from here saluted the flag, and the other people were talking. They did not show respect. That, we see negatively. Why do they do that if they are from here? Many people come feeling big. Some are children, and it is not so much their blame as their parents. They only speak English, English. Also, if they leave as children, they also have to know the language from here. (Conchita)

The *norteño* children feel superior to those who live in Xaripu. More than anything, it's because of the language. By speaking English they feel superior to everyone else. In fact, when they come here, the majority of them speak English among themselves. And many times they show off when some kid from here passes by them. They know that non-migrant kids do not understand them. So in that way they marginalize them [non-migrants]. (Lorena)

I have the impression that they want to make it understood that they are a bit superior to those who are here . . . by speaking to you in English and comparing everything from the US to Mexico. They always compare that over there they don't litter, that over there they have no potholes in the road, and that everything from over there is better than what we have here. (Samuel)

In contrast to these negative views, Nadia, who was one of the oldest respondents in Michoacán, did not have any problem with children speaking English. She said that they respect her and that she loves to hear them speak in English. She likes the sound of their language and how they are *"Bien arregladas y bonitas"* (all fixed up and pretty). She recalled how when some non-migrant neighbors get jealous and say, "Don't they remember when they slept on a *petate* [straw mat]?" she thought, "Yes, they remember, but now they earn money and have facilities. Why shouldn't they dress up?"

Nepantla is the inevitable and emergent social location that transnational Xaripus collectively occupy in relation to their non-migrant relatives in Michoacán. People on both sides of the border recognized that distances have grown between them because of social inequities and cultural changes. Material inequalities between nations place transnational Xaripus in between two unequal nations. Consequently, while Xaripus generally disapproved of assimilation, those in Mexico viewed *norteñas/os* as Americanized and perceived assimilation primarily in linguistic terms, whereby Spanish is replaced by English. A few linked other negative characteristics to assimilation: disrespect for authority and tradition (parents, elders, teachers, the flag), being self-centered, and adopting *chola/o* or other *norteño* dress styles. These critiques of *norteñas/os'* acculturation reflect a tendency to identify transnational migrants with the United States and its long history of imperialist acts toward Mexico and other third-world nations. National domination takes a concrete and emotional expression in the face-to-face interaction between migrants and non-migrants in Michoacán, whereby the former occupy more empowered positions than the latter and often even non-migrant Xaripus in California (see below).

EMPOWERMENT

Whereas some migrant scholars contend that transnationalism merely reflects painful dislocations brought about by the global division of labor (Parreñas 2001b; Hondagneu-Sotelo and Avila 1997; Portes and Rumbaut 1996; Levine 2006),[45] others document empowerment among transnational communities through their organized hometown associations

(Goldring 2003, 184–85; Smith 2003, 215–19) and their parallel structures of power, "scattered hegemonies" or "re-orient[ed] regimes of stratification" (Mahler 2003, 89, 91; Goldring 2003, 167, 173). Guarnizo and Smith suggest that "the dialectics of domination and resistance needs a more nuanced analysis than the celebratory vision allows" (2003, 6), and Mahler recommends that we examine "mass actions" (i.e., common behavior) and not just "organized actions" to understand "a more universal medium through which non-elites exercise power (albeit not necessarily toward the configuration of power)" (2003, 69–73). Following from these recommendations, the Xaripu case reveals that transnational migrants both reaffirm and challenge hegemony (see Mahler 2003; Guarnizo and Smith 2003). As we will see, they are also empowered in comparison to Xaripu non-migrants from both sides of the border, and their empowerment can be observed in their ability to weave together the best of very different worlds.

"*Dios y norte*" (God and the United States) is a common expression among Mexican migrants who credit these two forces with an improvement or expected betterment in their lives. Raúl, in the *retirada/o* cohort, invoked this expression when he declared, "Since I started to work in the United States my life has improved very much, as they say, *Dios y Norte.* The United States has helped me a lot, because I have been able to earn money to support my family and all, and I was able to legalize all my family. My life changed a lot, because now I am more relaxed with everything. Working in the US, I live more comfortably and relaxed, and I have not had any major obstacles finding work or anything."

While *Dios y norte* offer opportunities to some migrants, others report that *el norte* has shattered their dreams. Martha, a member of the *mayor* cohort, shared, "At work, everyone has suffered an accident. My husband was injured in 1985 and Marí [their older daughter] also in 1985. Alberto [their older son] also had an accident at work. This young man injured his knee while picking tomatoes, and then just like that he could not continue for anything. His knee gives out easily . . . a disjointing of bones. This is all we got in *el norte.*"

Raúl's and Martha's divergent views about life and empowerment in the United States are partly explained by their unique social location as transnational migrants. Even though both came from a similar context of exiting (a neocolonized nation) and experienced a similar context of

reception in the United States (labor and residential segregation and social marginalization), their world outlooks differ considerably (see also
Menjívar 2000, 2003; Portes and Rumbaut 1996; and Espiritu 2003b).

Raúl had uncles who had been among the first Xaripu migrants in the
early 1900s; his father died when his mother was pregnant with him in
the early 1930s. Like most of his town folk, he was born landless. Raúl,
however, was able to join the half-century-old, labor-migration experience of his male relatives in 1952. To this day, Raúl typically works ten-
hour days in the fields as a foreman, comes home to no other major
obligations, and receives appreciation for being a hard worker at his age.
He has been going to Mexico every year for about four to six months
since the early 1950s. Raúl's fluid and active movement across borders
provides him a relative sense of empowerment in contrast to Martha
and other Xaripus, who are more restricted by familial, labor market,
and political constraints (see chapter 6).[46]

Martha's father owned a blacksmith shop and would seasonally travel
to *el norte* for work in the 1930s and again through the Bracero Program
in the 1940s, leaving behind finished iron products for sale to help support Martha's mother and siblings. Martha did not first migrate until
after the passage of the family reunification provision of the Immigration Act of 1965. In California, her daily life consists of working a double
shift: one at a super-exploitative packinghouse and the other as a taken-
for-granted reproductive worker at home. She thus enjoys visiting Michoacán, in her words, "to change routine and to rest a little bit, because
here all we do is work all the time. Over there, we go to rest." Martha reported not being able to visit Xaripu as much as she wanted to because of
work constraints and because she helps look after her grandchildren.

In what follows I examine Xaripus' sense of empowerment on both
sides of the border and document how transnational migrants are advantaged over non-migrant Xaripus in both California and Michoacán.[47]
I explore both the objective and the subjective transnational experiences
that affect empowerment among Xaripus across borders through field
observations as well as two direct questions: Have things improved for
you in California? And have things improved for people in your sister
community in Michoacán?[48] I used structured survey questions in both
locations to compare participants' assessments of improvement in housing, health, work, education, social life, family, and future.[49] I define

Xaripu empowerment as (1) material improvement in housing, education, employment, etc., and (2) perception of material and social improvement. This definition helps compare Xaripus across nations, and illustrates how transnational subjects are thus empowered through their freedom to cross national borders, their economic ability to cross borders, and their relative experience with two unequal nations that creates a more positive outlook about the future for them.

Material Empowerment

Xaripu transnationals are materially more empowered than non-migrants.[50] A majority of the transnational migrants own houses in both Michoacán and California, whereas many of the non-migrants from California were less likely to have a house or at least a livable one in Michoacán. Moreover, those who visit Michoacán are usually more financially stable, whereas a majority of the California-based Xaripus who visit infrequently reported financial and employment constraints.

When migrants held seasonal jobs in the past, it made more sense to migrate back and forth rather than stay in California, where their money did not stretch as far. Their settlement experience in California provides insight into how transnational Xaripus became economically more independent (see chapter 3).[51] As labor migrants in those days, Xaripu farm workers who returned to Mexico did so out of necessity because their low pay, seasonal labor, and lack of unemployment insurance made it very difficult to settle more permanently. Conversely, in the twenty-first century only those with the economic means to travel south visit Michoacán regularly and tend to make such trips for pleasure. This was quite clear in my field observations in Stockton, particularly among the younger cohorts (the older ones have maintained a more consistent and persistent movement across borders): the siblings with higher incomes and more secure jobs were able to visit Michoacán, while those with lower paying jobs could not.

Non-migrants from Michoacán also have more difficulty than transnational migrants because of political constraints, lack of resources, and economic dependency. First, some of them do not have green cards to permit them to freely visit the United States. Second, they earn pesos, which do not match the earnings of even less-educated transnational migrants. And third, the economic dependency of non-migrants on *nor-teños* is pervasive. As noted above, employment opportunities arise when Xaripus who have settled in the United States come back to visit and employ non-migrants in construction projects, food preparation, or domestic work. Moreover, many non-migrants depend upon remittances from *norteño* relatives, which, as was evident in the interviews above, create unequal power relationships between them.

Transnational migrants, thus, have the better of two difficult worlds (see Guarnizo and Smith 1999, 91–92). On the one hand, in the United States they earn dollars and can access the public resources of a developed country (e.g., medical services, social security, and education), while in Mexico these public services were cut by the dominating influence of the World Bank and the International Monetary Fund on Mexican budget priorities (Sassen 2003; Gonzalez and Fernandez 2003). On the other hand, transnational migrants can reclaim a fuller humanity by visiting Michoacán, where they can relax, have fun, and even become their own bosses and create a play, a dance, a road, or a political program.[52] They experience a "status valorization"—in prestige, power, and influence— that they do not enjoy in their United States homes (Espiritu 2003b; Goldring 2003).

Perceived Empowerment

Transnational migrants and non-migrants generally agreed that people in California had material advantages over those in Michoacán. In California most Xaripus said their lives had improved in terms of food, consumption, housing, and employment opportunities, and non-migrants in Michoacán agreed that *norteños* had experienced material improvements. Both sides also agreed that life in Michoacán had improved for those with US connections,[53] but that employment opportunities and the economic future of the pueblo did not look good. In fact, those in Michoacán were nearly unanimous on these points.

In contrast, educational opportunities in California were perceived differently by transnational Xaripus and Michoacán non-migrants. Whereas almost all in California said that educational opportunities had improved and that they expected even more positive futures, permanent residents of the pueblo thought that very few Xaripu *norteños/as* had furthered their education and they did not believe that this would change anytime soon. Their pessimism about the opportunity to advance educationally and professionally in the United States was likely influenced by the high number of accidents and deaths of Xaripus at work in recent years in the United States (see chapter 4), and by the fact that more Xaripus have become professionals in Mexico than in the United States (see chapter 2).

Those in California and Michoacán also disagreed sharply about whether education and family had improved in Michoacán. Transnational Xaripus had more positive impressions of education and family in Mexico than those who actually live there. Two-thirds believed education was good in Mexico, and some felt it was better than in the United States. In contrast, only one-third of the persons interviewed in Michoacán felt the education there was good, possibly because even with a good education professionals struggle economically.[54] Furthermore, because the number of primary-school-aged children declined drastically from over a hundred in the 1960s to a handful in the twenty-first century,[55] classes and instructors have been reduced, and some children must now commute to the bigger cities—such as Jiquilpan or Zamora—for their education.

Concerning family life in Michoacán, a majority of the Xaripus in California said that family relations where better in Michoacán than in the United States, whereas only one-fifth of those in Michoacán agreed. The latter noted the strains of being separated from family members and expressed deep concern over the increasing trend of people leaving their community to work in the United States (see also Parreñas 2001b; Espiritu 2003b). Those who perceive Michoacán as a "happy place" that they wish to visit every year to get away from the hardships of *el norte* do not share this impression. Their experience with a relatively faster-paced life in the United States, characterized by work and more work, certainly shapes this view. It is not surprising to find that both groups perceived social life to be worse in California than in Michoacán. In California two-thirds indicated that they had seen no improvements in their social lives, half reported that their health had declined, and one-third claimed that they were experiencing deteriorating family relations as a result of living in the United States. Those from Michoacán also sensed that people in California had not improved in any of these areas.

Thus transnational Xaripus have improved their living conditions as compared to Xaripu non-migrants in the areas of work, housing, and food, but there was consensus that health and social life were better in Michoacán. Nonetheless, transnational migrants diverged from non-migrants on whether family, education, and future had improved for them in California and Michoacán. The former perceive more improvements on both sides of the border, basing their positive impressions on their relative experiences across borders. Clearly, transnational migrants experience a sort of social uplift in Mexico, while at the same time reproducing social inequities in Michoacán through their increased political-economic influence in the pueblo (see Smith 2003; Guarnizo and Smith 2003). *Dios y Norte* has been good to some, particularly to those who are able to weave together the best of two difficult worlds.

THE CHALLENGE OF BUILDING A CROSS-BORDER COMMUNITY: GLOBAL INEQUALITIES

The experience of *haciendo comunidad* (building community) was evident in both Michoacán and California, where Xaripus continue their *convivencia* and construct a sense of community through familial and pueblo social engagements at social gatherings, weddings, and funerals. The construction of community is thus a continuous process whereby some become part of it and others move away from it. *Convivencia* plays a more significant role in making community than either *raíces* or birthplace. While community formation processes were evident in both Michoacán and California, a single community across nations (or "transnational social fields") was more challenging to reproduce because emergent social inequalities complicate *convivencia* between non-migrant and transnational Xaripus. Divergent interests and conflicts reflect larger structural and national inequalities that take on intense and emotional expression at the local level, where transnational migrants and non-migrants meet. In effect, the sense of a community across borders varies among those whose *convivencia* has been strained by social inequities.[56]

Although transnational Xaripus resist assimilation to American culture, they nonetheless have undergone a collective *nepantla* transformation. They are materially and culturally distinct from those in Michoacán and from mainstream society in California. And though many say, "I'm from here and from there,"[57] they experience an inevitable change that simultaneously places them in between two unequal nations and empowers them over Xaripu non-migrants. While some scholars view migrants' agency to maneuver across oppressive contexts as resistance (Alicea 1997; Espiritu 2003b), others question that transnational migration constitutes a form of empowerment (Hondagneu-Sotelo and Avila 1997; Parreñas 2001b; Levine 2006). In this case study, transnational Xaripus were generally better off than relatives with less of a transnational experience across borders.[58] The former felt they had two homes, were socially connected to both sides, and had the financial and legal means to move across borders fluidly and constantly.

Most transnational Xaripus explain their returns to Mexico as a way to relax and escape the pressures of US society. Unlike non-migrants in California or Michoacán, they escape the year-round labor exploitation in these visits and thereby affirm their full humanity and spirituality through religious and cultural celebrations and as multidimensional family members and friends rather than just workers or anthropological ethnic curiosities.

Transnational Xaripus cross national borders, increase their labor value, and develop bicultural skills. They experience social valorization and relative empowerment, and their social transformations place them in an in-between position in a global hierarchy defined by racial, class, gender, and national inequalities. Their experience manifests both resistance and hegemony: while they resist social oppression in the United States, they often reproduce social hierarchies in Michoacán. The Xaripu challenge, in *haciendo comunidad* across borders, is for those empowered by their in-between position to construct egalitarian and just relationships with those unfairly relegated to the bottom of the global hierarchy.

Chapter Six

THE FAMILY ACROSS BORDERS

Exploring Gaps in Perception and Practice of Gender Empowerment

Men are more *machista* in Mexico, and women are more liberal in the United States. First of all, the man here thinks he is very macho, no? He wants the woman to shine his shoes, iron, cook, treat him well . . . like it's the obligation of the woman when in reality it should not be like that. . . . Because if you love your wife, you're not going to want a maid, but unfortunately they, because of their *machismo*, feel that the woman has to do it.

—Rita, a non-migrant woman from Michoacán

This chapter explores the gaps in perception and practice of gender equality across borders and addresses the question: What contributes to the perception, as articulated by Rita above, that men are more *machista* in Mexico and women more liberal in the United States? To frame this exploration, I first review and assess the dominant scholarly view on the impact of labor migration and settlement on gender equity within the family. I then examine how Xaripa women's perceptions of gender empowerment within the family, the adherence and practice of gender ideals, and the household division of labor vary across age cohorts and borders. This exploration of familial authority and equity in the household division of labor will thus help illuminate the impact of transnationalism on perceptions of family and gender equity across borders.

PERSPECTIVES ON GENDER RELATIONS WITHIN IMMIGRANT FAMILIES

Within gender and migration scholarship, the two most widely investigated areas have been the household and social networks. The question of gender empowerment has also been a central theme in this literature—specifically, whether migrant women experience some liberation from patriarchy when they migrate to the United States. Early scholarship noted that patriarchy within the family genders migration and determines migrants' access to social networks, which affects their level of empowerment: women's networks become broader and more diverse, creating better employment opportunities and thus independence from men (Hondagneu-Sotelo 1994, 121, 136, 138; Hagan 1994, 107–88; Menjívar 2000, 159–64).[1] Consequently, migration and settlement experiences affect the household patriarchy (Menjívar 2000, 162–63; Sarmiento 2002, 160). Migrant sons also challenge their fathers' authority (Grasmuck and Pessar 1991, 139–47). Women discover personal strength during periods of separation from their male family members (Curry-Rodriguez 1988; Hondagneu-Sotelo 1994) and eventually enjoy greater agency and opportunity after they migrate and settle in the United States because of its more open structure of opportunities for females (Grasmuck and Pessar 1991; Hondagneu-Sotelo 1994, 2003; Rouse 1992). Roles also change along age lines: younger generations assume important roles within the family as translators and mediators in public spaces, while older generations lose social status upon settling in *el norte* (Menjívar 2000; Espiritu 2003b; Rouse 1992). Ultimately, the youth are left to navigate two worlds, attempting to reconcile traditional family and gender ideals with the demands and practices of a new society (Toro-Morn and Alicea 2003, 204–7).

More recent studies advance the idea that "gender [is] a constitutive element in immigration" (Hondagneu-Sotelo 2003, 9) and point to how labor migration and settlement experiences can alternatively empower women or reconfigure patriarchy within the family (Pessar 2003, 31). This scholarship tends to fall into one of several competing conclusions: immigration and settlement empowers immigrant women more than men (Grasmuck and Pessar 1991; Hondagneu-Sotelo 1994, 2003; Hirsch 1999; De Genova and Ramos-Zayas 2003; Rouse 1992); immigration and settlement intensifies the exploitation of women through the "double shift"[2] (Alicea 1997; Fernández-Kelly 1983; Malkin 1999; Menjívar 2000; Palacios Franco 1987; Sarmiento 2002; Ybarra 1982; Zavella 1987); or immigration and settlement reconstitutes patriarchy without necessarily eliminating it (Curry-Rodriguez 1988; Espiritu 2003a, 2003b; George 2000; Malkin 1999; Parreñas 2001b; Pessar 2003; Soldatenko 1991).

The first perspective (that migrant women versus men are the winners in the reconfigured gender relations in the United States) remains the dominant scholarly and popular view regarding the impact of migration and settlement on the Mexican family and thus warrants careful review. Articulating this dominant position, Grasmuck and Pessar's study of Dominican migrants (1991, 148–51) found that migration and settlement in the United States had empowered women with more household authority and a more egalitarian division of household chores than nonmigrant women in the Dominican Republic. They claimed that material and cultural experiences help migrant women renegotiate their level of authority and division of labor within the household. They do concede that gender ideology privileges patriarchy (1991, 154–55) but insist that immigration, work, and settlement experiences advance gender equality for immigrant Dominican women. They further observed that these relational shifts contribute to Dominican men's tendency to favor return migration, while the women prefer postponing it or even sponsoring their children's immigration so that they can settle more permanently in the United States (Grasmuck and Pessar 1991, 156–58; Espiritu 2003b, 96).

With similar findings, Hondagneu-Sotelo popularized the view that migration and resettlement in the United States creates more egalitarian relations between male and female Mexican migrants: "Through the process of settlement, relatively speaking, women gain and men lose in family politics" (1994, 147). She further elaborates, "Gender is reconstructed in different ways, guided by the limits imposed by particular contexts and patterns of migration, but family and community relations exhibit a general shift in the direction of gender egalitarianism. This was indicated in the study by shifts in women's and men's spatial mobility, patterns of family authority, and in some instances, by transformations in the gendered division of household labor" (1994, 193).

Other qualitative and ethnographic studies of Mexican migration expand on these points and trace the changes in relationships between spouses prior to, during, and after their migration (Curry-Gonzalez 1988, 51; Palacios Franco 1987, 49–50; Hondagneu-Sotelo 1994, 12, 62, 195). These studies found that women whose husbands had been braceros gained greater independence and authority during their seasonal separations from their spouses. In the absence of their husbands these women performed tasks normally done by men, such as administering resources, making decisions about children's education and discipline, working in agriculture and with livestock, and engaging in other income-earning activities (Palacios Franco 1987; Mummert 1988; Curry-Gonzalez 1988; Alicea 1997). After the Bracero Program ended, wives and children began to join the men in migrating (known as family-stage migration), and their migration/settlement experiences in the United States eventually challenged traditional gendered spatial mobility (Rouse 1992; Hondagneu-Sotelo 1994; Hirsch 1999; Pessar 2003). Whereas in rural Michoacán women's spatial movement had been limited to the private domestic sphere, in the United States they were able to enter the public sphere by working outside the home, taking their kids to school, and participating with community organizations (Hondagneu-Sotelo 1994; Hondagneu-Sotelo and Avila 1997; Mummert 1994; Rouse 1992). Thus these scholars argue that immigration and settlement experiences created more gender egalitarian relationships (Hondagneu-Sotelo 1994, 12–14; Curry-Gonzalez 1988, 58–59) and point out how women's autonomy and self-sufficiency were increased by migration and settlement experiences, including urbanization and wage labor, which they also suggest have "begun to erode men's dominance over women in Mexican families" (Hondagneu-Sotelo 1994, 14, 196).

Despite the widespread appeal of this optimistic assessment of gender relations in the United States, there are six limitations that generally undermine this scholarly position. First, as Hondagneu-Sotelo (2003) and Pessar (2003) have noted (and reconsidered earlier views), some scholarship in this area is limited by its exclusive focus on households and social networks as the primary agents of gendering migration. Early scholarship especially noted that family-stage migration was male-initiated/-dominated and attributed much of the causality for migration to the family patriarch (e.g., Hondagneu-Sotelo 1994, 56–57), while overlooking other social factors like state policies and labor market demands that gendered large-scale migration (e.g., agribusiness and US government recruited and structured bracero migration).[3] Thus it seems illogical to attribute more gender equity to the very nation that produced the unequal access to migration and resources along gender lines in the first place. Instead, most of the power to gender migration was attributed to dislocated third-world subjects, which both neglected the institutional forces that gendered migration and reinforced the stereotype that third-world migrants epitomize patriarchy.

Second, in much of this scholarship immigrant experiences from the same geographic region are overly essentialized and homogenized (Guarnizo and Smith 2003), which calls into question the gender equity thesis and third-world stereotypes it presumes. For example, many studies focus on national groups (e.g., Dominicans, Mexicans, and Puerto Ricans) without elaborating the internal stratification that exists within such broad categories. While some scholars do observe that diversity within nationalities along class, gender, urban/rural, and generational lines mediates the experiences in the receiving society, many fail to examine the racial/cultural diversity within national immigrant groups and instead treat co-nationalists as undifferentiated masses. This essentialism weakens both quantitative and qualitative research and its inferences about so-called "Mexican" or other national groups' migration.

Many studies of Mexican migration, for example, continue to obscure the racial/ethnic diversity that exists within Mexico and to present a monolithic image of *"lo Mejicano"* even though this misrepresents and suppresses the nation's immense diversity.[4] People from Michoacán have a particular culture and history distinct from other Mexican regions in part because Purépechans, not Mexicans, historically dominated the region. The diversity found within each state, including Michoacán, reflects continued Indigenous presence as well as the cultural and racial varieties—*mestizaje*—produced during and after the colonial period.

Thus it is not sufficient to simply recognize gender differences between rural and urban experiences because the ethnically and racially diverse "Mexicans" who inhabit these spaces experience them differently.[5]

Third, and related to the last point about ethnic essentialism, the idea that settlement in the United States reduces the private and public spatial constraints for immigrant women is questionable on a number of fronts (e.g., Rouse 1992; Hondagneu-Sotelo 1994, 2003; Hirsch 1999; Min 1997). To begin with, the private-public binary (i.e., a feminine private sphere versus a masculine public one) is not an essential characteristic of all Mexican immigrant communities. Historical sources on "Mexican" patriarchy reveal that gendered domains were neither rigid nor universal (De la Coruña 1539/1541, 221; Pollard 1993, 142–43,178–80; Warren 1985, 54; Reyes García 1998, 35–36; Malkin 1999, 485), and contemporary studies have critiqued this stereotypical representation of Mexican families (Blea 1997, 38–39; Curry-Gonzalez 1988, 51; Fernández-Kelly 1983, 7–15; Fernández-Kelly and García 1989, 257–58; Melville 1988, 2–3; Palacios Franco 1987, 37–40; Sarmiento 2002, 80–81, 145). Moreover, for many immigrant women, entering the public workforce does not mean that they are freed from assuming responsibility for their households, nor are they necessarily regarded as equals in the workplace. Rather, unequal gender relationships continue to be reproduced through labor/class segmentation in various institutions, such as work, education, and government (Glenn 1994b, 5–8; Hesse-Biber and Carter 2000, 54–57, 67–72; Hondagneu-Sotelo 2003, 8; Pessar 2003, 28; Segura 1996, 149–64; Soldatenko 1991, 76–78), and as noted above, many immigrant women of color work a "double shift" (Ybarra 1982, 169–78; Zavella 1987, 136–37, 141; Palacios Franco 1987, 35; Alicea 1997, 601–2; Malkin 1999, 486; Menjívar 2000, 165–69)—one in the fields or factories, the other at home—which translates into increased wage and non-wage labor in comparison with non-migrant women in the sending countries (Barajas and Ramirez 2007).

Furthermore, the public-private split is often linked with other simplistic binaries such as host-home and market-family (Fernández-Kelly 1983; Alicea 1997; Barajas and Ramirez 2007). These dichotomies attribute liberation and independence with the first part of the pairing (the public domain, the host nation, and the marketplace) and identify repression and dependence with the latter (the private sector, the home nation, and the family). However, these binaries, as Alicea points out, misconstrue "the complexity of women's experiences and cultural differences" (1997, 600–601; see also Sarmiento 2002, 145). Moreover, these conceptual categories themselves reflect the very unequal power relationships they seek to explain: the privileged (US-based scholars who occupy the public space of the academy) represent themselves as the normal and ideal types while distorting and simplifying the reality of people who are marginalized (Glenn 2002; Collins 2003; Harding 2004).

Fourth, the claim that women who experienced a long separation from their migrant husbands became more empowered is not as straightforward as it appears. To begin with, some women continue to experience gender inequalities in their husband's absence because their husband's families assume the right to supervise them and their decisions (Palacios Franco 1987, 50; Mummert 1999b, 457–58, 462, 466; Georges 1992, 91–92). Further, some non-migrant women, as well as non-migrant men, actually quit income-earning activities and thus increasingly become dependent on remittances from the United States (Grasmuck and Pessar 1991; Parreñas 2001a; Fernández-Kelly 1983). Hence, although some women do grow more independent during these separations, others become even more economically dependent than they were before.[6]

Fifth, the view that "through the process of settlement, relatively speaking, women gain and men lose in family politics" is too optimistic.[7] Women's empowerment (or disempowerment) within the family cannot be attributed with certainty to the immigration or settlement experience without comparing them with those in the sending societies (Alicea 1997; Mahler 2003; Malkin 1999; Pessar 2003; Sarmiento 2002). Yet, with few exceptions (e.g., Hirsch 2003; Rouse 1992), gender and immigration scholars have studied women on just one side of the border, usually the United States (see Barajas and Ramirez 2007). Moreover, the question of whether intra-national migration and settlement experiences have the same impact as international migration has not been addressed. Also, the transformation of the Mexican family cannot be broadly inferred on the basis of the typically small samples of qualitative studies or without comparison to a control group of non-migrants.[8] Finally, because much of labor migration scholarship has exclusively focused on one social factor—typically class or gender—it has neglected race and its relationship to class and gender (Glenn 2002; Collins 2003;

Pessar 2003). As Pessar (2003, 36) argues, "we must develop theories and analytical frameworks that allow us to capture and compare the simultaneity of the impact of gender, race, ethnicity, nationality, class, and legal status on the lives of immigrants and native-born men and women."

Many scholars, however, continue to privilege one social category—i.e., race, class, or gender. To overcome this limitation, Sandra Harding (2004) recommends enlisting "standpoint theory." From a standpoint approach, qualitative and quantitative research begin from the views and experiences of immigrant women primarily because it is their perspectives and experiences that are omitted or distorted in scholarship when the male migrant experience is normalized and universalized. This woman-centered research approach has helped illustrate how patriarchy has both shaped and been shaped by migration experiences, particularly in the household and social networks. Nevertheless, although standpoint approach has helped develop a much-needed understanding of migration experiences, scholarship on migration and gender needs to apply it more broadly, since related and marginalized experiences that deserve much attention have been neglected. For instance, much of this scholarship has privileged the voices of immigrant women in the United States but paid less attention to the women who remain in Mexico and at the margins vis-à-vis their relatives in *el norte*.

To that end, this chapter examines how labor migration experiences affect the family, particularly gender equity among spouses,[9] and pays equal attention to women living on either side of the border. For this study the degree of power and empowerment that women experience within the household was ascertained through questions about who holds the *mando* (authority) at home and equity in the household division of chores.

The word *mandar* carries different and seemingly inconsistent meanings that are contingent on the syntax and context of the word. It can signify respect or esteem (Sarmiento 2002, 80, 211); for instance, if someone calls your name and you respond "*¿mande usted?*" (yes, can I help you?), it does not mean that the caller is dominant over you but rather that you respect his or her opinion and behavior. A more critical dimension of *mandar* implies that someone is giving orders to a subordinate who is expected to follow them, in which case the person receiving the orders replies with *"Mande Usted"* or "Yes, ma'am" (Rollins

1985).[10] In this extended case study, I was interested in identifying the second dimension of *mandar*, since, when a person is asked *"¿Quién Manda?"* in the context of household chores and decision making, it often reveals gender inequalities within the family. In what follows, I specifically examine gender equity within families and how familism and transnational migration shape perceptions of family and gender equity across borders.

¿QUIÉN MANDA? (WHO HAS THE AUTHORITY?)

¿Quién manda en la casa? (Who has the authority at home?) was asked of women on both sides of the border. In California, four of nineteen women interviewed said that they did, twelve answered both the man and the woman, and three said the man alone had *el mando*. In Michoacán, not one woman said the woman of the house had *el mando*, while seven of thirteen said both the woman and man shared household authority, and the remaining six stated that men alone held the *mando*. Although a majority of women in both places reported equally sharing *mando* with men, women in California appear to have more authority within their households than their counterparts in Michoacán.

Authority within the family was further explored through questions about who decides how money is used in large purchases and day-to-day home expenses.[11] A larger number of the women in California than in Michoacán reported having more say in these instances, though majorities in both places (twelve of the nineteen women in California and nine of the fourteen in Michoacán) indicated that such decisions are made on an equal basis. Hence, while women in California are more likely to enjoy individual authority (Hirsch 1999), men and women across borders tend to share *el mando* and decision making on an equal basis. This finding is consistent with other studies on marital decision-making and authority patterns among Mexican-origin families (Cromwell et al. 1973; Cromwell and Ruiz 1979; Sarmiento 2002; Ybarra 1982; Zinn 1980; Zavella 1987).

In-depth interviews and participant observation also reveal patterns of authority and gender relations in the family that descriptive survey questions alone do not uncover. Moreover, the findings on different age cohorts demonstrate more detailed understandings of patterns of inequity within the household across borders and the complex effect that migration has upon these.

Chicas (Ages Twenty to Twenty-nine)

In California, the *chicas*[12] provided insights about how authority within their homes was gendered and described how their mothers hold authority over the children while their fathers attempt to dominate their mothers. When asked "*¿Quién manda en la casa?*" these daughters reported observations about their parents, rather than commenting on their own relationships, because all but one were single at the time of the interview. Though most *chicas* said their parents shared authority, some said that their mothers seemed to hold more influence at home. Lucina, for example, reported that her mother had *el mando,* and when asked why, she said, "*porque ya lo amanzó*" (Because she has tamed him).

Although it is problematic to infer much about a couple's relationships based on their children's impressions, some of these young women's observations substantiate the stories of control and domination that their mothers (generally from the *mayores* cohort) experience in their conjugal relationships. *Chicas'* insights suggest that their mothers derive their power and authority from their roles as primary disciplinarians. For example, Tita said, "My dad wants to have my mom under his control, but in terms of who has authority over me, I'd say my mom, because she is the one who decides whether I can go out or not. My dad always says, 'Ask your mom.' My dad exerts *mando* over my mom, and my mom, over us." Valencia shared,

> My dad is the strong one in my house. I am more afraid of my dad than of my mom. In other words, I can't manipulate him as much, but at the same time I think my mom has *el mando.* Because my dad says, "Whatever your mom says." But my mom also says, "Whatever your dad says." She is the one who is more in touch with us; she is the one that does not sleep if we don't get home early. Then she is the one who we ask permission to go out, but we also ask our dad. But to buy something, my mom decides whether we are going to buy it or not. The two have *el mando* . . . but I think my mom has a little bit more

mando . . . in saying, "We are going to buy this; we're going to lend money to so and so . . ."

These cases offer insights about power struggles within the home. For example, Tita explained how conflict arose when her father wanted to have her mother "under his control."[13] Valencia initially stressed that her father has ultimate authority at home, but as she elaborated on the question, she also recognized that her father's *mando* is not all-encompassing. Rather, Valencia's mother exerts significant influence on how familial resources are shared within and outside of the family, though she may struggle to lend or give aid to her extended family over the objections of her husband.

In Michoacán, the *chicas* had similar views about household authority as their counterparts in *el norte*. They noted that their parents typically share *el mando* at home, but also follow traditional norms of authority. For example, Blanca explained, "When I want to go out, I ask my mom, and she says, 'Ask your father for permission, and if he lets you go out, well, go.' Both decide, but first we ask for permission from our dad, and if he lets us go, she also lets us. And if my dad doesn't give us permission, then she won't either." As in California, authority within the family is gendered in that the father has or tries to have *mando* over the mother and the mother over the children.

Hijas (Ages Thirty to Forty-nine)

In California, most of the *hijas*[14] interviewed were married and thus offered insights about their own marital relationships in discussing the household division of power. When asked *"¿Quién Manda?"* most of these women said they share authority with their husbands. Julia quipped, "Both of us [have authority], because if he has an opinion over something, I have to agree with it. And if I have an opinion, he has to agree with it." Similarly, Olivia noted, "If the decision involves something that he knows about, well, he has the say, but if it is something that I know more about, well, I decide. But what matters is that both of us reach an agreement."

Hijas in Michoacán also described sharing the *mando* with their husbands. When asked the same question as the women in California,

Miranda responded, "Both of us do. Well, look, sometimes neither him nor I, because we both make decisions together." Single women in this age group commented on their parents' relationship in similar ways to the *chicas* above. For example, Lorena reported, "We always gave the *mando* to our father, but we never had it, for example, if there was a problem. My dad was very good, but in a sense he never supported us. If we had a problem, we'd say, 'Papá, look at this,' but he would say, 'No, I don't know—you resolve it however you can.' But even like this, we'd say that who had the *mando* was my dad. . . . In practice we decided, but because of respect we'd say he had the *mando*. The man has to hold the authority." Lorena's discussion was insightful: even though her family did not experience a direct patriarchal authority, she accepted patriarchal expectations that the man ought to hold authority in the household. She and her family members constructed a symbolic patriarch because, in her words, "the man has to hold the authority," even though her father rarely occupied such a role.

But more common than Lorena's patriarchal ideal (despite the contradictory experience in her family) was the evident gap between holding to the ideal of egalitarian gender relations and the practice of gender inequality within one's family. For example, Chana, who was single, commented about men in both California and Mexico:

They have [sexism] in common. The men in Michoacán are used to having their laundry washed, clothes ironed, and ordering the women around. In reality they have the *mando*, even though they say that they are not *machistas*, that they help and support her. There are a few who do so, but there comes a moment when in their homes women do things for them. They get married, and now they have someone who will do things for them in the house. When those from the United States come, I have noticed the same thing. . . . Women come and are just inside the house, and men are out in fiestas. It is the same *machismo*. The woman wants to get liberated from the *machismo*, but why don't they do the same thing and go out?

Chana's comments highlight how men are privileged across borders with *mando* and an unfair division of household chores, particularly when married. Unlike Lorena, she is critical about patriarchy. Chana notes the gap between professed ideals of gender equity and the actual practice in relationship ("they [men] say that they are not *machistas*, that they help her"), and she critiques men's double standards, like staying out in fiestas ("why don't they [women] do the same thing and go out?").

Mayores (Ages Fifty to Sixty-four)

The *mayores*[15] provided more diverse responses to the question of household authority yet confirmed their *chica* daughters' impressions of their relationships. Although most said they share the *mando* with their husbands, gender relations in these marriages were more strained and contested and less egalitarian than found among the younger cohorts. For instance, María observed, "[My husband] is the one that screams, but who knows if the children listen to him. . . . The two of us have *el mando*. He doesn't even talk to [the children] much less supervise them." María decided to buy the house where they live, but she also revealed, with resentment, that he had greatly influenced where she worked. María had worked mostly in the fields and also performed the overwhelming majority of the household chores, but had recently begun working where she wanted—at a cannery and packinghouse. María shared that for several years she had asked her husband to fill out her job application to the cannery, but that he had filled it out incorrectly to jeopardize her chances of getting the job. Only after one of her daughters filled out the application was she called to work at the cannery. Her age and physical weariness had motivated her to persist in changing jobs because field work had become difficult for her to do.[16]

A few women in this cohort thought they had more *mando* than their husbands. Lupe, who was interviewed with her husband, asked him to respond to the question on *mando*, and he shyly said, "*Pues tu*" [Well, you]. Martha also felt she had the *mando* at home and believed that this was why her husband ultimately left her. She commented that "once a woman tries to take control of her life, men run away." Both women above worked a "double shift," working in the fields/canneries and then performing the majority of the household chores. Although they were outspoken and assertive at home, they were also busier, compared to the other family members, doing paid and unpaid work all day long.

Christina was an atypical *mayor* both because she was a full-time homemaker and because she evidently held the *mando* in her home.

Though she claimed that both she and her husband shared the *mando*, in separate interviews both her husband and her children insisted that she had more *mando*. Her husband said, "Why should I lie to you? The woman has more say in decisions. It is good for a person to be able to make decisions. She can more than I." His view was confirmed in my many visits to their house.[17] For example, on several occasions Christina would tell him, "Go to the store and bring me water" or "Watch your grandson. He is too close to the street." They sounded much more like orders than requests.

In Michoacán, Rosa said, "My husband has *el manda*, but right now I do, because he is not here." Her house was bought by her husband, a transnational migrant, who works most of the year in California. Rosa has a reputation in the pueblo for speaking her mind. People who get on her wrong side try to steer away from her path. My field notes document her non-compliance to patriarchal norms:

> I was walking on La Calle Nacional in Xaripu nearing the plaza, when I came across Gloria's store. She and her daughter Rosa sat just outside the store eating *pinzanes* or *guamuches* [a green bean-like fruit]. They invited me to sit with them and eat. I accepted, and they talked to me about my family, migrants, and US-Mexico relations, and also school. . . . While we sat there, Rosa and Gloria talked to people who passed by. Rosa appeared to be a strong and aggressive woman, with a good sense of humor. On one occasion a man was passing by across the street, and she screamed at him, "Hey *cabrón*! [expletive] I heard you were talking *chingaderas* [expletive], just keep it up, and *ya verás* [you'll see]!" The man seemed intimidated and denied the rumors. Later, a young woman was walking down the street with her baby, and Rosa graciously praised her for looking nice.

Another indication of Rosa's tendency to defy gender norms is the fact that it was she who approached her husband-to-be as a young teenager and told him that she liked him and that she wanted him as a husband when he got older. Her future husband was intimidated by her advances, but ultimately they eloped at her initiative, or as they say in Michoacán, *se lo robo* (she stole him).[18]

Rita, another *mayor* in Michoacán, was single and lived alone, so the question of who had the authority in her household was not asked.[19] However, in terms of authority in other social sectors, Rita held public office in Xaripu in the 1980s, and she wielded significant power in the pueblo. She was bold and assertive, and was not afraid to go against the influence of the Church or *ricos* (rich). She once scolded a priest for interfering in the politics of the pueblo, and some folks accused her of chasing the priest out of town. She is very religious, though she supports leftist politics and parties—e.g., Partido Revolucionario Demócrata (PRD). Although Rita's and Rosa's behaviors may not be generalizable, their cases challenge stereotypes of Mexican women as uniformly passive and submissive to patriarchal domination.

Retiradas (Ages Sixty-five and Older)

In contrast to other cohorts, a majority of *retiradas*[20] on either side of the border reported that men had the *mando* at home, though some reported sharing it with their husbands. This older generation appeared to adhere more to traditional patriarchal norms, but, again, there were gaps between professed ideology and practice. For example in California, Nena, who was interviewed with her husband, Luis, was assertive and quick to answer questions.[21] She would also interrupt and answer for him at times. During our conversations Luis would also turn to Nena seeking her approval and seemed to defer to her and look to her for answers. So when I asked her "*¿Quién Manda?*" I was surprised to hear her say "*él*" (him). Thus Nena and others apparently subscribed to traditional norms of male dominance even though they did not consistently practice them (see also Del Castillo 1996, 219).

Margarita, who was in her nineties and had been widowed at the age of twenty-three, offered an interesting take on the question of *mando*: "I spent so little time with a husband that I don't even know. But I believe that he had *el mando*; or did I have it? But always, the man goes by what the woman says. Always, always, by what the woman says. Does it not happen to you also? That you do what she tells you to do? Yes or no?" This interview was interesting not because the ninety-year-old widow did not remember who had *el mando* at home, but because she believed that women generally get their way. She even asked me to confirm it from my own experience as a Xaripu-origin person.[22] A clear pattern that emerged was that Xaripas were strong and assertive, and that many of them had been primarily responsible for buying the house in both Michoacán and California, some even against their husband's will.[23]

In Michoacán, most *retiradas* reported that their husbands had the *mando*, and only Consuelo—who lived in Zamora, about forty minutes from Xaripu—reported sharing the *mando* with her husband.[24] Her life experiences in a bigger city resembled those of women in *el norte*; she worked at her family's store and assumed most of the major household decisions. Consuelo tended the family store by herself, while simultaneously caring for her grandchildren. Her day began at five thirty AM preparing breakfast and organizing the store and assessing what was needed. She opened the store at seven AM, sent her husband to the *mercado* (open market) to get fresh vegetables, and at about eight AM received her grandchildren, whom she baby-sat while tending the store for most of the day. She only took breaks to eat and to run errands after her children came to retrieve their children. She would close the store around nine PM and clean up before going home.

Consuelo's example notwithstanding, most *retiradas* in Michoacán seemed to uphold and reinforce the ideal of male dominance to a higher degree than all the other groups across borders. For example, Gloria, who was widowed in the 1970s and owned her business, answered the question "*¿Quién manda?*": "My husband has the *mando*, even up to this date." She reflected, "Since he died, it seems to me, that the strength of the house died, but I talk to my children like friends . . . 'Look, this is not convenient,' and this and that. And they have listened to me." Although in practice her authority is respected, she and her children remain loyal to her deceased husband's symbolic authority.

Nadia, who was in her eighties, said with pride that her husband had the *mando*. Nadia confided that a woman shows respect to her husband by avoiding conversation with other men. She told me how, when they lived in Mexico City, she had never asked her husband if she could go visit Xaripu. When he asked her why she had not expressed interest in returning to her pueblo, Nadia had responded that in Xaripu everyone talked to her, and she thought it would be rude to have them talk to her and not her husband. "Out of respect," she said, "one should not be talking." And once in Xaripu, an old friend saw her and greeted her, and she told him, "I want you to talk to him [my husband] the same way you talk to me." According to Nadia, her husband didn't get jealous because the people from Xaripu also talked to him.

Modesta, who was 105 at the time of our interview, said her husband had the *mando*, and commented that "he had been a very jealous man, without end." She giggled and commented, "Just before he died he became a saint." Modesta laughed and said, "Today all the women have the *mando*; they even get into physical fights with their husbands." Modesta suggested that during her lifetime gender relations had changed in Michoacán and noted that this change did not come about peacefully.

Across cohorts and borders, Xaripas reveal that older generations uphold the ideal of male authority more than their younger counterparts. Nonetheless, on both sides of the border the majority of women expressed sharing the *mando* with their husbands, though women in California were more likely to report that they alone have the *mando*. The evidence suggests that there is a higher adherence to patriarchal ideals in Michoacán,[25] even though there are evident gaps in gender ideology and practice across borders (Malkin 1999; Benería and Roldán 1987; Ybarra 1982; Zinn 1980).

While the ideal of male authority constitutes one dimension of patriarchy, the patriarchal order is also expressed through the gendered division of labor. Generally, those who hold power shape the division of labor and the valuation of the tasks performed. In what follows, the gendered division of household labor is examined to more comprehensively assess gender equity and inequity among Xaripu families across borders.

THE DIVISION OF HOUSEHOLD LABOR

In both the United States and Mexico, men and women experience a division of labor both inside and outside of the home that unfairly privileges men with unearned material and cultural rewards over women. As Coltrane (1998, 70) observes, "Men's household chores, in contrast to women's, have tended to be infrequent or optional." However, he also notes, "Since the 1970s . . . men's average hourly contributions to inside housework have almost doubled in the past 20 years, and women's contributions have gone down by about a third, so that men now do about a quarter of the inside chores" (1998, 71). Despite this documented increase in the amount of time men spend on household chores, the overwhelming majority of housework continues to be performed by women in US society (Coltrane 2000).[26]

The Xaripu case reveals that neither work nor immigration nor women's authority at home has changed the unequal division of domestic labor among Xaripa women in the United States. On the contrary, women in the United States do more housework than those still living in Mexico.[27] When asked how many hours of household chores they performed per week, women in California reported significantly higher levels of domestic work (an average of fifty-four hours) than women in Michoacán (an average of thirty-one hours).[28] Thirteen of the nineteen women interviewed in California indicated that they perform thirty-six or more hours of household chores per week, whereas only four of the thirteen women interviewed in Michoacán reported spending this much time. So, too, the married women I spoke with in California spend more time on average doing household tasks (sixty-six hours per week) than the married women in Michoacán (who averaged forty-eight hours a week). In general, women in California report higher levels of domestic work per week and a double day of work (or double shift) than those in Michoacán, many of whom are unemployed or underemployed (See Tables 2.1 and 2.2 in the appendix).[29]

The comparatively large workload of Xaripa women in California is compounded for women in the *mayor* generation by the reality that their daughters and granddaughters frequently seek their social, financial, and emotional support (see also Hondagneu-Sotelo and Avila 1997, 559). For instance, young families commonly leave their children to be cared for by their mothers.[30] These grandmothers generally experience occupational segregation in secondary sector jobs and yet must put up with these conditions in order to earn an income. Despite this, they are still expected to perform most of the domestic work and nurture their spouses, their children, and frequently their grandchildren (see also Parreñas 2001a, 363–64). My field observations of María, a *mayor*, illustrate the exploitation of Xaripu women in California who performed both caring work and paid labor:

I was greatly moved by the unfair life conditions of immigrant mothers. For example, I gathered valuable qualitative information from a Mexican mother who coped with work at a tomato packinghouse and with her second shift job as a nurturing mother/wife. Her days began at 5:00 a.m. as she got up to prepare lunch for her husband, a farm worker. When he left, she rested for about half an hour, and then got up at 6:30 a.m. to take her younger son to summer school. Upon returning home, she washed dishes, cleaned the kitchen/house, and prepared meals for when her family returned from school and work. At 9:00 a.m. she left home to work at the tomato packinghouse from 9:30 a.m. to 9:00 p.m., six days a week (roughly 10 to 12 hours a day). After her job, she returned home to do house chores for another 2-3 hours: cooking, washing, cleaning, nurturing, etc. (5-6 hours a day). The two work shifts added up to 15 to 18 hours of work a day . . .

Martha, also a *mayor*, was going through a very difficult time in her life, taking care of her elderly father, a disabled brother, and two grandchildren while also working in an asparagus packinghouse. In addition, she was extremely discouraged and depressed because she had recently separated from her husband. Martha's grown children (two sons and two daughters), who still lived at home, did not help with the household responsibilities. Our interview was paused three times: twice to serve food to her small grandchildren who were playing in the living room, and once to pray for about fifteen minutes. Environmental stressors along with familial problems led her to seek spiritual guidance for support. This spirituality was very evident among many women in this age cohort, who search for a type of support they lack in their daily lives.

Although women in Michoacán also perform the bulk of housework and apparently have less *mando* at home,[31] they spend significantly less time on household chores and comparatively more time socializing outside the home than those in California. Most evenings they socialize in the plaza or *la plazuelita* (smaller plaza) or take walks along the streets of the pueblo. Most of the women interviewed in California reported that they miss these social activities. The general sense among those in California is that, in the United States, life is structured from the house to the workplace for adults, and for children from the house to school. Several reasons for not socializing outside the home in Stockton were pointed out, including high crime rates, no proximate public spaces to frequent, and busy work schedules. These observations clearly contrast with the common depictions of spatially bound women in Mexico and liberated and unrestrained women in the United States.

Despite living amid social conditions that make it possible to spend more time socializing outside of the home, Xaripas in Michoacán have significant experiential disadvantages because of Mexico's subordinate global position. Non-migrant Xaripas/os frequently rely on remittances from *norteños/as* for their incomes, which changes these relationships from those of equals to those of dependence. Unemployment and under-employment are typical conditions for both men and women in Xaripu, except during the months of December and January, when the trans-national *norteñas/os* visit the homeland. This period briefly stimulates the local economy, employing non-migrant women in domestic work, restaurants, and commerce, while incorporating men primarily in con-struction, commerce, and field work. This superficial economic stimula-tion encourages the smaller number of non-migrants into migration, because of the inflated cost of living related to the migrants' dollars. Thus, men and women who live in Michoacán year-round are economi-cally forced either into dependent relationships with their *norteño/a* relatives or into migration.

Overall, women's family experiences in Michoacán and California are shaped by different structures of opportunities within a global racialized division of labor.[32] Although *norteñas* perceive more *mando* for them-selves than those in Michoacán, women in California clearly perform more housework than those in Michoacán. In California, Xaripas find relatively more empowerment within the family than outside it, which may contribute to the perception of having more *mando* at home than outside. At home, women generally make the decisions about the disci-pline of children and over money matters, whereas outside the home they have comparatively less power negotiating work schedules, pay scales, and political/cultural citizenship. These discrepancies suggest that *norteñas* obtained their relative sense of empowerment—vis-à-vis their spouses—from their authority and influence at home, particularly over their children. Nonetheless, structural inequalities in society exert ex-treme levels of physical and psychological stress on them, particularly the *mayores* in California.[33] Below I further explore why women perceive more gender empowerment within the family and suggest that the transnational migration experience affects these perceptions of gender empowerment.

THE IMPACT OF TRANSNATIONALISM ON PERCEPTIONS OF FAMILY AND GENDER EQUITY

As many other researchers have documented, in contexts of social oppression people of color frequently consider their families to be units of survival (Espiritu 2003b; Kibria 1990; Lim 1997; Mirandé 1985; Toro-Morn and Alicea 2003). The familism[34] that takes hold in such situations reflects a desire to belong to an affirming group, real and/or imagined. The family then becomes a site that both serves as a refuge from external stresses and reproduces inequalities benefiting men over women. In this way, this family construct is dialectical. For instance, Xaripus search for material and affective support within the family, even though gender inequities are reproduced in the household. Although families are not unified, egalitarian institutions (Hondagneu-Sotelo 2003; Menjívar 2000; Parreñas 2001a), Xaripas generally find more support and equality within the home than outside of it. This was evident in Xaripas' affection for family, high levels of *convivencia* with nuclear and extended family, and high reliance on family for material and emotional support. Although family remains highly valued on both sides of the border, the transnational experience affects differing perceptions about the family and gender relations among relatives who cross borders and those who do not.

In California, transnational Xaripus typically described their families as being very close and unified. When asked how their families related across the borders, they answered, "[Our] family is very united," or "We are both very united. I'm very close to my brothers and sisters." Yet differences were also observed: "Here [in the US] we are employed, and over there only those who have businesses [work]. We are different because we speak English and they don't. I am working, and they are not." In Michoacán, on the other hand, the younger cohorts perceived greater differences between themselves and their families in *el norte*. All uniformly felt that about half of the youth who visit are showoffs and that families are more liberal in the United States in that they allow their children to stay up at night and to drink alcohol. Leopoldo, a *chico* in Michoacán, noted distances with *norteña/o* relatives who regarded him and his family as *"muy poca cosa"* (lowly). He also believed that *norteña/o* families were more liberal because, in his perception, they spent all day going out or partying. These perceptions partly stem from the reality that migrants go out and have fun during their visits to the pueblo while non-migrants have to work, and this differentiation creates conflict. Chana, a member of the *hija* cohort in Michoacán, elaborated:

> Migrants are different. Well, when they come here, those from Xaripu hang out with those from Xaripu, and those from the US, with those from the US. Without wanting, *norteños* shove you aside. I tell you this, because that is what I see. Even within the same family, when they leave for the United States, nothing in the relationship is the same; even though they might say it is, it is not. . . . My brothers changed—I don't know how to talk to them now, how to treat them, because now they come and it is not the same thing. . . . They need to stay here and not just come during the fiesta. They need to stay for at least three to four months like they used to before, so that things can be the same. Moreover, here you see how the youth are peaceful . . . just as you see them play here at the *plazuelita* [basketball court]. Once in a while they have a basketball tournament [and they mix] . . . but during the dances you see right away [the social apartness between] those from the US and those from here. I myself, just because of my personality, I talk to both groups.

Chana's discussion highlights two points: one, the significance of *convivencia* in the production of the transnational family, and two, how it suffers in the context of national inequalities—"without wanting, *norteños* shove you aside," even family.

Miranda, another *hija* cohort member in Michoacán, further elaborated Chana's point. She observed how, when a transnational *norteña/o* returns with new outfits and invites a non-migrant friend to go out, the latter gets discouraged from going out because he/she does not have the same quality of clothes. Moreover, with or without parents' permission, Miranda contends, migrant youth go out at night to neighboring towns such as Jiquilpan and San Antonio, whereas non-migrant youth do not go out without their parents' consent. Supposedly, young transnational *norteñas* do not ask for their parents' permission to go out, and non-migrants think it is the norm in the United States.

Despite the fact that transnational *norteñas/os* perceived their families to be similar to those in Michoacán, the latter believed that *norteña/o* families were more liberal, pointing to the lack of respect toward parents, to the liberated youth who stayed up at night and drank alcohol in public, and to the material spoiling of youth. Not only are perceptions about the family shaped by the transnational experience, but also the views on gender differences vary between those who cross borders and those who do not.

In California, the *chicas* with higher levels of transnational experience[35] saw few differences in gender relations between themselves and those who moved less frequently across the border. Tita, who was born in California, had briefly visited Michoacán only three times (week-long trips) in her almost thirty years and felt that there was more respect for women in the United States. In her view, women in Michoacán generally did not work outside the home, which she believed often translated into more male control. She also believed that men in Mexico were more demanding and wanted everything *en la mano* (handed to them). She cited her brothers as an example of this behavior, though they grew up in California. They were brought as young children from Michoacán to the United States and, in her view, manifested the kind of demanding behavior that she thinks is typical of men in the pueblo. Rosalía, a *chica* who recently had begun to visit Michoacán, saw similar gender patterns:

Well, they don't want their wives to work in Mexico. They want their wives to raise their kids and stuff like that. So the husband has to work extra hours, and sometimes they can't. . . . It depends on their situation—how they raise their kids, if both parents are there or not, it might be worse. They could be traditional, and over here the girls take off. . . . They just want to be with their friends and things like that. That's why I say it can be dysfunctional here in comparison to over there. You know what I'm thinking about, too, right now; I think that the guys are meaner in Mexico. It seems like they expect a lot from their wives. They expect everything. . . . They are going to be grouchy, because they want their wives to be home. But as women in Michoacán are becoming more independent they realize . . . "I'm not going to stay home." But sometimes it is the same as over here in California . . . because the women here, they want to be independent, too. And the younger generation in Mexico, they want to be more independent, I think.

Rosalía's assessment of gender relations across borders includes a reconsideration of the view that women are more liberated in the United States in her reflection that: "as women are becoming more independent, they realize . . . 'I'm not going to stay home.' But sometimes it is the same as over here."

Valencia, who has a longer and more active transnational experience than Rosalía, noted that youth in Xaripu do not display open affection in public, such as kissing. This difference was attributed to the lack of anonymity and the social control of a small town as opposed to the freedoms of a big city. Martina, who had become an infrequent visitor after her marriage,[36] felt that youth had more opportunities to go out and do different things in California, while in Michoacán the perceived lack of liberties was associated with lack of employment opportunities or big-city entertainment. Money seemingly serves as a liberator in the sense that those who have it have more freedom to move, to buy, to get out and have fun, whereas those without jobs or money are less mobile.

Lucina, who was born in the United States, visits Xaripu every year and believes that men on both sides of the border are *"igual de machistas"* (equally sexist). Delia, who also frequently visits, agreed that gender relations in California and Michoacán were similar. Thus, *norteña* perceptions of gender differences between Xaripus in California and Michoacán were affected by their direct experience and exposure across borders: those who were high on the continuum of transnational experience—frequent visitors, active social ties across borders, and a sense of dual homes—were less likely to see gender differences than those with less transnational experience.

In Michoacán, four young, single women (ages eighteen to twenty-nine) expressed mixed views about gender differences between migrants and non-migrants. Conchita and Paula said that they were free to go out with their boyfriends, while Blanca and Angélica said that their father only permitted them to do so if their brothers accompanied them during fiestas. All four young women described the double standard that exists for girls and boys in the pueblo and noted that their brothers are allowed to come home later at night than they are.[37] They also maintained that some Xaripa *norteñas* appear more dominant than their husbands, but then mentioned that they also knew of such women in Michoacán. When asked why they thought women dominated their husbands in the United States, they responded, laughing, "Because . . . women can call the police to intervene."

Miranda, a married woman in the *hija* cohort, said that she did not really know how gender relations functioned in California, but that she had heard that in the US couples cannot even scream at each other (because of the threat of intervention by the authorities). She went on to say that she had observed some US-based men hitting their wives when they were visiting the pueblo, which suggested to her that gender relationships among couples have changed very little in the United States. She had also heard visiting women say, "Why doesn't he treat me like that [mean] when we are in the United States?" Despite acknowledging that she did not have firsthand experience with gender relations among Xaripos/as in California, Miranda maintained that transnational men continue to be patriarchs, and that women have no more or less respect for men than they did before they migrated. She also noted that domestic abuse exists both in Michoacán and among transnational migrants (West 1998, 184–209; Sorenson 1996, 124; Jasinski et al. 1997, 814–31),[38] and though she believed the problem has lessened, fear continues to keep many women from reporting it. When asked whether there were protections for the women against domestic abuse in the pueblo, she said,

> Today there is, whereas before there wasn't. Before, if a husband hit the wife, because he was the husband, it was tolerated, but not in today's time. Today, if she complains and wants to punish him, she can. They will put him in jail. But women, many of us are often afraid that he will get out and will beat us again or will do something else. . . . I think that fear has to end today. One as a woman needs to confront the husband. Yesterday, I had a problem, and I stepped over board, with that young man I had told you about [who had beaten up his wife in a neighboring *ranchito*]. I got very angry, even though the

incident had taken place a few days ago, and I told the law officer, "With your permission, please excuse me," and then I slapped him good, that young man. I told him, "Now do what you screamed you would do to me in public." I told him, "Don't think I slap you because of my position as pueblo public official. I slap you because I'm a woman and I have dignity." . . . He didn't even lift his arms to protect himself when I slapped him. It could be because the law officer was there. My mother has warned me, "When this guy gets out from jail, you're going to have a problem." But I told her, "Mother, that's why we have a police!" I was nice to him; I didn't send him to a higher authority; we already filed two complaints against him, and if he does it again for a third time, he will go to court and jail. From that moment, I will not do anything for him.

Miranda in her public office position seemed empowered, and she assumed the role of a justice enforcer—even to the point of enforcing discipline herself at the risk of future retaliation. The "slapped him good" incident took place during my field visit to Michoacán and was confirmed by other witnesses, including Miranda's mother.

Also providing a critical view of unfair spousal relationships, Rita, a non-migrant who had been active in public office in Xaripu during the mid-1980s and who presently worked in commerce and farming, commented on how she thought economic independence affected gender relations across borders:

Let us not ignore . . . that there is a union [between a husband and wife] and that there should be respect for it. In the United States there is none. Over there once the woman starts to work, there is another mentality . . . possibly because she lacks reason or maybe she has more disposable money. But now, because she works, she can say "Go to hell" to the husband. "You and I are equal." But she does not see that they cannot be equal, because now they have children. If she as a mother distances herself from her children, well, they won't be able to develop properly. What is that child going to learn? The child is going to come up with [strange] ideas, no? It is more difficult and more different in the United States.

Rita's interpretation of gender relations in the pueblo and beyond simultaneously critiqued patriarchy for reducing women to the status of maids (see epigraph) and economic independence in the United States for reducing women's respect for their role as mothers and wives. Although Rita did not condone the exploitation of women in Mexico, she nevertheless believed that the family was breaking down in the United States, and she attributed this erosion to women gaining more economic freedom (see also Parreñas 2003a; Espiritu 2003a, 2003b), which led women to abandon their traditional role as mother and wife. Although Rita admired Xaripa *norteñas'* work ethic, she noted that they experience many hardships, particularly the double shift. Her views seemed conflicted: on the one hand she did not like women's economic dependency and subordination in Michoacán, while on the other she expressed concern about the presumed breakdown of motherhood in California— "they cannot be equals, because they have children"—that she perceived stemmed from their newfound economic independence. In spite of the economic contributions of mothers, Rita believes that they have more responsibility to their children than their husbands.

Implicit in Rita's view is an assumption that the division of labor between men and women is not the root of the problem, but rather the unequal values given to what they do. In other words, she suggests that if men only valued the work that women perform as wives and mothers, family relations would be vastly improved. While this point has some value, the rigidity of gendered separate spheres creates an oppressive social context for both women and men who are discouraged from developing a fuller human potential. Furthermore, in California, women in the *mayores* cohort continue to be subordinated both at work and at home, and, rather than the breakdown of the family, what appear to be breaking are women's backs from performing at least two work shifts: one paid and the other unpaid.

In 2000, I interviewed Modesta Salcedo, the oldest woman from Xaripu, who was born on February 24, 1895. She shared her experiences living in Xaripu and offered insights about social life and gender relations in her younger years. As a girl, Modesta had been very active climbing trees and in one jump was able to mount a donkey—"*Era una chiva me subía a los árboles y a los burros de un brinco.*" She laughed with glittering eyes, reminiscing, *"En aquel tiempo no había borrachos. Los muchachos nomás tenian la ilusión de tener una novia"* (In those times, people were not drunkards, and the only illusion young men had was of having a girlfriend). Her granddaughter asked how many boyfriends she had. *"Uno de Villamar, uno de Zamora, uno del Ajuate . . . ,"* she laughed. As a young woman she had enjoyed serenades and had many boyfriends before getting married in 1917: *"Antes llevaban serenata a las muchachas"* (In the past, young men serenaded the young women). I asked whether her parents got mad, and she responded, "Why should have they? The girls were inside and the guys outside on the street." Those who took a woman by force, she said, were severely punished. They were taken to *Las Islas Marias* (prison).

According to Modesta, her father, Andrés, worked hard and was very responsible. He gave all his earnings to his wife, Crisofola, so that she could administer the money and feed the family. They never lacked anything to eat, and they often had meat and *chicharrones* (pork skin). The pigs were fed with corn, unlike today, when people fatten pigs with *rastrojo* (ground-up corn plant). She said that back then food was better than today, and noted that they often ate fish and shrimp. Although life seemed better in those days, in Modesta's own home her husband had the *mando*. She laughed, *"Ahora todas mandan, se agarran a carambasos"* (Today all women have the *mando*; they even get into physical fights). Modesta thus suggested that during her lifetime, bridging three centuries, she has witnessed changes in gender relations in Xaripu, though these changes have often been wrought with conflict, as illustrated by the cases of domestic violence.

THE COMPLEXITIES OF GENDER EMPOWERMENT WITHIN THE FAMILY ACROSS BORDERS

Transnational migration experiences have affected Xaripus' perceptions of gender empowerment within the family, though not necessarily the practice of gender equity. When examining the relationship between perceptions of *mando* and household division of labor, the findings reveal that women in California were more unfairly burdened with housework and wage labor than those in Michoacán, who generally did not work for wages. The gap in perception and practice of gender equality raised this question: What contributes to the perception that women in the United States are more empowered? Mothers' familial influence—on household decisions over resources and children and in the reproduction of family—offers them a sense of *mando* and, thus, relative empowerment. Although women express strong positive views about their family, many recognize it as a dialectical site, offering them both support and burdens. Familism and the motherhood ideology, however, were equally present across borders. To further understand the perception of empowerment in *el norte*, one must observe how transnational migration experiences influence perceptions and practices of equality.

Only the infrequent visitors to Mexico maintain that gender relations in Michoacán were more unequal than they were in California, whereas the more frequent visitors and the older cohorts observed similar gender relations on either side of the border. Though women on both sides of the border suspected that in the US women have more liberties and rights, those in Michoacán often noted, "They say they are more equal, but when they come here, we don't see a difference." Non-migrants in Michoacán believed that *norteña/o* families are becoming more liberal, less traditional, less respectful to elders, and more sexually expressive.

As noted, these perceptions can partly be explained by the form of *norteñas/los'* visits to Michoacán. Transnational families visit Xaripu to relax, to have fun, and to go out. They enjoy their brief visit to the fullest, which is facilitated by their comparatively greater spending power. Non-migrants consequently interpret this transnational *norteña/o* behavior as *"muy liberales,"* basing their impressions on the latter's brief visits. Unknown to non-migrants, however, is that the "liberation" of *norteñas/los* does not often extend past the border into the United States, where money constraints, work or school schedules, and high crime rates, among other factors, limit women's social engagements in public settings. On the other hand, some *norteñas/los*, particularly infrequent visitors, may develop the impression that non-migrants in Mexico are timid and withdrawn and deduce that they are more traditional and conservative, while ignoring that those who reside in Michoacán year-round have to work while they are visiting them and that they do not have the same resources (e.g., money or cars) to go out and have fun.

The problem of gender inequality within the family is shared across the border, and Xaripus who are exposed to both social spaces do not see substantive differences in its level. Gender relations remain essentially similar on both sides of the border, and the perceived differences between them can be attributed in large part to the form of migrants' visits to Michoacán. Pueblo dependence on remittances and tourism intensifies the unequal relationships between migrants and non-migrants, yet money only creates an illusion of more liberal families and greater freedom for women. This extended case study reveals the gap between the ideals and practice of gender equity and thus the problematic notion that *"en el norte, la mujer manda"* (Hirsch 1999; Hondagneu-Sotelo 1994; Rouse 1992). The reality of patriarchy shows otherwise, at least for the participants of this case study.

To conclude, patriarchy is not particular to "Mexican" families, but rather a widespread institutional phenomenon reproducing male privilege across borders. The view that immigrant or non-immigrant families move to more egalitarian gender relations with migration, settlement, and labor experiences vastly simplifies the nature of institutionalized patriarchy across borders.[39]

Chapter Seven

A PUEBLO'S SEARCH FOR EMPOWERMENT ACROSS BORDERS

And one of the things that is, I think, tough for the American people to digest is that Mexicans, because it's next door, are holding onto their tradition and to their language much longer than the Polish did when they came over here, and the Germans and the Austrians when they came here, the French when they came here, because that was like you wanted to go and become part of America so quickly that you tried to learn the language.
—Governor Arnold Schwarzenegger (quoted in Yamamura 2007)

In the twenty-first century, Indo American people, including Mexican-origin, are the nation's fastest growing population—from 6.4 percent in 1980 to 15.1 percent in 2008 (US Bureau of the Census 2008a)[1]—and are among the poorest and most socially marginalized racial/ethnic groups in the United States (Almaguer 1994, 212).[2] In the context of globalization and a declining quality of life for US society in general (Collins and Yeskel 2005), concerns about immigrants taking away jobs, draining public resources, and not assimilating, as voiced by the governor, have fueled nativistic immigration policies and social mistreatment that complicate migrants' equal integration into society. The

213

Xaripu case dispels racial stereotypes and counters criticism that migrants of color are not "making it" in America by illustrating how their long historical (colonial) subordination continues to affect their labor, community formation, and family empowerment across borders.

I have proposed a conceptual framework, interactive colonization (XC),[3] that reflects the Xaripu experience and underscores the continuity of domination rooted in and universalized through various types of colonialisms. XC, moreover, looks beyond polarized conflicts (e.g., Europeans versus Indigenous people, capitalists versus workers, and women versus men) by exploring the internal diversity within social categories (e.g., Hispanic and Mexican) and examining the role of emergent intermediaries in reproducing, countering, and/or reconfiguring existing social hierarchies.

In the United States, Xaripus have historically encountered limited occupational opportunities and labor market segmentation. While the global economy affects the general population in similar ways (such as economic restructuring, declining real income, and increasing household debts), the unequal incorporation of racial minorities limits their access to resources and social valorization. The logic of colonialism[4] remains entrenched at work, where the racialization of workers and occupations correlates with labor conditions and wages. Whitened occupations offer the most stable and highest paid employment; diversified jobs, the fairest conditions; and Mexicanized, the most exploitative. The jobs themselves do not simply carry an inherent value or reflect supply and demand market forces, but rather reveal that who performs them determines the status and rewards associated with the job.

In-between workers—such as managers and contractors of color—facilitate and secure these labor hierarchies. This intermediary position is structured by racial, class, gender, and national hierarchies, and it appears in all Mexicanized, diversified, and Whitened occupations. In Mexicanized farm labor, for instance, the documented mestizos managed an increasingly undocumented Indigenous workforce. In packinghouses and factories, English speakers supervised the non-English speakers; men oversaw women; and the more European-looking Mexicans were put in charge of more Indigenous-looking ones. Similarly, in the diversified and Whitened labor settings, workers closer in race, gender, culture, and class to the administration experienced unearned advantages and rewards.[5]

The strategic employment of members of the marginalized group in intermediary positions[6] secures existing social hierarchies. At the global level, the historical recruitment of labor migrants from (neo-) colonized nations also reproduces labor hierarchies in the receiving nation (Ngai 2004), and it fragments communities/families in the sending nation (see López Castro 1986; Parreñas 2001a; Espiritu 2003b). Transnational Xaripus illustrate this complex reality through their in-between class position across borders.

Transnational Xaripus experience "contradictory class mobility" in relation to their counterparts in Michoacán (see Parreñas 2001b; Kearney 1996). That is, in California they are generally laborers, whereas in Michoacán they employ fellow Xaripu non-migrants in farming, domestic work, and construction. Although transnational Xaripus create economic opportunities in their pueblo, they also disrupt relationships that were once egalitarian and mutual. This rupture occurs because transnational *norteños/as* are relatively better off economically than their counterparts in Mexico, irrespective of their human capital differences. For instance, a farmworker from California earns more than a teacher from Michoacán. Furthermore, the non-migrants are hurt by inflation created by the flow of dollars into the local economy, underemployment, unemployment, and an uncomfortable dependence on remittances from relative *norteñas/os*. After the neoliberalism of the late twentieth century,[7] few non-migrants in Michoacán can subsist without remittances from *el norte*, and many consequently emigrate, searching for a better future and for equality vis-à-vis their *norteña/o* relatives.

While people from Michoacán seek material equality by escaping their neocolonial context, Xaripus in California search for a fuller humanity by reproducing community in California and remaining connected to Michoacán. Both community formation and transnational connections with Michoacán protect Xaripus from a complete reduction of their humanity to devalued labor hands. While Xaripu *norteñas/os* reject one-way assimilation, material and cultural changes occur that stratify them from non-migrants in Michoacán. These social inequities create distances between transnational and non-migrant Xaripus, which are particularly manifest among the younger generations, who undergo a more notable social differentiation—financially, linguistically, and in their dress styles.[8] Thus, nativist rejection of Xaripus in *el norte* nurtures their social ties with the homeland, yet their *nepantla* experience in between worlds places them above their non-migrant relatives and complicates their *convivencia*.

Transnational Xaripus thus occupy an in-between position vis-à-vis non-migrants from both Michoacán and California. They generally move more easily across borders—given their permanent residency in the United States—and have more stable economic positions than non-migrants. In addition, transnational Xaripus acquire more wealth in Michoacán than those who live there year-round. These material inequities began as early as the 1930s, when a small group of mostly Xaripu norteños claimed *ejido* lands.[9] In the latter part of the twentieth century, a neo-Porfiriato period again privileged the few over the many, particularly those most able to fluidly cross borders and accumulate wealth. While multinational corporate elites benefit primarily from these neoliberal policies, transnational migrants with much less power also benefit in the short run but ultimately facilitate the monopolizing of wealth for the global corporate elites. One example illustrates this point.

Tacho, a grandson of an old-time bracero, shared that his family had worked hard for many years and had painfully acquired much land around the pueblo, particularly after the neoliberal policies of the 1980s.[10] Tacho's desire was to continue his family's success. His vision was to establish an economic relationship with a foreign firm in which the family and the company could mutually prosper. In the post-NAFTA period, the family land—which took several decades of hard work to accumulate—shifted production from subsistence and varied crops (beans, corn, squash, and garbanzos) to the mono-production of maguey for export, with less orientation to local needs or environmental concerns. Other local transnational families also responded to promises of mutual prosperity and oriented their farmland production to export demands from foreign investors and collaborators (Mexican state/domestic producers). However, this export orientation threatened the local communities through the repression of diversified crops for subsistence, the overproduction of maguey and lowering of prices, a lack of security for markets given the newness of the producers, and ecological problems (such as the reduction of native plants, the suppression of genetic-varied magueys, and soil erosion) (Aguilera 2005, 1). Transnational Xaripus thus remain embedded within a web of political-economic and national hierarchies: at the bottom are non-migrant workers in Michoacán and at the top, foreign interests and Mexican state/corporate intermediaries. While advantaged over non-migrant relatives, transnational Xaripus like Tacho are much closer to them in fortune than to the global elites that manage the global division of labor and production (Sassen 2003). Transnational persons, nonetheless, feel empowered vis-à-vis their non-migrant relatives.

Transnationalism also affects Xaripu families' sense of empowerment in the area of gender relations. In the first two-thirds of the twentieth century, a mostly male migration created a remittance-dependent[11] community of women, elders, and children. When the US Immigration Act of 1965 was passed, women and families began to migrate to *el norte*.[12] Xaripu settlement soon began in the 1970s and was largely established in the 1980s. In the early '80s, structural adjustment policies in Mexico dislocated even a few middle-class Xaripus, who soon joined others in the United States.[13] In this global context, Xaripa women's experience with work, migration, and settlement in California produced among them a sense of empowerment, but the Xaripu study reveals a complex reality. The perception of gender empowerment is more of an illusion than a substantive reality (see also Barajas and Ramirez 2007).[14] In both nations, the family as a unit of affective and material support continues to benefit children and husbands over mothers, and has certainly enriched US employers with the unpaid work of women, who reproduce labor on both sides of the border.

Gender ideologies unfairly burden women with child care and household chores. While Xaripu men face intersecting systems of oppression along race and class, they reproduce and benefit from patriarchy's gendered double standards and unfair division of labor both at home and at work.[15] Men are privileged over women at home and work, similarly to how transnational Xaripus are empowered over non-migrants in Michoacán. Just as transnational migrants extend and create social inequities in Michoacán based on national inequalities privileging those from *el norte*, men access higher-paying and valued jobs outside the home more than women. Masculinized jobs in transportation and construction, for example, pay more than feminized ones in the service sector.

Thus, in terms of social location, Xaripu *norteño* men occupy an in-between position with significant power differentials vis-à-vis Xaripas in California and townsfolk in Michoacán.

Scholars have interpreted in-between individuals/groups whose identities are forged in the midst of cultural change in contrasting ways. In *Endangered Cultures,* for example, Miguel León-Portilla (1976/1990) examined the Nahuatl concept of *nepantla,* particularly in cases in which racial minorities were institutionally forced to assimilate the culture and values of the dominant group, and concludes that this resulted in minorities having a sense of being *"ni de aquí ni de allá"* (neither from here, nor from there). In this view, "The concept of *nepantlism,* to remain in the middle, is one of the greatest dangers of culture contact ruled by the desire to impose change" (León-Portilla 1990, 11). León-Portilla elaborated this in-between experience: "Subjected to sometimes violent processes of acculturation, many young Chicanos experience marked forms of cultural *nepantlism.* Thus in Mexico they were called by the derogatory term of *pochos,* meaning 'ridiculously Americanized Mexicans,' while in the United States discrimination against them was almost the norm" (1990, 16).

The idea of an emergent deviant ethnicity, which does not fit in the sending or receiving societies, is also reproduced by contemporary scholars focusing on immigrants of color. Portes and Zhou (1993), for example, elaborated how immigrants follow one of various paths of segmented acculturation, including full assimilation into the mainstream society, the selective acculturation[16] of traditional cultures, or acculturation into an underclass group (i.e., culturally defective). Although acknowledging that immigrant children can become bicultural and operate successfully in various cultures, Portes and Rumbaut suggest that those who fail to resemble either the sending or receiving society become culturally defective: "Many years of uninterrupted migration have created a sizable Mexican population in southern California, but the relegation of its members to the bottom of the labor market and unabated discrimination have turned some Mexican-American areas into the core of inner cities in this region. The adversarial reaction to this permanent situation of subordination has its clearest expression in the emergence of Chicano and Cholo subcultures" (1996, 255–56). Furthermore, "young adults caught in a cycle of menial jobs, low incomes, early childbearing, and frequent confrontations with the police face immense obstacles of the future, reinforcing the same racial and ethnic stereotypes that contributed to their situation in the first place" (2006, 280). But while admitting the great majority of Chicanos/as do not engage in deviance (2006, 280), the authors nonetheless reproduced a racial stereotype (the culture of poverty) in their effort to help the "second-generation youths at risk of downward assimilation" (2006, 283). From this perspective those in-between—e.g., "Chicano and Cholo subcultures"—apparently have damaging consequences to themselves and society.

José Vasconcelos in *La Raza Cosmica* (The Cosmic Race; 1948) offered an alternative interpretation of cultural change, which countered Social Darwinist ("scientific" racist views) and cultural purist ideologies of the late nineteenth and early twentieth centuries by inverting the racial hierarchies of the former and claiming that mestizas/os—those of mixed races/cultures—were superior to those who were not of mixed ethnic ancestry. His objective was to advance a nationalistic and unifying identity in postrevolutionary Mexico. Though Vasconcelos' universal melting pot concept, *raza cosmica*, briefly[17] challenged the racial purist ideologies of the pan-European empires, it nonetheless reproduced social hierarchies, only with mestizas/os at the top. For example, Vasconcelos's notion of the superiority of *la raza cosmica* led to the suppression of Indigenous ethnicities (see also Urrieta 2003, 151).

A postmodern version of the *raza cosmica* was popularized by Gloria Anzaldúa (1987/1999) in a literary essay, "La Conciencia Mestiza." Like Vasconcelos, Anzaldúa claimed that the future belonged to the mestiza, but she distinctly moved away from static melting pot concepts (and nationalism) and instead highlighted the notion of a fluid self who has "tolerance for ambiguity" and the ability to weave the best of multiple worlds into a mestiza way (Anzaldúa 1999, 101–5). Anzaldúa contended that the mestiza becomes empowered when "she learns to transform the small 'I' into the total 'Self'" (1999, 105).[18] Without group loyalties, then, individuals who are in between clashing worlds feel the urgency for dialogue and reconciliation. Anzaldúa elaborated, "That focal point or fulcrum, that juncture where the *mestiza* stands, is where phenomena tend to collide. It is where the possibility of uniting all that is separate occurs. . . . En unas pocas centurias, the future will belong to the mestiza" (1999, 101–2).[19]

Anzaldúa's view of *nepantla,* though optimistic and humanistic, has conceptual limitations, foremost its neglect of structured power inequalities and of collective *nepantla* processes. It emphasizes individual choice and critiques collective culture, ironically suggesting the possibility of universal melting pot culture like *la raza cosmica,* i.e., "the future will belong to the *mestiza.*" The self, however, is a collective construct, and even valued individualism requires a group culture. Moreover, such an emphasis on individuals' capacity to determine their own identities is frequently enlisted to critique minority ethnicities who insist on maintaining their distinction in the midst of a dominant culture that is presumed to be both universal and universally accessible and desirable, e.g., "Don't be tribalistic," "just be an individual," "ethnic identities balkanize and thus threaten the nation." These claims obscure the reality that diverse group cultures have always coexisted and that privileging and institutionalizing one national culture reproduces the logic of colonialism, subordinating the full humanity of ethnic minorities.

I thus offer a third way: a *collective nepantla*—based on the Xaripu experience—that adds to these earlier conceptual insights. Borrowing from León-Portilla's view, the collective *nepantla* underscores how group identities are forged amid a context of unequal power relationships and global inequalities, and it underscores that social transformations occur within entrenched racial, class, gender, and national hierarchies. The collective *nepantla* view also embraces Anzaldúa's optimism that the *conciencia de la mestiza* can help create a better world and that a world without national borders is possible and was indeed the norm for most of human history (Anderson 1991; Nevins 2002; Winant 2001).

To begin with, every ethnicity—or, more broadly, social formation—is the product of *mestizaje* and, thus, *nepantla.* The concept of existing in a state of *nepantla* or inbetweenness, captures this process, and expects and allows for change. Cultural diversity and change have not been perceived as problematic in all places throughout the world but rather are considered normal among many Indigenous people (León-Portilla 1990).[20] For example León-Portilla documents an early colonial encounter between a Spanish priest and Nahua elder in which the priest expresses concern about the Indigenous people's inability to fully assimilate into Spanish culture, and the Native replies, "We are still in 'nepantla' . . . 'in the middle' . . . 'we are neutral'" (León-Portilla 1990, 10). The word *nepantla* here underscores the normality of diversity and acceptance of cultural change—though in this case, it was an oppressive colonial context.

The logic of colonialism, however, remains entrenched in the twenty-first century and reduces society's openness to human differences and consequently limits equality, freedom, and justice. The forced imposition of unequal relationships creates emergent selves, communities, and organizations whose ideals and practices reflect *con quién conviven más* (with whom they interact more) in a very unequal terrain of power, economic, and cultural relations.[21] A minority community with dense social ties, like Xaripu, can better defend itself from stigmatizing images imposed upon it than can isolated minority individuals, but given the institutional power inequalities, it will nonetheless be transformed. Therefore, while considering the historical/structural realism of León-Portilla and the humanism of Anzaldúa, the collective *nepantla* departs from the broad claims that emergent identities and cultures of individuals and groups are either good or bad. The emergent in-betweens, nonetheless, are critical in shaping history: they can advance the interests of those at the bottom, those at the top, or their own. But only the support of the interests of those at the bottom offers a hope for a more just world. Those at the margins clearly want respect, freedom, and equal valorization across borders at work, in the community, and in the family.

Although those "in between" may be strategically positioned to relate to the broadest scope of views and experiences, power inequalities jeopardize a fair and objective valuation of all views. Identifying one's location in the social hierarchy is necessary in order to understand the breadth and limits of our social relations, ideals, values, and thus analyses, because this awareness brings attention to the blind spots and/or instrumental pragmatism (opportunism) created by the privileges of unfair systems and unearned advantages (Collins 2004; hooks 2004; McIntosh 1997). For instance, some *norteña/o* youth comment on how they are put down in their homeland for not being "Mexican" enough, but it is important to recognize who has power and benefits there. In the Xaripu case, it was not the non-migrants but the transnational families. Those in between conflicting interests (race, class, gender, and nation) can serve social justice and maximize objectivity if their analysis begins from the standpoint and interests of those at the bottom and if they pursue projects that narrow the gap in wealth, power, and prestige differences rather than reconfigure social hierarchies in their favor. This task is the challenge. Historically, social justice has been advanced by those at the margins of power, because insights of human rights arise from that position that intimately understands oppression as unnatural and unacceptable (King [1963] 2003).[22] The quality of *convivencia* with the marginalized, therefore, is indicative of how immersed or removed one is from an objective understanding of their experiences and also from informing social justice.

The hope for justice lies not necessarily with new *nepantlas* or a universal melting pot, but rather with the ideals and practices that embrace human differences and that advance egalitarian, democratic, and ethical social relations at work, community, and family across borders. Although the movement for justice has come from the margins, the emergent *nepantla*(s) can contribute in dismantling vertical social relationships based on unearned privileges and domination. Xaripus' transnationalism reveals a strategy for reclaiming a fuller humanity and empowerment: the right to exist and to belong to a community as human beings of equal worth. Their movement across the border affirms their relations and heritage with those in Michoacán. However, the global inequalities—which are preserved by national borders—stratify and divide them within the nation and across nations.[23] While there is a desire for community among transnational and non-migrant Xaripus, systemic global inequities complicate it. In the twenty-first century Xaripu empowerment rests on *un mundo sin fronteras* (a world without borders) that allows diverse people to relate with mutuality, equality, and respect.

APPENDIX

Figure 1 Theatrum Orbis Terrarum

Xaripu ("Xaouripo" on the map) appears in Abraham Ortelio's 1579 map of New Spain. Below Chapala Lake, Xaripu appears slightly southeast of Xiquilpa and southwest of Xacona (two more noticeable points on the map).

223

Table 2.1 Background Information of Participants in California

	Name	Birth Year	Birthplace	Education	Marital Status	Work	Migration
1	Olivia	1960	Xaripu	14	married	service	infrequent
2	Julia	1968	Xaripu	12	married	service	frequent
3	Anita	1968	Xaripu	8	married	factory	frequent
4	Cecilia	1969	Xaripu	12	married	agriculture	frequent
5	Delia	1972	Aguas	6	married	agriculture	frequent
6	Martina	1972	Xaripu	16	married	service	infrequent
7	Rosalía	1974	Stockton	18	married	service	somewhat
8	Tita	1974	Stockton	18	single	service	infrequent
9	Valencia	1975	Stockton	16	single	service	frequent
10	Lucina	1976	Stockton	12	single	service	frequent
11	Elias	1962	Xaripu	12	single	factory	infrequent
12	Alberto	1968	Xaripu	12	married	factory	somewhat
13	Margarita	1910	Xaripu	5	widow	retired	frequent
14	Carolina	1925	Xaripu	3	married	homemaker	frequent
15	Nena	1925	Xaripu	0	married	homemaker	frequent
16	Paz	1928	Xaripu	4	married	homemaker	frequent
17	Ana	1937	Xaripu	4	married	homemaker	frequent
18	Martha	1940	Xaripu	5	separated	agriculture	somewhat
19	María	1941	Xaripu	5	married	agriculture	infrequent
20	Lupe	1941	Xaripu	5	married	agriculture	frequent
21	Cristina	1943	Xaripu	7	married	homemaker	somewhat
22	Luis	1923	Xaripu	0	married	agriculture	frequent
23	Armando	1923	Xaripu	2	married	retired	frequent
24	Alejandro	1924	Xaripu	0	married	agriculture	frequent
25	Raul	1932	Xaripu	4	married	agriculture	frequent
26	Juan	1934	Xaripu	2	married	agriculture	frequent
27	Gregorio	1939	Xaripu	3	married	agriculture	infrequent
28	Lionel	1943	Jalisco	5	married	agriculture	infrequent
29	Danilo	1947	Xaripu	14	single	retired/but	frequent
30	Luis	1956	Xaripu	8	married	agriculture	frequent

Education: number of years completed in school

Migration: refers to the frequency of movement across borders as "frequent" (at least once every one to three years), "somewhat" [frequent] (once every four to six years), and "infrequent" (every seven or more years)

Table 2.2   Background Information of Participants in Michoacán

	Name	Birth Year	Birthplace	Education	Marital Status	Work	Migration
1	Nico	1951	Xaripu	18	single	teacher	frequent
2	Fidel	1935	Xaripu	0	separated	retired	frequent
3	Angelica	1981	Xaripu	10	single	unemployed	never
4	Chana	1960	Xaripu	10	single	unemployed	never
5	Miranda	1962	Xaripu	10	married	commerce	never
6	Alondra	1964	Pachuca	16	married	teacher	never
7	Lorena	1967	Xaripu	14	single	notary	never
8	Conchita	1976	Xaripu	10	single	unemployed	never
9	Blanca	1977	Xaripu	10	single	unemployed	never
10	Paula	1979	Xaripu	10	single	unemployed	never
11	Samuel	1956	Xaripu	20	married	doctor	never
12	Alfredo	1964	Zacapu	16	married	teacher	never
13	Jesus	1971	Xaripu	10	married	butcher	frequent
14	Antoñio	1979	Tecolote	12	single	unemployed	never
15	Leopoldo	1980	Tarimoro	10	single	construction	never
16	Nadia	1914	Xaripu	2	widow	homemaker	never
17	Gloria	1929	Xaripu	0	widow	commerce	never
18	Consuelo	1931	Xaripu	0	married	commerce	never
19	Rita	1941	Xaripu	5	single	commerce	never
20	Rosa	1949	Xaripu	6	married	commerce	never
21	Marcos	1927	Cancun	0	retired	agriculture	somewhat
22	Victor	1943	Xaripu	3	married	commerce	never
23	Valentin	1947	Xaripu	2	married	agriculture	never
24	Felipe	1947	Xaripu	12	single	unemployed	never
25	Modesta	1895	Xaripu	0	widow	homemaker	never

Education: number of years completed in school

Migration: refers to the frequency of movement across borders as "frequent" (at least once every one to three years), "somewhat" [frequent] (once every four to six years), "infrequent" (every seven or more years), and "never" (never migrated)

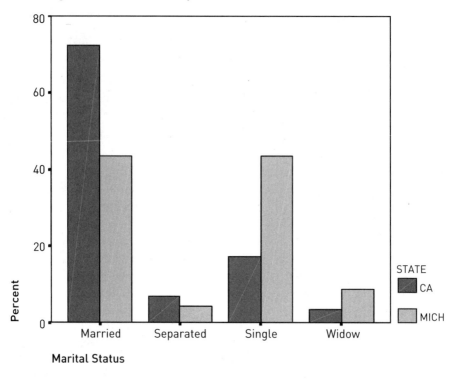

Figure 2   Marital Status by State

Table 4.1   Family Farmwork Piece-Unit Productivity: Summers 1978, 1980, and 1981

	Crop	Pay by piece	Papá	Mamá	Sylvia	Luis	Jorge	Total $
06-JUL-78	tomato	.35	80	78	0	74	76	107.80
07-JUL-78	tomato	0.35	80	78	68	80	84	136.50
08-JUL-78	none	.00	0	0	0	0	0	.00
09-JUL-78	none	.00	0	0	0	0	0	.00
10-JUL-78	cucumber	.60	42	0	48	46	54	114.00
11-JUL-78	tomato	.35	54	0	44	54	56	72.80
12-JUL-78	tomato	.35	94	88	64	98	100	155.40
13-JUL-78	tomato	.35	62	68	54	62	70	110.60

Table 4.1 continued

	Crop	Pay by piece	Papá	Mamá	Sylvia	Luis	Jorge	Total $
14-JUL-78	tomato	.35	58	60	0	58	60	82.60
15-JUL-78	tomato	.35	68	68	0	70	72	97.30
16-JUL-78	none	.00	0	0	0	0	0	.00
17-JUL-78	tomato	.35	92	82	0	92	92	125.30
18-JUL-78	tomato	.35	118	108	0	108	108	154.70
19-JUL-78	tomato	.35	100	92	68	80	0	119.00
20-JUL-78	tomato	.35	124	100	98	106	0	149.80
21-JUL-78	tomato	.35	86	0	74	86	94	119.00
22-JUL-78	tomato	.35	50	0	46	54	0	52.50
23-JUL-78	none	.00	0	0	0	0	0	.00
24-JUL-78	tomato	.35	80	78	0	70	78	107.10
25-JUL-78	tomato	.35	66	66	54	26	68	98.00
26-JUL-78	tomato	.35	80	84	72	0	88	113.40
27-JUL-78	tomato	.35	100	86	76	88	92	154.70
28-JUL-78	tomato	.35	88	84	48	84	92	138.60
29-JUL-78	tomato	.35	12	0	0	24	0	12.60
30-JUL-78	none	.00	0	0	0	0	0	.00
31-JUL-78	tomato	.35	64	54	0	58	58	81.90
01-AUG-78	cucumber	.60	62	0	64	70	76	163.20
02-AUG-78	cucumber	.60	44	0	50	52	62	124.80
03-AUG-78	cucumber	.60	50	0	50	52	60	127.20
04-AUG-78	cucumber	.60	28	0	44	36	44	91.20
05-AUG-78	none	.00	0	0	0	0	0	.00
06-AUG-78	none	.00	0	0	0	0	0	.00
07-AUG-78	cucumber	.60	74	0	72	72	94	187.20
08-AUG-78	cucumber	.60	72	0	70	74	82	178.80
09-AUG-78	cucumber	.60	50	0	50	54	60	128.40
10-AUG-78	cucumber	.60	32	0	38	34	44	88.80
11-AUG-78	cucumber	.60	32	0	40	34	42	88.80
12-AUG-78	cucumber	.60	36	0	36	38	42	91.20
13-AUG-78	none	.00	0	0	0	0	0	.00
14-AUG-78	tomato	.35	70	72	0	72	80	102.90
15-AUG-78	tomato	.35	60	64	0	0	66	66.50
16-AUG-78	tomato	.35	48	42	0	40	44	60.90
17-AUG-78	cucumber	.60	30	0	34	34	44	85.20
18-AUG-78	cucumber	.60	40	0	54	38	44	105.60
20-AUG-78	none	.00	0	0	0	0	0	.00

Table 4.1   continued

	Crop	Pay by piece	Papá	Mamá	Sylvia	Luis	Jorge	Total $
22-AUG-78	red tomato	.30	54	72	0	60	66	75.60
23-AUG-78	red tomato	.30	54	48	0	54	48	61.20
24-AUG-78	red tomato	.30	34	0	34	44	44	46.80
25-AUG-78	red tomato	.30	0	0	0	0	0	.00
26-AUG-78	red tomato	.30	47	0	47	50	54	59.40
27-AUG-78	none	.00	0	0	0	0	0	.00
28-AUG-78	tomato	.35	84	86	0	90	90	122.50
29-AUG-78	tomato	.35	95	95	0	96	90	131.60
30-AUG-78	tomato	.35	82	70	62	76	80	129.50
31-AUG-78	tomato	.35	84	84	70	70	78	135.10
01-SEP-78	cucumber	.60	28	0	34	0	46	64.80
02-SEP-78	cucumber	.60	50	0	0	0	0	30.00
03-SEP-78	none	.00	0	0	0	0	0	.00
08-JUL-80	tomato	.35	72	78	0	84	98	116.20
09-JUL-80	tomato	.35	60	68	0	50	70	86.80
15-JUL-80	tomato	.35	88	92	0	82	94	124.60
16-JUL-80	tomato	.35	86	94	0	84	104	128.80
17-JUL-80	tomato	.35	102	92	0	78	94	128.10
18-JUL-80	cucumber	.60	54	0	0	54	72	108.00
19-JUL-80	cucumber	.60	64	0	0	68	0	79.20
21-JUL-80	tomato	.35	126	120	0	120	130	173.60
22-JUL-80	tomato	.35	108	104	0	96	108	145.60
23-JUL-80	tomato	.35	60	60	0	58	70	86.80
24-JUL-80	tomato	.35	100	0	0	92	104	103.60
26-JUL-80	tomato	.35	68	0	56	76	82	98.70
28-JUL-80	tomato	.35	110	114	0	118	156	174.30
29-JUL-80	tomato	.35	98	94	0	86	108	135.10
30-JUL-80	tomato	.35	100	100	0	92	108	140.00
31-JUL-80	tomato	.35	70	68	0	66	80	99.40
01-AUG-80	tomato	.35	0	54	40	54	60	72.80
04-AUG-80	tomato	.35	0	120	0	102	134	124.60
05-AUG-80	tomato	.35	0	108	0	105	133	121.10
06-AUG-80	tomato	.35	0	136	0	130	164	150.50
07-AUG-80	tomato	.35	0	132	0	132	154	146.30
08-AUG-80	tomato	.35	0	146	0	134	166	156.10
09-AUG-80	tomato	.35	0	88	76	80	96	119.00
11-AUG-80	tomato	.35	0	100	0	84	100	99.40

Table 4.1 continued

	Crop	Pay by piece	Papá	Mamá	Sylvia	Luis	Jorge	Total $
12-AUG-80	tomato	.35	54	54	0	42	60	73.50
14-AUG-80	cucumber	.60	42	0	0	30	36	64.80
16-AUG-80	cucumber	.60	60	0	0	42	48	90.00
18-AUG-80	cucumber	.60	58	0	0	42	50	90.00
19-AUG-80	tomato	.35	76	68	0	64	80	100.80
20-AUG-80	tomato	.35	70	74	0	66	76	100.10
22-AUG-80	tomato	.35	78	78	0	76	98	115.50
24-AUG-80	tomato	.35	72	0	0	102	108	98.70
26-AUG-80	tomato	.35	110	96	0	90	128	148.40
28-AUG-80	tomato	.35	56	0	0	62	76	67.90
29-AUG-80	tomato	.35	40	0	0	44	50	46.90
02-SEP-80	tomato	.35	74	0	0	66	90	80.50
03-SEP-80	tomato	.35	58	0	0	66	80	71.40
04-SEP-80	tomato	.35	62	0	0	60	78	70.00
05-SEP-80	cucumber	.60	19	0	0	20	24	37.80
08-SEP-80	tomato	.35	65	73	0	67	85	101.50
09-SEP-80	tomato	.35	73	72	0	0	88	81.55
06-JUL-81	tomato	.35	31	35	27	54	62	73.15
07-JUL-81	tomato	.35	80	40	35	82	90	114.45
08-JUL-81	tomato	.35	54	30	27	118	132	126.35
09-JUL-81	tomato	.35	48	26	21	122	152	129.15
10-JUL-81	tomato	.35	104	48	43	124	146	162.75
11-JUL-81	tomato	.35	82	41	37	98	106	127.40
13-JUL-81	tomato	.35	126	0	60	142	154	168.70
14-JUL-81	tomato	.35	112	55	50	154	172	190.05
15-JUL-81	tomato	.35	108	58	51	190	200	212.45
16-JUL-81	tomato	.35	104	45	35	170	210	197.40
17-JUL-81	tomato	.35	46	23	0	70	74	74.55
20-JUL-81	tomato	.35	48	25	21	138	162	137.90
21-JUL-81	tomato	.35	82	41	38	128	150	153.65
22-JUL-81	tomato	.35	100	104	92	96	118	178.50
23-JUL-81	tomato	.35	108	108	90	98	144	191.80
24-JUL-81	tomato	.35	76	84	76	74	96	142.10
27-JUL-81	tomato	.35	78	80	80	178	200	215.60
28-JUL-81	tomato	.35	96	108	100	140	158	210.70
29-JUL-81	tomato	.35	120	116	102	144	170	228.20
30-JUL-81	tomato	.35	92	100	100	120	140	193.20

Table 4.1   continued

Crop	Pay by piece	Papá	Mamá	Sylvia	Luis	Jorge	Total $
04-AUG-81 red tomato	.30	0	35	0	74	0	32.70
05-AUG-81 red tomato	.30	0	0	0	72	86	47.40
06-AUG-81 red tomato	.30	0	0	0	112	117	68.70
07-AUG-81 red tomato	.30	0	0	0	26	44	21.00
08-AUG-81 cucumber	.60	45	0	0	0	0	27.00
09-AUG-81 cucumber	.60	0	0	35	61	35	78.60
10-AUG-81 tomato	.35	0	0	0	110	126	82.60
11-AUG-81 cucumber	.60	55	0	31	0	0	51.60
12-AUG-81 tomato	.35	0	0	0	80	96	61.60
13-AUG-81 tomato	.35	0	0	0	114	136	87.50
14-AUG-81 tomato	.35	0	0	0	132	156	100.80
17-AUG-81 tomato	.35	98	100	0	78	94	129.50
18-AUG-81 tomato	.35	36	0	0	30	36	35.70
21-AUG-81 tomato	.35	70	70	0	32	36	72.80
22-AUG-81 cucumber	.60	40	0	27	32	37	81.60
24-AUG-81 tomato	.35	69	92	0	74	84	111.65
26-AUG-81 cucumber	.60	0	0	30	0	0	18.00
tomato	.35	0	0	0	61	57	41.30
27-AUG-81 cucumber	.60	58	0	0	0	0	34.80
tomato	.35	0	0	0	70	74	50.40
28-AUG-81 cucumber	.60	36	0	23	28	35	73.20
31-AUG-81 tomato	.35	92	124	116	82	100	179.90
01-SEP-81 tomato	.35	96	100	82	118	146	189.70
02-SEP-81 tomato	.35	100	102	62	100	104	163.80
03-SEP-81 tomato	.35	120	126	0	128	150	183.40
04-SEP-81 tomato	.35	134	132	0	128	150	190.40
05-SEP-81 tomato	.35	106	0	106	94	174	168.00
07-SEP-81 red tomato	.30	154	0	124	0	0	83.40
tomato	.35	0	0	0	116	132	86.80

Numbers under individual names indicate number of piece-units picked per person each day.

These field notes and data were gathered by Jorge Barajas (the author's brother).

Table 4.2 Total Family Earnings for Farmwork: Summers 1978, 1980, and 1981

		Papá	*Mamá*	*Sylvia*	*Luis*	*Jorge*	*Total Family $*
N	Total days	154	154	154	154	154	154
Mean		21.8214	15.1769	9.8247	25.4153	29.2523	101.4906
Median		24.5000	13.1250	7.525	25.9000	29.4000	100.4500
Sum		3360.50	2337.25	1513.00	3913.95	4504.85	15,629.55

Numbers under individual names indicate number of piece-units picked per person each day.

These data were derived from Jorge Barajas's field notes.

Figure 4 Family's Farmwork Concentration: Summers 1978, 1980, and 1981

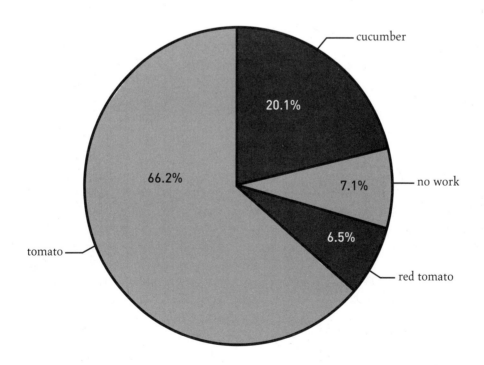

NOTES

1. Introduction

1. See Ngai 2004 and Zolberg 2006, who document how immigration policies were used to construct and privilege a White nation.

2. Employer sanctions—first introduced in the Immigration Reform and Control Act of 1986—are likely to continue being unenforced. Less than one-fifth of 1 percent of the employer violations were inspected.

3. The Naturalization Act of 1790 excluded nonwhites from citizenship, and the Alien and Sedition Act of 1798 extended the abilities of the state to deport perceived national threats and complicated the naturalization process for non-Protestant Europeans. The 1864 Immigration Act and the Homestead Act of 1862 encouraged European immigrants to populate the west and to claim land for small family farming, while the Immigration Act of 1924 reasserted race-based (via national-origin) immigration quotas privileging northern Europeans, while excluding other populations. Filipinos and Mexicans were exempted and imported as colonial labor, experiencing occupational segregation, class segmentation, and dual wages. "Colonial labor" refers to racialized minorities from within or outside the nation who experienced formal or legal mistreatment based on race and nation in terms of access to social resources, jobs, housing, legal rights, education, and political representation.

4. Levitt and Waters 2002 and Smith and Guarnizo 2003 include excellent transnational community studies.

5. Scholars' sampling approach partly explains this situation. Researchers, as outsiders, have easier access to migrants in the receiving society, where information of the sending communities is obtained. During a researcher's visit to sending communities, migrants often facilitate other interview contacts through snowball sampling, which affects the content of the interviews.

6. "Colonialism" is commonly used to refer to the European colonialism of the Americas, in which a violent conquest of people, land, and resources was

undertaken for several centuries to the benefit of European kingdoms (this concept is elaborated in chapter 2). In line with an abundant body of historical and sociological literature (see Blauner 1972; Almaguer 1971; and Barrera 1979), I argue that colonial domination continued after the independence of externally colonized territories, creating new forms of colonial relations between newly developed nations (neocolonialism) and within nations (internal colonialism) and sometimes overlapping ones (a subordinated nation with internal colonies—as in the cases of many Indo [Latin] American nations). These colonialisms have affected the experiences of modern labor migrants.

7. The colonial model marks the initial labor migration of Indigenous people to their dislocation by European colonizers (Bonfil Batalla 1987, 1996), and in the Southwest additional displacements were experienced after Anglo conquest (Barrera 1979; Mirandé 1985), converting feudal peasants into migrant agricultural workers (Montejano 1987; Glenn 2002). In addition, the colonial model stresses the continued imbalance in relationships between descendants of the colonized and colonizers, which affects their economic opportunities and social integration (Blauner 1972).

8. This chapter demonstrates how, although these perspectives advance the understanding of migration, they are not without limitations. Specifically, structural and transnational views unwittingly reduce complex historical processes to a single dimension. Structural analyses underscore imperialism, or monopoly capitalism, as the central factor stimulating labor migration; while capitalism is an important factor, prioritizing it relegates to secondary importance the structural dimensions of patriarchy and racism in the labor migration experience. Moreover, it tends to treat global regions as socially homogenous. Transnational perspectives, on the other hand, emphasize that social networks are the primary shaper of modern international migration and argue that, after the initial structural cause of mass migration has passed, migration is maintained through social relationships across borders. This emphasis overshadows the continued significance of global inequality and of its central role in the labor migration experience.

9. Braudel conceptualizes the *longue durée* as a historical perspective that privileges "the very long time span" and trends rather than brief, dramatic, individual events. For example, instead of focusing on key individuals and a brief period of the US-Mexican War (1846–48), the *longue durée* approach examines several centuries of European colonial expansionism from the East to the West.

10. See Crenshaw 1997; Glenn 2002; Collins 2003. Intersecting or integrated systems of oppression have been elaborated by all these scholars as they examine how various systems of oppression relate to each other.

11. Bonacich and Appelbaum (2000, 20, 140–42, 290–91) elaborate on the concept of the "middleman minority," who play an opportunistic role between workers and manufacturers/retailers: they focus on how different racial/ethnic groups occupy different social/class locations (e.g., Whites at the top, Asians in the middle, and Mexicans at the bottom). In my application, I further focus on emergent middlemen from within those at the bottom, middle, and top.

12. "Mestiza/o" is used to refer to a hybridity of different ethnicities/races, though it traditionally refers to the offspring of Indigenous people and Europeans.

13. "Criollos" refers to Europeans born in America.

14. The Bracero Program was a US guest-worker program with Mexico that imported Mexican workers to work in agriculture and railroads for seasonal periods (see McWilliams 1990; Galarza 1964).

15. The deterioration of labor conditions occurs when Mexicans become a majority of the workforce. This process is significantly a racist process, intensifying capitalistic exploitation (see chapter 4).

16. *Norteña/o* is used to refer to Xaripus who reside in the United States. Most *norteñas/os* in my study were transnational.

17. The 2000 *XII Censo de Población y Vivienda* (a regional census) registered 641 people living in Xaripu; Fonseca and Moreno (1984) took a census of Xaripus living in Stockton in the early 1980s, and counted about the same number (624). I conservatively estimate that from natural growth and migration the Xaripu community in Stockton has more than doubled since the early 1980s. The majority of households I interviewed had added two to three new members since then.

18. The critique falls more severely on young women, who are perceived as more liberal than those in Michoacán. However, what the non-migrants do not see is that this "liberation" occurs primarily in the hometown, while in California the *norteña/o* experiences with spatial/social mobility are more restricted. *Norteño* working-class wages typically do not stretch as far as in Michoacán, so the outings and parties become more limited in California and not an everyday thing like in Michoacán.

19. Transnational migrants are materially and politically more empowered than non-migrants because they have the freedom to cross the border as documented residents or citizens of the United States. Moreover, many are bilingual, and in a context of national inequalities English is perceived by non-migrants as a language that is used to assert superiority, which carries a different and greater social distance and resentment than toward the urbanized co-nationals in Mexico (see chapter 5).

20. Cohorts are used as ideal type categories that provide general characteristics. These categories, however, are not all-encompassing. Although the category of *retiradas/os* implies migrants who have the longest migration experience and have experienced more diversified types of work in the United States, in a few cases *mayores* may have the longer experience and the more diverse work experience. Nonetheless, the cohort category does convey the general characteristics of the various age groups and the unique historical events that shaped their lives.

21. The first Xaripu international migrants came immediately at the turn of twentieth century. Most of these first international migrants have passed away, but Mexican anthropologists Fonseca and Moreno (1984) were able to interview some. Oral history traditions were very common with this generation, particularly because many did not go to school. I was privileged to have been exposed to their experiences through my grandfather, Elias Barajas (1900–91), and great-uncles. Moreover, their children (now *retiradas/os* and *mayores*) have been able to share their parents' oral histories.

22. These *retiradas/os* followed an earlier wave of Xaripus who migrated to *el norte* prior to and during the first Mexican guest-worker program between 1917 and 1921 (see also Fonseca and Moreno 1988; Torres 1998, 171–72).

23. Labor migrants come to the United States primarily to work, and they consider Mexico their home. Xaripus were labor migrants during the Bracero Period, and after the program ended, their migration included their families, beginning a settlement process in the United States.

24. Transnational migrants entail the following characteristics: (1) having a dual-home base in two nation-states, (2) having physical, mental, and/or emotional connections with both regions, and (3) making these material, cultural, and emotional relations constant and active across the border. All these conditions generally apply more to the older generations (ages fifty and over) than to the younger ones (ages forty-nine and under). Members of the two older cohorts were more frequent visitors than members of the two younger cohorts: twelve of seventeen compared to seven of thirteen. They had the same number of somewhat frequent visitors (two from each group), and only three members of the two older cohorts were infrequent visitors as compared to four members of the younger groups.

25. In the late 1960s, one medical doctor made two weekly visits of one hour each, and a dentist visited three times a week. The most frequent illnesses documented were parasites, gastrointestinal infections, respiratory infections (e.g., colds and pharynx-tonsilitis), pneumonia and bronchopneumonia, tuberculosis, measles, chicken pox, German measles, scarlet fever, and diphtheria.

26. See Grasmuck and Pessar 1991, 102–4. The authors discuss that Dominican families with land grants were not able to support themselves with the lands over time, because the division of land among children made the allocations smaller and smaller. Thus, male children were forced to migrate to make a living. Likewise, the few Xaripus who obtained *ejido* land were never really able to make a living off it, and their children had little land to work with.

27. In an effort to regulate the movement of migrants dislocated as a result of global capitalism, the Immigration Reform and Control Act was enacted in 1986. Prior to 1986 *cuadrillas* (field work teams) in the cucumber fields had numbered thirty to forty workers on each side of a field, and after IRCA over fifty workers on each side were allowed to work. (I grew up doing this work from ages four to twenty, so these trends were very evident to me and all of the participants in my study.) Farm workers had to walk further distances carrying heavy buckets (from twenty-five yards to about forty yards); the trucks were loaded more quickly, and the wait for trucks to arrive was longer; the number of work hours declined from about eight to six; wages declined from about twenty-five dollars a day to under twenty dollars a day. Overall labor conditions declined (see chapter 4).

28. While there are younger Xaripus who display a more substantive transnationalism, I underscore the general patterns in my sample.

29. She was newly pregnant at the time and learned shortly before her baby was due that she had received a perfect score on her application exam.

30. This car trek was long, fatiguing, and extremely dangerous, particularly in the passages of La Romorosa and Plan Barrancas, which have narrow passes through high mountain cliffs. Entire migrant families have died on their way to Mexico.

31. By "meaning" I am referring to the changing view of Xaripu: from considering it a primary home to seeing it as a vacationing homeland, particularly for the younger cohorts.

32. Warren (1985) documents the Purépechas' linkage to Zuñi Indians in New Mexico.

2. Theoretical Perspectives on Labor Migration

1. Fonseca and Moreno, two Mexican anthropologists, based their book on their binational ethnographic study of "Jaripas/os" (Xaripus) across borders. They interviewed some of the first Xaripu migrants to the United States, including some of my grandparents and great uncles, who were in their eighties at the time.

2. Transnational social ties are relations across borders with family members and friends as well as economic interests (land, home, employment), political involvement (lobbyist, voter, activist), and emotional or symbolic affinities with the homeland.

3. See Lenin 1950, 89. He defined imperialism as the monopoly stage of capitalism: "Imperialism is capitalism in that stage of development in which the dominance of monopolies and finance capital has established itself; in which the export of capital has acquired pronounced importance; in which the division of the world among the international trusts has begun; in which the division of all territories of the globe among the great capitalist powers has been completed."

4. See Portes and Rumbaut 1996, 272–76. They use "structural imbalancing" to point to a history of political-economic and military interventions that shaped the economy and labor of colonized nations for the benefit of the colonizing one, which also dislocates labor migrants and incorporates them into its developing economy. I instead use the term "global sharecropping" because it provides clear images of the imposed "imbalanced" relationship between the colonizing nation and the colonized one and of all the related disadvantages to the marginalized nations, including debt, super-exploitation, and poverty.

5. Ngai (2004) elaborates that though the national origin quotas exempted Mexicans from the restrictive immigration act, the law nonetheless created the concept of "illegality," which became primarily applied to Mexican migration, irrespective of individual immigration status.

6. See Gonzalez and Fernandez 2003; Sassen 2003. SAP augments debts in developing countries, disrupts local economies, orients production for export, and cuts public services. It creates the conditions for migration and facilitates cross-border movement through the infrastructure created by foreign "investors."

7. Some structural theories (dependency and world systems) focus on unequal exchanges that maintain the historical inequities and global division of labor between nations. Others (such as articulation theory) consider how capitalism subordinated and integrated diverse modes of production (tributary system, slavery, debt peonage, etc.) into a global economic system through wage labor, appropriation of surplus value, and labor exploitation.

8. Ngai provides an excellent discussion of a devaluation of Filipino workers not based on supply and demand principles or the workers' willingness to work for less, but rather through the racism of employers.

9. The United States historically has enacted immigration laws and policies that favor Northern Europeans (Whites) and exclude or integrate others as unequal members of the nation. These laws include the Naturalization Act of 1790, Chinese Exclusion Acts of 1882 and 1892, Alien Act of 1913, Immigration Acts of 1921 and 1924, Bracero Program 1942–64, Operation Gatekeeper 1994, Pa-

triot Act of 2001, and HR 4437 (Sensenbrenner House Bill) in 2005. These and other nation-state political acts reproduce racial, gender, and class hierarchies within the nation.

10. Although scholarship has focused mostly on migrants and their communities, transnationalism also includes the cross-border movement/networks of capitalists and their corporations. Their transnational agency has been elaborated by Gonzalez and Fernandez's agents of empire (2003), Sassen's administrators of global cities (2003), and Robinson's transnational capitalists (2003).

11. I place the transnational perspective within the general theoretical framework of interactionism for several reasons. Social ties, networks, and circuits are constructs of the former framework, and these ties can only exist through social interaction, including shared symbols and meanings. For instance, Rumbaut (2002, 81–82) finds that adult children of immigrants' use of language (including their preferences and proficiency) is a significant predictor of their level of transnationalism. The interactionist perspective elaborates how networks across borders facilitate migration and re-create notions of community that may transcend the nation.

12. Patriarchy shapes the networks that influence migration and settlement opportunities for women, whereby they rely on women's networks to immigrate and settle (Hondagneu-Sotelo 1994, 121, 136, 138; Hagan 1994, 107–8; Menjívar 2000, 159–64). Women's access to social networks is determined by their limited opportunities to generate income and the cultural prescriptions that regulate their relationships with nonrelative males (Hagan 1994, 60–68). Furthermore, a patriarchal context of reception creates greater opportunities for males, giving them "good bargaining chips in exchanges" with their female co-nationals such as ownership of cars, discretionary income, and legal documents (Menjívar 2000, 162–63; see also Sarmiento 2002, 160). Women's unequal access to power and resources within their community encourages some to seek "a wider variety of resources" outside of it (Menjívar 2000, 164, 171), while others remain restricted to fewer resources and information (Hagan 1994, 68, 119–20).

13. Sarmiento also found that Tzintzuntzeño families had interdependent survival strategies, in which women's work in Michoacán provided a safety net for migrant men in seasonal and low-paid work in the United States (2002, 80–82).

14. Both the economic contributions of older children and the family's stable employment facilitated settlement.

15. In the Xaripu case study, non-migrants in Michoacán, particularly the youth, generally underscored the desire to emigrate as a way to increase their labor value.

16. See also Glick-Schiller et al. 1992a, 1; Levitt 2001, 197.

17. For example, colonial history is indicative of how migrants are incorporated into the receiving society: with or without political rights, labor opportunities, cultural citizenship, etc. While Xaripus began migrating in the early 1900s, it was after two-thirds of a century that women and children joined the migration experience to the United States. Whereas a structural perspective appropriately identifies political-economic factors displacing Indigenous communities from central Mexico and later recruiting them as workers to the United States and whereas a transnational perspective highlights the significance of social networks in facilitating/gendering their migration, neither of these perspectives alone explains why Indigenous Mexican communities differ from Northern and Eastern European migration that began about the same time but quickly settled in the United States.

18. While patriarchy was not particular to Europe, colonialism universalized it in the conquered areas and among the colonizers. Espiritu (2003b, 50–55) elaborates that colonialism was not only an economic project of domination but also racial and gender projects that constructed some as masculine and rational civilizers and others as dependent and unfit for self-governance. Pollard (1993, 178–79) notes that the gendered division of labor and of religious/political leadership roles was not as rigid among Purépechans in Michoacán as it came to be.

19. For an exception to resistance see Grosfoguel 2003a, 356–58. Grosfoguel adds complexity, noting that Puerto Rico experiences "modern colonialism" under the United States. Because of US geopolitical interests, Puerto Ricans have experienced a better quality of life than other Caribbean nations—Haiti and Dominican Republic—that have achieved national independence. These nations, Grosfoguel argues, remain neocolonized by imperial powers but do not receive any imperial benefits (e.g., social security, welfare, federal aid, labor rights), which Puerto Ricans do. Hence, Puerto Ricans in general engage in "subversive complicity," remaining attached to the United States to enjoy these benefits and avoid the great costs that other neocolonized nations endure.

20. Neocolonialism also refers to the domination of a nation by controlling its political-economy without having to invade it in a comprehensive way (i.e., militarily), as in classical colonialism.

21. I use "Indo America" instead of "Latin America" as a way of recognizing the continued existence and influence of Indigenous people in the Americas. In my view the use of "Latin America" privileges only the contributions and influences of Latin European nations in the American continents and neglects those of the Indigenous.

22. Grosfoguel argues that maintaining a modern colony like Puerto Rico is more costly for the United States than relating to it as a neocolonizer and

taking wealth without any responsibilities to it. This choice of domination— neocolonialism over colonialism—was also possibly conditioned by the costly U.S. Civil War in the 1860s.

23. The internally colonized were reduced to a numeric minority through racist violence, labor exploitation, and migration policies.

24. See Cervantez 2003, 336, 339–49. For example, Cervantez contends that colonized territories, having incorporated as states and experienced a change in "the social relations of production," transition to a postcolonial status. Therefore, Chicanas/os should not be considered as internally colonized given that they were incorporated into the state and wage labor. See San Juan 1998 for an extensive critique of the postcolonial concept.

25. Blauner asserts, "The colonial order in the modern world has been based on the dominance of white Westerners over non-Western people of color; racial oppression and the racial conflict to which it gives rise are endemic to it, much as class exploitation and conflict are fundamental to capitalist societies" (1972, 12).

26. McIntosh illustrates the many parallel ways that racial and gender privileges offer unearned advantages and benefits to Whites and males, whether they are ever aware of it.

27. Lipsitz documents that minority experiences with historical exclusion of resources and unequal treatment have increased the wealth and status of Whites vis-à-vis people of color.

28. Natives went from being externally colonized by Spain to internally colonized by criollo/mestizo elites within the newly constructed nation.

29. Indigenous people and mestizas/os were internally colonized in the Southwest immediately after Mexican independence in 1821, and after the 1848 US conquest, they became part of a new internal colony that included the downwardly mobile criollos (Mirandé 1985; Menchaca 1995). "Mexicans" thus were differentiated by race, gender, culture, and class in both the Southwest and in Mexico (Pitt 1966; Meier and Ribera 1972; Camarillo 1979; Montejano 1987; Padilla 1993; Limón 1994; Menchaca 1995; Ochoa Serrano 1997; Moreno García 1994; Alvarez del Toro 1988; Lugo 1995; Bonfil Batalla 1996; Cockcroft 1998; Purnell 1999).

30. High rates of residential segregation of Blacks in the United States continue (Massey and Denton 1993; Yinger 1991), as do high rates of Mexican segregation (Camarillo 1979; Montejano 1987; Menchaca 1995; Fields and Herndon 2001).

31. After the Mexican Revolution (1910–17), Xaripus and many other Indigenous and mestizo people remained landless and exploited by the existing haciendas. Those monopolizing the land continued to be primarily of European descent and the more Hispanicized mestizos (see chapter 3).

32. For instance, I focus on how structural inequalities affect transnational migrants and non-migrants' relationships; whereby even though both identify with their pueblo, the fact that the former are transformed culturally in the United States and benefit from relative higher wages creates social distances between them and emergent stereotypes of each other (see chapter 5).

33. Domination is central to the analysis, because inequality of power does not necessarily translate into abuse and oppression, though it is an essential component.

34. See Almaguer 1994, 114–15. He elaborates how the Ohlone Indians from California in the mid-nineteenth century were egalitarian, nonmaterialistic, and spiritual. See also Zinn 1999, 5–6. Zinn quotes de las Casas's documentation that Natives did not place "a special value on gold and other precious things." The *Chronicles of Michoacán* also offers many examples of how materialism was not the dominant ideology among some Chichimecans and Purépechans.

35. Structural theories stress dialectical relations between empires and neo-colonies, between different modes of economic production, between nation-state and global capitalism, and so on. The transnational perspective also elaborates dialectical social ties between women and men, older and younger generations, and homeland and host cultures.

36. No structure can exist without a culture patterning behavior, and no ideology can exist without a structure reproducing it. More concretely, capitalism cannot exist without the ideologies of private property and utilitarianism, and those ideologies cannot exist without their reproduction by relevant institutions, such as government and education. The base and superstructure are two sides of the same coin.

37. Mead ([1934] 1962) conceptualized human beings as being interactive (with self, environment, and others), reflective (able to direct attention toward the past and future or any object—physical or abstract), communicative (verbally and nonverbally through significant symbols), creative (builders or constructors of their line of action) (see also Charon 1998; Blumer 1969; Meltzer et al. 1975). Also significant to Mead's perspective are the interrelated concepts of self, mind, and society, which are only possible through social interaction and ability to be reflective and interpretative.

38. See Limón 1994, 34–36, 71–74. He provides helpful illustrations of both dialectical and interactionist processes in his examination of three individuals whose race, class, and gender experiences shaped their standpoint views or points of view. In a context of dominant group influences (e.g., serving in the US military and/or attending a predominantly White male university), they often reflected an ambivalent "political unconscious" producing ideological inconsistencies (34–35). "Bourke" and "Dobie," both US soldiers of Irish origin, often

expressed racist and ethnocentric claims about Mexicans in south Texas, but at times they also displayed inconsistencies in the "element of political unconscious in textual abundance" (36). These tensions reveal contradictory experiences based on dialectical relationships and identifications. Though they were serving in the US military and advancing "Manifest Destiny," they could also identify with and admire the colonized subjects' abilities to survive and be creative, partly because of a shared historical experience with Anglo domination.

The third individual in Limón's study, Jovita Gonzalez, was from an elite Tejano family and was quick to distinguish her own class from the "half-breeds," Indigenous people, and *vaquero* hired hands. She also resented those who displaced *los ricos* (the rich), but she repressed her feelings within the White male–dominated University of Texas at Austin. Hence, much of her early literary work on Mexican folklore reproduces the ethnocentric views of her White colleagues at the university. Upon returning to south Texas, however, Jovita found more freedom of expression to write about characters such as *traga-balas* (bullet eater) that revealed courage and honor, something denied to Mexicans in her old academic setting (Limón 1994, 71–74). Yet this freedom of expression was not a full one. Limón notes that Jovita's "complete exclusion of women and her nearly exclusive devotion to the description of male experience" reveals "another kind of paradoxical and repressive position, this one keyed on gender politics" (74).

39. The idea of ethnic purity in the twenty-first century is very unlikely of any of the major racial constructs (Asian, Black, Native, and White) that have a long history in the Americas (see Piper 1997; Forbes 1982).

40. See Sarmiento 2002, 28. She makes similar observations.

3. A Social-Historical Context of Xaripu's Land Displacement and Labor Migration Experience

1. *Tarasco* is another term used to refer to Purépecha, though the latter is preferred by those who maintain their Indigenous heritage.

2. I was able to identify many of the last names of present Xaripus with long roots to the pueblo and was able to identify the newer names (from the twentieth century and on) in the pueblo. The church books are very old, with the oldest going back to 1797, and the print was not readable at times. I was fortunate, however, because Dr. Alvaro Ochoa Serrano, a historian at the Colegio de Michoacán, had a list he was able to produce himself.

I found my paternal last name "Barajas" and traced its long history in Xaripu and its classification with Indigenous heritage, while "Pulido," my maternal last name, first appears in the 1930s, and no racial/ethnic identity is reported at the time. (Racial identification in these church records was outlawed after the Mexican Independence, but it persisted into the late nineteenth century.) The physical appearance of my mother's side is more mestizo, though she recalls her father speaking Purépecha. Establishing the racial composition of Xaripus was not a goal of this study, but analyzing racial and ethnic heritage helps to trace the Xaripu pueblo identity and changes across time. Although not racially or ethnically "purely" Indigenous, Xaripus' collective memory and direct experience with Indigenous relatives and heritage root them in Xaripu and generally identify them as Xaripus. This identity is dominant and unusually manifest even among the second- and third-generation Xaripus in California.

3. See Romero Flores 1939, 24; Fonseca and Moreno 1984, 56–57. "Xaripu" means *alumbre* (aluminum sulfate), which also means enlightenment.

4. See maps in León-Portilla 1995, 63, 65.

5. See also De la Coruña 1539/1541, 204–6. While Purépechans spoke the language of the islanders of Pátzcuaro, they worshiped the Chichimecan sun god, Cueracuri; the Purépechan mother of all gods, Cuerauáperi; and the daughter goddess of fertility Xaratanga.

6. According to Warren, the *Codex Plancarte* (colonial record) also suggests that at one time the "Tarascan kingdom included a large part of northwestern Mexico and even extended as far as Zuñi, in New Mexico" (1985, 4).

7. See Purnell 1999, 30–31. She notes some general Purépecha traits in the second half of the nineteenth century: "The communal property regime, in which land was owned by the community as a whole, even as individual families held long-standing use rights; the offices (*cargos* or *mayordomías*) and confraternities (*cofradías*) through which religious practice was organized and financed; the hospital, with its own confraternity, generally dedicated to the Virgin of the Immaculate Conception; and the council of politico-religious elders, or *cabildo*" (30–31).

8. The words are translated as the following: large red ants, red dirt and/or water, green grasshopper, basket, a large grayish or brown bird with a loud whistle, round tamale, sweet tamale, dried up, like a turkey, mite-like insects, plot of land, sandal, a bird type, wrapped up in a small bundle, and a small, long banana-looking fruit from the maguey.

9. The relational images in the context of colonialism produced binary representations of "them and us," whereby "they" were savage, immoral, irrational, pagan, nonwhite, and "we" were civilized, moral, rational, Christian, and White.

10. Lee and Navarrete 1978, 124, 126. Although the first accounts of the Purépechans were documented in *The Chronicles of Michoacán* by De la Coruña

(1538/1539), Xaripus were not included in those chronicles. The first documentations of Xaripu were included in Friar Alonso Ponce's chronicles of his travels in Michoacán in 1585 and 1586.

11. The *encomienda* system consisted of Spanish administrators, usually generals, who managed land, resources, and labor for the Crown in Europe. While the *encomendados* were not owners, they prospered tremendously.

12. See also Cook and Simpson (1948, 47–48), who estimated that 80 percent of the Natives were killed, and later revised their calculations to 90 percent (Borah 1951; Cook and Borah 1960, 3, 50–56).

13. The Spanish texts generally use "mulatto" to refer to a person with Black and White heritage, but because it is an offensive term I replaced it with "mestiza/o," which is more commonly used to refer to the Indigenous-European mix. Thus, I refer to the various racial mixtures as *mestizaje*, though I specify which heritages are involved.

14. "Criollo" is used to refer to the Spanish who were born in the Americas, whereas *peninsulares* were those born in Spain.

15. Hidalgo is credited with beginning the independence movement in Mexico.

16. See also Keen 1994, 40; Cockcroft 1998, 25. Since the sixteenth century, criollo *encomendados* had considered breaking ties with Spain to end sharing their profits with the Crown. In 1565, they plotted to kill the viceroy and members of the royal *Audiencia*, and to appoint the son of Hernán Cortés, Marquéz Martín Cortés, as the monarch of a new independent Mexican kingdom.

17. Her only son, *el chino* (curly-haired one), became a bracero during the 1940s, and her grandchildren and great-grandchildren continue to maintain social ties across the borders. For years her son and his family lived the life of labor migrants, moving back and forth to the United States; Michoacán was their home and California a place to work. This orientation changed once Chino's family settled in Stockton. They now have two homes across the border from each other.

18. The exchange rate in 2007 was about ten pesos.

19. From Michoacán, they went to Irapuato, Guanajuato, and Guadalajara, Jalisco.

20. See Ochoa Serrano 1995, 15. Because of Díaz's devaluing of the Mexican peso in 1905, workers earned less than a peso a day, while they could earn at least twice as much in the United States.

21. See Fonseca and Moreno 1984, 90–91. They also documented that the landowning families were headed by Justo Acevedo, Wenceslao Rivas, and Benito Higadera. The last two families were related and left Xaripu around the time

of the Mexican Revolution, selling "their" land before they lost it to the Agrarian Reform. Only the Acevedos were affected by the land reform, and their land was used to form three *ejidos*.

22. In conversations with Elias Barajas Muratalla in 1990, Esther Pulido Carrillo in 1999, and Gilberto Acevedo Barajas in 2000, they recalled that their parents and/or grandparents had spoken the Purépecha language and followed other Indigenous traditions.

23. Marta Durán de Huerta describes how various Indigenous groups coalesced to form the Zapatistas, and highlights that one of the main cultural features that is shared is the collectivist orientation—in which the individual is obligated to help out the group (1994).

24. Interestingly, diverse ethnicities coming from Mexico in the early twentieth century, were classified as "Mexican" regardless if they were Purépecha, Huichol, Chichimec, etc. What marked them as such was their Indigenous appearance and the fact that they came from the southern border, since the Indigenous from within the United States were regarded as "Native American."

25. See Fonseca and Moreno 1984 and De Bernal 1969. Based on my own conversations and interviews, the Ines Garcia Chavez attack on San Antonio Guaracha is the only revolutionary conflict that Xaripu elders recall.

26. The following people were involved: José Muratalla (chief of the guard), Mariano Ruiz (sub-supervisor), Juan y Ramón Muratalla, Guillermo Manzo, Trinidad Larios, Rafael Orejel, Juan Torres, Julián Ceja, Gregorio Medina, Francisco Bautista, Florencio Chávez, Gregorio Alcántar, Juan Vega, Francisco Meza, and Jesus de Bernal (De Bernal 1969, 173–74).

27. The casualties included Mariano Ruiz, Ramon Muratalla, Trinidad Larios, Juan Vega, Julián Ceja, and Gregorio Alcántar.

28. See Purnell 1999. The state policy to secularize government and to reduce the power of the Church produced the Cristero Revolt (1926–29). This rebellion is thought to have influenced President Cárdenas into enforcing the land reform during his administration (1934–40), so as to gain the favor of the *agraristas* (land grantees) and reduce future rebellions.

29. For another view on the relation between land claims and migrant status, see López Castro 1986, 47. Unlike the Xaripu case, Castro noted that in Puentecillas (Michoacán) migrants were more likely to recognize *hacendados'* private property and thus not make land claims. My discussion on land distribution in Michoacán benefits from Fonseca and Moreno's research (1984).

30. Consequently, in 1929 the number of eligible men in Xaripu was reduced from 126 to 101.

31. See also De Bernal 1969. An early example of the evasion of the Agrarian Reform was when the *hacendado* Manuel F. Moreno transferred his Platanal

Hacienda to his son-in-law Alfonso Fernández Somellera in 1919, and success-fully evaded the *reparto's* demands of dividing large landholdings among the peasants. By transferring land to a son-in-law, the Moreno family secured the land concentration among close family friends and allies and thus was able to keep its northeast Michoacán haciendas: Guaracha, San Antonio Guaracha, and El Cerrito Pelón.

32. See Fonseca and Moreno 1984, 115. The lands given to Xaripus were La Liebrera, La Loma, La Presa (part of this was reduced because of flooded land), La Ortiga, La Raya, Las Viviendas, and La Palobera. Another formal request to am-plify the Xaripu *ejido* was made in May 1937. A census was taken, documenting 979 residents, 187 heads of households, and 281 qualified for *dotaciones*. From 1921 to 1925, Wenceslao Rivas, the affected proprietor, had acquired lands from Xaripu's neighboring communities. About 20 of his 333 acres were authorized to be given to Xaripus, from which six parcels would be made. President Lázaro Cárdenas approved this request on October 26, 1938, but in the final stage the *ejido* claims were denied by the agrarian authorities on December 20, 1945.

33. The physical and linguistic differences among the populations are appar-ent when visiting the surrounding communities of Xaripu. A large majority of the Xaripu community have marked Indigenous features and heritage. Com-munities inhabiting the lands of the former Hacienda Guaracha (San Antonio Guaracha and La Presa) have notable Black ancestry and traditions, while many of the family *ranchitos* on the neighboring hillsides (to Xaripu) have stronger European features and linguistics, as do pueblos without pre-Columbian roots. Generally, all these communities have interacted and experienced ethnic trans-formation, but even so there remains these kinds of distinctions among them.

34. These factors were obtained in interviews with seven braceros: three who came in 1942 and four who came in the 1950s.

35. They were the fathers and uncles of those in the second wave of guest workers (braceros), who came to the United States in the 1940s.

36. Before wives came to the United States, braceros attained legal residency for them. This legal status was a significant factor in deciding to bring their fa-mily to the United States. Seven bracero families in my study shared this migra-tion experience. See also Sarmiento 2002.

37. Her maternal grandfather and great-grandfather had migrated to the United States long before the Bracero Period, and her father followed this mi-gration in the late 1940s. Valencia's mother joined this migration immediately after the 1965 Immigration Act.

38. The first factors—education, stress of familial separation, housing—were not sufficient in themselves to encourage settlement because they had been present for over two-thirds of a century before Xaripus began to settle. The

more crucial factors, I argue, were at the national and state institutional level—the Immigration Act of 1965 and extension of labor rights and benefits to farm workers in the 1970s. A clear trend of settlement is apparent when Xaripus had access to unemployment insurance in the mid-1970s. This benefit allowed them to subsist when not all members were working in the fields in the off-season.

39. See Palerm 1991, 85. This migratory pattern was also observed among some of the seventy-two migrant farm worker families in Palerm's study.

40. "Cheap" connotes low cost, and it also implies worthless. I prefer the term "devalued labor," which shifts the responsibility to the employer who chooses to pay low wages.

41. In the Stockton area, harvesting the asparagus crop begins in February and ends in June; whereas the tomato harvest starts in late June and ends in late October or early November, depending on when the rain begins. Both crops last for about four months each, and in between these two crops, most Xaripus preferred picking cherries over other crops like cucumbers or apricots. In San Joaquin County, the cherry crop begins in May and lasts about one month, usually extending into late June.

42. See Menchaca 1995, 132. The California Occupational Safety Act, Menchaca outlines, "mandated three provisions: (1) portable rest rooms must be provided to the farm workers in the fields, (2) drinking water must also be available in the work place, and (3) employers must adhere to safety standards to protect their workers from pesticides."

43. When eighteen parents were asked if they thought their children/grandchildren would continue visiting Xaripu, they all said yes.

4. The Logic of Colonialism in Modern Labor Relations

1. See Ngai (2004, 129, 166), who refers to Filipino and Mexican migrants as "imported colonialism," because they came from nations that had experienced US colonialism and had been incorporated as unequal subjects into the labor market and society. Xaripus came from a neocolonized nation where historically they had been internally colonized (see chapter 3). Mexico was politically and economically subordinated to its northern neighbor; Indigenous people were displaced from their lands by haciendas that produced for export; and foreign investors monopolized railroads, natural resources, and political influence over Mexican government leaders (see Gonzalez and Fernandez 2003). Hence, when the dictator Porfirio Díaz further devalued Mexican labor in 1905 (one peso devalued to fifty US cents) to benefit foreign and hacienda interests (Hart 2002), peasants readily responded to the recruiting efforts of agriculture, mining, and

railroad industries in the United States (Portes and Rumbaut 1996). Mexicans entered the United States as colonial labor (Ngai 2004 and Barrera 1979), and were "differentially included" (unequally integrated) as exploitable laborers into the nation (Espiritu 2003b).

2. See Menchaca 1995 and Ngai 2004. Farmworkers were denied the rights/ legal protections that were offered to all other workers: collective bargaining, minimum wage, and unemployment insurance.

3. This occupational segregation was shaped by immigration policy, housing segregation, labor market opportunities, and class segmentation.

4. See Harding 2004, 132, 136–38. This standpoint approach attempts to maximize objectivity by privileging the point of view of the marginalized (such as Xaripu workers) when speaking of the institutions that exploit them, because it recognizes that the social locations of the researcher and subjects of study significantly influence the completeness of the reality captured. It assumes that those who are privileged by class, gender, and race will be less able to identify/ critique a racial/gender/class abuse than those who experience it directly, and will excuse it as attributable to the faulty perception of the victim(s), character problems of the individual(s), and irrational claims of victim(s). They will deny that a systemic/institutional problem exists and privileges them with unearned and unfair advantages/rewards. See also McIntosh 1997, 298–99; Lipsitz 1998, 18.

5. See US Bureau of the Census 2000. In the Stockton, California, region the demographics were as follows: Stockton's population included Asians (23 percent), Blacks (12.5 percent), Hispanics (32 percent), and Whites (32 percent); in neighboring cities—Lodi/Galt (north) and Manteca/Lathrop (south)—at least a third of the population was of a minority group. Although the census notes that the category "Hispanic" is composed of any racial combination, the more appropriate term would be *India/o* to make it comparable to the other racial/ethnic categories (White, Black, and Asian). Each racial classification reflects a racialization whereby specific meanings/values have been assigned to it, even though there is a tremendous amount of diversity and hybridity within each racial/ ethnic category. It is problematic to use a cultural category, "Hispanic," and compare it to racial categories that also reflect a *mestizaje*. See Piper 1997; Forbes 1982; Ochoa Serrano 1997.

6. See Neckerman and Kirschman 1999 and US Commission on Civil Rights 1994. These studies document employer and institutional practices and values that reproduce occupational segregation and inequities.

7. See Glenn 2002 and Piper 1997. For example, the 1896 Supreme Court decision *Plessy v. Ferguson*, making "separate but equal" the law of the land, affirmed a structure of segregation in which one drop of Black ancestry made some

White people Black. The in-between category of Black-White mix became insignificant to mainstream society as racial purist ideologies shaped national race relations. Furthermore, Irish, Italians, and Eastern Europeans were at first considered nonwhite ethnicities, but through immigration and labor practices they were eventually reclassified as White. See Omi and Winant 1994; Ngai 2004.

8. See Palerm 1991, 42. Observing the Mexicanization of labor in the fields, Palerm noted the ongoing historical reliance on Mexican migrant labor by US agribusiness: "In sharp contrast with the dominant practices that have characterized the development of US agriculture throughout the 20th century, California's agricultural industry is being transformed because manual labor—mostly Mexican migrant workers—is needed instead of being replaced by mechanization. We call the transformation 'Mexicanization.'" While Palerm's use of 'Mexicanization' merely underscores an increasing number of "Mexican" farmworkers in a time marked by changes in technology and mechanization in the fields, I use the term to also stress the colonial logic—racism—that dehumanizes people beyond labor exploitation.

Also revealing processes that devaluate Mexican-origin communities, Allensworth and Rochin (1999) empiricize the Mexicanization of rural California towns and document how towns that experienced both Latino growth and White flight became increasingly impoverished, while towns that became Whitened became wealthier. They found that "the relationship between ethnicity and community well-being was stronger in 1990 than in 1980" (1999, 4). My chapter, however, focuses only on labor relations and contextualizes them in the history of colonialism (see theory in chapter 4).

9. See Aguirre Beltrán 1972; Gómez-Quiñonez 1977; León-Portilla 1995; Cockcroft 1998; Keen 1994; Ochoa Serrano 1997. Although the term "Mexican" refers to a nationality, people more commonly use it to connote ethnicity and race, in spite of the fact that people from Mexico (as well as those from Latin America) are racially and culturally diverse. The same is true for Cubans, Puerto Ricans, and other Caribbean nationals. Nonetheless, those from the Caribbean have a strong African influence, while in Indo America, the Indigenous influence is greater. However, "mestizas/os" (referring to various racial hybridities), an ever increasing segment of the "Latino" population since the times of European colonization in the sixteenth century, are not the only Latinas/os. Throughout the Americas, a racial hierarchy persists, with fluid and overlapping rankings with *Indias/os* and Blacks at the bottom and their offshoots (mestizas/os) in between, but with a clear white supremacist marking (see Cockcroft 1998 and Warren 1985). See also Lugo 1995, 40–41. He notes that generic terms like "Mexican" or "Latino," and even "American," are indicative of a melting pot ideology that obscures rather than reveals the hierarchies of race, class, and gender. To under-

stand and move beyond constraining conceptual frameworks like the Black-White binary (see Perea 1997), we need to examine the particular histories of those homogenized as "Latinos." Looking at some basic, descriptive US Census statistics, we can identify the diversity and recognize the significance of the "context of reception" (as discussed by Portes and Rumbaut 2006) and of the particular political-economic histories of "Latinos."

10. Allensworth and Rochin (1999, 12, 58) similarly document that a town's socioeconomic well-being was significantly correlated with the percent of Latinos in a community. They observed that community well-being factors (income, education levels, unemployment, and poverty) and levels of Latinos were more strongly correlated than community well-being and levels of immigrants. Their findings suggest that race and ethnicity shape access (via social capital) to resources, as predominantly Mexican towns (or sections of towns) were poorer than predominantly White communities, irrespective of immigrant levels. Their study found that White flight—more than Mexican immigration—significantly affected both the economic health and the ethnic composition of a town (1999, 53–54, 58). Moreover, the Mexican-origin, US-born population contributed more to the Latino population growth than did immigration of foreign-born Mexicans.

11. This process, I contend, follows the logic of colonialism, which dehumanizes diverse Natives/ethnicities into a racial "Other" and reduces them to exploitable laborers and servants. Although the term "Mexican" is not an ethnicity or a race but rather a nationality, it has become racialized with the meanings of alien, brown, and laborers.

12. For example, some Mexican-origin persons blame their ethnic group for lack of social mobility and explain their poor status as resulting from their "crab syndrome," nepotism, *envidia* (envy), or a backward and pathological culture.

13. After World War II, the Filipina/o and Mexican experiences began to diverge. The US military recruited Filipinos (from the Philippines) into the navy, while it recruited Mexicans (from Mexico) into farm labor. After the Immigration Act of 1965, their experiences further diverged with US policy and labor market opportunities. The United States opened its doors to professionals from Asia and Africa and continued to recruit primarily Mexican migrants into the laboring/service sectors. The overall impact of changing US institutional policies (immigration policy and labor recruitment) shifted the stereotypical representations shared by Filipinos and Mexicans, whereby the former was constructed as a model minority and the other remains the manual- and service-labor type.

14. Among the Mexicans, 17 percent were US-born and 71 percent, Mexican-born.

15. Given the historical relations between the United States and Mexico, people from Central America are often wrongly assumed by Americans to be Mexicans because of their Indigenous appearance and immigrant status. Moreover, it is not the nationality that matters in the Mexicanization thesis, but rather the historical fact that people from Indo America who appear Indigenous and are not Americanized or Europeanized suffer from specific forms of racialization, which constructs them as perpetual aliens, unintelligent, manual workers, servants, and unorganized, among many other racially specific stereotypes.

16. Many of these early migrants—Purépechas, Chichimecas, Huicholes, etc.—became "Mexicanized" in both Mexico and the United States as they went through common experiences (Mexican Revolution, Bracero Program, Great Depression) and interacted with each other in racially segregated communities and employment (Weber 1998).

17. By the 1930s, Mexican students were segregated in 85 percent of schools; see Menchaca 1995, 74.

18. Ibid., 73–74.

19. Ibid., 76.

20. Now even Central Americans are racialized as "Mexicans," which many find offensive because it erases their national and cultural distinctions.

21. Menchaca 1995, 75–77.

22. This condition—extending labor rights to farmworkers—resembled the end of de jure (legal) racism, which did not end de facto (norms and practices) racism in the post-'60s period. Farmworkers' rights are generally neglected by employers and government agencies.

23. One of my earliest memories of farm labor exemplifies the harshness of agricultural working conditions. In late May 1975, when I was six years old, I went with my two older brothers and sister to pick cherries with our parents in the San Joaquin Valley. Since the growers did not provide child care and babysitters were expensive, it was common for children to accompany their parents to the fields. I spent the day playing with my young friend Greñas, who was five, using cherry stems as "arms" and "legs" in our own make-believe world. At the end of the day, we said good-bye and promised to bring our toys to the fields the following day.

But the next day I did not accompany my parents to the fields because I had to go to school. I spent the day feeling terrible for breaking my promise to Greñas, who was too young to attend school. When my parents returned from work that evening, they faced me with deep concern and told me to never fall asleep under a cherry tree. (It was a common practice for children to sleep in the cars during cold hours in the morning, and once the sun got hot, they would place two boxes [about two feet by one and a half feet] together, face down, to make a comfortable bed under a tree.) They hugged me, and nothing else was said. A few days later, I learned that I wouldn't be seeing my friend again—a distracted grower had been looking at his cherry trees while driving a truck and had run over Greñas while he played with two toy trucks on the side of a dirt road. Though this was my first and most traumatic experience in the fields of the San Joaquin Valley, it would not be my last.

24. Piece-rate wages are based on production levels and not on an hourly basis. For example, see Tables 4.1 and 4.2 (in the Appendix), which document my family's piece-rate production for five members during the summers of 1978, 1980, and 1981. The earnings reflect the number of units (buckets in this case) picked and the pay for each one: $0.35 per tomato bucket, and $0.60 per cucumber bucket. One can get an hourly average of piece-rate production by dividing the amount earned in one day by the number of hours worked. For instance, on July 6, 1978, my mother worked eight hours and earned $27.30 by the piece rate, which came out to $3.40 an hour. My brother was a bit less productive, earning $26.40 total and averaging $3.30 an hour (for an eight-hour period).

25. They are able to do this by paying workers in cash. Some workers need immediate cash to get by in the day (gas, food, shelter, etc.), so they may willingly sell their piece-unit tokens or tickets after work, though they may then receive a lower rate for their work than if they follow formal procedures.

26. While Sancho was a successful contractor, it was evident that a supervisor position within the tomato company offered a more secure and better income.

27. See Osterman 2005b. She reports that state enforcement—the Agricultural Labor Relations Board—is negligent, partly because of the lack of governmental funding.

28. *Owens v. Local 169, Association of Western Pulp and Paper Workers.*

29. Another abuse occurs when workers are told to be on the fields at a certain time, only to have to sit and wait to begin work because the buyers and sellers of produce have not yet set a price on the fruit or vegetable. While the companies and growers haggle over prices, workers stand by without being compensated for their on-call time.

30. A 2004 policy required compensation, but enforcement is generally absent.

31. Cal. Labor Code § 11140 (4)(B) (IWC Order 14).

32. In the summer of 1987 in Stockton, my father and I worked picking cucumbers for at least twenty-one days straight without a day off. This problem is more common with *regadores* (irrigators), who spend up to sixteen hours a day, seven days a week, watering endless miles of field rows.

33. IWC Orders § 7(b).

34. Farmworkers make up 1 percent of the national workforce; see Rose 2000.

35. Ngai elaborates on the racist devaluation of wages for Filipinos and Mexicans and argues that an oversupply of workers, job competition, easy acceptance of lower wages, and passivity contributed to their lower wages. Many of conflicts between Filipinos/Mexicans and White society occurred because of the former's resistance to being devalued at work. While growers generally did not distinguish between foreign- and US-born Mexicans in the 1930s, they felt Mexican Americans demanded too much, and were finally able to import contract labor during World War II.

36. The profits were gained by the agribusiness and multinational corporations, while producers (growers) and farm workers who create the surplus value have been the major losers.

37. A disabling injury is one that leads to death or physical impairment or that incapacitates a worker from working a full day beyond the day of the injury.

38. I was also able to witness this period while working in the fields throughout the 1980s, and there was a dramatic difference after the passage of IRCA 1986 in the number of workers allowed in the fields. This oversupply of workers took place in the IRCA context and did not necessarily continue, as many workers—especially those coming from an urban experience in Mexico—moved out from the fields in the late 1990s. These observations come from my direct experiences in the fields and interviews with Xaripus who remain in farm labor, including my father. See other collaborating evidence from Palerm 1991 and Magaña 1988.

39. SAW offered migrants more opportunities to legalize if they did not meet the amnesty requirements under LAW (general legalization for those who had continuously lived in the United States since January 1, 1982). Migrants were able to prove they had labored in the fields for ninety days prior to 1986 more easily than proving they had resided in the United States for five years continuously since 1981.

40. This finding was consistent with Villarejo and Runsten 1993, 19, and Rothenberg 1998, 24. However, in my assessment, the impact on the amount of work was temporary in the 1990s, as the new farmworkers from urban settings in Mexico transitioned to nonagricultural jobs in the United States.

41. Although Palerm (1991) assessed that mechanization was not replacing Mexican workers, many of the new technologies—tomato planter, weeding technologies, cucumber harvester—were not introduced until later in the 1990s. Technological changes in agriculture have certainly had an impact on some spe-

cific jobs that Xaripus had worked before, particularly weeding tomato fields and picking cucumbers.

42. In my interviews with Xaripus, including my parents, this trend was observed in Stockton in the mid-1990s, and it is also confirmed in Mines's report (2006).

43. See Rothenberg 1998, 67: "75 percent of the nation's vegetables [are] produced by 6 percent of the farms and nearly 80 percent of all fruit [is] produced by 10 percent of the country's growers."

44. The knife has a four-inch wooden handle attached to a two-foot thin rod with a three-inch flat blade that is two inches wide at the end.

45. When the weather gets warmer, the asparagus plants are more plentiful.

46. While some of these strategies were not new, they became more widespread and common among Xaripu families.

47. See also Campbell 2000. In July 2000, Chapter 11 offered Tri Valley Growers protection from creditors and time to reorganize its operations, though two tomato processing plants were closed. (Cecilia was one of the affected workers of an estimated eleven thousand.) One problem was that Tri Valley—a cooperative of four hundred grower members—overproduced fruits and vegetables, hurting their price, and did not have a market for their oversupply of tomatoes. Another major and related problem was attributed to global competition, which priced imported food below the cost of production for growers in the United States. See Schnitt 2002 and Sinton 2000.

48. In colonial times the forced extraction of tribute (surplus labor) was clearly manifest, as opposed to today's form, where the extraction of surplus value is abstracted or clouded with empty notions of individual choice, contract labor, and natural market forces.

49. See Menchaca 1995, 132: C.O.S.A. "mandated three provisions: (1) portable rest rooms must be provided to the farm workers in the fields, (2) drinking water must also be available in the work place, and (3) employers must adhere to safety standards to protect their workers from pesticides."

50. The Agricultural Labor Relations Act (1975) gave California farmworkers collective bargaining rights (which had been excluded in the NLRA of 1935) for the first time in US history, allowed union representatives to enter the growers' fields, mandated that union elections be taken seven days from when they are petitioned for, required contract negotiations to be between workers and growers (not contractors), and made growers liable for not bargaining in good faith.

51. The association was named after President Lázaro Cárdenas (1934–40), who during his administration expropriated Mexican national resources from

foreign capitalists and intensified the agrarian reform that broke down large haciendas and gave land to the peasants (see chapter 3).

52. These are the persons distributing the tickets or punching the production card for workers, usually the contractor's or supervisor's relatives.

53. See http://shop.safeway.com/superstore.

54. Subcommandante Marcos was among the central leaders of the Zapatista Rebellion in Chiapas on January 1, 1994. This was the first day of NAFTA, and the Indigenous people feared losing more of their land and resources to global capitalism.

55. OTAC's goals are as follows:

1. Support and assessments in the transmission of documents to migrant workers and families in their place of origin and destination.

2. Empower farmworkers with the basic knowledge needed to defend their civic, labor, political, and human rights (Mundo Hispano 1992, 13; Magaña 1997a).

3. Promote communal projects of sustainable economic development to help migrants seeking stability in their home communities. On February 25, 2001, OTAC sponsored the first binational encounter, Encuentro de Migrantes Para Alternativas de Desarrollo Economico y Por los Derechos Humanos (Binational Encounter of Migrants for Alternative Economic Development and for Human Rights) at the Center for Studies of the Mexican Revolution, Jiquilpan, Michoacán. On April 27 and 28, 2001, they sponsored the second binational encounter in Stockton, California (Magaña 2001a, A6).

4. Promote binational educational programs advancing the retention of Mexican culture and its diversity. This approach is exemplified in the organization's embracing the diversity of Indigenous campesinas/os rather than imposing a homogenous organizational project from the top.

5. Maintain a cooperative relationship involving information and referrals services with offices of the consulate, embassy, and supportive organizations to migrants on both sides of the border. Many of the conferences (e.g., the binational ones mentioned in number 3, above) have included representatives from diverse grassroots and social/public agencies so as to advance information sharing and networking.

6. Assist in the transportation of deceased migrants to their communities of origin. OTAC helps with fund raisers to help families transport the bodies of their deceased. (Historically, Indigenous and Indio-mestizos have been relegated to the most dangerous occupations, typically characterized as colonial labor.)

7. Advance the voting rights of migrant workers such as the right to vote in US elections while abroad without losing Mexican citizenship (Vasquez 1991; Magaña 1996, 1997b, 1997c).

8. Advance health programs for migrants and their families in their communities of origin and abroad (Nichols 1991).

9. Promote community forums discussing and analyzing topics related to migrants and prioritizing issues concerning undocumented immigrants (Sierra Reyes 1997).

56. In response to the labor organizing and labor rights gains of the 1970s, corporate agribusiness Mexicanized the fields in the last quarter of the twentieth century, and it simultaneously shifted production to Mexico, producing a neo-Porfiriato period (see chapter 2).

57. Theoretically, the idea behind the sanction provision was that if employers were fined for hiring undocumented workers, employers would not hire them, and the latter would have no incentive to immigrate to the United States.

58. While all workers experience the impacts of global capitalism and the related economic restructuring that has deteriorated the standard of living for the average person, these economic processes are not race- or gender-neutral.

59. The wages were depressed before they were hired, as part of the restructuring of the factory; this case was similar to that of Cecilia, who was laid off from the Triple E cannery in 1999.

60. According to Elías, shortly after the company's restructuring, the Immigration and Naturalization Services had targeted the factory. Thus, the new workers who remained proved their legal residency. Even so, there was a distance between older immigrants and the newer immigrants, often referred derogatorily to as *amestialldos* (those who legalized—via SAW or LAW—through IRCA). Such intragroup conflicts reflect the pressures from nativism and national policies that influence some immigrants or US-born children to disassociate from the newer immigrants. See also Menchaca 1995.

61. The complete Mexicanization was beneficial to the company, because the top-down racialized dehumanization—which was previously manifest in a class-segmented workforce with White supervisor(s)—was reproduced by intragroup coworkers. Thus, the further devaluation based on race—overlapping class oppression—became obscured.

62. He changed work from Death Tile Company to Money Tile Company in 1996, and his experience revealed three basic reasons why he changed companies: the negative working environment from the first company, the better pay from the second factory, and his encouragement from a friend already working in the second factory.

63. Death Tile was completely Mexicanized in labor, whereas Money Tile Company was also becoming Mexicanized, but not completely. Whites and Blacks worked in the second company as forklifters and managers, as had been the situation in the first company before full Mexicanization of labor. And when Money Company became fully Mexicanized, foremen were selected from among the workers. This approach enhanced the company's control of the workers by splitting their loyalties from each other and shifting it to their company.

For almost every day for a whole summer in 1994, I conversed with about six Xaripus after work, including Keletos, who had the fatal accident in 1998, who shared the same views about the worsening working conditions at the roofing tile factory.

64. He is a "situational in-between" also because at the structural level those who would call themselves "Americans" perceive Indigenous-looking people like Elías as aliens (see chapter 2 for elaboration of the in-between status).

65. These assimilated minorities are in between Whites and less assimilated minorities, and may not necessarily be assimilated but are closer in cultural form and style to those with more power. Rosalía, for instance, was interviewed in English and reflected excellent fluency in both languages, and some may regard her English as being nonaccented, yet she herself observed a coworker who spoke more Anglicized English and acted more Americanized being favored over her.

66. More generally, however, Whitened occupations reflect larger structural trends organized around primary sector (high pay, security, benefits) and secondary sector (low pay, unstable, few or no benefits) jobs (see Amott and Matthaei 2007, 289–92). People of color and White women are generally found in secondary-sector jobs, while White men typically monopolize the primary-sector ones.

67. See Kivel 1995, 8–48. He highlights four concepts underlying the ideology of Whiteness, including purity, Christianity, conflation of "American" with "White," and gender.

68. The starting wage on the post office application was $10 an hour in 1984, yet she was paid $9 an hour. At that time, President Reagan had decided to lower federal service salaries. In August 1998, she earned about $18.90 an hour, yet she forfeited seniority benefits by transferring to the San Joaquin area from San Jose. As a full-time employee, she earned about $38,000 a year.

69. Three stages of Mexicanization were observed. In the first stage, Mexicans enter a diverse workforce where the pay and benefits are relatively equal to those of non-Mexicans. Production, wages, and benefits remain stable. In the second stage of Mexicanization, the company may either (a) close, laying off workers and rehiring them at lower pay and reduced benefits; or (b) increase production while not increasing wages, thus weeding out senior workers. The

new workers in both cases were largely Mexicans who had come from more exploitative labor experiences.

70. They were the only ones taking the jobs.

71. In the fields with a more undocumented labor force, productivity was also achieved by increasing the number of workers.

72. Liberation movements from oppression have also benefited tremendously from the efforts of individuals in the privileged classes who forgo their benefits and risk their lives for those at the bottom, e.g., De las Casas, Marx, abolitionists, etc. (see chapter 2).

73. The income returns of higher education are significantly lower for "Mexicans," regardless of generation, than for Whites. See US Bureau of the Census 2006; Levine 2006, 12–13.

74. The highest paid Xaripu was a young man earning $200 a day in a monopoly-sector utility company with stable employment, health coverage, and a retirement plan. His experiences were exactly similar to Olivia's: unfair schedules and burdens and racial marginalization. However, his Whitened masculinized job, while in just as racially hostile an environment, was more highly compensated.

75. Indirectly, non-migrant women and family in Mexico subsidized US employers by reproducing labor in Mexico at no cost to the United States.

76. Supply and demand models do not explain why, for example, farmworkers, who make up less than 1 percent of the national workforce, feed the US population, and perform the most dangerous work, are undervalued.

5. *Haciendo Comunidad* across Borders

1. See Rosaldo 1997, 30–38. He elaborates the politics of recognition and cultural citizenship as essential for a more complete national citizenship. With cultural citizenship, individuals from minority groups have not only political rights but the right to reproduce culture and feel free and safe to express it without being marginalized or stigmatized by the dominant society.

2. Interactive colonialism highlights the overlapping colonialisms across borders (see chapter 2). After Mexico's independence it was politically and economically subordinated to foreign nations and interests (particularly the United States), which had a tremendous influence on the Mexican government. Within Mexico, Indigenous and indo-mestizo communities were further subordinated by criollo and Europeanized mestizo elites. The former were internally colonized within a neocolonized nation and were easily absorbed by the northern nation

to meet its labor demands as imported colonialism or internal colonial labor. See Ngai 2004 and Barrera 1979.

3. Emerging identities are in the making, and most identities are emerging; however, I use "emergent identities" to convey the idea that there is a sense of continuity and normalcy in the ethnic identity that has developed from competing social influences (culture, race, nation, etc.) to form a new and distinct one, i.e., *nepantla.*

4. Reincorporation by sending states refers to the policies and programs created by the sending nations to encourage migrants to return or to remit money to the homeland. These programs and policies also include dual citizenship, consulate services, and tourism advertisement.

5. Racist nativism refers to hostile, nationalist sentiments directed against those perceived as foreigners that often lead to anti-immigrant laws, programs, and policies. What makes this nativism racist is that those marked (normalized profiling) as foreign are distinguished by color and ethnicity.

6. Benedict Anderson (1991) examines the development of the nation-state as a social and modern construct during the independence movements in the Americas in the late eighteenth and early nineteenth centuries. Although the nation-state does not represent or include as equals all within its borders, the power of the modern nation relies on the widespread identification with it ("imagined community") by people who do not even know each other and who may have divergent interests (based on, for example, class differences). The Xaripu community is a much smaller unit, but in some ways it is imagined as a unified collectivity by members who are also stratified and may have different social-political interests. Nevertheless, there are important distinctions between the nation-state and smaller ethnic communities like Xaripu. Xaripus have a tremendous level of *convivencia* (qualitative and social interaction) with other members of the community, though not everyone knows each other, especially in a transnational context and with the growing younger generations. Furthermore, unlike the larger nation-state, the Xaripu community's most well-off have and maintain high levels of *convivencia* with other community members who are less well-off, and many are related directly and indirectly through kinship ties. It is the inequities across nations that seem to strain the relationships between transnational and non-migrant Xaripus in Michoacán.

7. My use of "dual home base" does not imply home ownership in either place, but rather a sense of belonging and being connected to family, friends, community, and institutions in both countries.

8. Members of the two older cohorts were more frequent visitors than members of the two younger cohorts, twelve of seventeen compared to seven of thir-

teen. They had the same number of somewhat frequent visitors (two from each group), and three of the two older cohorts were infrequent visitors as compared to four of the younger groups.

9. Another factor affecting migration patterns is home ownership in Michoacán. Those with homes were more likely to visit. Generally, the elder cohorts were more likely to have a home in Michoacán.

10. See Rumbaut 2002, 79–89. In a study of various ethnicities from the "1.5"—foreign-born children raised in the United States—and second generations, Rumbaut found that homeland language use was the most significant predictor of transnationalism (frequency of visits/remittances to the country of origin and sense of dual homes across nations). He concluded that less than 10 percent of the various ethnicities fit the transnational experience and that with time and new generations the sense of two homes fades into a one-American-home orientation.

11. While older Xaripus remained racially segregated in agricultural jobs and housing, younger Xaripus are more integrated in housing, employment, and education, though still subjected to similar social hierarchies as their elders (see chapter 4). This difference partly explains the social or cultural transformations between the various cohorts.

12. See Espiritu 2003b, 11. The expression "symbolic transnationalism" was coined by Espiritu: she elaborates how second-generation Filipinos unfamiliar with the homeland might feel mental and/or emotional transnationalism in the context of social rejection in the receiving society.

13. These observations took place in the summers of 1999 and 2001.

14. Overwhelmingly, most Xaripus across the various cohorts reported social rejection or discrimination at work, in school, and in stores, and also expressed concern over the perceived high crime rates in their neighborhoods, particularly with robberies, violence, and drugs.

15. Relatives appreciate the remittances, but not their dependent statuses. In my assessment, they would prefer economic independence and equality with their relatives, and these goals are unattainable without migrating to *el norte*.

16. Although the social distances between transnational and non-migrant Xaripus might arise even without national inequalities, I contend below that these inequities intensify the distances and conflicts.

17. *Convivir* is a concept commonly used by Xaripus.

18. The Xaripu label classifies Xaripus as a community, and even though individuals may not regard or label themselves as such, they are called "a Xaripu" by others familiar with the Xaripu community. While in high school, I didn't think of myself as a Xaripu, though I was enmeshed in a dense network of

extended family and friends—not to say my life was exclusively lived within this community in Stockton. Many of my neighbors and friends in a racially segregated neighborhood and school were African Americans and Chicanas/os of other Mexican or Latino origins. When I visited friends after school in their homes, their parents and siblings would refer to me as a Xaripu: "Oh, your friend 'el Xaripu' came to visit," or "Be careful," and "Don't hang out with that Xaripu, because he is a *callejero* [street kid]." Also, when associating with other Xaripu friends or family, I often heard them refer to others as "*las/los Xaripus*": "In Los Bukis concert, there were a whole bunch of Xaripus. I saw *la chavela, la chata, el gabino* . . ." or "After school *las/los Xaripus* went on a field trip to Escalon Lake." The Xaripu label continues to be used by Xaripus and by those who know the community.

19. In the section on the meaning of "Xaripu" I focus on the two younger cohorts (ages twenty to twenty-nine and thirty to forty-nine) on both sides of the border, because their responses were more diverse than the older Xaripus.

20. *Caciques* are pueblo members perceived as having a tremendous amount of power, influence, and money, as well as the ability to shape pueblo politics to their interests. The pueblo Xaripu does not appear to have *caciques* that fit the definition above, though there are competing influential people.

21. The question of who belongs here and who doesn't has been traced to nation-state building, in which new notions of community were introduced, including more extreme ideas about its homogeneity and purity. Like their fellow Purépechans, Xaripus of today are products of diverse cultural and political-economic influences (see chapter 3). The imperialistic project of advancing the nation-state, however, erased Xaripus' historical identities and replaced them with empty and generic "post"-colonial ones such as "Mexicans," "Hispanics," and "Latinos." Although these generic constructs allegedly have been designed to create more inclusive identities, diverse people are subjected to homogenizing forces and encouraged to think in more exclusive terms, becoming intolerant toward cultural differences. Consequently, these terms serve as melting-pot concepts that obscure racial, class, and gender inequalities in both countries.

22. Betty, Lorna, and Lilly began to exclude Tita from conversations and outings, and appeared to hold grudges against Tita. The culmination of their fallout occurred in a classroom where Lilly wrote on the chalkboard that Tita was a "bitch." Tita confronted her and ended her friendship with them. The emergent inequities in number of friends and popularity between Tita and her childhood friends appear to have been the root of the fallout. Her ex-friends responded by reaffirming their close ties, placing borders between themselves and others, and excluding Tita, whose Xaripu connections were alien to them.

23. The bonding after work is more common for these working-class men than for Xaripu women, who typically interact with their families after work. In a way, *la calle* (the street) is masculinized.

24. In my respondents' estimation over 80 percent of the attendees in large community celebrations were of Xaripu-origin.

25. As one of the many *padrinos,* I witnessed the wedding ceremony and reception in 2001.

26. See Smith 2003, 207–11. He elaborates similar processes among a transnational community from Ticuani, Puebla, and Brooklyn, New York, and suggests that Ticuanenses' ability in forming community in New York is partly rooted in their Indigenous communal heritage.

27. *Quinceañera* is the fifteenth-birthday celebration for a young woman, who marks her entrance into adulthood. The ceremony consists of a special Mass, *chambelanes* and *damas* (participating friends) accompanying the *Quinceañera,* and a party after the church services.

28. Xaripu-origin or -related persons from California, Texas, Chicago, and even New York attend the religious festivities in January. These activities reunite people in Michoacán who are spread across the United States and still have ties after being away for many years.

29. Mexican influences are observed in *peregrinaciones* in which they integrate Aztec dancers. This representation contrasts with the fact that during the pre-Hispanic period the Mexican nation had attempted to subdue the Purépechans, to no avail. As Michoacán became engulfed by the "Mexican nation" under criollo and later mestizo rule, however, it has also come to identify itself as "Mexican."

30. See, for example, Limón, who suggests that "the cultural logic of late capitalism" fragments notions of a "community" among Mexicans in south Texas as well as in California (1994, 106).

31. See Bordo 1997, 346–48. She elaborates:

All the elements of what I have here called postmodern conversation—intoxication with individual choice and creative jouissance, delight with the piquancy of particularity and mistrust of pattern and seeing coherence, celebration of "differences," suspicion of the totalitarian nature of generalization along with a rush to protect difference from its homogenizing abuses—have become recognizable and familiar in much of contemporary intellectual discourse.... (346) What this celebration of creative reading as resistance effaces is the arduous and frequently frustrated historical struggle that is required for the subordinated to articulate and assert the value of their "difference" in the face of dominant meanings—meanings that often offer a pedagogy directed at reinforcement of feelings of inferiority, marginality, ugliness. . . . (347)

32. See Glenn 2002. "Relationality" refers to how race and gender gain meaning in relation to each other. Yet Western culture creates dualisms—for example, man/woman, Anglo/Mexican, white/black—that gain meaning in opposition to one another. These dualisms suppress variability and normalize the dominant category, producing hierarchies.

33. Moreover, racial/ethnic identities do not impede coalition building, as has been illustrated in the twenty-first century by Los Zapatistas, who are made up of various Indigenous ethnic groups—Tzeltal, Tzotziles, Choles, Tojolabales—who often are multilingual (see Durán 1994).

34. For example, W. E. B. Du Bois's concept of "double consciousness" (1903), Patricia Hill Collins's "outsider within" (2004), bell hooks "spaces of radical openness" (2004), and Chela Sandoval's "differential oppositional consciousness" (2004) all elaborate how marginalized people develop strategies of survival and resistance in oppressive environments while creating and maintaining safe spaces of affirmation and support.

35. The experiences with transnationalism produce not so much a condition of extreme fluidity and variability, but rather a condition of *nepantla*. While some scholars situate *nepantla* in "'blurred zones in-between' patterns of culture" (see Lugo 1995, 125; Rosaldo, *Culture and Truth*, 207–17) and/or interpret it as a perpetual "mestiza consciousness" (see Anzaldúa 1999) fluidly living, maneuvering, and weaving multiple social worlds, I use *nepantla* to mark emergent patterned and popularized ethnic forms. For instance, Xaripus together experience new emergent cultural patterns within racial, gender, and economic subordination (see Guarnizo and Smith 1999, 100–103; Guarnizo and Smith 2003, 21). While *norteña/o* Xaripus may be seen as *agabachados* (Whitened) in Michoacán, in California these same Xaripus are identified as *Mexicanized*. Their experiences reflect not a substantial change in their self-concept, but rather a unique relational position between several cultural and national influences. Xaripus' code-switching from Spanish to English or mixing languages does not change their skin color, class, gender, or personality, but rather reflects the influences of various social contexts. Individualistic interpretations of identity formation, as contingent on always shifting choices of a postmodern reality, neglect the normalizing forces of structured inequalities and hegemonic "dominant meanings" (Bordo 1997, 346–48).

36. In an ideal world of justice and equality, multiculturalism and multilingualism would be more accepted than monolingualism and a dominant culture,

and the emergent *nepantla(s)* would be regarded as normal and natural. Xaripus' ability to reproduce community allows them a greater ability to reproduce and retain culture—though not unchanged culture.

37. This section relies on interviews and participant observation with persons from California and Michoacán.

38. Smith (2003) and García Canclini and Villalobos (1985) elaborate on the changing meaning of pueblo celebrations as a result of commercialization.

39. The nicknames can be translated, respectively, as the devil, the rat, the possum, the cod's chin, the fox, the donkey, and the eagle.

40. Other interesting names highlighting physical or personality traits of persons include: *la prieta, el amarillo, el corto, el diablo, mishúmo, el troncón, el rápido, el zurdo, el zambo, el compañero, la balita, la naila, la chata, el morisqueto* (the dark one, the yellow one, the short one, the devil, I am sinking, the trunk, the fast one, the left-handed one, the Black-Indian, the partner, the bullet, a song, the small nose, the rice eater).

41. In addition, the racial/cultural composition of their neighborhoods has influenced the rate and form of cultural transformation. As mentioned earlier, most Xaripus live in working-class and racially segregated communities and within walking distances from each other.

42. This barrio-dress style was featured in the films *American Me* and *Blood In, Blood Out*. However, the Xaripus who follow this style do no fit the racist stereotypes of an "oppositional culture," underclass, or segmented assimilation that devalues working-class minorities.

43. "Mexicanness" appears in quotation marks here because I have argued that it is a broad category that homogenizes tremendous internal diversity within Mexico, yet in the usage above I associated it with speaking Spanish, continuing to eat typical foods (chile, beans, and corn tortillas), participating in cultural celebrations (*Quinceañeras* and religious celebrations), etc.

44. "Mexican" appears in quotation marks because Xaripus' Indigenous heritage is Purépechan rather than Nahuatl or Mexica. Although Spanish is neither Mexica nor Purépecha, the emergent Spanish varieties in Mexico reflect the Indigenous regional influences, which Xaripus reflect in their day-to-day speech—e.g., *chunde, chisquilina, corunda,* etc.—and more communal behavior.

45. These scholars critique the claim that transnationalism is a form of resistance, pointing out that national borders and politics of exclusion block the full integration of immigrants into the receiving society.

46. Immigrant women of color from working-class backgrounds have experienced a different type of social incorporation in the receiving society. Some scholars have observed an empowerment in familial politics experienced by women (see Rouse 1989; Hondagneu-Sotelo 1994; Hirsch 1999), while others

document a double shift burdening women of color more than men in the United States (see Espiritu 2003b; Parreñas 2001b; Sarmiento 2002). What is certain is that there are diverse experiences among and within racial immigrant groups in how they experience life in the United States (see González-López 2003; Menjívar 2003; Pessar 2003), though they clearly enter a nation with structured racial, gender, and class inequalities (see Gonzalez and Fernandez 2003; Guarnizo and Smith 2003; Glenn 2002). Their context of exiting and arrival has greatly determined their success in the United States (see Menjívar 2000; Portes and Rumbaut 2006; and Espiritu 2003a).

47. This claim does not apply to all migrants, but only to those from communities, like Xaripu, with a long history of crossing national borders and who are mostly documented US residents or US citizens with extensive social networks in the United States and Mexico.

48. The non-migrants in Michoacán were asked the inverse questions.

49. Their responses help understand how transnational migration shapes a sense of empowerment and ideologies (e.g., *Dios y Norte*).

50. Material empowerment does not necessarily mean absolute and total empowerment, because even Xaripus with low levels of material wealth (across borders) may have more social wealth (social capital and networks) than those with more material wealth. Their social capital can achieve what an individual's wealth cannot, e.g., fix a roof or build a room with the help of friends rather than paying someone to do it.

51. Xaripus' social conditions changed in the 1970s, when favorable legislation improved conditions in the fields, established the right of farm workers in California to union representation, and extended federal unemployment insurance to farm workers (see also chapter 4). These developments contributed to changing migration patterns, as a significant number of Xaripu migrants opted to settle more permanently in the United States. Another key factor contributing to Xaripu settlement was their interest in furthering their children's education, which became more possible when unemployment insurance and other public services were extended to them.

52. In California, transnational migrants also display more civic engagement than non-migrant Xaripus. The former are more actively involved in Church activities, labor organizing, and other cultural/social events.

53. Thirteen out of nineteen Xaripus in California believed food had improved; fifteen out of nineteen saw improvements in housing; twelve out of seventeen, in health; and twelve out of sixteen, in social life. Whereas among non-migrants in Michoacán, fifteen out of nineteen saw improvements in food; seventeen out of nineteen, in housing; and sixteen out of eighteen, in health.

54. Several professionals—e.g., a lawyer, accountant, and teacher—had begun to migrate to work in the fields during the 1980s.

55. See Corona Hurtado 1967–68, Table "Cuadro de concentración de calificaciones" [Grades] 1967–68. I also interviewed three teachers in Xaripu during the summer of 1999, winter of 2000, and summer of 2001.

56. Although materially they have all experienced differentiation from those who remain in Michoacán, culturally the oldest group members are more similar in traditions and beliefs to those in Mexico, while the younger members have experienced linguistic, behavioral, and ideological changes.

57. They say this rather than "*no soy de aquí, ni de alla*" (I'm neither from here nor from there).

58. My observations and claims are more applicable to small-town pueblos with a long migratory history in the United States. Thus, claims that more recent "immigrants" or "migrants" have it better than non-migrants cannot be made because of the greater stressors they face: unfamiliarity with a new environment, weaker connections to US social institutions, greater vulnerability as possibly undocumented immigrants, emotional pain from being recently separated from family and/or community, etc.

6. The Family across Borders

1. In first-stage migration, for instance, women rely on bracero men's networks to legalize—via the 1965 Immigration Act—and their (women's) employment and housing opportunities are significantly shaped by male-dominated networks and information. Over time, however, women build their own social networks of support, and sometimes women's networks are broader and more diverse (e.g., community and public services, employment), offering them opportunities beyond those provided by their male counterparts.

2. The "double shift" refers to women doing non-wage work at home and wage work outside the home. The two work settings constitute the double shift.

3. See Menchaca 1995, 94, 129; Sarmiento 2002; and Gonzalez and Fernandez 2003. For example, the Bracero Program was designed by US agribusiness (e.g., Agricultural Labor Law No. 45 in 1942 and Public Law No. 78 in 1951). This program recruited male migrants. After the Bracero Program ended in 1964, employers continued to recruit ex-braceros from Michoacán and other Mexican states, even offering housing for their families.

4. Bonfil Batalla (1996) elaborates the Indigenous and *mestizaje* diversity. The construction of a monolithic "Mexican" parallels the discourse of the normal and undifferentiated "American" (see Kivel 1995; Lipsitz 1998; McIntosh 1997).

5. See Menjívar 2003, 109. For example, Menjívar compared Guatemalan and Salvadorian migrants and found that Indigenous Guatemalan migrants were more gender egalitarian than their fellow Ladino (mestizo) co-nationals; the latter often experienced relational strains and inequity in their households, resulting from men's frustrations with their limited and unstable economic opportunities, whereas women more easily found employment in feminized occupations.

6. How the increasing dependence on remittances affects women and families in Mexico requires a more systematic comparative and bi-national study.

7. See Hondagneu-Sotelo 1994, 196; see also Pessar 2003, 27. This claim is based on the idea that women gain equality by increasing gender spatial mobility, gaining more family authority, and transforming the gender division of labor at home.

8. A similar critique applies to quantitative approaches, but in their case their large samples become meaningless when they fail to identify the internal diversity within their broad categories—Mexican, Latino, Hispanic. Quantitative approaches may also fail to compare with a control group of non-migrants.

9. I specifically focus on spousal relationships among Xaripus. Although other familial relationships—both between generations and between parents and children (Menjívar 2000, 210–11; Espiritu 2003b, 172–73; Rouse 1992, 38–40)—are important, spousal relationships are a particularly powerful means through which children learn gender roles, including whether to relate to each other across gender as equals or unequals. Thus this chapter focuses on spouses and examines other familial relationships only as they relate to these.

10. See Hirsch 1999. She examines the more narrow conception of respect, implying hierarchy. However, the usage of *respeto* encompasses a sense of honoring and caring for others as well, not necessarily affirming social hierarchies.

11. In California, out of eighteen women, three said the man decided over large purchases; four said the woman; and eleven said both equally decided. In regards to day-to-day purchases, of sixteen women, three said the man decided; six reported the woman decided, and seven noted both man and woman decided. In Michoacán, of eleven women, three women said the man decided over large purchases; one said the woman; and seven said both equally decided. Regarding daily expenditures, of eleven women, three said the man decided; one reported the woman decided, and seven claimed both decided.

12. Generally, these young women were born in the United States and are second generation.

13. One area of conflict was Tita's mothers' visits to her sisters over her father's objection. Her mother won the battle, but not without a fight.

14. Most of these women were brought to the United States as children under twelve years of age and are also regarded as the "one-point-five" generation.

15. *Mayores* typically came during family-stage migration, in which parents or husbands first migrated to the United States and then women in the *mayores* cohort and their children followed (particularly after the Immigration Act of 1965).

16. Moreover, pay by the hour guarantees a minimum wage, which becomes more difficult to achieve through piece-rate work, especially for the older farm workers.

17. I am good friends with their sons and visit their home at least two or three times a year. We grew up in the same housing projects, and I attended elementary school with three of their sons. We also worked in the fields during the summers and weekends from our elementary school years to after we graduated from high school.

18. I do not intend to trivialize the serious topic of kidnapping spouses (*robar*). This practice was known to have occurred especially during the times of war: the Mexican Revolution and the Cristero Revolt. The capturing and forcing of a person into an undesired marriage is apparently a form of slavery. However, the term *robar* has also been used to describe the experiences of young couples that mutually agree to run off together without their parents' consent. Typically, the family will say that the young woman was stolen: "*se la robaron.*" Sometimes, when it was known that it was the young woman who insisted on the eloping, they will say "*se lo robo*" (she stole him).

19. Rita is a good friend of mine, and during my field research and visits to Xaripu I would go to her house on a daily basis just to talk and relax. She would sometimes go to my hosting house to share information she thought would be useful to my research or just to talk. Her supportiveness may be related to the fact that she and my mother were good friends when they were growing up in the pueblo, and also to the fact that I remain a close friend to many members of her family in California.

20. This group of women is mostly retired, and many had husbands who participated in most of the Bracero Program from 1942 to 1964. Some even had husbands who had come earlier in the century, around the time of the Great Depression. Many of their parents had been intra-national migrants within Mexico, working for haciendas in the Michoacán region.

21. When I asked Nena ¿*Quién manda?*, she said her husband. Yet it was obvious that she was not a submissive woman and that Luis was not a domineering person. It appears practice and gender ideology are not necessarily consistent. In practice, she asserted over, corrected, and interrupted Luis, and received

deference from him. He looked shyly at her for approval when answering questions (bowing his head and timidly looking up to her from across the small kitchen table). Yet in line with the hegemonic ideology of western societies, she said the "patriarch" has *el mando*.

22. I agreed, but this claim cannot be generalized.

23. For instance, Ana and María pressured their husbands into buying a house in the United States. In Ana's case, her husband, Raul, lives an active transnational life and was happy with life in the farm labor camps, which suited that lifestyle—six months in California and six in Michoacán. In María's case, whose family was less transnational and frequented Mexico less frequently, her husband, Gregorio, did not think they could make the payments, as they even struggled with rent in the low-income housing projects. However, both María and Ana persisted and identified Housing and Urban Development (HUD) federal programs for low-income families that helped subsidize their home payments.

24. She was interviewed in a commercial city about forty minutes from Xaripu.

25. This situation may be attributed to both men's and women's dependence on remittances and lack of wage labor opportunities.

26. Household chores thus continue to be unequally distributed and performed in US society, and studies have shown that Anglo families are no more gender egalitarian in their household division of labor than Latino families (see Coltrane 2000, 1208–33). Some studies encountered more sharing of household chores among Latino families (see Mirandé 1997; Shelton and Daphne 1993), others less (Golding 1990), and most found similar levels of sharing of household chores among Mexican and Anglo families (Coltrane and Valdez 1993; Herrera and del Campo 1995; and John et al. 1995). More recently, Adams and Coltrane (2000) found that Mexican mothers performed 49.5 hours of weekly housework compared to White mothers' 38.7; Mexican fathers, 11.8 hours, compared to White fathers' 10.1; and Mexican children, 12.9 hours, compared to White children's 9.1. Claims that Mexican gender equity is enhanced in the United States—either through structural conditions (see Hondagneu-Sotelo 1994; Grasmuck and Pessar 1991; Pessar 2003; Rouse 1992) and/or cultural assimilation (see Foner 1998; Lim 1997; Min 1997)—need to be examined more systematically and comparatively across nations, and to be historically situated (see Malkin 1999; Smith and Guarnizo 2003; Pessar 2003).

27. Household chores were measured with a ten-item index listing home chores performed by women and men, and respondents are asked to report the number of hours per week they spend doing the specified chores: cooking, washing dishes and laundry, cleaning the house, going to the market, doing home

repairs, paying bills, fixing the car, transporting household members, and supervising children.

28. The eight men interviewed in California performed an average of twenty-three hours of domestic work per week, compared to an average of sixteen hours among the eight men interviewed in Michoacán. Although men in California performed more household chores than men in Michoacán, men in California share only a marginally higher level of household chores with their wives than men in Michoacán. For example, men in California perform only 57 percent of what women do in household chores per week, compared to men in Michoacán, who performed 52 percent of what women do. Again, these proportions are not inferential, and only serve to compare those in my sample.

29. Their household chore differences may be attributed to the growing dependence on United States remittances rather than on local employment, and to the fact that families in Michoacán are smaller in size as a consequence of widespread emigration.

30. *Retiradas* had more family support, because they had older children and grandchildren to provide diverse types of support. When asked who they turned to for emotional and financial support, all of them referred to family members, primarily children and siblings. Hence, although the family does not equally support all its members (e.g., mothers in *mayores* cohort), it remains a place of support in a context of social oppression (see chapters 4 and 5).

31. Although no woman in Michoacán reported having *el mando* at home, of the nine who reported doing low levels of domestic work, four said the man had *el mando* at home, and five said they shared *el mando*. Four reported high levels of domestic work; two said the man had *el mando*, and two said they shared it.

32. Occupational stratification and segmentation were elaborated in the chapters on theory (2) and labor (4).

33. See also Parreñas 2001b, 386–87, and Alicea 1997, 597–626. Alicea insightfully documents that "caring work and kin work bring with them [mothers] power and recognition and are important to building a sense of belonging and connectedness, and at the same time they are oppressive because women are held accountable for doing an unfair share of this work" (621).

34. Familism refers to being family-oriented and actively involved with family. It was observed through questions about (1) feeling of closeness to family, (2) level of contact with family and extended family, (3) comparing friendships with nonrelatives and family members, (4) and identifying the source of emotional and material support. As in *Haciendo Comunidad* (see chapter 5), individuals make family through high levels of *convivencia*.

35. As explicated in chapter 5, Xaripu transnational members (1) have a dual home base or sense of home in two nation-states, (2) maintain physical, mental,

and/or emotional connections with both regions, and (3) make material, cultural, and emotional relations constant and active across the border. Transnationalism thus varies in intensity, and Xaripus fitting the three dimensions above and with frequent (or somewhat frequent) visits to Michoacán are regarded as more transnational. In the case study, thirty participants had settled permanently in California, though twenty-three travel to Michoacán frequently (once every one to three years) or somewhat frequently (once every four to six years) and seven infrequently (every seven or more years). Most of the frequent visitors reflect dual-home orientations and maintain active social ties across borders, and the infrequent visitors to Michoacán are classified as less transnational (see Tables 2.1 and 2.2 in the appendix).

36. Martina's transnationalism changed from being a frequent to an infrequent transnational. While she was growing up, she traveled to Michoacán more often than after she married. Her visits became more infrequent with her work schedule and young children.

37. This situation was also true in California: patriarchal norms of regulating young women's behavior and sexuality continue across borders. In my personal and informal conversations, gendered double standards with dating, going out at night, and household chores were common in California as well. See also Espiritu 2003b; Toro-Morn and Alicea 2003.

38. This serious problem also exists in the United States, affecting women of all class and racial backgrounds.

39. This optimistic view is in line with color-blind and class-blind approaches, which suggest that structural inequalities will disappear over time without any conscious and formalized intervention.

7. A Pueblo's Search for Empowerment across Borders

1. See also Pew Hispanic Center 2008, Table 4. Mexican-origin people in the United States make up over 64 percent of those classified Hispanics, followed by Puerto Ricans at 9 percent, Cubans at 3.5 percent, and Salvadorans at 3 percent.

2. See Pew Hispanic Center 2006, Table 14. Hispanics had the lowest median weekly earnings at $423, compared to Whites' $624, Blacks' $480, and Asians' $665. Of all the foreign-born racial categories, Hispanics were the only ones earning less than their counterparts born in the United States (other foreign-born racial groups earned more than their US counterparts).

See US Bureau of the Census 2008a, Table 682. Hispanics also had a lower per capita income at $14,483 compared to Blacks' $16,874, Asians' $27,331, and Whites' $28,946.

See US Bureau of the Census 2000, Tables 45, 318. Only 7 percent of the Mexican population had four years of college—the lowest as compared to other Latino and non-Latino-groups. For example, 11 percent of the Puerto Ricans had four years of college; 15.4 percent of African Americans; 24 percent of Cubans; 26 percent of Whites; and 42 percent of Asians.

See US Bureau of the Census 2006. Even when controlling for education, Hispanics' earnings were significantly lower than other racial groups; for instance, Hispanics with a professional degree average $78,190 compared to Blacks' $103,155 and Whites' $119,712.

3. Interactive colonialism (XC) is elaborated in chapter 2. XC highlights interacting forms of colonialism: neocolonialism, internal colonialism, and other forms rooted in classical colonialism.

4. This expression refers to the logic and practice of dehumanizing distinct categories of people.

5. The racialization of occupations and workers creates the most disadvantageous conditions for Xaripa women, who experience occupational segregation that limit them to stereotypical and devalued roles.

6. This limited employment—also referred to as tokenism—is not substantive in quantity or quality and helps convey the illusion of inclusion just as long as the minority employee does not challenge the existing social order.

7. Neoliberalism is used to refer to laissez-faire policies; for example, the government diminishes its role in the free market, advances privatization of public resources, reduces regulations of environment/labor protections to create a business-friendly environment, ends subsidies to domestic industry, and cuts public service expenditures in health and education. The structural adjustment programs and free trade agreements of the 1980s and 1990s were guided by a neoliberal philosophy.

8. Xaripus creatively integrate various cultural forms into new emergent dress and speech styles. For instance, Xaripu youth may start a sentence in Spanish and finish it in English (e.g., "*no me vas a creer,* I saw so and so") and often use Spanglish words (e.g., pushar, liquiar, parquear, etc). At work and school, their broad language skills allow them to speak in one or the other language, but when in the company of family and friends they incorporate their multiple realities in a creative and normalized way. Their cultural in-between position, in contrast to the older cohorts, gives them more social mobility at work, in school, and in society.

9. See chapter 3 for more elaboration. *Ejidos* were collective land grants gained through the land reform policies (Plan de Ayala 1917) that resulted from the Mexican Revolution.

10. These policies dismantled the *ejido* system created by the Mexican Revolution that had been designed to protect associated small landholders from larger monopolistic and/or foreign interests.

11. It can be more accurately described as interdependent, because male migrants also depended on families' reproduction of labor and support while unemployed in Michoacán (see Sarmiento 2002). Over time, *norteños* have become more empowered over non-migrants in Michoacán, though the former continue to benefit from the social ties with the homeland.

12. This migration was permitted through the family reunification provision.

13. See Sassen 2003, 56. Structural adjustment programs (SAP) (1) augmented the national debt in poor countries, (2) disrupted local economies, (3) oriented production for export, and (4) reduced public services. In short, SAP established the conditions for migration and facilitated cross-border movement through infrastructure created by globalization from the top. In the Xaripu case, they had a long history with migration to the United States and had already been far along in the settlement process. However, when Mexico followed SAP in the early 1980s, Xaripus, who had lived comfortably in Mexico, were forced into migration and connected with relatives already settled in California.

14. See chapter 6 for elaboration. This perception is influenced by the home-host dichotomies paradigm and the level of transnationalism among Xaripa women.

15. The multiple disadvantages are acutely experienced by unemployed and underemployed women in Michoacán, who directly face the entangled systems of gender, class, and national oppression.

16. See Portes and Rumbaut 2006, 350. Selective acculturation "means the acquisition of English fluency and American cultural ways along with preservation of certain key elements of the immigrant culture, of which language is paramount" (350). This approach allows children to integrate into mainstream culture and remain connected to their parents and older generations, which is viewed as important for healthy child development.

17. See Krauze 1997, 502, 508. Vasconcelos later supported Nazi Germany. Krauze interprets this shift to Vasconcelos's intense hate of capitalism, communism, liberalism, and Semitism. He shared those feelings with Hitler.

18. See Mead [1934] 1962; Blumer 1969; and Charon 1998. In sociological social psychology (e.g., the theory of symbolic interactionism), the self is composed of three related components: I, me, and generalized other (G.O.). The "I"

is the most individualistic/spontaneous/fluid component, and it is engaged in a dialectical relationship with an internalized collective attitude of society or "generalized other." The outcome of this tension (I and G.O.) produces actions (me's) that in reflection and the long-term trajectory constitute the total self. The equivalent terms of "I, me, and self" in psychological social psychology are the respective Freudian terms id, ego, and superego.

19. See also Moraga 1983, 34. She also expresses urgency for bridging her Anglo culture and her newly embraced Chicana one: "I am a woman with a foot in both worlds; and I refuse to split. I feel the necessity for dialogue. Sometimes I feel it urgently" (34).

20. See Shorris 2004, 77–86. Shorris contends that the Nahuas' belief system in the "god of corn" was more inclusive of cultural differences and change as compared to the Europeans' "god of bread."

21. See Du Bois 1903 and Fanon 1967. In the early twentieth century, W. E. B. Du Bois's concept of double consciousness illustrated the movement between two unequal worlds, in which Blacks were forced into deference and demeanor desired by White society and could only express their full humanity in the safety of their Black communities. The existence of a Black community provided an alternative space of positive images and affirmations, which to some degree resisted the dehumanizing forces from the dominant society. Blacks' double consciousness allowed them to survive, but the neutrality and health of such an experience were placed into question by Fanon, who noted the psychological injuries suffered by Black Martiniquais' lack of a supportive community in France.

22. See King [1963] 2003. Those who are privileged and have power never give up their comforts without organized pressure to do so. In history, for instance, slaves fought for the abolition of slavery; workers, for the right to collective bargaining and fair labor standards; women, for the right to vote and gender equity in the private and public spheres; immigrants, for freedom of movement.

23. See Nevins 2002 and Winant 2001. National boundaries are remnants of a brutal history of conquest, they are oppressive, and they continue to reproduce unfair and unearned advantages along racial, cultural, gender, and class lines. While the discourse justifying national boundaries lauds law and order, this rhetoric facilitates what classical colonialism accomplished: dehumanizing a people in a very comprehensive way. Hence, the pursuit of law and order without dismantling the colonial hierarchies left by a history of genocide, forced occupation, and slavery is negligent and oppressive.

WORKS CITED

Acuña, Rodolfo. 1981. *Occupied America: A History of Chicanos*. 2nd ed. New York: Harper & Row.

———. 1988. *Occupied America: A History of Chicanos*. 3rd ed. New York: HarperCollins.

Adams, Michele, and Scott Coltrane. 2000. "Housework in Mexican American and European American Families." Paper presented at 11th Annual Meeting of the California Sociological Association, Riverside, California, October 20.

Aguilera, Antonio. 2005. "Clonación y cambios del clima ponen en riesgo producción de agave tequilero." *La Jornada Michoacán*, February 22.

Aguirre, Adalberto Jr., and Manuel Barajas. 2000. "Intimate Social Contact, Cultural Proximity, and Prejudice toward Mexican Origin Persons: A Modified Application of Contact Theory." *Latino Studies Journal* 11 (2): 67–87.

Aguirre Beltrán, Gonzalo. 1972. *La Población Negra de México*. 2nd ed. Mexico City: Fondo de Cultura Económica.

Alcalá, Jerónimo de. 2000. *Relación de Michoacán, o, Relación de las ceremonias y rictos y población governación de los indios de la Provincia de Mechuacán*. Coordinación de edición y estudios Moisés Franco Mendoza. Zamora, Michoacán: El Colegio de Michoacán.

Alicea, Marixsa. 1997. "A Chambered Nautilus: The Contradictory Nature of Puerto Rican Women's Role in the Social Construction of a Transnational Community." *Gender & Society* 11 (5): 597–626.

Allensworth, Elaine M., and Refugio I. Rochin. 1999. *The Mexicanization of Rural California: A Socio-Demographic Analysis, 1980–1997*. East Lansing: Julian Samora Research Institute, Michigan State University.

Almaguer, Tomás. 1971. "Toward the Study of Chicano Colonialism." *Aztlan: Chicano Journal of Social Sciences and the Arts* 2 (Spring): 7–21.

———. 1994. *Racial Fault Lines: The Historical Origins of White Supremacy in California*. Berkeley: University of California Press.

Alvarez del Toro, Jesus. 1988. *Guarachita Ayer . . . Villamar Hoy: Monografía Municipal de Villamar, Michoacán*. Coordinación de Apoyo Municipal Centro Estatal de Estudios Municipales.

Amott, Teresa, and Julie Matthaei. 2007. "Work and Economic Transformation." In *Race, Class, and Gender: An Anthology*, edited by Margaret L. Andersen and Patricia H. Collins, 283–91. 6th ed. Wadsworth Sociology Reader Series. Belmont, CA: Thomson/Wadsworth.

Anderson, Benedict R. O'G. 1991. *Imagined Communities: Reflections on the Origins and Spread of Nationalism*. Rev. and extended ed. New York: Verso.

Anderson, Nick. 2001a. "Senate Overturns Ergonomics Rules on Worker Safety." *Los Angeles Times*, March 7: A1, A8.

———. 2001b. "House Kills Worker Ergonomics Rules." *Los Angles Times*, March 8.

Anzaldúa, Gloria. 1987. "La Conciencia de la Mestiza/Towards a New Consciousness." In *Borderlands: The New Mestiza = La Frontera*. San Francisco: Aunt Lute Books.

———. 1999. "La Conciencia de la Mestiza/Towards a New Consciousness." In *Borderlands: The New Mestiza = La Frontera*. 2nd ed. San Francisco: Aunt Lute Books.

Arax, Mark. 1994. "California Farm Workers' March Marks Return to Their Roots." *Chicago Sun-Times*, March 28: 42.

Arizpe, Lourdes. 1978. *Migración, Etnicismo y Cambio Económico*. Mexico: El Colegio de Mexico.

———. 1981. "The Rural Exodus in Mexico and Mexican Migration to the U.S." *International Migration Review*. 15: 626–49.

Arizpe, Lourdes, and Josefina Aranda. 1981. "The Comparative Advantages of Women's Disadvantages: Women Workers in the Strawberry Export Agribusiness in Mexico." *Signs: Journal of Women in Culture and Society 7*: 453–73.

Associated Press. 2004. "Concern over Safety of Mexican Workers." *Sacramento Bee*, March 19: A20.

Avalos, Manuel. 1995. "Economic Restructuring and Young Latino Workers in the 1980s." In *Chicanas and Chicanos in Contemporary Society*, edited by Roberto De Anda, 25–40. Boston: Allyn & Bacon.

Barajas, Manuel. 1997. "Prejudiced Attitudes towards Mexicans in the 1990s: Modified Contact Hypotheses." Professional paper for master's degree, University of California, Riverside.

———. 2002. "An Extended Case Study of the Xaripu Community across Borders: Interactive Colonization in the 21st Century." PhD diss., University of California, Riverside.

Barajas, Manuel, and Elvia Ramirez. 2007. "Beyond Home/Host Dichotomies: A Comparative Examination of Gender Relations in a Transnational Mexican Community." *Sociological Perspectives* 50 (3): 367–92.

Barndt, Deborah. 2002. *Tangled Routes: Women, Work, and Globalization on the Tomato Trail*. Lanham, MD: Rowman & Littlefield.

Barrera, Mario. 1979. *Race and Class in the Southwest: A Theory of Racial Inequality*. Notre Dame, IN: University of Notre Dame Press.

Barrera, Mario, Carlos Muñoz, and Charles Ornelas. 1972. "The Barrio as Internal Colony." In *People and Politics in Urban Society*, edited by Harlan Hahn, 465–98. Urban Affairs Annual Reviews, vol. 6. Beverly Hills: Sage Publications.

Bazar, Emily. 2004. "Migrants Live in Shadowy World of Hard Toil." *Sacramento Bee*, March 21: A1, A12.

Bell, Derrick. 2002. *Ethical Ambition: Living a Life of Meaning and Worth*. Bloomsbury, NY: Holtzbrink Publishers.

Bellah, Robert N., R. Madsen, W. M. Sullivan, A. Swindler, and S. M. Tipton. 1996. *Habits of the Heart: Individualism and Commitment in American Life*. Berkeley: University of California Press.

Benería, Lourdes, and Martha Roldán. 1987. *The Crossroads of Class and Gender: Industrial Homework, Subcontracting, and Household Dynamics in Mexico City*. Chicago: University of Chicago Press.

Bernard, William S. 1998. "Immigration: History of U.S. Policy." In *The Immigration Reader: America in a Multidisciplinary Perspective*, edited by David Jacobson, 48–71. Malden, MA: Blackwell Publishers.

Besserer, Federico. 1999. "Estudios Transnacionales y Ciudadanía Transnacional." In *Fronteras Fragmentadas*, edited by Gail Mummert, 215–38. Zamora, Michoacán: El Colegio de Michoacán.

Blauner, Bob. 1972. *Racial Oppression in America*. New York: Harper & Row.

———. 2001. *Still the Big News: Racial Oppression in America*. Rev. and exp. ed. Philadelphia: Temple University Press.

Blea, Irene I. 1997. *U.S. Chicanas and Latinas within a Global Context: Women of Color at the Fourth World Women's Conference*. Westport, CT: Praeger.

Blumer, Herbert. 1969. *Symbolic Interactionism: Perspective and Method*. Berkeley: University of California Press.

Bonacich, Edna. 1972. "A Theory of Ethnic Antagonism: A Split-labor Market." *American Sociological Review* 37: 547–59.

———. 1976. "Advanced Capitalism and Black/White Race Relations in the United States: Split Labor Market Interpretation." *American Sociological Review* 41: 34–51.

————. 1999. "The Site of Class." In *Race, Identity, and Citizenship: A Reader,* edited by Rodolfo D. Torres, Louis F. Mirón, and Jonathan Xavier Inda, 297–303. Malden, MA: Blackwell Publishers.

Bonacich, Edna, and Richard P. Appelbaum. 2000. *Behind the Label: Inequality in the Los Angeles Apparel Industry.* Berkeley: University of California Press.

Bonacich, Edna, and Lucie Cheng. 1984. "Introduction: A Theoretical Orientation to International Labor Migration." In *Labor Immigration under Capitalism: Asian Workers in the United States before World War II,* edited by Lucie Cheng and Edna Bonacich, 1–56. Berkeley: University of California Press.

Bonfil Batalla, Guillermo. 1987. *México Profundo: Una Civilización Negada.* Mexico City: Centro de Investigaciones y Estudios Superiores en Antropología Social.

————. 1996. *México Profundo: Reclaiming a Civilization.* Translated by Philip A. Dennis. Translations from Latin America. Austin: University of Texas Press.

Bonilla-Silva, Eduardo. 2001. *White Supremacy and Racism in the Post-Civil Rights Era.* Boulder: Lynne Rienner Publishers.

————. 2003. *Racism without Racists: Color-Blind Racism and the Persistence of Racial Inequality in the United States.* Lanham, MD: Rowman & Littlefield.

Borah, Woodrow. 1951. "New Spain's Century of Depression." In *Ibero-Americana,* vol. 35, edited by C. O. Sauer et al., 1–58. Berkeley: University of California Press.

Bordo, Susan. 1997. "'Material Girl': The Effacements of Postmodern Culture." In *The Gender/Sexuality Reader: Culture, History, Political Economy,* edited by Roger N. Lancaster and Micaela di Leonardo, 335–58. New York: Routledge.

Bowler, Mary. 1999. "Women's Earnings: An Overview." *Monthly Labor Review,* December: 13–21.

Braudel, Fernand. 1980. *On History.* Translated by Sarah Mathews. Chicago: University of Chicago Press.

Bravo Ugarte, José. 1960. *Inspección Ocular en Michoacán: Regiones Central y Sudoeste.* Mexico City: Editorial Jus.

Brecher, Jeremy, Tim Costello, and Brendan Smith. 2000. *Globalization from Below.* Cambridge, MA: South End Press.

Brewer, Anthony. 1990. *Marxist Theories of Imperialism: A Critical Survey.* 2nd ed. New York: Routledge.

Buitrago Ortiz, Carlos, and Eva Villalón Soler. 1999. "Transnacionalismo y Fragmentación." In *Fronteras Fragmentadas*, edited by Gail Mummert, 185–94. Zamora, Michoacán: El Colegio de Michoacán.

Burawoy, Michael. 1979. *Manufacturing Consent: Changes in the Labor Process under Monopoly Capitalism*. Chicago: University of Chicago Press.

———. 1991. "The Extended Case Method." In *Ethnography Unbound: Power and Resistance in the Modern Metropolis*, by Michael Burawoy, Alice Burton, et al., 271–88. Berkeley: University of California Press.

Burawoy, Michael, Joseph A. Blum, et al. 2000. *Global Ethnography: Forces, Connections, and Imaginations in a Postmodern World*. Berkeley: University of California Press.

Burawoy, Michael, Alice Burton, et al. 1991. *Ethnography Unbound: Power and Resistance in the Modern Metropolis*. Berkeley: University of California Press.

Burns, Robert. 2001. "Pentagon Celebrates Direct Hit." [Riverside] *Press-Enterprise*, July 15: A1, A11.

Bustamante, Jorge A., et al. 1978. *Análisis de algunos resultados de la primera encuesta a trabajadores mexicanos no documentados devueltos de los Estados Unidos*. México: Centro Nacional de Información y Estadísticas del Trabajo, Secretaría de Trabajo y Previsión Social.

Calavita, Kitty. 1998. "Gaps and Contradictions in U.S. Immigration Policy: An Analysis of Recent Reform Efforts." In *The Immigration Reader: America in a Multidisciplinary Perspective*, edited by David Jacobson, 92–128. Malden, MA: Blackwell Publishers.

Camarillo, Albert. 1979. *Chicanos in a Changing Society*. Cambridge, MA: Harvard University Press.

Campbell, Dan. 2000. "Tri Valley Growers Files Chapter-11 Bankruptcy." *Rural Cooperatives* (July/August). http://www.rurdev.usda.gov/rbs/pub/aug00/tri.htm.

Carens, Joseph H. 1998. "Aliens and Citizens." In *The Immigration Reader: America in a Multidisciplinary Perspective*, edited by David Jacobson, 365–87. Malden, MA: Blackwell Publishers.

Carr, Leslie G. 1997. *"Color-Blind" Racism*. Thousand Oaks, CA: Sage Publications.

Castañeda Medina, Liborio. 1983. "A un Rincón Michoacano." *El Heraldo de Jaripo*. April 1: 8.

Castells, Manuel. 1997. *The Power of Identity*. Information Age, vol. 2. Malden, MA: Blackwell Publishers.

Castells, Manuel, and Alejandro Portes. 1989. "World Underneath: The Origins, Dynamics, and Effects of Informal Economy." In *Informal Economy: Studies in Advanced and Less Developed Countries,* edited by Alejandro Portes, Manuel Castells, and Lauren A. Benton, 11–37. Baltimore: Johns Hopkins University Press.

Castillo, Ana. 1994. *Massacre of the Dreams: Essays on Xicanisma.* New York: Penguin.

Caulfield, Norman. 1998. *Mexican Workers and the State: From the Porfiriato to NAFTA.* Fort Worth: Texas Christian University Press.

Cervantez, Fred A. 2003. "Chicanos as a Postcolonial Minority: Some Questions Concerning the Adequacy of the Paradigm of Internal Colonialism." In *Latino/a Thought: Culture, Politics, and Society,* edited by Francisco H. Vasquez and Rodolfo D. Torres, 331–42. Lanham, MD: Rowman & Littlefield.

Chacón, Justin Akers, and Mike Davis. 2006. *No One Is Illegal: Fighting Racism and State Violence on the U.S.–Mexico Border.* Chicago: Haymarket Books.

Chang, Grace. 2000. *Disposable Domestics: Immigrant Women Workers in the Global Economy.* Cambridge, MA: South End Press.

Charon, Joel M. 1998. *Symbolic Interactionism: An Introduction, An Interpretation, and Integration.* 6th ed. Upper Saddle River, NJ: Prentice Hall.

Chavez, Leo R. 1992. *Shadowed Lives: Undocumented Immigrants in American Society.* Forth Worth: Harcourt Brace Jovanovich College Publishers.

———. 1997. "Immigration Reform and Nativism: The Nationalist Response to the Transnational Challenge." In *Immigrants Out! The New Nativism and the Anti-Immigrant Impulse in the United States,* edited by Juan Perea, 61–77. New York: New York University Press.

———. 2001. *Covering Immigration: Popular Images and the Politics of the Nation.* Berkeley: University of California Press.

Chavez, Leo R., and Rebecca M. Martínez. 1996. "Mexican Immigration in the 1980s and Beyond: Implications for Chicanas/os." In *Chicanas/Chicanos at the Crossroads,* edited by David Maciel and Isidro D. Ortiz, 25–51. Tucson: University of Arizona Press.

Cho, Sumi K. 1997. "Converging Stereotypes in Racialized Sexual Harassment: Where the Model Minority Meets Suzie Wong." In *Critical Race Feminism: A Reader,* edited by Adrien Katherine Wing, 203–20. New York: New York University Press.

Ciudad Real, Antonio de. 1976. *Tratado curioso y docto de las grandezas de la Nueva España.* Mexico: UNAM.

Claiborne, William. 1997. "Labor Picks California Strawberry Fields as Organizing Battleground." *Washington Post,* May 11: A3.

Cockcroft, James D. 1998. *Mexico's Hope: An Encounter with Politics and History*. New York: Monthly Review Press.

Collins, Chuck, and Felice Yeskel. 2000. *Economic Apartheid in America: A Primer on Economic Inequality and Insecurity*. New York: New Press.

———. 2005. *Economic Apartheid in America: A Primer on Economic Inequality and Insecurity*. 2nd ed. New York: New Press.

Collins, Patricia Hill. 1991. *Black Feminist Thought: Knowledge, Consciousness, and the Politics of Empowerment*. New York: Routledge.

———. 1994. "Shifting the Center: Race, Class, and Feminist Theorizing about Motherhood." In *Mothering: Ideology, Experience and Agency*, edited by Evelyn Nakano Glenn, Grace Change, and Linda Rennie Forcey, 45–66. New York: Routledge.

———. 2003. "Toward a New Vision: Race, Class, and Gender as Categories of Analysis and Connection." Chapter 56 in *The Social Construction of Difference and Inequality: Race, Class, Gender, and Sexuality*, edited by Tracy E. Ore. 2nd ed. Boston: McGraw-Hill.

———. 2004. "Learning the Outsider Within: The Sociological Significance of Black Feminist Thought." Chapter 7 in *The Feminist Standpoint Theory Reader: Intellectual and Political Controversies*, edited by Sandra Harding. New York: Routledge.

Collins, Randall. 1992. *Sociological Insight: An Introduction to Non-Obvious Sociology*. New York: Oxford University Press.

Coltrane, Scott. 1996. *Family Man: Fatherhood, Housework, and Gender Equity*. Oxford: Oxford University Press.

———. 1998. *Gender and Families*. Thousand Oaks, CA: Pine Forge Press.

———. 2000. "Research on Household Labor: Modeling and Measuring the Social Embeddedness of Routine Family Work." *Journal of Marriage and the Family* 62 (November): 1208–33.

Coltrane, Scott, and Elsa Valdez. 1993. "Reluctant Compliance: Work/Family Role Allocation in Dual-Earner Chicano Families." In *Men, Work and Family*, edited by Jane C. Hood, 151–74. Research on Men and Masculinities 4. Newbury Park, CA: Sage Publications.

Connell, Rich, and Robert J. Lopez. 2001a. "Mexico to Look into Missing Millions Saved for Braceros." *Los Angeles Times*, January 28: A1, A9.

———. 2001b. "Mexican Report Contradicts Claims that 40s War Workers Weren't Paid." *Los Angeles Times*, March 30: A3.

Cook, Sherburne F., and Woodrow Borah. 1960. "The Indian Population of Central Mexico: 1531–1610." In *Ibero-Americana*, vol. 44, edited by C. O. Sauer et al. Berkeley: University of California Press.

Cook, Sherburne F., and Lesley Byrd Simpson. 1948. "The Population of Central Mexico in the Sixteenth Century." In *Ibero-Americana*, vol. 31, edited by C. O. Sauer et al. Berkeley: University of California Press.

Cornelius, Wayne A. 1976. *Mexican Migration to the United States: The View from Rural Sending Communities*. Cambridge, MA: Center for International Studies, Massachusetts Institute of Technology.

Corona Hurtado, Froylán. 1967–68. *Memoria*. Teacher thesis, Secretaría de Educación Publica, Morelia, Michoacán.

Couey, Anna. 2001. "Women of Color and the Growth of Low-Wage Labor in the United States." In *Time to Rise: US Women of Color: Issues and Strategies*, edited by Maylei Blackwell, Linda Burnham, and Jung Hee Choi. Report to the UN World Conference Against Racism, Racial Discrimination, Xenophobia and Related Intolerances, Durban, South Africa (August–September): 39–41.

Crenshaw, Kimberlé. 1995. "Race, Reform, and Retrenchment: Transformation and Legitimation in Anti-Discrimination Law." In *Critical Race Theory: The Key Writings that Formed the Movement*, edited by Kimberlé Crenshaw et al. New York: New Press.

———. 1997. "Beyond Racism and Misogyny: Black Feminism and 2 Live Crew." In *Feminist Social Thought: A Reader*, edited by Diana Tietjens Meyers. New York: Routledge.

Cromwell, Ronald E., Ramon Corrales, and Peter M. Torsiello. 1973. "Normative Patterns of Marital Decision-Making Power and Influences in Mexico and the United States: A Partial Test of Resource and Ideology Theory." *Journal of Comparative Family Studies* 4:177–96.

Cromwell, Ronald E., and Rene A. Ruiz. 1979. "The Myth of Macho Dominance in Decision Making within Mexican and Chicano Families." *Hispanic Journal of Behavioral Sciences* 1 (4): 355–73.

Curry-Rodríguez, Julia E. 1988. "Labor Migration and Familial Responsibilities: Experiences of Mexican Women." In *Mexicanas at Work in the United States*, edited by Margarita B. Melville, 47–63. Mexican American Studies Monograph 5. Houston: University of Houston.

De Anda, M. Roberto, editor. 1996. *Chicanas and Chicanos in Contemporary Society*. Boston: Allyn & Bacon.

De Barbieri, Teresita M. 1984. *Mujeres y vida cotidiana*. Mexico: SEP 80 (60).

De Bernal, Jesus V. 1969. *Tierra mía: Recuerdos de adolescencia*. Mexico City: Los Talleres de Gráfica Panamericana, S. de R.L.

De Genova, Nicholas, and Ana Y. Ramos-Zayas. 2003. *Latino Crossings: Mexicans, Puerto Ricans, and the Politics of Race and Citizenship*. New York: Routledge.

De la Coruña, Martin de Jesus. 1538/1539. *Cronicas de Michoacán*. Mexico: Ediciones de la Universidad Nacional Autonoma, 1954.

———. 1539/1541. *The Chronicles of Michoacán*. Translated by Eugene R. Craine and Reginald C. Reindorp. Norman: University of Oklahoma Press, 1970.

De las Casas, Bartolomé. 1552. *The Devastation of the Indies: A Brief Account*. Translated by Herma Briffault. Baltimore: Johns Hopkins University Press, 1974.

Del Castillo, Adelaida R. 1993. "Covert Cultural Norms and Sex/Gender Meaning: A Mexico City Case." *Urban Anthropology* 22 (3–4): 237–58.

———. 1996. "Gender and Its Discontinuities in Male/Female Domestic Relations: Mexicans in Cross-Cultural Context." In *Chicanas/Chicanos at the Crossroads: Social, Economic, and Political Change*, edited by David R. Maciel and Isidro D. Ortiz, 207–30. Tucson: University of Arizona Press.

Delgado, Richard. 2003. *Justice at War: Civil Liberties and Civil Rights during the Times of Crises*. New York: New York University Press.

Delgado, Richard, and Jean Stefancic. 1995. "Why Do We Tell the Same Stories? Law Reform, Critical Librarianship, and the Triple Helix Dilemma." In *Critical Race Theory: The Cutting Edge*, edited by Richard Delgado, 206–16. Philadelphia: Temple University Press.

Delgado, Sergio Torres. 1995. "Convenencia del régimen: Condena a los emigrados a la esclavitud." *Porqué*, February 15: 3.

Dill, Bonnie Thornton. 1988. "Our Mother's Grief: Racial Ethnic Women and the Maintenance of Families." *Journal of Family History* 13:415–31.

Donato, Rubén, M. Menchaca, and R. R. Valencia. 1991. "Segregation, Desegregation, and Integration of Chicano Students: Problems and Prospects." In *Chicano School Failure and Success: Research and Policy Agendas for the 1990s*, edited by Richard R. Valencia. Stanford Series on Education and Public Policy. London: Falmer Press.

Driscoll, Barbara A. 1999. *The Tracks North: The Railroad Bracero Program of World War II*. Austin: CMAS Books.

Du Bois, W. E. B. 1903. *The Souls of Black Folk*. New York: Signet.

Durán de Huerta, Marta. 1994. *Yo, Marcos*. Mexico City: Ediciones del Milenio.

Edelman, Marc. 2002. "Price of Free Trade: Famine." *Los Angeles Times*, March 22: B17.

Espiritu, Yen Le. 2003a. "Gender and Labor in Asian Immigrant Families." In *Gender and U.S. Immigration: Contemporary Trends*, edited by Pierrette Hondagneu-Sotelo, 81–99. Berkeley: University of California Press.

———. 2003b. *Home Bound: Filipino American Lives across Cultures, Communities, and Countries*. Berkeley: University of California Press.

Espiritu, Yen Le, and Thom Tran. 2002. "'Viet Nam, Nuoc Toi' [Vietnam, My Country]: Vietnamese Americans and Transnationalism." In *The Changing Face of Home: The Transnational Lives of the Second Generation*, edited by Peggy Levitt and Mary C. Waters, 367–400. New York: Russell Sage Foundation.

Fanon, Frantz. 1967. "The Negro and Language." Chapter 1 in *Black Skin, White Masks*. New York: Grove Press.

Feagin, Joe R. 1997. "Old Poison in New Bottles: The Deep Roots of Modern Nativism." In *Immigrants Out! The Nativism and the Anti-Immigrant Impulse in the United States*, edited by Juan Perea. New York: New York University Press.

———. 2000. *Racist America: Roots, Current Realities, and Future Reparations*. New York: Routledge.

Feagin, Joe R., and Clairece Booher Feagin. 1999. "Theoretical Perspectives in Race and Ethnic Relations." In *Racial and Ethnic Relations*. 6th ed. Upper Saddle River, NJ: Prentice Hall.

Feagin, Joe R., and Hernán Vera. 1995. *White Racism: The Basics*. New York: Routledge.

Fernández-Kelly, Maria Patricia. 1983. *For We Are Sold, I and My People: Women and Industry in Mexico's Frontier*. Albany: State University of New York Press.

Fernández-Kelly, M. Patricia, and A. N. García. 1989. "Informalization at the Core: Hispanic Women, Homework, and the Advanced Capitalist State." In *The Informal Economy: Studies in Advanced and Less Developed Countries*, edited by Alejandro Portes, Manuel Castells, and Lauren A. Benton, 247–64. Baltimore: Johns Hopkins University Press.

Fetzer, Joel S. 2006. "Why Did House Members Vote for H.R. 4437?" *International Migration Review* 40 (3): 698–706.

Fields, Robin, and Ray Herndon. 2001. "Segregation of a New Sort Takes Shape." *Los Angeles Times*, July 5: A1, A17.

Florescano, Enrique et al. 1983. *Atlas histórico de Mexico*. Mexico City: Siglo Veintiuno.

Foner, Nancy. 1998. "Benefits and Burdens: Immigrant Women and Work in New York City." *Gender Issues* 16 (4): 5–24.

Fonseca, Omar, and Lilia Moreno. 1984. *Trabajando en tierras ajenas . . . que antes eran nuestras: Jaripo pueblo de migrantes*. Jiquilpan de Juarez, Michoacán: Centro de Estudios de la Revolución Mexicana, Lázaro Cárdenas, A.C.

————. 1988. "Consideraciones Historico-Sociales de La Migración de Trabaja-dores Michoacanos a Los Estados Unidos de America: El Caso de Jaripo." In *Migración en el Occidente de Mexico,* edited by G. López Castro and S. Pardo Galvan, 65–84. Zamora, Michoacán: El Colegio de Michoacán.

Forbes, Jack. 1964. *The Indian in America's Past.* Englewood Cliffs, NJ: Prentice Hall.

————. 1982. *Native Americans of California and Nevada.* Rev. ed. Happy Camp, CA: Naturegraph Publishers.

Fouron, Georges E., and Nina Glick-Schiller. 2002. "The Generation of Identity: Redefining the Second Generation within a Transnational Social Field." In *The Changing Face of Home: The Transnational Lives of the Second Genera-tion,* edited by Peggy Levitt and Mary C. Waters, 168–208. New York: Russell Sage Foundation.

Frank, Andre Gunder. 1967. *Capitalism and Underdevelopment in Latin America.* New York: Monthly Review Press.

————. 1969. *Latin America: Underdevelopment or Revolution.* New York: Monthly Review Press.

————. 1978. *Dependent Accumulation and Underdevelopment.* London: Mac-millan.

Froylán Corona, Cecilio. 1967–68. *Memoria: Secretaria de Educación Publica: Dirección General de Enseñanza Normal.* Morelia, Michoacán: Escuela Nor-mal Urbana Federal.

Galarza, Ernesto. 1964. *Merchants of Labor: The Mexican Bracero Story.* Santa Barbara, CA: McNally and Loftin.

Gamio, Manuel. 1930. *Mexican Immigration to the United States.* Chicago: University of Chicago Press.

————. 1931. *The Mexican Immigrant: His Life-Story: Autobiographic Docu-ments.* Chicago: University of Chicago Press.

García, Alma M. 1993. "Studying Chicanas: Bringing Women into the Frame of Chicano Studies." In *Chicana Voices: Intersections of Class, Race, and Gen-der,* edited by Teresa Córdova et al, 19–29. Albuquerque: University of New Mexico Press.

García, Brígida, H. Muñoz, and O. de Oliveira. 1982. *Hogares y trabajadores en la cidudad de México.* Mexico City: El Colegio de México, Instituto de Inves-tigaciones Sociales, UNAM.

García, Ignacio M. 1997. *Chicanismo: The Forging of a Militant Ethos among Mexican Americans.* Tucson: University of Arizona Press.

Garcia-Bahne, Betty. 1977. "La Chicana and the Chicano Family." In *Essays on La Mujer,* edited by Rosaura Sanchez. Los Angeles: Chicano Studies Center Publications, UCLA.

García Canclini, Néstor, and A. S. Villalobos. 1985. *Mascaras, Danzas y Fiestas de Michoacán.* Morelia, Michoacán: Comité Editorial del Gobierno de Michoacán.

Geertz, Clifford. 1964. "The Transition to Humanity." In *Horizons of Anthropology,* edited by Sol Tax, 37–48. Chicago: Aldine.

George, Sheba. 2000. "'Dirty Nurses' and 'Men Who Play': Gender and Class in Transnational Migration." In *Global Ethnography: Forces, Connections, and Imaginations in a Postmodern World,* edited by Michael Burawoy, Joseph A. Blum, et al., 144–74. Berkeley: University of California Press.

Georges, Eugenia. 1992. "Gender, Class, and Migration in the Dominican Republic: Women's Experiences in a Transnational Community." In *Towards a Transnational Perspective on Migration: Race, Class, Ethnicity, and Nationalism Reconsidered,* edited by Nina Glick Schiller, Linda Basch, and Cristina Blanc-Szanton, 81–99. Annals of the New York Academy of Sciences, vol. 645. New York: New York Academy of Sciences.

Gledhill, John. 1999. "El Reto de la Globalización." In *Fronteras Fragmentadas,* edited by Gail Mummert, 23–54. Zamora, Michoacán: El Colegio de Michoacán.

Glenn, Evelyn Nakano. 1994a. "Racial Ethnic Women's Labor: The Intersection of Race, Gender, and Class Oppression." In *Race and Ethnic Conflict: Contending Views on Prejudice, Discrimination, and Ethnoviolence,* edited by Fred L. Pincus and Howard J. Ehrlich. Boulder: Westview Press.

———. 1994b. "Social Construction of Mothering: A Thematic Overview." In *Mothering: Ideology, Experience, and Agency,* edited by Evelyn Nakano Glenn, Grace Chang, and Linda Rennie Forcey, 1–30. New York: Routledge.

———. 2002. *Unequal Freedom: How Race and Gender Shaped American Citizenship and Labor.* Cambridge, MA: Harvard University Press.

Glick-Schiller, Nina, Linda Basch, and Cristina Blanc-Szanton. 1992a. "Towards a Definition of Transnationalism: Introductory Remarks and Research Questions." In *Towards a Transnational Perspective on Migration: Race, Class, Ethnicity, and Nationalism Reconsidered,* edited by Nina Glick Schiller, Linda Basch, and Cristina Blanc-Szanton, ix–xiv. Annals of the New York Academy of Sciences, vol. 645. New York: New York Academy of Sciences.

———, editors. 1992b. *Towards a Transnational Perspective on Migration: Race, Class, Ethnicity, and Nationalism Reconsidered.* Annals of the New York Academy of Sciences, vol. 645. New York: New York Academy of Sciences.

———. 1992c. "Transnationalism: A New Analytic Framework for Understanding Migration." In *Towards a Transnational Perspective on Migration: Race, Class, Ethnicity, and Nationalism Reconsidered,* edited by Nina Glick Schiller, Linda Basch, and Cristina Blanc-Szanton, 1–24. Annals of the New York Academy of Science, vol. 645. New York: New York Academy of Sciences.

Golding, J. M. 1990. "Division of Household Labor, Strain, and Depressive Symptoms among Mexican American and Non-Hispanic Whites." *Psychology of Women Quarterly* 14:103–17.

Goldring, Luin. 2003. "The Power of Status in Transnational Social Fields." In *Transnationalism from Below*, edited by Michael Peter Smith and Luis Eduardo Guarnizo, 165–95. Comparative Urban & Community Research, vol. 6. New Brunswick, NJ: Transaction Publishers.

Gómez-Quiñones, Juan. 1977. *On Culture.* Popular Series No. 1. Los Angeles: UCLA Chicano Studies Center Publications.

———. 1994. *Mexican American Labor, 1790–1990.* Albuquerque: University of New Mexico Press.

Gómez-Quiñones, Juan, and David R. Maciel. 1998. "What Goes Around Comes Around: Political Practice and Cultural Response in the Internationalization of Mexican Labor, 1890–1997." In *Culture across Borders: Mexican Immigration and Popular Culture*, edited by David R. Maciel and María Herrera-Sobek, 17–66. Tucson: University of Arizona Press.

Gonzalez, Gilbert G., and Raul A. Fernandez. 2001. "Empire and the Origins of Twentieth Century Migration from Mexico to the United States." *Pacific Historical Review* 71 (1): 19–57.

———. 2003. *A Century of Chicano History: Empire, Nations, and Migration.* New York: Routledge.

González, Luis. 1995. *Un Pueblo in Vilo.* Zamora, Michoacán: El Colegio de Michoacán.

Gonzalez, Manuel G. 1999. *Mexicanos: A History of Mexicans in the United States.* Bloomington: Indiana University Press.

Gonzalez, Manuel G., and Cynthia M. Gonzalez, editors. 2000. *En Aquel Entonces = In Years Gone By: Readings in Mexican-American History.* Bloomington: Indiana University Press.

González-López, Gloria. 2003. "De Madres a Hijas: Gendered Lessons on Virginity across Generations of Mexican Immigrant Women." In *Gender and U.S. Immigration: Contemporary Trends*, edited by Pierrette Hondagneu-Sotelo, 217–40. Berkeley: University of California Press.

Gordon, David M., Richard Edwards, and Michael Reich. 1982. *Segmented Work, Divided Workers: The Historical Transformation of Labor in the United States.* New York: Cambridge University Press.

Gramsci, Antonio. 1988. *An Antonio Gramsci Reader: Selected Writings 1916–1935.* Edited by David Forgacs. New York: Schocken Books.

Grasmuck, Sherri, and Patricia R. Pessar. 1991. *Between Two Islands: Dominican International Migration*. Berkeley: University of California Press.

Greenhouse, Steven. 2001. "Senate Kills Work Safety Rules." [Riverside] *Press-Enterprise*, March 7: A1, A12.

———. 2007. "U.S. Seeks Rules to Allow Increase in Guest Workers." *New York Times*, October 10: A16.

Griswold del Castillo, Richard. 1979. *The Los Angeles Barrio, 1850–1890: A Social History*. Berkeley: University of California Press.

———. 1984. *La Familia: Chicano Families in the Urban Southwest, 1848 to the Present*. Notre Dame, IN: University of Notre Dame Press.

Grosfoguel, Ramón. 2003a. *Colonial Subjects: Puerto Ricans in a Global Perspective*. Berkeley: University of California Press.

———. 2003b. "The Divorce of Nationalist Discourse from the Puerto Rican People." In *Latino/a Thought: Culture, Politics, and Society*, edited by Francisco H. Vasquez and Rodolfo D. Torres, 348–64. Lanham, MD: Rowman & Littlefield.

Guarnizo, Luis Eduardo, and Michael Peter Smith. 1999. "Las Localizaciones del Transnacionalismo." In *Fronteras Fragmentadas*, edited by Gail Mummert, 87–112. Zamora, Michoacán: El Colegio de Michoacán.

———. 2003. "The Locations of Transnationalism." In *Transnationalism from Below*, edited by Michael Peter Smith and Luis Eduardo Guarnizo, 3–34. Comparative Urban & Community Research, vol. 6. New Brunswick, NJ: Transaction Publishers.

Gutiérrez, David G. 1995. *Walls and Mirrors: Mexican Americans, Mexican Immigrants, and the Politics of Ethnicity*. Berkeley: University of California Press.

———. 1996. *Between Two Worlds: Mexican Immigrants in the United States*. Jaguar Books on Latin America 15. Wilmington, DE: Scholarly Resources.

Gutiérrez, Natividad. 1999. *Nationalist Myths and Ethnic Identities: Indigenous Intellectuals and the Mexican State*. Lincoln: University of Nebraska Press.

Hagan, Jacqueline Maria. 1994. *Deciding to Be Legal: A Maya Community in Houston*. Philadelphia: Temple University Press.

Harding, Sandra. 2004. "Rethinking Standpoint Epistemology: What Is 'Strong Objectivity'?" Chapter 8 in *The Feminist Standpoint Theory Reader*, edited by Sandra Harding. New York: Routledge.

Hart, John Mason, editor. 1998. *Border Crossings: Mexican and Mexican-American Workers*. Latin American Silhouettes. Wilmington, DE: SR Books.

———. 2002. *Empire and Revolution: The Americans in Mexico since the Civil War*. Berkeley: University of California Press.

Harvey, David. 1990. *The Condition of Postmodernity: An Enquiry into the Origins of Cultural Change*. Cambridge, MA: Blackwell.

Hastings, Maribel. 1990. "Perredistas critican convenio de UFW con Mexico." *La Opinion*, April 24.

Herrera, R. S., and R. L. del Campo. 1995. "Beyond the Superwoman Syndrome: Work Satisfaction and Family Functioning among Working-Class, Mexican American Women." *Hispanic Journal of Behavioral Sciences* 17:49–60.

Hesse-Biber, Sharlene, and Gregg Lee Carter. 2000. *Working Women in America: Split Dreams*. New York: Oxford University Press.

Heyman, Josiah M. 1991. "Introduction: Fieldwork, Data Analysis, and Presentation." In *Life and Labor on the Border: Working People of Northeastern Sonora, Mexico, 1886–1986*. Tucson: University of Arizona Press.

Hightower, Jim. 1978. *Hard Tomatoes, Hard Times: The Original Hightower Report, Unexpurgated, of the Agribusiness Accountability Project*. Cambridge, MA: Schenkman Publishing.

Hirsch, Jennifer J. 1999. "En el Norte la Mujer Manda: Gender, Generation, and Geography in a Mexican Transnational Community." *American Behavioral Scientist* 42 (9): 1332–49.

Hondagneu-Sotelo, Pierrette. 1994. *Gendered Transitions: Mexican Experiences of Immigration*. Berkeley: University of California Press.

———, editor. 2003. *Gender and U.S. Immigration: Contemporary Trends*. Berkeley: University of California Press.

Hondagneu-Sotelo, Pierrette, and Ernestine Avila. 1997. "'I'm Here, but I'm There': The Meaning of Latina Transnational Motherhood." *Gender & Society* 11 (5): 548–71.

hooks, bell. 1995. *Killing Rage: Ending Racism*. New York: Henry Holt.

———. 2004. "Choosing the Margin as a Space of Radical Openness." Chapter 10 in *The Feminist Standpoint Theory Reader: Intellectual and Political Controversies*, edited by Sandra Harding. New York: Routledge.

Hubner, John. 2001. "Hispanic Indians Spur State Growth." [Riverside] *Press-Enterprise*, August 4: A1.

Hurtado, Aída, and Patricia Gurin. 2004. *Chicana/o Identity in a Changing U.S. Society: Quién soy? quiénes somos? Mexican American Experience*. Tucson: University of Arizona Press.

Ibarra, Maria de la Luz. 2003. "The Tender Trap: Mexican Immigrant Women and the Ethics of Elder Care Work." *Aztlan: A Journal of Chicano Studies* 28 (2): 87–113.

Jacobs, Harriet A. 1987. *Incidents in the Life of a Slave Girl: Written by Herself*. Cambridge, MA: Harvard University Press.

Jasinski, Jana L., N. L. Asdigian, G. K. Kantor. 1997. "Ethnic Adaptations to Occupational Strain: Work Related Stress, Drinking, and Wife Assault Among Anglo and Hispanic Husbands." *Journal of Interpersonal Violence* 12 (6): 814–31.

John, D., B.A. Shelton, and K. Luschen. 1995. "Race, Ethnicity, Gender and Perceptions of Fairness." *Journal of Family Issues* 16:357–79.

Johnson, Gordon. 2001. "One Tribe, Two Nations." [Riverside] *Press-Enterprise,* January 4: C1 and C4.

Johnston-Hernandez, Beatriz. 1991. "The UFW Eagle Has Landed: Stockton's Luis Magaña and His 'Alianza Campesina' Replacing Cesar Chavez's UFW and Traditional Unions." *Stockton Record,* July 21: A13.

———. 1993. "Cesar's Ghost." *California Lawyer,* July: 48–90.

Jones, James M. 1972. *Prejudice and Racism.* Reading, MA: Addison-Wesley.

Kasinitz, Phillip, Mary C. Waters, John H. Mollenkopf, and Merih Anil. 2002. "Transnationalism and Children of Immigrants in Contemporary New York." In *The Changing Face of Home: The Transnational Lives of the Second Generation,* edited by Peggy Levitt and Mary C. Waters, 96–122. New York: Russell Sage Foundation.

Kay, Cristobal. 1989. *Latin American Theories of Development and Underdevelopment.* London: Routledge.

Kearney, Michael. 1986. "From the Invisible Hand to the Visible Feet: Anthropological Studies of Migration and Development." *American Review of Anthropology* 15:331–61.

———. 1996. *Reconceptualizing the Peasantry: Anthropology in a Global Perspective.* Boulder: Westview Press.

———. 1998a. "Immigrants' National Origins and Transnational Ties: Mexican in the United States." Work in progress presented at Social Science Research Council, May 15–17.

———. 1998b. "Rural Oaxaca and California Agribusiness: The Transfer of Economic Value from Mexican Villages to the U.S. Suburbs." Work in progress presented at colloquium series of the Program in Agrarian Studies, Yale University, February 6.

Kearney, Michael, and Carole Nagengast. 1989. "Anthropological Perspectives on Transnational Communities in Rural California." Working paper 3, Discussion of Bi-National Aspects of California Rural Labor, California Institute for Rural Studies, Davis.

Keefe, Susan E., and Amado M. Padilla. 1987. *Chicano Ethnicity.* Albuquerque: University of New Mexico Press.

Keen, Benjamin. 1994. "Editor's Introduction." In *Life and Labor in Ancient Mexico,* by Alonzo de Zorita. Norman: University of Oklahoma Press.

————, editor. 1996. *Latin American Civilization: History and Society, 1492 to the Present.* 6th ed., rev. and updated. Boulder: Westview Press.

Kibria, Nazli. 1990. "Power, Patriarchy, and Gender Conflict in the Vietnamese Immigrant Community." *Gender & Society* 4 (1): 9–24.

King, Martin Luther Jr. [1963] 2003. "Letter from Birmingham Jail." In *Imprisoned Intellectuals: America's Political Prisoners Write on Life, Liberation, and Rebellion,* edited by Joy James, 34–47. Lanham, MD: Rowman & Littlefield.

Kivel, Paul. 1995. *Uprooting Racism: How White People Can Work for Racial Justice.* Philadelphia: New Society Publishers.

Kraul, Chris. 2002. "Free Trade Proves Devastation for Mexican Farmers." *Los Angeles Times,* October 26: A11.

Krauze, Enrique. 1997. *Mexico: Biography of Power: A History of Modern Mexico, 1810–1996.* Translated by Hank Heifetz. New York: HarperCollins.

Kurien, Prema. 2003. "Gendered Ethnicity: Creating a Hindu Indian Identity in the United States." In *Gender and U.S. Immigration: Contemporary Trends,* edited by Pierrette Hondagneu-Sotelo, 151–73. Berkeley: University of California Press.

Lee, Thomas A. Jr., and Carlos Navarrete, editors. 1978. *Mesoamerican Communication Routes and Cultural Contacts.* Provo, UT: New World Archaeological Foundation, Brigham Young University.

Lenin, Vladimir I. 1950. "Imperialism, the Highest Stage of Capitalism." In *Selected Works,* vol. 1. Moscow: Foreign Languages Publishing House.

León-Portilla, Miguel. 1976. *Culturas en Peligro.* Mexico City: Alianza Editorial Mexicana, S.A.

————. 1990. *Endangered Cultures.* Translated by Julie Goodson-Lawes. Dallas: Southern Methodist University Press.

————. 1995. *La Flecha en el Blanco: Francisco Tenamaztle y Bartolomé de las Casas en lucha por los derechos de los indeginas 1541–1556.* Mexico City: El Colegio de Jalisco.

————. 2001. "Aztlan: From Myth to Reality." In *Road to Aztlan: Art from a Mythic Homeland,* edited by Virginia M. Fields and V. Zamudio-Taylor, 20–33. Los Angeles: Los Angeles County Museum of Art.

Levine, Elaine. 2006. "Transnationalism and Labor Market Conditions for Mexican Workers in the US." Paper presented at National Association of Chicanas/os Studies Conference, July 29.

Levitt, Peggy. 2001. "Transnational Migration: Taking Stock and Future Directions." *Global Networks* 1 (3): 195–216.

Levitt, Peggy, and Mary C. Waters. 2002. *The Changing Face of Home: The Transnational Lives of the Second Generation.* New York: Russell Sage Foundation.

Lim, In-Sook. 1997. "Korean Immigrant Women's Challenge to Gender Inequality at Home: The Interplay of Economic Resources, Gender, and Family." *Gender & Society* 11 (1): 31–51.

Limón, José E. 1994. *Dancing with the Devil: Society and Cultural Poetics in Mexican-American South Texas*. Madison: University of Wisconsin Press.

Lipsitz, George. 1998. *The Possessive Investment in Whiteness: How White People Profit from Identity Politics*. Philadelphia: Temple University Press.

Loewen, James W. 1995. *Lies My Teacher Told Me: Everything Your American History Textbook Got Wrong*. New York: Simon & Schuster.

López, Alfredo Austin. 1981. *Tarascos y mexicas*. Mexico: Fondo de Cultura Económica.

López, Ann Aurelia. 2007. *The Farmworkers' Journey*. Berkeley: University of California Press.

López, Antoinette Sedillo. 1999. *Latina Issues: Fragments of Historia(ella) (Herstory)*. New York: Garland Publishing.

López Castro, Gustavo. 1986. *La casa dividida: Un estudio de caso sobre la migración a Estados Unidos en un pueblo michoacano*. Zamora, Michoacán: El Colegio de Michoacán y Asociacion Mexicana de Población.

———. 1988. "La migración a Estados Unidos en Gomez Farias, Michoacán." In *Migración en el Occidente de Mexico*, edited by G. López Castro and S. Pardo Galvan. Zamora, Michoacán: El Colegio de Michoacán.

Lowe, Lisa. 1996. *Immigrant Acts: On Asian American Cultural Politics*. Durham, NC: Duke University Press.

Lugo, Alejandro. 1995. *Fragmented Lives, Assembled Goods: A Study in Maquilas, Culture, and History at the Mexican Borderlands*. PhD diss., Stanford University.

Maciel, David R., and María Herrera-Sobek. 1998. "Introduction: Culture across Borders." In *Culture across Borders: Mexican Immigration and Popular Culture*, edited by David R. Maciel and María Herrera-Sobek, 3–16. Tucson: University of Arizona Press.

Magaña, Luis. 1988. "Agriculture and Its Forgotten People." *Stockton Record*, September 14.

———. 1993. "Human Rights Lost to NAFTA Shuffle." *Stockton Record*, October 3: C1, C6.

———. 1996. "Los Trabajadores Agrícolas Mexicanos en California y La Doble Nacionalidad." Report presented in "III Foro Regional de Análysis en Materia de Nacionaldad," Oaxaca, Oaxaca, March 1.

———. 1997a. "Justicia laboral para los indocumentados." *El Tiempo*, December 18: A2.

———. 1997b. "Luchando por el derecho de votar en el 2000." *El Tiempo*, July 24.

————. 1997c. "Doble Nacionalidad o Nacionalidad de Segunda." *El Tiempo*, December 25: A2.

————. 2001a. Interview with Manuel Barajas on Labor Activism. April 29.

————. 2001b. "Encuentro de Migrantes para Alternativas de desarrollo Economico y por los Derechos Humanos." *El Informador,* April 19–25: A6.

Mahler, Sarah J. 1995. *American Dreaming: Immigrant Life on the Margins.* Princeton, NJ: Princeton University Press.

————. 2003. "Theoretical and Empirical Contributions toward a Research Agenda for Transnationalism." In *Transnationalism from Below,* edited by Michael Peter Smith and Luis Eduardo Guarnizo, 64–100. Comparative Urban & Community Research, vol. 6. New Brunswick, NJ: Transaction Publishers.

Malik, Kenan. 1996. *The Meaning of Race: Race, History, and Culture in Western Society.* Washington Square: New York University Press.

Malkin, Victoria. 1999. "La reproducción de relaciones de género en la comunidad de migrantes Mexicanos en New Rochelle, Nueva York." In *Fronteras Fragmentadas,* edited by Gail Mummert, 475–96. Zamora, Michoacán: El Colegio de Michoacán.

Martinez, Elizabeth, and Ed McCaughan. 2001. "Chicanas and Mexicanas within a Transnational Working Class." In *Re-emerging Native Women of the Americas,* edited by Yolanda Broyles-Gonzalez, 41–64. Dubuque, IA: Kendall/ Hunt Publishing.

Marx, Karl. 1970. *The German Ideology.* New York: International Publishers.

Massey, Douglas S., R. Alarcón, J. Durand, and H. González. 1987. *Return to Aztlan: The Social Process of International Migration from Western Mexico.* Studies in Demography 1. Berkeley: University of California Press.

Massey, Douglas S., and Nancy A. Denton. 1993. *American Apartheid: Segregation and the Making of the Underclass.* Cambridge, MA: Harvard University Press.

Massey, Douglas, Jorge Durand, and Nolan J. Malone. 2002. *Beyond Smoke and Mirrors: Mexican Immigration in an Era of Economic Integration.* New York: Russell Sage Foundation.

McIntosh, Peggy. 1997. "White Privilege and Male Privilege: A Personal Account of Coming to See Correspondences through Work in Women's Studies." In *Critical White Studies: Looking Behind the Mirror,* edited by Richard Delgado and Jean Stefancic, 291–99. Philadelphia: Temple University Press.

McWilliams, Carey. [1935] 1971. *Factories in the Field: The Story of Migratory Farm Labor in California.* Santa Barbara: Peregrine.

————. 1990. *North from Mexico: The Spanish Speaking People of the United States.* Edited by Matt S. Meir. New ed. New York: Praeger.

Mead, George. [1934] 1962. *Mind, Self, & Society*. In *Works of George Herbert Mead: Mind, Self, and Society from the Standpoint of a Social Behaviorist*, edited by C. W. Morris, 1–336. Chicago: University of Chicago Press.

Meier, Matt S., and Feliciano Ribera. 1972. *Mexican Americans, American Mexicans: From Conquistadors to Chicanos*. New York: Hill and Wang.

Meltzer, Bernard N., John W. Petras, and Larry T. Reynolds. 1975. *Symbolic Interactionism: Genesis, Varieties, and Criticism*. Boston: Routledge & Kegan Paul.

Melville, Margarita B. 1988. "Mexican Women in the U.S. Wage Labor Force." In *Mexicanas at Work: In the United States*, 1–11. Mexican American Studies Monograph No. 5. Houston: University of Houston.

Memmi, Albert. 1965. *The Colonizer and the Colonized*. Translated by Howard Greenfeld. Boston: Beacon Press.

Menchaca, Marta. 1995. *The Mexican Outsiders: A Community History of Marginalization and Discrimination in California*. Austin: University of Texas Press.

Menjívar, Cecilia. 2000. *Fragmented Ties: Salvadorean Immigrant Networks in America*. Berkeley: University of California Press.

———. 2003. "The Intersection of Work and Gender: Central American Immigrant Women and Employment in California." In *Gender and U.S. Immigration: Contemporary Trends*, edited by Pierrette Hondagneu-Sotelo, 100–126. Berkeley: University of California Press.

———. 2004. "Living in Two Worlds? Guatemalan-Origin Children in the United States and Emerging Transnationalism." Unpublished paper.

Miles, Robert. 1989. *Racism*. London: Routledge.

Min, Pyong Gap. 1997. "Korean Immigrant Wives' Labor Participation, Marital Power, and Status." In *Women and Work: Exploring Race, Ethnicity, and Class*, edited by Elizabeth Higginbotham and Mary Romero, 176–91. Thousand Oaks, CA: Sage Publications.

Mines, Richard. 2006. *Family Settlement and Technological Change in Labor-Intensive U.S. Agriculture*. Davis: California Institute of Rural Studies.

Mines, Richard, Jackie Hausman, and Lisett Tabashouri. 2005. "The Need for Targeted Survey of Farm Workers: A Comparison of the California Health Interview Survey (CHIS) and the California Agricultural Worker Health Survey (CAWHS)." Report for the California Program on Access to Health. Davis: California Institute for Rural Studies.

Mines, Richard, and Michael Kearney. 1982. "The Health of Tulare County Farm Workers: A Report of 1981 Survey and Ethnographic Research of the Tulare County of Public Health." State of California Department of Health Services, Rural Health Division and Tulare County Department of Health.

Mirandé, Alfredo. 1985. *The Chicano Experience*. Notre Dame, IN: University of Notre Dame Press.

———. 1987. *Gringo Justice*. Notre Dame, IN: University of Notre Dame Press.

———. 1997. *Hombres y Machos*. Boulder: Westview Press.

Montejano, David. 1987. *Anglos and Mexicans in the Making of Texas, 1836–1986*. Austin: University of Texas Press.

Montoya, Maria E. 2000. "Beyond Internal Colonialism: Class, Gender, and Culture as Challenges to Chicano Identity." In *Voices of a New Chicana/o History*, edited by Refugio I. Rochín and Dennis N. Valdés, 183–95. East Lansing: Michigan State University Press.

Moore, Joan W. 1976. "American Minorities and 'New Nation' Perspectives." *Pacific Sociological Review* 19: 448–55.

Moraga, Cherrie. 1983. "La Guera." In *This Bridge Called My Back: Writings by Radical Women of Color*, edited by Cherrie Moraga and Gloria Anzaldúa, 27–34. New York: Kitchen Table Women of Color Press.

Mora-Torres, Juan. 2001. *The Making of the Mexican Border: The State, Capitalism, and Society in Nuevo León, 1848–1910*. Austin: University of Texas Press.

Moreno García, Heriberto. 1994. *Guaracha: Tiempos Viejos, Tiempos Nuevos*. 2nd ed. Zamora, Michoacán: El Colegio De Michoacán.

Mummert, Gail. 1988. "Mujeres de migrantes y mujeres migrantes de Michoacán: Nuevos papeles para las que se quedan y las que se van." In *Movimientos de población en el occidente de México*, edited by Thomas Calvo and Gustavo Lopez, 451–73. Zamora, Michoacán: El Colegio de Michoacán.

———. 1994. "From *Metate* to *Despate*: Rural Mexican Women's Salaried Labor and the Redefinition of Gendered Spaces and Roles." In *Women of the Mexican Countryside, 1850–1990*, edited by Heather Folwer-Salamini and Mary K. Vaughan, 192–209. Tucson: University of Arizona Press.

———, editor. 1999a. *Fronteras Fragmentadas*. Zamora, Michoacán: El Colegio de Michoacán.

———. 1999b. "Juntos o Desapartados: La Fundación del Hogar." In *Fronteras Fragmentadas*, edited by Gail Mummert, 451–73. Zamora, Michoacán: El Colegio de Michoacán.

Mundo Hispano. 1992. "Conmemorando el 82 aniversario de la revolución mexicana de 1910 en Stockton." Report on event sponsored by Union Campesina Lázaro Cárdenas, November/December, 13.

Muñoz, Carlos, Jr. 1989. *Youth, Identity, Power: The Chicano Movement*. New York: Verso.

National Farmers Union. 2005. *The Farm Crisis and Corporate Profits*. A report by Canada's National Farmers Union, November 30, 1–16.

Neckerman, Kathryn M., and Joleen Kirschman. 1999. "'We'd Love to Hire Them But . . .': The Meaning of Race for Employers." In *Rethinking the Color Line: Readings in Race and Ethnicity*, edited by Charles A. Gallagher, 276–87. Mountain View, CA: Mayfield Publishing.

Nevins, Joseph. 2002. *Operation Gatekeeper: The Rise of the "Illegal Alien" and the Making of the U.S.-Mexico Boundary*. New York: Routledge.

Ngai, Mae. 2004. *Impossible Subjects: Illegal Aliens and the Making of Modern America*. Princeton, NJ: Princeton University Press.

Nichols, Dana. 1991. "Saturday Profile: Luis Magaña." *Stockton Record*, April 6.

Obsatz, Sharyn. 2001. "Inland Group Helping Ex-Braceros in Suit for Pay Withheld in 1940s." [Riverside] *Press-Enterprise*, April 12: A1, A8.

Ochoa Serrano, Álvaro. 1995. *Repertorio Michoacano, 1889–1926*. Zamora, Michoacán: El Colegio de Michoácan.

———. 1997. *Afrodescendientes: Sobre Piel Canela*. Zamora, Michoacán: El Colegio de Michoacán.

———. 1999. *Jiquilpan-Huanimban: Una historia confinada*. Morelia, Michoacán: Morevallado Editores.

Ollman, Bertell. 1976. *Alienation: Marx's Conception of Man in Capitalist Society*. 2nd ed. Cambridge, UK: Cambridge University Press.

Omi, Michael, and Howard Winant. 1994. *Racial Formation in the United States: From the 1960s to the 1990s*. 2nd ed. New York: Routledge.

Ong, Aihwa. 1999. "Cultural Citizenship as Subject Making." In *Race, Identity, and Citizenship: A Reader*, edited by Rodolfo D. Torres, Louis F. Mirón, and Jonathan Xavier Inda, 262–93. Malden, MA: Blackwell Publishers.

Orozco, Cynthia. 1993. "Sexism in Chicano Studies and the Community." In *Chicana Voices: Intersections of Class, Race, and Gender*, edited by Teresa Córdova et al., 11–18. Albuquerque: University of New Mexico Press.

Ortelio, Abraham. 1579. *Theatrum orbis terrarium*. Antwerp: Plantin Ayer.

Osterman, Rachel. 2005a. "Landmark Farm Labor Law Sees Mixed Legacy." *Sacramento Bee*, June 12: A1, A6.

———. 2005b. "UFW Ready to Boycott Gallo—Again." *Sacramento Bee*, June 14: D1, D3.

Padilla, Genero M. 1993. *My History, Not Yours: The Formation of Mexican American Autobiography*. Madison: University of Wisconsin Press.

Palacios Franco, Julia Emilia. 1987. "Vámonos Pa'l Norte. Migración Feminina Mexicana a Estados Unidos: Un Estudio de Caso." Master's thesis, Universidad Iberoamericana.

Palerm, Juan Vicente. 1991. *Farm Labor Needs and Farm Workers in California 1970 to 1989*. Report prepared for State Employment Development Department, April.

————. 1994. *Immigrant and Migrant Farm Workers in the Santa Maria Valley, CA.* Report submitted to Center for Survey Methods Research, September.

Parreñas, Rhacel Salazar. 2001a. "Mothering From a Distance: Emotions, Gender, and Inter-Generational Relations in Filipino Transnational Families." *Feminist Studies* 27 (2): 361–90.

————. 2001b. *Servants of Globalization: Women, Migration and Domestic Work.* Stanford, CA: Stanford University Press.

Paz, Octavio. 1959. *El Laberinto de la Soledad.* Mexico: Fondo de la Cultura Económica.

Perea, Juan F. 1997. "The Black/White Binary Paradigm of Race: The Normal Science of American Racial Thought." *California Law Review & La Raza Law Journal* 85 (5): 1213–58.

Pesquera, Beatríz M. 1993a. "Chicanas' Work Identity." *Aztlan: A Journal of Chicano Studies* 20 (1–2).

————. 1993b. "In the Beginning He Wouldn't Lift Even a Spoon: The Division of Household Labor." In *Building with Our Hands: New Directions in Chicana Studies,* edited by Adela de la Torre and Beatríz M. Pesquera, 181–96. Berkeley: University of California Press.

Pessar, Patricia R. 2003. "Engendering Migration Studies: The Case of New Immigrants in the United States." In *Gender and U.S. Immigration: Contemporary Trends,* edited by Pierrette Hondagneu-Sotelo, 20–42. Berkeley: University of California Press.

Pew Hispanic Center. 2006. "Latino Labor Report, 2006: Strong Gains in Employment." Washington, DC: Pew Research Center.

————. 2008. "A Statistical Portrait of Hispanics at Mid-Decade." Washington, DC: Pew Research Center. http://pewhispanic.org/reports/middecade/.

Piper, Adrian. 1997. "Passing for White, Passing for Black." In *Critical White Studies: Looking Behind the Mirror,* edited by Richard Delgado and Jean Stefancic, 425–31. Philadelphia: Temple University Press.

Pitt, Leonard. 1966. *The Decline of the Californios: A Social History of the Spanish-Speaking Californians, 1846–1890.* Berkeley: University of California Press.

Pollard, Helen. 1993. *Taríacuri's Legacy: The Prehispanic Tarascan State.* Norman: University of Oklahoma Press.

Portes, Alejandro. 1998. "From South of the Border: Hispanic Minorities in the United States." In *The Immigration Reader: America in a Multidisciplinary Perspective,* edited by David Jacobson, 130–39. Malden, MA: Blackwell Publishers.

Portes, Alejandro, and Robert L. Bach. 1985. *Latin Journey: Cuban and Mexican Immigrants in the United States.* Berkeley: University of California Press.

Portes, Alejandro, and Ruben G. Rumbaut. 1996. *Immigrant America: A Portrait.* 2nd ed. Berkeley: University of California Press.

———. 2006. *Immigrant America: A Portrait.* 3rd ed. Berkeley: University of California Press.

Portes, Alejandro, and Min Zhou. 1993. "The New Second Generation: Segmented Assimilation and Its Variants." *Annals* 530:74–96.

Pritchard, Justin. 2004. "Mexican Workers' Deaths Soar in U.S." *Sacramento Bee,* March 14: A1, A19.

Puerner, John P., John S. Carroll, and Janet Clayton. 2001. "Give Braceros Back their Money." *Los Angeles Times,* February 6: B8.

Purnell, Jennie. 1999. *Popular Movements and State Formation in Revolutionary Mexico: The Agraristas and Cristeros of Michoacán.* Durham, NC: Duke University Press.

Quijano, Anibal. 2000. "Coloniality of Power, Eurocentrism, and Latin America." *Nepantla: Views from South* 1 (3): 533–80.

Quiñonez, Sam. 2001. *True Tales from Another Mexico: The Lynch Mob, the Popsicle Kings, Chalino, and the Bronk.* Albuquerque: University of New Mexico Press.

Raum, Tom. 2001. "Test Wins in Fueling Missile Plans Debate." [Riverside] *Press-Enterprise,* July 15: A11.

Redfield, Robert. 1956. *The Little Community, and Peasant Society and Culture.* Phoenix Books. Chicago: University of Chicago Press.

Reyes García, Cayetano. 1998. *Tzacapu: Las Piedras Universales: Los Procesesos de Dominación y Desertización.* Zamora, Michoacán: El Colegio de Michoacán.

Richter, Paul. 2001. "Test of Antimissile System Scores a Hit." *Los Angeles Times,* July 15: A1, A27.

Robinson, William I. 2003. *Transnational Conflicts: Central America, Social Change, and Globalization.* New York: Verso.

Rodríguez, Luis. 2001. *Hearts and Hands: Creating Communities in Violent Times.* New York: Seven Stories Press.

Roediger, David R. 1991. *The Wages of Whiteness: Race and the Making of the American Working Class.* New York: Verso.

Rollins, Judith. 1985. *Between Women: Domestics and Their Employers.* Philadelphia: Temple University Press.

Romero Flores, Jesus. 1939. *Nomenclatura Geografica de Michoacán.* Morelia: Sociedad Geográfica e Historica de Michoacán.

Rosaldo, Renato. 1989. *Culture and Truth: The Remaking of Social Analysis.* Boston: Beacon Press.

————. 1997. "Cultural Citizenship, Inequality, and Multiculturalism." In *Race, Identity, and Citizenship: A Reader,* edited by Rodolfo D. Torres, Louis F. Mirón, and Jonathan Xavier Inda, 253–61. Malden, MA: Blackwell Publishers.

Rose, Stephen J. 2000. *Social Stratification in the United States: The New American Profile Poster.* Rev. and updated ed. New York: New Press.

Rosenberg, Howard R., V. J. Horwitz, and D. L. Egan. 1995. *Labor Management Laws in California Agriculture.* Cooperative Extension, University of California, Division of Agriculture and Natural Resources, Davis.

Rosenblum, Karen E., and Toni-Michelle C. Travis. 1996. *Meaning of Difference: Race, Sex and Gender, Social Class, and Sexual Orientation in Contemporary America.* New York: McGraw-Hill.

Rothenberg, Daniel. 1998. *With These Hands: The Hidden World of Migrant Farmworkers Today.* New York: Harcourt Brace.

Rouse, Roger. 1989. *Mexican Migration to the United States: Family Relations in the Development of a Transnational Migrant Circuit.* PhD diss., Stanford University.

————. 1991. "Mexican Migration and the Social Space of Postmodernism." *Diaspora* 1 (1): 8–23.

————. 1992. "Making Sense of Settlement: Class Transformation, Cultural Struggle, and Transnationalism among Mexican Migrants in the United States." In *Towards a Transnational Perspective on Migration: Race, Class, Ethnicity, and Nationalism Reconsidered,* edited by Nina Glick Schiller, Linda Basch, and Cristina Blanc-Szanton, 25–52. Annals of the New York Academy of Science, vol. 645. New York: New York Academy of Sciences.

————. 1996. "Mexican Migration and the Social Space of Postmodernism." In *Between Two Worlds: Mexican Immigrants in the United States,* edited by David G. Gutiérrez, 247–63. Jaguar Books on Latin America 15. Wilmington, DE: Scholarly Resources.

Rumbaut, Rúben G. 2002. "Severed or Sustained Attachments? Language, Identity, and Imagined Communities in the Post-Immigrant Generation." In *The Changing Face of Home: The Transnational Lives of the Second Generation,* edited by Peggy Levitt and Mary C. Waters, 43–95. New York: Russell Sage Foundation.

Runsten, David, Roberta Cook, Anna Garcia, and Don Villarejo. 1993. "The Tomato Industry in California and Baja California." U.S. Commission on Agricultural Workers, Case Studies and Research Reports, Appendix I, February: 1–6.

Sahagun Sahagun, Enrique. 1967. "Investigación Medio-Sanitaria de la Comunidad de Jaripo, Edo. De Michoacán." Informe del Servicio Social presentado para el Departamento de Sociología Medica y Medicina Preventiva, Universidad Nacional Autonoma de Mexico.

Salcedo Zaragoza, Mariano. 1988. "Hagamos de la Tecomaca un jardin lleno de flores por todo el tiempo que nos quito la sed." *El Heraldo de Jaripo,* April 1: 8.

Samora, Julian. 1971. *Los Mojados: The Wetback Story.* Notre Dame, IN: University of Notre Dame Press.

Sandoval, Chela. 2004. "U.S. Third World Feminism: The Theory and Method of Differential Oppositional Consciousness." In *The Feminist Standpoint Theory Reader,* edited by Sandra Harding, 195–210. New York: Routledge.

San Juan, Epifanio. 1992. *Racial Formations/Critical Transformations: Articulations of Power in Ethnic and Racial Studies in the United States.* Atlantic Highlands, NJ: Humanities Press.

———. 1998. *Beyond Postcolonial Theory.* New York: St. Martin's Press.

Sarmiento, Socorro Torres. 2002. *Making Ends Meet: Income-Generating Strategies among Mexican Immigrants.* New York: LFB Scholarly Publishing.

Sassen, Saskia. 1988. *The Mobility of Labor and Capital: A Study in International Investment and Labor Flow.* Cambridge, UK: Cambridge University Press.

———. 1996a. *Losing Control? Sovereignty in an Age of Globalization.* New York: Columbia University Press.

———. 1996b. "U.S. Immigration Policy toward Mexico in a Global Economy." In *Between Two Worlds: Mexican Immigrants in the United States,* edited by David G. Gutiérrez, 213–27. Jaguar Books on Latin America 15. Wilmington, DE: Scholarly Resources.

———. 1998. "Foreign Investment: A Neglected Variable." In *The Immigration Reader: America in a Multidisciplinary Perspective,* edited by David Jacobson, 250–64. Malden, MA: Blackwell Publishers.

———. 2003. "Strategic Instantiations of Gendering in the Global Economy." In *Gender and U.S. Immigration: Contemporary Trends,* edited by Pierrette Hondagneu-Sotelo, 43–60. Berkeley: University of California Press.

Savage, David G. 2002. "Anti-Bias Agency Can Sue, Despite Arbitration Deals." *Los Angeles Times,* January 16: A13.

Schnitt, Paul. 2002. "Gridley Plant Closing to Cost Scores of Jobs." *Sacramento Bee,* April 23: D1.

Scott, James C. 1985. *Weapons of the Weak: Everyday Forms of Peasant Resistance.* New Haven, CT: Yale University Press.

Segura, Denise. 1990. "Chicanas and Triple Oppression in the Labor Force." In *Chicana Voices: Intersections of Class, Race, and Gender,* edited by Teresa Córdova et al., 47–65. Albuquerque: University of New Mexico Press.

————. 1991. "Ambivalence or Continuity? Motherhood and Employment among Chicanas and Mexican Immigrant Women Workers." *Aztlan: A Journal of Chicano Studies* 20 (Spring/Fall): 119–50.

————. 1994a. "Inside the Work Worlds of Chicana and Mexican Immigrant Women." In *Women of Color in U.S. Society,* edited by Maxine Baca Zinn and Bonnie Thornton Dill, 95–112. Women in the Political Economy. Philadelphia: Temple University Press.

————. 1994b. "Working at Motherhood: Chicana and Mexican Immigrant Mothers and Employment." In *Mothering: Ideology, Experience, and Agency,* edited by Evelyn Nakano Glenn, Grace Chang, and Linda Rennie Forcey, 211–35. New York: Routledge.

————. 1996. "Chicana and Mexican Immigrant Women at Work: The Impact of Class, Race, and Gender on Occupational Mobility." In *Race, Class, and Gender: Common Bonds, Different Voices,* edited by Esther Ngan-Ling Chow, Doris Wilkinson, and Maxine Baca Zinn, 149–64. Thousand Oaks, CA: Sage Publications.

Sexton, Richard. 2004. "The Canning of Tri Valley: What Went Wrong at Tri Valley Growers, and What Can Other Co-ops Learn from It?" *Rural Cooperatives,* September–October, 20–24.

Shelton, Beth Anne, and John Daphne. 1993. "Race, Ethnicity and Difference: A Comparison of White, Black, and Hispanic Men's Household Time." In *Men, Work, and Family,* edited by Jane C. Hood, 131–50. Research on Men and Masculinities 4. Newbury Park, CA: Sage Publications.

Shibutani, Tamotsu. 1955. "Reference Groups as Perspectives." *American Journal of Sociology* 60:562–69.

Shorris, Earl. 2004. *The Life and Times of Mexico.* New York: W. W. Norton.

Sierra Reyes, Arturo. 1997. "XIX Jornadas de Historia de Occidente, en el ERLC de Jiquilpan." *Guía,* September 14: 20.

Silva Herzog, Jesús. 1960. *Breve historia de la revolución mexicana: Los antecedentes etapa maderista.* Mexico City: Fondo de Cultura Económica.

Sinton, Peter. 2000. "Farmers Face Hard Facts: Falling Prices, Foreign Competition Are Strangling Growers." *San Francisco Chronicle,* November 29: B1.

Sirota, David. 2006. "NAFTA and Immigration." *San Francisco Chronicle,* April 9: E7.

Smith, James. 2001. "Ex-Migrants Sought for Class-Action." *Los Angeles Times,* March 15: A10.

Smith, Michael Peter, and Luis Eduardo Guarnizo, editors. 2003. *Transnationalism from Below.* Comparative Urban & Community Research, vol. 6. New Brunswick, NJ: Transaction Publishers.

Smith, Robert C. 2003. "Transnational Localities: Community, Technology and the Politics of Membership within the Context of Mexico and U.S. Migration." In *Transnationalism from Below*, edited by Michael Peter Smith and Luis Eduardo Guarnizo, 196–238. Comparative Urban & Community Research, vol. 6. New Brunswick, NJ: Transaction Publishers.

Sneider, Daniel. 1997. "Strawberry Fields Become a Fresh Union Battleground." *Christian Science Monitor*, April 16: 3.

Soldatenko, Maria Angelina. 1991. "Organizing Latina Garment Workers in Los Angeles." In "Las Obreras: The Politics of Work and Family," special issue, *Aztlan: A Journal of Chicano Studies* 20 (1–2): 73–96.

Sorenson, Susan B. 1996. "Violence Against Women: Examining Ethnic Differences and Commonalities." *Evaluation Review* 20 (2): 123–45.

Sosa Riddell, Adaljiza. [1974] 2001. "Chicanas and El Movimiento." In *The Chicano Studies Reader: An Anthology of Aztlán, 1970–2000*, edited by Chon A. Noriega et al., 359–70. Los Angeles: UCLA Chicano Studies Research Center Publications.

SourceMex. 2004. "Surplus of Agave Cactus Threatens the Tequila Industry." October 20.

Taub, Nadine, and Elizabeth M. Schneider. 1998. "Women's Subordination and the Role of the Law." In *The Politics of Law: A Progressive Critique*, edited by David Kairys, 328–55. 3rd ed. New York: Basic Books.

Thompson, Ginger. 2002. "NAFTA to Open Floodgates, Engulfing Rural Mexico." *New York Times*, December 19: A3.

Tienda, Martha. 1975. "Diferencias socioeconómicas regionales y tasas de participación de la fuerza de trabajo femenina: El caso de México." In *Revista Mexicana de Sociología* 37 (4): 911–29.

Toro-Morn, Maura I., and Marixsa Alicea. 2003. "Gendered Geographies of Home: Mapping Second and Third-Generation Puerto Ricans' Sense of Home." In *Gender and U.S. Immigration: Contemporary Trends*, edited by Pierrette Hondagneu-Sotelo, 194–214. Berkeley: University of California Press.

Torres, María de los Angeles. 1998. "Transnational Political and Cultural Identities: Crossing Theoretical Borders." In *Borderless Borders: U.S. Latinos, Latin Americans, and the Paradox of Interdependence*, edited by Frank Bonilla et al., 169–82. Philadelphia: Temple University Press.

Torres Delgado, Sergio. 1995. "Conveniencia del régimen: Condena a los emgirados a la esclavitud." *Porqué*, February 15: 3–4.

Trueba, Enrique T. 2004. *The New Americans: Immigrants and Transnationals at Work*. Lanham, MD: Rowman & Littlefield.

Tyner, James A. 2003. "The Global Context of Gendered Labor Migration from the Philippines to the United States." In *Gender and U.S. Immigration: Contemporary Trends*, edited by Pierrette Hondagneu-Sotelo, 63–80. Berkeley: University of California Press.

United Farm Workers of America, AFL-CIO. 1992. *No Grapes*. Video. La Unión de Campesinos de America, AFL-CIO, Keene, CA.

Urrieta, Luis Jr. 2003. "Las Identidades También Lloran, Identities Also Cry: Exploring the Human Side of Indigenous Latina/o Identities." *Educational Studies: A Journal of the American Educational Studies Association* 34 (2): 147–68.

US Bureau of the Census. 2000. "45. Social and Economic Characteristics of the Hispanic Population." In *Current Population Reports: P20-475*. http://allcountries.org/uscensus/45_social_and_economic_characteristics_of_the.html.

———. 2003. "The Relationship between the 1990 Census and Census 2000 Industry and Occupation Classification Systems, Technical Paper 65: Table 9." Prepared by Thomas S. Scopp. http://www.census.gov/hhes/www/ioindex/ioindex.html

———. 2006. "Table 217: Mean Earnings by Highest Degree Earned, 2003." In *Current Population Reports: P20–550*. http://www.census.gov/compendia/statab/2006/tables/06s0217.xls.

———. 2008a. "U.S. Hispanic Population Surpasses 45 million: Now 15% of Total." Washington, DC: Department of Commerce. http://www.census.gov/Press-Release/www/releases/archives/population/011910.html

———. 2008b. "Workers Killed or Disabled on the Job: 1970–2005: Table 635." Istaca, IL: National Safety Council. http://www.census.gov/compendia/statab/cats/labor_force_employment_earnings.html.

US Commission on Civil Rights. 1994. "Employment Discrimination Against Asian Americans." In *Race and Ethnic Conflict: Contending Views on Prejudice, Discrimination, and Ethnoviolence*, edited by Fred L. Pincus and Howard J. Ehrlich, 133–44. Boulder: Westview Press.

US Department of Agriculture. 2007a. "Increased US Imports of Fresh Fruit and Vegetables." A Report from the Economic Research Service by Sophia Huang and Kuo Huang: No. (FTS-32801) 21 pp, September 10.

———. 2007b. "Foreign Agricultural Trade of the United States (FATUS): Table 819: Agricultural Exports and Imports—Volume, by Principal Commodities: 1990 to 2005." www.census.gov/prod/2006pubs/07statab/agricult.pdf.

Vasconcelos, José. 1948. *La Raza Cosmica: Mision de la Raza Iberoamericana*. Mexico City: Espasa-Calpe.

Vasquez, Daniel. 1991. "Mexican Citizens in U.S. Fight for Vote at Home." *San Francisco Chronicle,* August 21: A14.

Velasco Vargas, Luis. 1945. *Exploración Sanitaria del Poblado de Jaripo Tenencia del Municipio de Villamar Estado de Michoacán.* Mexico City: Universidad Nacional Autónoma de México.

Vélez-Ibáñez, Carlos. 1996. *Border Visions: Mexican Cultures of the Southwest United States.* Tucson: University of Arizona Press.

Verástique, Bernardino. 2000. *Michoacán and Eden: Vasco de Quiroga and the Evangelization of Western Mexico.* Austin: University of Texas Press.

Villarejo, Don. 1989. *Farm Restructuring and Employment in California Agriculture.* Report published by the California Institute for Rural Studies, February.

Villarejo, Don, D. Lighthall, D. Williams, A. Souter, R. Mines, B. Bade, S. Samuels, and S. A. McCurdy. 2000. *A Report from the California Endowment: Suffering in Silence: A Report on the Health of California's Agricultural Workers.* California Institute for Rural Studies, November.

Villarejo, Don, and Dave Runsten. 1993. *California's Agricultural Dilemma: Higher Production and Lower Wages.* California Institute for Rural Studies, December.

Wallerstein, Immanuel. 1974. *The Modern World-System.* Volume 1: *Capitalist Agriculture and the Origin of the European World-Economy in the Sixteenth Century.* Studies in Social Discontinuity. New York: Academic Press.

———. 2003. *The Decline of American Power: The U.S. in a Chaotic World.* New York: New Press.

Warren, Benedict J. 1985. *The Conquest of Michoacán.* Norman: University of Oklahoma Press.

Watson, George. 2002. "Cancer: Migrant Workers Are Found to Have Higher Incidence than Other Hispanics." [Riverside] *Press-Enterprise,* April 16: A1, A12.

Weber, Devra. 1994. *Dark Sweat, White Gold: California Farm Workers, Cotton, and the New Deal.* Los Angeles: University of California Press.

———. 1998. "Historical Perspective on Transnational Mexican Workers in California." In *Border Crossings: Mexican and Mexican-American Workers,* edited by John M. Hart, 209–33. Latin American Silhouettes. Wilmington, DE: SR Books.

Wellman, David. 1977. *Portraits of White Racism.* Cambridge: Cambridge University Press.

West, Carolyn M. 1998. "Lifting the 'Political Gag Order': Breaking the Silence Around Partner Violence in Ethnic Minority Families." In *Partner Violence:*

A Comprehensive Review of 20 Years of Research, edited by Jana L. Jasinski and Linda M. Williams, 184–209. Thousand Oaks, CA: Sage Publications.

Williams, Kimberlé Crenshaw. 1993. "Beyond Racism and Misogyny: Black Feminism and 2 Live Crew." In *Words that Wound: Critical Race Theory, Assaultive Speech, and the First Amendment,* by Mari J. Matsuda et al., 111–32. Boulder: Westview Press.

Wilson, Thomas, and Hastings Donnan, editors. 1998. *Border Identities: Nation and State at International Frontiers.* Cambridge, UK: Cambridge University Press.

Wilson, William Julius. 1980. *The Declining Significance of Race: Blacks and Changing American Institutions.* 2nd ed. Chicago: University of Chicago Press.

Winant, Howard. 1994. *Racial Conditions: Politics, Theory, Comparisons.* Minneapolis: University of Minnesota Press.

———. 2001. *The World Is a Ghetto: Race and Democracy since World War II.* New York: Basic Books.

Wirth, Louis. 1938. "Urbanism as a Way of Life." *American Journal of Sociology* 44:8–20.

Wolf, Eric R. 1956. "Aspects of Group Relations in a Complex Society: Mexico." *American Anthropologist* 58:1065–78.

———. 1957. "Closed Corporate Communities in Mesoamerica and Central Java." *Southwestern Journal of Anthropology* 13:1–18.

———. 1959. *Sons of the Shaking Earth.* Chicago: University of Chicago Press.

Wright, Angus. 1990. *The Death of Ramón González: The Modern Agricultural Dilemma.* Austin: University of Texas Press.

Wylie, Alison. 2004. "Why Standpoint Matters." Chapter 27 in *The Feminist Standpoint Theory Reader: Intellectual and Political Controversies,* edited by Sandra Harding. New York: Routledge.

Yamamura, Kevin. 2007. "More Blunt Talk on Tapes: In New Transcripts of Office Conversations, Governor Calls Perata 'A Very Sick Man' and Discusses Cultural Assimilation." *Sacramento Bee,* February 5: A1.

Ybarra, Leonarda. 1982. "When Wives Work: The Impact on the Chicano Family." *Journal of Marriage and the Family* 44 (1): 169–78.

Yinger, John. 1991. *Housing Discrimination Study: Incidence of Discrimination and Variation in Discriminatory Behavior.* Washington, DC: U.S. Department of Housing and Urban Development, Office of Policy Development and Research.

Zabin, Carol, M. Kearney, A. García, D. Runsten, and C. Nagengast. 1993. *Mixtec Migrants in California Agriculture: A New Cycle of Poverty.* Research Report presented to the Rural Economic Policy Program of the Aspen Institute and the Ford Foundation.

Zachary, Pascal G. 1995. "Farm Workers Find New Life after Death of Union Founder." [Toronto] *Globe and Mail*, December 21.

Zamora, Emilio. 1993. *The World of the Mexican Worker in Texas*. College Station: Texas A & M University Press.

Zavella, Patricia. 1982. *Women, Work and Family in the Chicano Community: Cannery Workers of the Santa Clara Valley*. PhD diss., University of California, Berkeley.

———. 1987. *Women's Work and Chicano Families: Cannery Workers of the Santa Clara Valley*. Ithaca: Cornell University Press.

———. 1994. "Reflections on Diversity among Chicanas." In *Race*, edited by Steven Gregory and Roger Sanjek, 199–212. New Brunswick, NJ: Rutgers University Press.

Zentgraf, Khristine. 2002. "Immigration and Women's Empowerment: Salvadorans in Los Angeles." *Gender & Society* 16 (5): 625–46.

Zinn, Howard. 1999. *A People's History of the United States: 1492–Present*. 20th anniversary ed. New York: HarperCollins.

Zinn, Maxine Baca. 1975. "Political Familism: Toward Sex Role Equality in Chicano Families." *Aztlán: Chicano Journal of the Social Sciences and the Arts* 6 (Spring): 13–26.

———. 1979. "Chicano Family Research: Conceptual Distortions and Alternative Directions." *Journal of Ethnic Studies* 7 (Fall): 59–71.

———. 1980. "Employment and Education of Mexican-American Women: The Interplay of Modernity and Ethnicity in Eight Families." *Harvard Educational Review* 50 (1): 47–62.

———. 1982. "Mexican-American Women in the Social Sciences." *Signs: Journal of Women in Culture and Society* 8 (Winter): 259–72.

———. 1996. "Family, Feminism, and Race in America." In *Race, Class, & Gender*, edited by Esther Ngan-Ling Chow, Doris Wilkinson, and Maxine Baca Zinn. Thousand Oaks, CA: Sage Publications.

Zolberg, Aristide R. 2006. *A Nation by Design: Immigration Policy in the Fashioning of America*. Cambridge, MA: Harvard University Press.

Zorita, Alonso de. [1512–85] 1994. *Life and Labor in Ancient Mexico*. Translated by Benjamin Keen. Norman: University of Oklahoma Press.

INDEX

MANUAL BARAJAS

is associate professor of sociology

at California State University, Sacramento